CAREER

OPPORTUNITIES

in

THE FOOD AND BEVERAGE INDUSTRY

CAREER OPPORTUNITIES in

THE FOOD AND BEVERAGE INDUSTRY

KATHLEEN THOMPSON HILL

Ferguson

An imprint of Infobase Publishing

Career Opportunities in the Food and Beverage Industry

Copyright © 2010 by Kathleen Thompson Hill

Ferguson
An imprint of Infobase Publishing
132 West 31st Street
New York NY 10001

Library of Congress Cataloging-in-Publication Data

Hill, Kathleen, 1941–
  Career opportunities in the food and beverage industry / Kathleen Thompson Hill.
    p. cm.
  Includes bibliographical references and index.
  ISBN-13: 978-0-8160-7612-3 (hbk. : alk. paper)
  ISBN-10: 0-8160-7612-X (hbk. : alk. paper)
  1. Food service—Vocational guidance—Juvenile literature. 2. Food industry and trade—Juvenile literature. I. Title.
  TX911.3.V62H55 2010
  647.95023—dc22   2009033934

Ferguson books are available at special discounts when purchased in bulk quantities for businesses, associations, institutions, or sales promotions. Please call our Special Sales Department in New York at (212) 967-8800 or (800) 322-8755.

You can find Ferguson on the World Wide Web at http://www.fergpubco.com

Text design by Kerry Casey
Cover design by Takeshi Takahashi
Composition by Hermitage Publishing Services
Cover printed by Sheridan Books, Ann Arbor, MI
Book printed and bound by Sheridan Books, Ann Arbor, MI
Date printed: June 2010
Printed in the United States of America

10 9 8 7 6 5 4 3 2 1

This book is printed on acid-free paper.

CONTENTS

INDUSTRY OUTLOOK

People's discretionary spending habits change with the times, including what they spend on food, how they spend it, and where they spend their food and beverage dollars.

Everyone needs to eat. While food and beverage workers in some sectors have lost their jobs during economic downturns—also known as recessions—many of the restaurants that have survived are rehiring workers, snack food producers have more business than ever, breweries can barely keep up with demand, and many chain food restaurants are hiring, making the food business hopeful. Some wine sales have increased as well.

Lots of new culinary programs have popped up nationally at art institutes, community colleges, and at cooking schools, presenting more and better training for those interested in getting into a field that will always have jobs. Trends toward linking sustainable and organic growing and "greening" of restaurants, clubs, and resorts also present new opportunities.

In the farming field, one can grow herbs in pots on a balcony or window ledge at home to sell at farmers' markets, make a deal with a cheese maker to grow vegetables in vacant parts of his or her property, grow vegetables around a restaurant, or even plant olive trees between rows in an existing vineyard to make an agricultural living with a direct connection to the food industry and consumers.

New opportunities abound as ethnic restaurants, food carts and trucks, and agritourism and other culinary travel industries grow.

With a trend toward eating food grown or produced closer to home, individual entrepreneurs can even start a farmers' market where one doesn't exist, or start a jam, baked goods, or catering company from home.

With a little initiative, food fans can even start their own food and beverage blog, Facebook page, or Twitter site and develop a following without any culinary education or experience at all. Or they may manage those services for a restaurant, winery, caterer, club, casino, cruise ship, or hotel.

There is the opportunity to help start a school vegetable garden, which will teach children how plants grow, what we put into our vegetables to help them grow, how that product, vegetable, or fruit affects our bodies, and how we can become independent and interdependent by growing our own food.

Working in a wide range of careers in the food and beverage industries proves to be emotionally and financially rewarding for millions of people throughout the world.

While chefs, winery workers, and bartenders were laid off or had their work days reduced in number during the recession, more home cooking led to more entry-level jobs in massive food preparation and packaging plants, as well as beverage production at some levels.

Just as car manufacturers closed automobile dealerships, some of the largest coffee chains shut hundreds of outlets, and some small chain restaurants folded completely or eliminated their least productive stores. On the other hand, chains focusing on doughnuts and coffee and other cheap thrills opened new stores.

The mere fact that chain eateries refer to their outlets impersonally as "stores" with remote connection to themselves rather than "restaurants" to which they are committed and with which they identify reveals a mountain of information about changes in the food industry.

Throughout history, hunting, gathering, shopping, cooking, and sharing meals have been the center of social life, whether in tribal villages or large metropolises, from sub-Saharan Africa to Manhattan and Sonoma.

Food plays an important role in conversation, family, diplomacy, politics, and friendship. And beverages, whether beer at a football game, wine at a White House dinner, or tea or coffee in a ceremony in Berkeley, Tokyo, or London, set the tempo and regulate the warmth of any interaction.

The American food system has moved full circle in nearly 400 years, from American Indians teaching newly arriving British mistresses of the house and their imported kitchen help what to do with corn and beans and rural farmers growing organically and naturally and trading with neighbors everything they needed to survive. We "progressed" to microwave diet meals and toaster-popped pies, and then back to "slow food" and growing and purchasing local foods and trading with neighbors.

At the same time, restaurants, food producers and packagers, and beverage companies pay notoriously little to workers. Culinary aspirants may spend a good (or bad) $100,000 going to cooking school and become totally deflated when they can only find a $9-an-hour job cooking on a line in some restaurant kitchen.

More and more immigrants from many countries, particularly from Latin America and Asia where food and eating together play a major role in family life, gravitate toward working in food, from minimum-wage meat packing plants to the kitchens of high-end restaurants. Many great immigrant cooks learned the use of fresh-ground spices from helping their mothers and using a mortar and pestle, while others cooked for the rest of their siblings while their parents worked.

Often the rest of the kitchen crew is from the same country, or even the same region, such as Michoacán in Mexico. We see Mexicans preparing Chinese food at Panda Express and Asians cooking at Taco Bell.

The kitchen strata have changed, from the hierarchical old French *brigade de cuisine* devised by the late Auguste Escoffier to fuzzier lines of author-ity today in many restaurants and hotel kitchens. Still, few immigrants and women get the higher positions in a male-dominated field. Ironically, many American men think cooking is feminine work, although most chefs in America are male.

Knowledge of English is definitely an asset, and bilingual talents in English and Spanish can put a person high on the kitchen ladder as translator from the chef de cuisine to the rest of the crew. It is also important to be able to read—in any language. We know of elegant restaurants where all orders are printed out in the kitchen with no words, only numbers. Some immigrant kitchen workers know the meaning of the numbers (if only their shapes) and symbols and know what to do to prepare their part of the meal, but cannot read an order in English, or possibly in any language.

A cook with both cooking and translating skills can rise rapidly to sous-chef or chef de cuisine so that he or she can teach the rest of the staff how and when to do things.

Some employers offer language classes, and others recommend that kitchen or hotel supervisors attend Spanish or other language classes so the English speaker can communicate with the immigrant worker.

We know winery, restaurant, and deli owners who take Spanish classes to communicate with workers rather than invest in the workers' education, sort of like throwing them a fish instead of teaching them to use a fishing pole. Some local high schools offer adult education or community college classes in English as a second language and in Spanish to help employers learn employees' languages or help the employees learn English.

While one may be able to get a minimum-wage job in a fast-food joint or packing plant without English, English is essential to move up in most systems. Our favorite example is the Robledo family of Sonoma Valley, who came here as migrant vineyard workers, saved their money, bought some land, established the first vineyard worker–owned winery in the United States, and now have been featured in *People* magazine and in *Readers' Digest.*

Many small and large ethnic restaurants were started by first-generation immigrants who learned English and how to cook in quantities "from the bottom up," washing dishes, sweeping, busing tables, and serving.

Notices in American restaurant kitchens and wineries are often posted in English, Spanish, Chinese, or Vietnamese, while in Canada they appear mostly in English and French.

Trends and New Issues in the Food Industry

Fast Food versus Slow Food

Food trends and science change as often as hemlines go up and down. Currently one of the hottest trends, which hopefully will stay around awhile, is growing organic vegetables and purchasing vegetables and meats grown close to home. Eating locally—sometimes described as being a "locavore"—is variously described as buying food grown within five, 10, 25, 50, or 100 miles from where one lives. The possibilities of knowing the person who grew the food and what they put into it, freshness of the produce, and saving the environment from and costs of transporting vegetables from another continent are among the benefits.

So there are more and more opportunities to work for dedicated growers, develop sales and delivery programs, or start your own bakery or route close to home. Even people growing plums or zucchini in their backyards can sell at some farmers' markets.

Fast-food outlets, for which massive potato growing, slicing, and packing plants consume a large part of the country's potato supply, have been the fastest growing segment of the food industry. As Eric Schlosser pointed out so profoundly in his book *Fast Food Nation*, much of the country's beef production is committed to these same chain fast-food stores.

Popular demand and local government regulations have forced chain restaurants and many cracker, cookie, and baked goods producers to abandon cooking with trans fats and to substitute other oils. New York City has banned trans fats altogether, forbidding restaurants to use them in cooking.

Grains that many Americans still haven't heard of, such as quinoa, amaranth, faro, and oat groats, will become more prominent in our diets and restaurants.

Restaurant owners reduce serving sizes and plate sizes to cut back on calories and food costs and fatten up profits, such as serving hanger steak instead of filet mignon, sometimes to avoid raising prices while lowering costs.

Watch for more vegetarian restaurant opportunities, or open your own.

Organic food production is the hottest trend this decade and offers many job opportunities, both in small production facilities and large plants. Whole Foods Markets are the first national certified organic grocers, while chains such as Safeway keep increasing their organic "O" offerings, from crackers to peanut butter, and recently committed to converting all of their trucks to biodiesel fuel.

Italian Carlo Petrini started the official "slow food" movement 30 years ago, although various segments of society had already "gone back to the earth." Petrini has maximized publicity opportunities and spread the word through a vast network of conviviums (clubs) that discuss ways to grow, cook, and enjoy food grown at or close to home and hold educational events to enlighten others. His annual "Terra Madre" (Mother Earth) conference draws thousands, and a 2008 Slow Food Nation conference in San Francisco did the same.

Some of Petrini's basic points about growing food naturally, organically, and slowly and purchasing food close to home dovetail into consciousness of global warming and the so-called green movement. Many "slow food" ideas are close to what our parents, grandparents, and great-grandparents considered common practice.

Genetic engineering and chemical research industries now make seeds that produce corn and other crops, but are engineered to not produce more seeds, forcing the farmer or grower to purchase seeds from those companies every year. These same seed companies offer new food chemist jobs in the industry.

Other food scientists and food chemists work to create the appearance and taste of natural flavors in order to add chemical and artificial flavoring in place of the real thing, intending to reduce the cost of producing popular foods without the cost of real ingredients, thus creating new jobs to develop the stuff. Some now even add fiber to replace fiber they removed during processing.

The enormous advertising and marketing industries offer thousands of food- and beverage-related jobs, from assistants to artists, cooks, food designers, photographers, copy editors, and a whole slew of other categories. For instance, I used to write labels for a major restaurant chain's food product line.

The U.S. federal government, through the Department of Health and Human Services' Food and Drug Administration and its Center for Food Safety and Applied Nutrition offer food-related jobs that rarely attract the romantic envy of those working in wineries and restaurant kitchens. In fact, proprietors often dread seeing inspectors approaching, as these officials are responsible for inspecting the U.S. poultry and beef supplies and encouraging "voluntary" recalls. In 2009 the Obama administration vowed to reorganize the USDA and FDA departments, with a suggestion that the United States put all inspections under one agency as is done in Canada and with the goal of better protecting the consumer.

And then, of course, you might enjoy the wildly independent jobs of cattle ranching, starting as a ranch hand, saving to buy your own land and developing your own business, or growing organic vegetables on someone else's land and selling them commercially or at farmers' markets.

The food world is wide open with prospects for jobs that presently exist and for creating your own employment opportunities and careers.

Restaurants

For decades, restaurant jobs in the U.S. and Canada followed the hierarchical *brigade de cuisine* system created in France by Georges Auguste Escoffier, thought possibly to have been the world's greatest chef. Escoffier modernized and simplified the cuisine of Marie-Antoine Carême (1784–1833), an original refiner of French *haute cuisine.*

Escoffier is credited with elevating cooking to a respected profession, having begun his career at age 13 as an apprentice at his uncle's restaurant, Le Restaurant Français, in Nice. Eventually he combined his skills with those of César Ritz (1850–1918) and directed the kitchens at Ritz's Grand Hotel in Monte Carlo, the London Savoy, the Hotel Ritz in Paris and New York, and the Carlton in London, where he introduced the concept of an à la carte menu.

Escoffier's brigade system, still found in restaurants and hotels throughout France and America, draws clear lines of job descriptions and outlines responsibilities of the entire kitchen staff, with everyone specializing in certain tasks and rarely moving outside those lines.

In the United States and Canada the traditions still exist, with the lines blurred slightly by the widespread use of immigrant cooks, who often learn the system and the job but do not get the formal brigade titles or pay.

Cooks in all of these jobs, except for the top famous chefs, work for far less than the public thinks they do.

Here is a brief outline of modern versions of the *brigade de cuisine* system to describe many of the positions available in restaurant kitchens today. The word *chef* has loosened tremendously from the title of the top person in a kitchen to define anyone who cooks in that kitchen.

- **Executive chef:** Responsible for managing everything that relates to the kitchen, from creation of the menu, ordering supplies, overseeing all staff, to reporting to owners and higher managers. The chef de cuisine, sous-chef, and all others report up the kitchen ladder to this person.
- **Chef de cuisine, or kitchen chef:** A chef who is the head chef of a kitchen or restaurant, usually when it is one of several restaurants within a hotel or resort, or at one of many restaurants under the same owner and overseen by an executive chef, or when an owner wants to hold out another step before the chef may truly have control.
- **Sous chef:** Under chef or deputy chef of a kitchen, or assistant or second in command to the executive chef or chef de cuisine, whichever is the top chef in that kitchen. An executive sous-chef in a large operation or in a hotel with several kitchens and room service works directly for the executive chef, executes orders from the executive chef, and troubleshoots wherever needed, including filling in positions below his or hers, such as chefs de partie or line cooks.
- **Expediter or announcer (aboyeur):** Takes orders from guests or servers in the dining room and relays them to each cooking station in the kitchen in order to coordinate communication. With sev-

eral languages spoken in one kitchen, this person may need foreign language skills. The expediter also may make a final check on a dish to make sure it is perfect, apply finishing touches to spruce up the dish, and even deliver it to the diner.

- **Chef de partie:** In sophisticated or large restaurant kitchens, the chef de partie is also called a station chef or line cook and is in charge of one facet of the kitchen's total cooking picture. In some kitchens, mainly those that follow the brigade system more closely, station chefs and line cooks are divided into sub-hierarchies, with head cooks for each in charge of a specialty as follows:

  1. **Saucier or sauté chef or sauce maker:** Responsible for all sauces and sautéed foods, sometimes with assistants specializing in each sauce or sautéing. Makes warm hors d'oeuvres or appetizers; finishes off meat dishes.

  2. **Poissonier or fish chef:** Oversees cooking of fish or cooks fish only, including occasionally recommending fish dishes or ordering specific fish, butchering the fish, and preparing sauces to go on or with the fish. In some cases the saucier will make these sauces.

  3. **Rôtisseur or roast chef:** Oversees or prepares roasted and braised meats and their sauces. Again, the sauces maybe made by the saucier.

  4. **Grillardin or grill chef:** grills all foods, which now can mean on a smooth stove surface or on a barbecue grill. Job may be done by rôtisseur or vice versa.

  5. **Friturier or fry chef:** Cooks or oversees all frying, from fish to potatoes.

  6. **Entremetier, legumier, or vegetable chef:** A position gaining in importance with the trend toward more healthful eating, sometimes preparing soups, egg dishes, and vegetable dishes.

  7. **Potager or soup chef:** Few kitchens have soup chefs any longer, and these duties and pasta preparation might be absorbed by the vegetable chef.

  8. **Cuisinier, cuisinier de partie, or cook:** Works under chef de partie making specific or singular dishes in a station on the line.

  9. **Tournant or roundsman or swing cook:** Rover who fills in at any station in a kitchen; a great place to learn.

  10. **Garde-manger or pantry chef:** This person oversees the "pantry" of fresh vegetables, washing and careful preparation of salad greens and fresh vegetables to be cooked; might also contribute ideas for vegetarian dishes, and is of great importance in vegetarian or raw vegetable restaurants. Also oversees or creates cold appetizers, pâté, and charcuterie (sausages or salumi) when a kitchen makes its own, a growing trend.

  11. **Boucher or butcher:** Butchers meats, fish, and poultry. Needs to recognize the finest meats, recognize any disease or defects, and know how to best use every part. Duties may include breading or performing other meat or fish preparations if those practices are used in the restaurant.

  12. **Pâtissier or pastry chef:** Often thought to be second most important staff member because customers remember desserts. Keeps up with trends and prepares all baked goods, sometimes from breads and muffins to ciabatta, focaccia, and luxurious, sumptuous cakes and other specialized desserts. In large establishments, the pastry chef may oversee his or her own kitchen or even have a separate shop for retail sales.

      - **Confiseur:** Makes petits fours and candies in restaurants with large staffs.
      - **Glacier:** Makes cold and frozen desserts in restaurants with large staffs.
      - **Décorateur:** Decorates showy cakes and possibly even ice sculptures in large restaurants.
      - **Boulanger:** Makes breads, cakes, and breakfast pastries in restaurants or hotels with large staffs.

  13. **Commis, junior cook, or apprentice:** May work under a chef de partie to learn each station's techniques and responsibilities.

  14. **Apprentice:** Usually a culinary student learning theory and getting practical experience working under more experienced chefs and doing food preparation (prep) or clean-up jobs.

15. **Communard**: May specifically prepare a meal for the staff during each shift. The food served in a restaurant kitchen is sometimes experimental and almost always good.

16. **Escuelerie, plongeur, or dishwasher**: In charge of keeping dishes and utensils clean and unbroken, stacked appropriately, and handy to cooks who need them, and keeping the kitchen clean. Sometimes a marmiton specializes in washing pots and pans and making them ready for cooks.

17. **Garçon de cuisine**: Does prep and an abundance of small jobs in large restaurant or hotel kitchens.

On the other hand, many positions in modern kitchens in restaurants and large hotels are simply called "cook."

Most restaurants are run with a person or host, occasionally still known as the *maître d'hotel* or *maître d'* ("dee"), managing the dining room or "front of the house" while the restaurant's chef runs "the back of the house" or kitchen. Often couples who own and run restaurants divide up their duties along those diplomatic and slightly territorial lines.

The Beverage Industry

Some of the biggest changes and fads in the food and beverage industries have developed recently on the beverage side of the business. People are looking for new sources of nutrients and energy, leading us to more widely available organic and fortified milk, colas with more and less caffeine and sugar, juices with less sodium and sugar, chain coffee drink products in bottles and boxes, wine in boxes, wine bottles with screw tops instead of corks from cork trees, and healthy and flavored teas.

Food producers and packagers have always been aware of marketing and shelf placement in grocery stores, but the tea and coffee industries seem to have had their collective eyes opened to possibilities by Seattle, Washington–based Starbucks.

Specialty teas have skyrocketed in popularity, with importers blending and packaging all over the country. Artisinal coffees and roasters compete on flavor, organic-ness, how sustainably grown the beans are, and occasionally on price. As economic trends ebb and flow, enormous coffee chains such as Starbucks have had to cut back on new store openings and hot breakfast sandwich offerings, and have even closed some outlets, while McDonald's moved into the coffee beverage field with inexpensive espresso drinks.

The wine industry also swings with trends and fads that affect the popularity of varietals. The movie *Sideways* temporarily put the kibosh on merlot sales, resulting in an effort to produce a movie in which the characters love merlot, all to save the wineries that make that varietal.

One can still start small, learn as an apprentice or "cellar rat" working at wineries or study winemaking and enology at a community college or university, then open one's own winery, rent space in a winery to blend your own, and stick your own labels on bottles. Giant bottling plants make up the other end of the spectrum, sometimes filling and sealing thousands of wine bottles an hour, and usually offer assembly-line jobs.

Regional breweries continue to spring up with great enthusiasm and near-cult followings. There are few beer-making programs at universities, although some community colleges offer classes. The best way to learn is to get a job, any job, in a brewery, learn from the brewmaster, and work your way up.

Sake, the Japanese alcoholic beverage made from rice, has become more popular in North America, partly because it is sometimes served warm and has a soft impact, and partly because it produces minimal hangover headaches. Several sake breweries opened around North America in the 1990s, and some closed in the early 2000s.

There is a well-established saying in the wine industry, which probably also pertains to starting a beer or sake brewery: "The way to make a small fortune in the wine industry is to start with a large one."

Kathleen Thompson Hill

ACKNOWLEDGMENTS

Several friends and colleagues helped me in many ways to create this new version of a book originated by Barbara Sims-Bell.

I thank agent Elizabeth Pomada for linking Jim Chambers of Facts On File to me to write the book. It was a natural relationship since my husband and I had already written two other books for the same publisher.

Project manager Sarah Fogarty Dalton and Jim both shared guidance and patience that waited out a surgery and this writer's wrist in a brace.

Beth Hadley, whom I met as the volunteer engineer on my radio show, was a gigantic help in developing the appendixes of this book and as a general member of my support team.

Among those I would like to thank for their generosity are Michelle Heston of the Fairmont Sonoma Mission Inn and Fairmont Hotels, Curtis Dorsett of Sunflower Caffé, Ignazio Vella of Vella Cheese, Joanne Filipello of Wild Thyme Events and Dining Club Rive Gauche, sommelier Christopher Sawyer and Chef de Cuisine Janine Falvo of Carneros Bistro & Wine Bar, Roger Declercq of Sonoma Gourmet, James Marshall Berry of JMB Web Consulting, Paul Bergna and John Calmeyer of Foley Family Wines, Marc Cuneo formerly of Sebastiani Vineyards & Winery, Lisa Lavagetto of Ramekins Culinary School, cookbook author and good friend Paula Wolfert, Jacqueline Buchanan of Laura Chenel Chèvre, Françoise Hodges of The Basque Boulangerie, and Linda Carucci of the Art Institute of San Francisco.

My husband, Gerald N. Hill, deserves the most thanks for putting up with my intense focus on this book, for sharing our experience writing a series of food and wine lovers' guidebooks to wine regions of the West Coast, sharing teaching duties with me in our courses on the politics and history of food and wine, and making excellent coffee every morning.

HOW TO USE THIS BOOK

The job descriptions in this book will give anyone interested in getting into the food, wine, and beer industries the tools to make good decisions on how to proceed, whether going to school or using the get-the-foot-in-the-door approach.

Here are explanations of the sections of each job entry.

Career Profile: Career profiles give bullet descriptions that are expanded later in each section.

Duties: This gives brief descriptions of what the person in this job does.

Alternate Title(s): This lists other names for the job described that might be found in job listings or in the food and beverage industry hierarchy.

Salary Range: This is an approximate range of salaries for each position throughout the United States. Salaries or hourly wages vary widely in different geographic regions of the country.

Employment Prospects: This rates the realistic potential opportunities of each job, although these vary greatly with region and the state of the national and local economies.

Advancement Prospects: This gives realistic assessment of the chances to move up the ladder in the kitchen, lab, winery, or brewery.

Best Geographical Location(s): This section suggests what parts of the United States or Canada are best for a particular job or industry.

Prerequisites

Education or Training—This section covers whether you need formal school training and at what level, or whether you can do the job by working your way up the ladder.

Experience—This offers obvious and alternative skills and job experience that employers will look for or which might get you the job ahead of someone else.

Special Skills and Personality Traits—This tells what work and people skills, temperament, physical abilities and other traits put you in the best position to get the job and succeed at it.

Career Ladder

This sidebar in each job section tells the position above and below the one being discussed to give applicants an idea of whom they might supervise and who might supervise him or her.

Position Description

This section expands the duties outline with great detail and realistically gives a full description of everything wonderful and not so wonderful about each job, and describes what an interested person can expect on the job and in his or her future.

Salaries

This section gives realistic estimates of what earnings in various positions in the food, wine, and beer industries might be, considering fluctuations in the economy, language abilities, and skill sets.

Employment Prospects

This section helps a job applicant put all of the above information together and assess true prospects of getting the job after going through all the training available. Some of these prospect assessments understate reality, but they also vary along with the national or North American economy.

Advancement Prospects

This section makes realistic assessments of how easy or difficult it is to move up the kitchen, winery, or brewery ladder and alternate ways to get there.

Education and Training

This is an expanded version of the prerequisites outline with optimistic prospects that will enhance a job candidate's prospects.

Experience, Skills, and Personality Traits

This section gives more information on how all of these traits can combine to give a person a leg up on the job ladder in addition to, or sometimes in place of, education and training.

Unions and Associations

This section lists all unions related to certain jobs if any exist in that field, as well as all associations from which one can learn or get information. See more such opportunities in the appendices.

Tips for Entry

This section gives a list of smart tips to work your way into whatever job level is your goal in the food, wine, and brewing industries. Most of the recommended steps cost little and are meant to help you get the job or develop skills inexpensively.

Other Resources in This Book

Appendix I includes more than 400 culinary schools and academies, from community colleges to private culinary schools, in the United States. Appendix II offers wine- and beer-making schools and classes. Appendix III lists all contacts for culinary organizations, professional societies, and trade associations. Appendix IV includes many magazines and periodicals covering the food and beverage fields. The bibliography lists all books, articles, and Web sites used as references in *Career Opportunities in the Food and Beverage Industry*.

CATERING, FAST FOOD, DELIS, AND TAKEOUT

CATERER

CAREER PROFILE

Duties: Establishes relationships with potential clients; meets with clients to learn their needs for a party, meal, or event; coordinates rental and fees for space, furniture, sound equipment, music, photographer, table covers, and place settings; coordinates cooking and serving staff; arranges for décor and flowers; coordinates cleanup after event

Alternate Title(s): Event Planner

Salary Range: $30,000 to millions

Employment Prospects: Fair for full time to good for part time; fluctuates with economic prosperity as people feel festive or cut back on spending

Advancement Prospects: Fair to good, depending on commitment, language skills, cooking or serving training, people skills

Best Geographical Location(s): High-income cities or suburbs, particularly on the East and West coasts

Prerequisites:

Education or Training—In event management and coordination, knowledge of cooking for numbers of people, contacts with food and setup sources, accu-

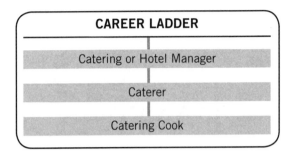

CAREER LADDER

Catering or Hotel Manager

Caterer

Catering Cook

rate cost estimating and knowledge of current prices of supplies, staff, and public relations

Experience—Cooking experience required in order to cook or supervise and understand on-site or off-site cooking; experience in coordinating people and in event organization and management

Special Skills and Personality Traits—Enjoyment in making people happy; diplomacy; ability to juggle party givers' demands, dreams, and visions; creative imagination; working relationships with suppliers to get best provisions at best price; unflappability; enjoyment in satisfaction from successful coordination of the many elements that make up the whole event

Position Description

A Caterer's role is to take the responsibility for organizing a party or event from the host, whether the event is an intimate dinner party for two, a wedding, or a corporate event for hundreds or thousands of guests; it could mean thousands of meals for all the flights of an airline, or catering events within a facility such as a hotel.

A Caterer needs to develop relationships with clients and potential clients, with representatives of organizations and companies that can provide a wide range of food, beverage, and supply sources, and with competent and reliable staff.

Depending on the region of the United States or Canada, the Caterer needs to determine his or her target market or specialty, which may range from small dinner parties to corporate cafeteria service. Some Caterers will need to build those relationships with a set of party-givers who want to either pretend they are good cooks or are willing to be honest, and occasionally even boast that they have hired a caterer to provide appetizers and drinks for their party.

Developing these relationships takes time as one builds a reputation for providing good food, appropriate decor, great service, punctuality, diplomacy, and smoothness. Sometimes to gain good exposure, new Caterers might have to underbid others to land a job to get started, perhaps "eating" some costs to show off their abilities.

Clients hire Caterers for a variety of reasons. They may just want to be served, or may lack confidence in their own cooking and entertaining capabilities, or are "too busy" to bother with organizational details. They might want to put on a "show" for a wedding or other occasion and do not know how to do it, or simply need assistance while managing other tasks. Hence, the Caterer often has to be an amateur psychologist and therapist to understand the client's needs, anxieties, desires, and goals.

Once a Caterer is established, clients will call him or her to make an initial inquiry. Caterers know that potential clients, who may be first-timers, may "shop around," comparing prices and determining what they will get for their money in terms of presentation, decor, food, and beverages.

At the initial meeting between Caterer and client, the client expresses what she or he wants or imagines, the estimated number of guests, the location of the party or event, the date, time of day, and whether they want buffet or table service, the estimated length of event, whether they want live music or a DJ, a magician, or other entertainment.

Some Caterers offer complete service, meaning their business owns all the equipment imaginable or necessary for an event. On the Caterer's checklist will be questions such as whether the venue has an on-site kitchen or whether it will be a "camp-out" situation in which grills and other portable kitchen equipment must be brought. The Caterer may also be asked to provide chairs, table linens, table settings, flatware, umbrellas for shade, tents, ice sculptures, and arranged flowers.

At events with large numbers of people, the Caterer will need clients to think about whether they want everyone served at once, whether they want people to wait in lines at buffet tables, and if so, how many buffet "stations" should be placed around the event space to keep buffet lines short and guests happy.

Experienced Caterers will have a set of menus, often in a binder or on a Web site, that they can recommend for a variety of occasions, from their least expensive appetizer combination to their most costly several-course dinner, including vegetarian and organic alternatives depending upon the client's choices. Often the Caterer will consider the client's ideas and suggestions and add their favorites to menus or create new ones.

By the end of that initial meeting, the Caterer will take home the client's desires, while the client will take home a list of ideas to consider. The Caterer then prepares a cost estimate and a contract for the client, keeping in mind that clients often change their minds, that the number of guests often changes up or down, and that weather can affect everything, and details who will perform what function and makes certain that expenses are all understood. The Caterer usually collects a deposit from the client at this stage.

Once a menu and price are agreed upon and the contract is signed, the Caterer has several organizational functions to perform. If the Caterer owns all materials and props required, he or she must schedule those within the organizational operation. If the Caterer has to rent everything from wine and water glasses to chairs, tables, stage, bartenders, musicians, sound equipment, flowers, ice sculptures and piñatas, those items must be reserved from purveyors.

Caterers must schedule cooks, setup staff, prep cooks, flower deliveries, bartenders, servers, cleanup crew, and takedown staff.

Many Caterers have a stable of reliable part-time cooks, servers, and bartenders who gladly work their parties, with some of the prep and setup required the day before the event. Especially talented and valued workers can do food prep the day before and then serve or bartend on party day.

Timing is everything in the catering business. A Caterer can lose a client if setup and preparations are not up to his or her expectations, or if the party is not ready to roll when the proverbial bell rings.

Caterers usually attend and supervise the events they stage to make sure everything runs as close to perfectly as possible. Even if the owner of the venue or of the catering company sends an assistant as event manager, that person should have the Caterer's authority. Celebrity Caterers usually make an appearance, take credit and occasional applause, and pass out business cards when asked. The Caterer or their supervisor stays until cleanup is complete, schmoozes and assesses the client's reaction, and then presents a bill or returns the next day to give the client the financial news, smooth over details, and hopefully book the next event the host wants to throw.

Salaries

Catering wages and earning power vary greatly according to regions and even neighborhoods. Caterers operating alone may make anywhere from $15 to $100 an hour, depending on where they live and on their experience, contacts, and reputation. A family working out of its home kitchen can produce interesting food to be picked up by the customer and pocket a few hundred dollars.

Catering companies with several employees can make several hundred thousand dollars a year, but must be good business managers to consider costs and overhead of food, transportation, and staff.

Earning power also varies by season. Some larger or specialized Caterers develop the ability to cater through all entertainment seasons and can keep staff working throughout the year. Most Caterers are busy during late spring, summer, and early fall, working graduation parties, weddings, and summer entertaining. Others have developed holiday clientele and do a great job of putting on Christmas and Hanukkah parties, as well as Easter and Passover events.

Generally, Caterers can earn from $30,000 to $500,000 annually, although profit margins depend on gasoline prices and inflation.

Employment Prospects

There are always job prospects for Caterers, especially those who have perfected an all-American menu or a particular ethnic cuisine. Cooking and event management skills transfer well, even if you relocate your residence. When Caterers displaced by Hurricane Katrina showed up in California, many of them found work and even created their own companies successfully because they brought a cuisine that was either familiar to Louisiana natives who had moved to California or they introduced new tastes to foodie Californians.

Usually it is believed that big cities offer the best catering opportunities, just because of the number of people and complexity and varieties of activities. But an individual in a small town can find a need and fill it, perhaps beginning to cook or bake at home.

Wealthy communities, nonprofit organizations, and certain ethnic communities tend to present the most catering job opportunities, although baking cakes for birthday parties also works in less affluent areas.

One negative is that when the economy suffers and corporations and individuals cut back on entertaining, the catering business can suffer as well. Some Caterers resourcefully host dinner clubs to take up the slack. On the other hand, when people are feeling flush, they are happy to call a Caterer to put on their parties.

Some Caterers thrive on catering nonprofit organizations' fund-raising events and gain a reputation in this field by starting out charging less than they might. After preparing food for such events, Caterers often meet wealthy individuals or company executives who like the food and event and ask for a card to make future contact.

A Caterer can also stir up business by visiting and leaving cards or brochures at party supply stores, party equipment rental businesses, florists, and farmers' markets, focusing on the best vegetable and flower vendors.

In good economic times, large Caterers keep full-time staff, including prep cooks, cooks, servers, sommeliers, bartenders, cleaners, and drivers. Smaller Caterers have a stable of on-call part-timers. Those who have shown up reliably and serve the customers well get called back to work first.

Some Caterers advertise their services and availability in either the phone book or online yellow pages or on Web sites such as Craigslist and many others.

Some Caterers require staff to get themselves to events at their own expense, while others transport staff to make sure they know where they are.

Advancement Prospects

If you are owner of a catering company, your advancement falls on your own shoulders. Your advancement can depend on making good decisions regarding what events you take on and for whom, what food and beverages can make a profit and still please the client, choosing the best staff you can for the particular event, and developing personal relations skills with clients and staff.

If you are an employee of a Caterer, your advancement within the company depends on your food, beverage, or service skills, your punctuality, people skills, willingness to show up at the last minute if called, and your eagerness to learn. As each staff member contributes his or her best to the whole, business grows and, hopefully, so does employment.

Education and Training

Catering education and training comes in two ways: experience and school. Some Caterers have grown their businesses from cooking or baking cookies with their mothers at home to huge catering operations with industrial warehouse kitchens. Others have studied at culinary schools or in college hospitality programs, of which there are hundreds around North America (see Appendix I), started to work for Caterers or restaurants, and then spun off their own catering operations.

Occasionally neighborhood or farm women have banded together to cook for multitudes to raise money for local charities, found that their collaboration works, and turn casual cooking into a formal business or a cookbook.

Experience, Skills, and Personality Traits

While catering is a business in which one can start with no experience, having worked in food or events somewhere, somehow, is best. If you have knife skills, you can work prep, or chop and cut vegetables and fruit.

Newcomers to catering should know or learn quickly the language of food and cooking, the difference between tastes, and the differences between the techniques and terms of roasting, sautéing, frying, steaming, poaching, braising, blanching, boiling, and rinsing.

Caterers and catering staff need to enjoy people, enjoy service, and enjoy making other people happy, take pride in diplomacy skills, and be flexible and considerate of others' needs and tastes. Caterers, similar to restaurant workers, have the chance to raise food service to the high levels of respect it once enjoyed.

Caterers and their staff should realize that they are the de facto hosts of the party. Their reputation and that of their client, the host, rests on how the Caterer performs and treats guests.

Obviously a Caterer must have organizational skills and enjoy coordinating and putting on a good party. If the Caterer is organized enough for every dish, drink, and feature of the party to go perfectly, the Caterer can even have a good time making other people happy.

Unions and Associations

Several national organizations provide associations through which information and certification are offered for cooks, chefs, kitchen workers, waiters, and bartenders. The International Association of Culinary Professionals (www.iacp.com) provides an examination and certification of cooking professionals called certified culinary professional. The American Culinary Federation (ACF) accepts Caterer members at the same level as chefs and has teamed with the Culinary Institute of America (CIA) to develop the ProChef Certification program. The CIA developed this effort to parallel the certified master chef exam in a quicker, shorter four-day format. Those who pass receive certification by both ACF and CIA (www.afchefs.com; www. culinary.edu). The ACF Web site also has a job board for both employers and job seekers. Culinary workers and bartenders each have unions, both of which have affiliated with Unite Here (http://www.unitehere.org), which includes food service and casino workers as well as the Hotel Employees and Restaurant Employees International Union. Unionized restaurants and Caterers are much more prevalent in big cities than elsewhere. The National Association of Catering Executives (NACE; www.nace.net) is a good source for information.

Tips for Entry

1. Get a start by volunteering to cook at a local meals-on-wheels program, soup kitchen, church, or nonprofit, or offer to do menial tasks for a Caterer, even for free, just to get your foot in the door and begin to learn the business.

2. To find Caterers from whom you can learn or with whom you can apprentice, look in the yellow pages of the locale where you want to be, visit party supply and rental stores where, hopefully, Caterers have left their cards, ask the store's staff who the good Caterers are, and then get up your nerve and call them.

3. Enroll in cooking, catering, or hospitality classes at a local junior or community college, the most inexpensive and directly related education available. These colleges often have job counselors with knowledge of job openings for when you finish.

4. If you have even fleeting thoughts of becoming a Caterer or working for one, ask questions of the staff at the next catered event you attend if and when you do.

CATERING COOK

Duties: Fulfill caterer's and client's agreed-upon menu with caterer's recipes, sometimes with the responsibility for recommending a menu, bearing in mind other parties the client has given; order ingredients, schedule delivery, and reserve the use of on-site equipment such as heating trays; schedule kitchen help; get food ready with ample time to transport to event; supervise presentation and serving; make sure servers know ingredient details of the food they are serving

Alternate Title(s): Catering Chef

Salary Range: Depending on region of the country, from $15 to $30 an hour and occasional shared tips; pay depends upon ability and experience

Employment Prospects: Depends on state of the national economy; good in many urban or wine-centric regions

Best Geographical Location(s): Urban areas; food and wine centers

Prerequisites:

    Education and Training—Study in a community college, junior college, or cooking school environ-

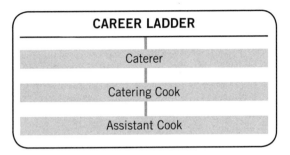

CAREER LADDER

Caterer

Catering Cook

Assistant Cook

ment, having cooked somewhere under direction of a chef, especially in situations where food is prepared for large numbers of people. Computer knowledge is helpful.

    Experience—Professional cooking experience outside the home, preferably in a cooking line in a restaurant or catering situation

    Special Skills and Personality Traits—Good organizational skills, humility, cool temperament, reliability, ability to work well with others, ability to enjoy teamwork

Position Description

A Catering Cook works with the caterer to develop menus that will please their clientele, designs and advises about new menu items and recipes that keep the caterer up to date, works with the caterer, and helps make a cost estimate of the menu. The product created by the cook for the public contributes to the caterer's and the cook's reputation. How the cook presents food at an event is all-important to the caterer's company success. If a client's guests rave about the food, the client will hire the caterer again, and guests may also hire the caterer in the future. Often recipes created by a cook working for a caterer become the property of the caterer, since the cook or chef was in the caterer's employ at the time.

    After the caterer and the client agree on a menu, the cook talks with the caterer on the client's expectations for buffet or table service, oversees gathering the recipes, forms a list of products required, and orders from the best vendors, which means that the cook or chef

has to know the vendors and which carry the best of each item at the best price for organic and conventional foods. The cook also schedules necessary kitchen help for prep and cooking phases or days.

    The caterer may have all of his or her recipes on a computer so that recipes can be mixed and matched, which is where computer writing and reading ability is increasingly important. Otherwise, arranging recipes for the meal might be done simply on recipe cards.

    A Catering Cook might work with a sommelier or wine specialist to select wines to go with each course. The cook will also make sure all cooking equipment and serving dishes will be available.

    If there are menu changes, either due to the client changing his or her mind or unavailability of ingredients, the cook seeks the new required ingredients, revises the cost estimate, and works with the caterer to inform the client.

    The cook arranges for or lists all food-related equipment needed at the event site, which ranges from steam tables to serving spoons, outdoor grills, cold chests, and condiments.

If a Catering Cook is the whole operation, he or she has to do all of the above. If a Catering Cook works for a large catering company, he or she may be in charge of organizing, preparing and directing staff for several events on the same day, ranging from a kids' Mad Hatter's tea party to a tiki party in the snow.

Salaries

Salaries for Catering Cooks vary widely by urban, suburban, or rural area; where in the country they are located, with coastal caterers generally paying higher; by experience leading staff members and cooking; how busy the caterer is; whether the job is full-time, part-time, or on-call; and how frequently they work.

Catering Cooks' salaries have not increased with inflation over the last few years. Catering Cooks, prep cooks, and other kitchen staff receive from $15 to $30 per hour, usually do not get in on tip distribution, and rarely get benefits. While the pay may not sound alluring, it is a great entry into the culinary world if a person has not worked in a restaurant and would like to get into cooking.

Employment Prospects

Many caterers are innovative individuals who do what they do because they love it or reinvented themselves after leaving another job. Sometimes these culinary entrepreneurs need help, so once one gets into the field one has a better chance of getting frequent calls.

Large catering companies often employ cooks and chefs full time or part time with long, intense hours adding up to making a living. Many cooks work occasionally for more than one caterer in their home area, sort of a "have knife, will travel" situation.

Job availability depends on local and national economic circumstances, while certain clients are not affected by swings in the economy. When things are bad, some larger caterers have to cut back on full-time cooking staff, and then when business picks up again they hire people back. In the interim, some cooks get the idea of starting their own companies.

Employment possibilities also depend upon how many caterers there are in an area. The more there are, the more opportunities there are, probably because there is enough business to spread around. The best opportunities exist in affluent urban areas or suburbs and in places popular for second homes or where there are few people with culinary talent. In many areas, a bilingual (Spanish/English) cook or chef has the best chance for employment if supervising Latino prep cooks or other kitchen staff.

Advancement Prospects

Good workers who show up on time or early, learn quickly, and are curious will advance in the food industry and in catering, especially someone willing to speak or learn Spanish.

If a caterer has good staff, good service, and good food, they will get more jobs and hire and promote good workers. Those workers who make the caterer look good will get promoted and called back to work most often.

During tough economic times, caterers—and all business people—may need to get innovative and find ways to keep busy and keep staff working. Such tactics might include a willingness to travel farther for jobs, which is complicated by gas and rising food costs, cultivate a clientele in large cities, or branch out beyond their normal clientele comfort zone.

Education and Training

You can acquire culinary and catering education two ways: by taking courses or apprenticing under someone in the field who will teach you. Some high schools and community colleges offer culinary training programs, while some culinary schools offer courses specific to catering.

One can also learn by cooking alongside more experienced cooks, such as cooking on a line or at the right or left hand of someone with more time at the stove.

Experience, Skills, and Personality Traits

Many of the best restaurant and Catering Cooks learned at home from one or both parents. Usually a Catering Cook needs to either take direction well or be able to read recipes in English. Reading cookbooks, books on catering, watching videos, and learning on the Internet can all help an ambitious cook.

Willingness—even excitement—to learn is an essential personality trait for an aspirant to do well and rise in the cooking end of catering. One must acquire knowledge of basic sauces, knife skills, and the nuanced differences among sautéing, frying, braising, roasting, grilling on various devices (from stoves to gas, wood, or charcoal barbecues and Big Green Eggs), smoking, and steaming to do well as a Catering Cook. The more you learn and know, the more people will want to hire you.

Showing up on time (or early), being reliable, acting responsibly, being ambitious, having a willingness to work with others as a team, taking direction, being well organized, wanting to learn, not smoking or drinking on the job, and having an even-keeled personality that can handle pressure and culinary crises are perfect traits for being a Catering Cook.

Unions and Associations

Some regions of the United States have strong culinary unions, but most do not. Local food-oriented interest groups have developed regionally and nationally to form networks of caterers, cooks, instructors, writers, chefs, and growers. Very few caterers outside big cities are unionized. The American Culinary Federation (www.acfchefs.org) and International Association of Culinary Professionals (www.iacp.com) both offer information online.

Tips for Entry

1. Volunteer at local charity kitchens to get experience. Then you can list that job as part of your cooking experience.
2. Be willing to start at the bottom washing dishes, busing dishes, or cleaning up if you want to get into the field but have no experience or training.

You can learn on the job from people next to and above you on the food chain of command.

3. Visit local party rental, supply stores, farmers' markets, and even retail kitchen stores where caterers may leave their cards hoping to attract new clients with referrals by the stores. Store staff may have heard of leads to caterers who need new cooks or other food-related employees. Call those caterers and ask to meet with them or find out whether they need help.
4. If you are a guest at catered events, from large parties to bridal showers to baseball games or even auto races, venture into the kitchen, look for whoever seems to be in charge, and ask if the staff needs help.
5. Find the nearest cooking school, whether private or at a community college, offer to enroll, and ask staff if they know of job opportunities.
6. Improve your computer skills. Many kitchens' recipes are now on computers, so knowing how to print, enter, or write recipes on a computer will be advantageous.

CORPORATE CATERER

Duties: Serve as in-house chef or executive chef and prepare all food for company employees, usually only on weekdays, and often only breakfast and lunch; depending upon the corporate culture, the Corporate Caterer or chef might have to also prepare dinner

Alternate Title(s): Corporate Chef; Company Cook; Executive Chef

Salary Range: $40,000 to $160,000, usually with benefits

Employment Prospects: Corporate Caterer or chef jobs are hard to find since the number of companies supporting in-house dining are rare; there are many more jobs as support or backup to the top caterer or chef, and working for big-name companies can add as much prestige to one's résumé as well-known restaurants.

Advancement Prospects: Advancements usually come in form of better title and small salary increases; while some high-tech companies have shut down satellite offices altogether, other high-tech companies that downsized in the past few years have dismissed expensive chefs and replaced them with lower paid cooking staff.

Best Geographical Location(s): Large cities and "Silicon Valley"–type centers for high-tech business campuses, where corporate culture provides

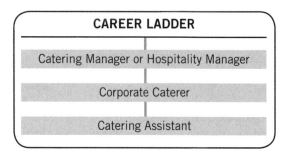

CAREER LADDER

Catering Manager or Hospitality Manager

Corporate Caterer

Catering Assistant

everything from fine food to gyms, massages, and concerts

Prerequisites:

Education or Training—Professional culinary training or experience in restaurants with high-volume production; knowledge of nutrition, ethnic foods, and a second language such as Spanish also would be helpful

Experience—Work in high-volume and varied culinary environment would be especially helpful, either for catering companies or restaurants

Special Skills and Personality Traits—Full knowledge of how a commercial kitchen works; ability to work with corporate leaders; patience; diplomacy; ability to deal with last-minute change; interest in health foods and ethnic foods; flexibility; confidence in capabilities; familiarity with foreign language (especially Spanish) handy

Position Description

Some corporations want to keep employees "on campus" and please employees in every way possible, including providing food to meet dietary needs, preferences, or whims. A Corporate Caterer or corporate executive chef runs all food service for a company, from morning coffee to mid-morning snacks (fruit to nuts and granola or whatever the corporate culture demands), lunch, afternoon snacks, power drinks, and occasionally dinner.

The Corporate Caterer usually develops and writes menus (sometimes multiethnic), oversees purchasing and inventory, cooks in a fairly up-to-date kitchen at the corporate offices or "campus," supervises chefs and cooks, may oversee smaller dining venues, and on rare occasions cooks at an outside catering kitchen.

Many Corporate Caterers serve in a cafeteria atmosphere, while others only have to cook and serve special private lunches for executives and their guests, or for special occasions and holiday parties.

Unlike outside caterers and restaurant chefs who only occasionally know their clients and guests well, in-house Corporate Caterers or chefs know they have the same clientele every day. Restaurant customers or catering clients often revisit a restaurant or rehire a caterer because they know the caterer's food and like it. In the corporate atmosphere, chefs have to vary the menu in order not to bore the corporate staff and keep their jobs.

In-house corporate dining and food preparation is rarely done to make a profit, except by an outside catering company. An in-house corporate chef has to prepare the best food possible at the lowest cost possible, sometimes just to break even financially. A corporate caterer from an outside company likely will be more profit motivated but will still have to produce good to excellent food while keeping prices low for the customer/employee.

Many businesses now hire outside catering companies that provide packages of chefs, vending machines, and food supplies. Some of the largest Corporate Caterers are massive international corporations that employ chefs or an executive chef who oversees café chefs for each dining facility or café within the corporate complex. Check out Compass Group (www.compass-group.com or www.cgnad.com), Bon Appétit Management Company (www.bamco.com), Canteen Food Service (www.canteen.com), or Aramark (www.aramark.com). As an example, Canteen owns Blimpie, Tony Roma's, Au Bon Pain, Sbarro, Krystal, Mamma Leone's, Rally's, Coyote Jack's Grill, Outtakes, and Nathan's, all of which technically can fall into the "Corporate Caterer" category.

Many jobs exist below the corporate chef level in company food service, from assistant cooks and cooks to prep cooks, drivers, dishwashers, food servers, and packagers.

Salaries

Salaries vary geographically, with the highest being on the coasts and in upscale industries that employ highly educated staff. Salaries also vary by whether the job is Corporate Caterer or chef working directly for the company or working for an outside mega-caterer, or whether the job is at the executive chef, café chef, or kitchen worker level.

Corporate Caterer salaries often include health care and 401(k) benefits, which many restaurant chefs and private smaller catering staff members do not receive. Annual salaries can range from $40,000 to $160,000, depending on the name and reputation of the executive chef, his or her experience, and the size of company and its location.

Employment Prospects

Corporate Caterer jobs are limited but worth looking for on U.S. coasts, in large cities with big businesses that are thriving and in Silicon Valley tech centers where good food is demanded and expected. Companies that like to keep their employees on campus may also offer free or inexpensive food so that their minds stay somewhat within corporate confines and mealtime can produce great ideas.

Corporate catering may also include vending machine operation. Some hospitals and other businesses offer alternatives to candy bar vending machines. These may include sandwich preparation, procuring baked goods, sourcing organic fruit, or even sale and placement of the machine in a business location.

Advancement Prospects

Depending upon where a Corporate Caterer or chef begins, he or she may climb up the kitchen ladder by gaining experience, learning the trade, learning a second language, and playing the corporate game.

As a contract caterer, the salary of the executive chef or corporate chef may rise or fall depending upon the addition of new sites within a corporation or on locations downsized or lost. Professional titles, positions, and job availability also play a role in determining pay.

It is also possible for Corporate Caterers and chefs to move up the in-house corporate hierarchy, while out-of-house caterers and chefs may also climb the kitchen ladder within the catering company.

Education and Training

The job of Corporate Caterer requires training at a culinary school or in a culinary program at a vocational school or community college, as well as experience working in a high-volume restaurant or for a private catering company. Knowledge and experience in preparing ethnic foods can be advantageous, as might knowledge of a second language.

Workers at the kitchen's lower levels should have some experience or training and can learn on the job and rise through the corporate ranks.

Experience, Skills, and Personality Traits

Experience working as a caterer or for a caterer or in a high-volume restaurant is necessary. A Corporate Caterer or chef must have diplomatic skills to deal with corporate higher-ups and company staff who want their culinary whims met. This person must also be able to build a team able to change directions quickly, write menus, translate to kitchen staff, plan long-range menus so as to not repeat offerings, and have an even personality so that temperament is not an obstacle to producing the best food possible.

Unions and Associations

The American Culinary Federation (www.acfchefs.org) offers membership and certification to chefs, cooks, and pastry chefs with hundreds of chapters around the United States. The International Association of Culinary Professionals (IACP; www.iacp.com) offers membership to anyone in a field even related to cooking and now provides certification in conjunction with the Culinary Institute of America. IACP provides lots of online community communication and information for its members. In many regions of the country, no unions exist to advocate for standardization of work conditions, pay, or benefits.

Tips for Entry

1. Many Web sites post current culinary jobs online.

2. Often cooks and chefs hear of corporate catering or chef jobs by word of mouth, as they do of restaurant job openings. As people leave a position because it has finished serving a purpose in their lives, they often tell someone else for whom they think the job would be appropriate to apply.

3. Visit corporate catering Web sites mentioned above and click on their job opportunity pages, which are often organized by region or state, and be willing to take a job at your skill level and work your way up the kitchen ladder.

4. If your culinary training is limited, get a job with a local caterer, be willing to start at the bottom, learn on the job, and work your way up. Once you have some experience in this specialized field of cooking for lots of people, you will have a better chance at the top jobs.

CATERING OPERATIONS MANAGER

Duties: Seeks new business for a hotel, convention center, golf club, or institution; books major banquets, events, and parties; works with chefs to develop and update menus to be presented to potential clients with sensitivity to trends, fads, and clients' needs; works with chefs to assign parties and kitchen duties to balance with what else is going on in the institution and within the catering operation; oversees general business and financials of department; schedules waitstaff; and works with public clientele

Alternate Title(s): Catering Manager; Catering Sales Manager; Special Events Coordinator; Catering Director, Catering and Conference Services Manager; Food Services Director

Salary Range: $40,000 to $150,000, sometimes on commission, and usually with benefits if working for a large institution

Employment Prospects: Fairly good, as hotels, golf clubs, convention centers, and large restaurants need to expand their sales and food service; in hard times, the catering manager position may be eliminated with duties distributed to other employees

Advancement Prospects: If one does well as Catering Operations Manager for one institution, meaning one increases sales and produces fine food and service, that person will be in demand by other organizations; catering personnel may work up to Catering Operations Manager and then into general hotel and chain hotel management

Best Geographical Location(s): Large cities with large food-serving hotels, entertainment/gambling cen-

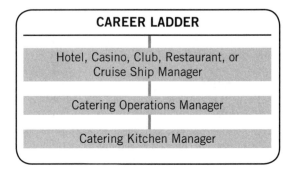

CAREER LADDER

Hotel, Casino, Club, Restaurant, or Cruise Ship Manager

Catering Operations Manager

Catering Kitchen Manager

ters, areas that have at least one hotel with in-house dining, preferably as part of a chain of hotels, or golf courses with dining facilities

Prerequisites:

Education or Training—Some catering operations or catering managers' employers require a bachelor's degree or equivalent experience; others want the potential employee to have culinary school credentials.

Experience—Many employers want at least two to five years' catering or banquet sales and supervisory experience, including business management, management of purchasing and cost control, and team building.

Special Skills and Personality Traits—Diplomacy skills to manage diverse employees, a second language, concern with details, multitasking ability, people skills to focus on client and customer service and develop lasting professional relationships with management and staff, communication skills and computer skills, creativity, diplomacy, flexibility, and tact are all skills for success

Position Description

Catering Operations Managers are supposed to cater to current clients' culinary needs and wishes; schmooze everyone and anyone as if he or she is a potential client; sign up new clients; book all business, whether within a club membership, museum, hotel, or university; find new clients for an international kitchen management or serving contract; and keep the events calendar and make sure the facility and staff can handle the combination of events so well that the business will get new and repeat client bookings. This person must also have firsthand knowledge of room or space capacities, ser-

vice such as flatware and tableware, and what needs to be rented where.

Whether in a private catering business or in a large institution, the Catering Operations Manager or catering manager has to keep booking new events and keeping existing clients happy to keep everyone else in the catering employment food chain working. At the same time, it is this person's responsibility to balance demand on the kitchen and serving staffs.

The Catering Operations Manager develops menus and recipes that combine tradition and new fads and helps create the budget and cost for the client. This person also works with the head chef to schedule sous-chefs, cooks and waitstaff, and calculates logistical needs such as tables and linens, space heaters or fans, decorators, and florists.

Assuming the party reservations are made several months ahead, the Catering Operations Manager may have to deal with changing costs of supplies and make plans for changes in clients' expectations.

The Catering Operations Manager may have to deal with city or county authorities for special event permits including one for loud music, deal with health and cleanliness inspectors, and select security firms, portable toilet rental companies, and musicians.

Keeping ahead of competitors in food and presentation trends while being able to produce traditional parties and have excellent community relations should maintain a flow of small to large parties or events through inexpensive word-of-mouth publicity.

This person also manages the catering office and keeps up on food trends nationally and internationally through magazines, dining at new and ethnic restaurants, and by frequently checking food and hospitality management Web sites (see p. 292).

Salaries
Depending on the size of the company or institution, Catering Operations Managers can receive $40,000 to $150,000, sometimes adding commissions on sales, and usually including benefits. This person might also share in company profits if negotiated in advance.

Employment Prospects
Since there is usually only one operations manager or manager in each catering company, catering department, hotel, or golf club, there are few jobs available compared to other positions. In large urban areas, one can move from one hotel or institution to another, while in large hotel chains, a catering manager can move to different hotels within the chain and move from catering manager to restaurant manager.

Ideal locations include large resort enclaves and urban areas where many weddings, bar and bat mitzvahs, graduations, winery events, and huge annual events take place, especially where wealthy people live or have extra homes, such as San Francisco and the Sonoma-Napa wine country; Lake Tahoe, New York; Palm Beach, Florida; Malibu, California; Newport, Rhode Island; coastal Connecticut; and mainline Philadelphia.

Advancement Prospects
One can work oneself up the kitchen ladder to the position of Catering Operations Manager from dishwasher

if one works hard. People in these positions occasionally rise into the hierarchy of corporate management of either the parent catering company or a hotel chain.

Education and Training
Some employers require a bachelor's degree in business or a related field, two to five years of experience, or a hospitality, hotel, restaurant, or beverage management degree. Good verbal skills in English and computer knowledge will be helpful, as might conversational Spanish.

Experience, Skills, and Personality Traits
Individuals interested in this position must be collaborative workers experienced in team building; be able to manage finances; have an even temperament; be perceptive and a good leader with well-developed verbal, computer, and written communication skills; have flexibility to respond to market demands; be creative; and be good at public relations.

Unions and Associations
The National Association of Catering Executives (www.nace.net) offers online networking at all levels, from bakers working at home to huge catering companies, as well as annual conferences and local chapters with meetings and (catered) parties. The International Association of Culinary Professionals (www.iacp.com) also offers online networking support groups and annual conventions. State winery, viticultural regions, and wine associations may also provide networking and new clients for luncheons, dinners, and parties given at individual wineries as well as association events. Every state now has wineries, so check them out for catering and catering management opportunities.

Tips for Entry
1. If you do not have culinary or catering education or training, get your foot in the door by taking the first job with a local catering company or restaurant that you can get in the industry, even if it is as a dishwasher or cleaner, and learn from those around you.
2. Volunteer at large soup kitchens or for meals-on-wheels to get ground-level experience and offer to work into a managerial role or to do scheduling of meals or of volunteer shifts, ordering, and coordinating people to gain experience.
3. Take outside courses in accounting or business as you work your way up the kitchen ladder. Human resources training or courses will be most helpful.

4. Read local or urban newspapers' Wednesday food sections or weekly style sections to learn who is giving parties and who is catering them. Watch for which industries and businesses feed their employees on-site, and which civic agencies host large parties and who provides the food. Call or e-mail those caterers and offer your services. Keep your own records of potential clients to pass on to an employer, or even develop your own catering service.

5. If catering manager or Catering Operations Manager positions are not available where you live, move to locations full of opportunities.

TAKEOUT STORE COOK/MANAGER

Duties: These two jobs may be one person or separate individuals. The manager and cook work with the store manager or owner to develop a menu, recipes, and prices; hire and schedule kitchen and sales staff; oversee display, presentation, and rotation of foods offered on steam tables or salad bars as well as deli meats, cheeses, and other food supplies; and hire and manage deli sandwich makers. If the operation is a stand-alone deli, a cook/manager might do everything, including keeping financial records. If the establishment is the deli or grab 'n' go counter in a grocery store, the staffer is more likely to lead the cooking and serving staff.

Alternate Title(s): Deli Cook; Deli Chef; Grab 'n' Go Cook or Chef; Catering Chef; Hot Food Cook or Chef; Takeout Food Manager or Chef

Salary Range: $20,000 to $60,000, occasionally with benefits

Employment Prospects: Excellent

Advancement Prospects: Good, depending on at what level one enters the deli kitchen workforce

Best Geographical Location(s): Urban areas, high-income suburbs, wine regions, groceries near resorts

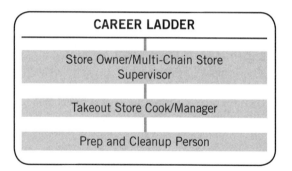

Prerequisites:

Education or Training—High school graduation, culinary or business training at the community college level, on-the-job-learning, some business management

Experience—Sometimes no experience is necessary at sandwich maker level; ideal experience is working for fast-paced restaurant or catering company, preferably having hired personnel

Special Skills and Personality Traits—Human relations skills and experience to spot good, tidy employees; interest in developing teamwork; desire to please customers and sensitivity to their needs; some business and financial management skills; even temperament; passion for working in food

Position Description

Deli and fast-food takeout opportunities range from 7-Eleven to Whole Foods and beyond, and from corner delis to elegant counters at chic restaurants. Gas stations stock sandwiches that may be made thousands of miles away in a sandwich factory or high-end organic sandwiches catered by a nearby popular deli, along with cult-chic coffee.

Even delis sometimes carry potato and macaroni salads produced by manufacturers hundreds of miles away, and others make all of their salads on-site. Some salad bars are stocked with trucked-in bulk provisions, while in other stores kitchen staff make everything from scratch, tearing lettuce, boiling eggs, and roasting turkey breasts, which provides positions for cooks at every level.

When you consider food prepared for sale in vending machines, food cooked and served at baseball and football games, food packaged for gas stations or convenience stores, ethnic specialty stores, and all levels of grocery stores from clapboard shops to large chains preparing more and more food for people in a rush, there are millions of job opportunities and positions up for grabs.

A Takeout Store Cook/Manager has to know the local clientele, what they like to buy on the run, what quality or ethnicity of food they prefer, and how little they like to cook at home. Deli and grocery store hot-food tables now provide substantial meals, as do ethnic markets, occasionally better than those purchasers might cook at home, or close enough for customers to decide to go for convenience and pay more for it than they would if they cooked the food themselves.

The cook/manager needs to consider what customers might want to purchase for breakfast, lunch, and dinner and everything in between, from hot soups and chili, sandwiches, salads, muffins and bagels, to cookies and conscience-free single-servings of lush desserts and donuts. The cook/manager also needs to order popular snacks such as chips, energy bars and drinks, and even scrambled eggs, frittatas, and breakfast sandwiches and burritos.

The Takeout Store Cook/Manager orders ingredients, cheeses, and cooked meats; organizes and coordinates kitchen and serving staff; and keeps up with espresso, power drinks, and green and "bubble" tea trends.

Early morning work includes prep and cooking for breakfast and the earliest lunch crowd, while dinner entrées are prepped and cooked in late morning and early afternoon, with many hot tables closing down by 6:30 or 7:00 P.M. The cook/manager coordinates all staff, from prep cooks and sandwich makers to cooks who make Indian entrées, salmon casseroles, enchiladas, and rotisserie chickens, as well as the cleanup crew who gets the sales, service and kitchen areas clean for the whole process to begin again the next day. A Takeout Store Cook/Manager may be responsible for department employees' pay scale, punctuality, and time cards as well.

Salaries

Cook/manager salaries vary tremendously, both by region of the country and specific job. Sandwich makers and line cooks may make only minimum wage on a per-hour basis, which varies by state and even by city, hence attracting many people new to the workforce, including first-job immigrants and students.

Takeout Store Cook/Managers can make between $20,000 to $100,000, depending on region and quality of store, with background and experience important. A profitable high-end store might pay dearly for a name chef to attract foodie customers, while other stores might have in-house recipes and have a lead cook who teaches everyone else the formulas and procedures. On a per-hour basis, these cook/managers may earn from $15 to $35.

Employment Prospects

There are millions of food preparation, cooking, and management positions in the deli/fast-food/grab 'n' go stores throughout North America. These jobs are great entry-level jobs to get initial experience and start one's climb up the kitchen ladder.

There is a lot of turnover in this stand-up work. Working as a deli sandwich maker, assistant cook, or chef is a great way to enter the profession. Some well-known restaurant chefs and even owners have opted to shed responsibility for losing or making money for themselves and to work for someone else in hot-food or

deli sections, which also usually prepare catered party trays for customers' events.

More affluent communities tend to have more commuters and residents with more income to spend on food cooked by others. Those neighborhoods can be found in urban areas, wealthy suburbs, gourmet food- and wine-centric regions, or in grocery stores near resorts where guests might want to pick up good food less expensively than at their hotels or resorts.

Advancement Prospects

If one begins making sandwiches in the deli of a fine chain grocery store, there is lots of opportunity to rise to cook, chef, manager, multi-branch supervisor, and maybe even be asked to open the next deli in the store's chain.

Education and Training

Culinary education and training would be ideal but are not necessarily required. High school, community college, and junior college business and culinary programs offer full- or part-time courses that would be handy. Knowledge of English and sanitation practices is a must, as is familiarity with the purchasing of fresh foods, whether conventional or organic.

Experience, Skills, and Personality Traits

Experience making sandwiches or cleaning up in a deli constructively contributes to the expertise to become chef/manager a deli or store hot-food counter, as would be working for a caterer, fast-food business, or even in the food line of a vending machine company to increase one's appreciation for what workers need to do.

Unions and Associations

Larger cities may have culinary unions to represent culinary employees, including cooks and managers of delis, whether stand-alone storefronts or in large grocery stores. In smaller cities, towns, and communities, people working in the world of food often form their own networks to share information, sources, employee pools, and occasionally purchasing power.

Tips for Entry

1. If you have no training or experience at all in the food industry but want to get into deli work, get a job at a fast-food joint and learn all you can. You might find that you want to work your way up to management and franchise ownership, or you might learn that you never want to work in those circumstances again.

2. Get a job in a deli, even if you have to start at the cleanup, dishwashing, or sandwich making level. You can learn loads from each job, and each job counts on your résumé of credentials for the next job up the kitchen ladder.

3. Take community college classes in food and business management while working at a deli, in a store, or for a caterer.

4. Work for a caterer who makes lots of picnic box lunches or delivers breakfast or lunch to work-places to learn how this part of the business works and what customers want.

5. Look for a stand-alone deli where the manager might bow out of his commitment or for a new grocery store opening that will include a deli or hot-food section and hang around and bug them until they hire you. Take the best job you can get just to get your foot in the door. There is lots of turnover in this field since the pay can be low.

DELI PREP/CLEANUP PERSON

CAREER PROFILE

Duties: A deli prep person may chop or slice vegetables, cheeses, or meats, boil pasta for salads, prepare all ingredients for salads, package them in plastic or biodegradable containers, make sandwiches, tend a bakery area, and refresh hot tables. A deli cleanup person might be expected to constantly tidy the to-go counters or clean up the kitchen and service areas at the end of the day. In some establishments, deli prep and cleanup are handled by one person.

Alternate Title(s): Assistant Cook; Deli Worker

Salary Range: Minimum wage to $30,000 annually

Employment Prospects: Excellent

Advancement Prospects: Excellent

Best Geographical Location(s): Everywhere in North America, with more positions available in larger cities, university towns, or in foodie or wine-centric regions

Prerequisites:

Education or Training—High school diploma; English, Spanish, or both; the more kitchen or cook-

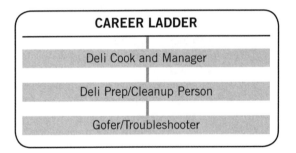

CAREER LADDER

Deli Cook and Manager

Deli Prep/Cleanup Person

Gofer/Troubleshooter

ing training the better, even a high school culinary program

Experience—A good entry-level position, but any kitchen experience is helpful; volunteering at a soup kitchen or meals-on-wheels will help

Special Skills and Personality Traits—English language skills, if the supervisor speaks English; good standards of cleanliness and interest in food and service; willingness to work hard; interest in learning; punctuality; reliability

Position Description

Beginning Deli Prep/Cleanup Workers have to be willing to do some of the most unglamorous work in the food business, but the jobs are excellent get-your-foot-in-the-door learning opportunities. A deli or delicatessen was one of the original fast-food markets in the United States, combining the grocery store with fast food and takeout, originally with an ethnic flare, ranging from the French-German origins of the word itself, to Jewish, kosher, Dutch, Italian, Middle Eastern, and other regions and ethnicities. The word *delicatessen* translates roughly to "good eats," "top quality food," or "stores for delicacies."

Delicatessens or delis either exist as stand-alone businesses that primarily feature cooked meats and cheeses along with salads and sandwiches and carry some more diverse groceries, or they consist of a deli counter in a grocery store. The latter may be small with hand-sliced meats or with vacuum-packed sliced meats, or huge with arrays of organic and conventional offerings from pizza and macaroni with blue cheese, Indian food, rotisserie or fried chicken, to salad makings of all kinds and varieties.

Some delis offer both packaged and made-to-order sandwiches, while a gas station may have what it calls a "deli" of food premade and packaged several states away. In some cases, pickles, coleslaw, and potato and macaroni salads come premade from deli suppliers, while other delis make salads and pickles on the spot, which is where on-site deli prep cooks are in demand.

In super urban neighborhoods, residents divide according to their favorite deli, while in less discriminating areas, the Subway chain qualifies as a "deli."

Currently, some delis serve cold and hot take-out food, while others have seats for customers. The greater the variety of prepared foods sold, the greater the job opportunities. Others make their own sausages or provide hot take-home entrées for singles and families every night,

First-time deli employees will learn to chop vegetables without chopping their fingers, slice meats in electric slicers (accommodating customers' demands for see-through to thick slices), keep the slicer clean and oiled, keep knives sharp and keep all counter surfaces clean, while all the time wearing rubber gloves to comply with health laws.

Once a deli prep person has developed basic skills of slicing, dicing, following recipes, and mixing, he or she can gain huge knowledge about various cheeses, sausages, salads, hot dishes, side dishes, and ethnic cooking and dining, all of which skills will count for next rungs up the kitchen ladder.

Besides sandwiches, some delis make everything from meatballs with tomato sauce and stuffed grape leaves to chopped chicken liver, chow mein, lasagna, tamales, fried chicken, mashed potatoes, and casseroles, as well as salads and espresso drinks.

A deli cleanup person may have prepped food in the morning, or all day, and then gets responsibility for keeping all publicly visible slicers, dicers, and countertops clean, as well as sweeping and washing floors and floor mats at night.

Salaries

Pay for Deli Prep/Cleanup People in delis or at in-store deli counters is usually low, ranging upward from minimum wage to $15,000 to $30,000 annually with few benefits. Pay varies from state to state and city to city. It is possible to begin at the bottom and work your way up if you are punctual, careful, and do a good job, learning along the way. Store owners often employ deli workers part time to avoid paying for health insurance and other benefits. Some large grocery chains have unionized clerks, which inches wages higher and may help provide benefits.

Employment Prospects

Employment prospects are good. There is always turnover as deli workers learn skills and move up the kitchen ladder, or get a better job elsewhere. Some large chain grocery stores allow deli workers to progress up the store's employment line, including grocery bagger, checker, supervisor, and assistant manager, although it rarely happens. Many corner or ethnic delis are run by family members, so it is often hard to break into the staff. Large chain coffee companies have established kiosks in chain groceries near deli counters or near the checkout stands, with more entry-level jobs available through the store or the coffee retailer.

There are many deli prep, sandwich making, and cleanup jobs throughout North America, although the delis and the jobs vary tremendously. In a highly urban area, corner delis have regular clientele, while other delis cater to in-office deliveries to individuals or to large groups at meetings. Towns with universities also have lots of delis or stores with take-out food, where students, staff, and professors look for a good lunch and sometimes quickie food to take home for dinner.

Advancement Prospects

Advancement prospects are excellent, if you are conscientious, ambitious, and learn well. Both deli prep and cleanup are entry-level jobs in the food industry, so you can only move upward. The more one learns about a deli's ethnic cuisine or various recipes along the way, the more one has to bring to another deli or restaurant. One can learn basic knife and other skills to move up the kitchen ladder to cook, chef, or manager, either within the deli operation or in restaurants or the highest-quality deli shops.

Education and Training

A high school diploma would be handy, with English and another language helpful. No real culinary training is required for deli prep and cleanup jobs, but high school or community college culinary program training would be advantageous. In real life, these jobs are often filled by first-time job holders right out of high school or immigrants. Both of these jobs provide on-the-job learning and training that can be helpful in getting the next job, especially if the person sticks to the job for a year or more.

Experience, Skills, and Personality Traits

Kitchen experience, even in a mother's kitchen helping to feed numerous siblings, can be valuable. One way to get experience to prepare for employment is to volunteer at a soup kitchen or meals-on-wheels in your community, where many of the same techniques are used for mass production. While these positions do not pay, they are great for learning skills and to put on your résumé.

It is important to take direction well, understand the language of your supervisor, be able to read numbers and measurements, be on time and attentive, have good standards of cleanliness, have an interest in food and learning, and have the temperament to make the same salad or casserole day after day.

Unions and Associations

Some large grocery store deli workers are members of unions, but there are rarely unions present in small family delis. When a person progresses to cook or manager, there are union and association memberships and networking groups available.

Tips for Entry

1. Visit grocery stores with in-house delis and ask if they are hiring. Fill out an application and make a good impression, because there is lots of turnover in this field.

2. Check jobs on craigslist.com or other online resources and in local newspapers.
3. Volunteer at a local soup kitchen or meals-on-wheels to get experience.
4. Get books from the library and teach yourself knife skills, such as slicing and dicing vegetables. In the process you can make salads and soups for your family.
5. If still in high school, enroll in a culinary skills class. Find a community or junior college program, both of which are relatively inexpensive, and take some classes in basic culinary skills. Most of these schools and culinary academies have job placement offices and a network of resources through which they can help you get a job close to home.

FOOD CART OWNER

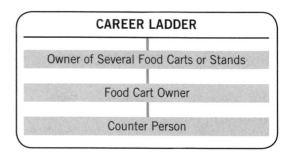
Position Description

The owner or manager of a food cart has to possess initial aggressiveness and determination to find, lease, or purchase the truck or cart. Once this person has a business vehicle and local government health licenses, he or she needs to fully furnish, clean, maintain, and decorate the business to make it sanitary and appealing to customers. The owner must know the clientele, order adequate supplies for slow- and fast-paced business days, make or have food delivered, take orders, serve customers, make change, hire any staff, pay bills, and build a satisfied repeat customer base.

Salaries

Steady income can be chancy or regular, depending upon the quality of products sold, how long the business has been established, and employees may start at minimum wage or higher, especially if they are part of the family. Some well-known chefs have started their own sausage carts and do very well by adding their established names and reputations to the name of the cart. Salaries range from $20,000 to $60,000 annually depending on locale and type of product, usually with no benefits.

Employment Prospects

Employment prospects are limited, unless a person is willing to set up a business, guaranteeing himself or herself a job, which is sort of like buying a franchise to buy a job. Once someone's first taco truck, sandwich or sausage cart, or espresso stand succeeds, and the owner saves his or her profits, that person often opens at a second venue, creating a management or worker position. Usual employees include family members and high school or college students.

Taco trucks, sandwich or sausage carts, and espresso stands can work in large urban centers as well as in more rural areas. If Costco can sell tons of kosher Polish sausages, anyone can. Corners near beaches, college campuses, high schools, high-traffic shopping districts, gas stations, hardware stores, and large buildings where many people walk by are fine locations, as are roadways where agricultural workers and truckers pass or anywhere people are looking for inexpensive good food.

Advancement Prospects

Advancement prospects are excellent if you are a successful self-starter, can manage money properly and create new units of the food or beverage stands. Many of these entrepreneurs expand to own several outlets. Possible expansion locations might include hospital lobbies or entryways, in or near bookstores, office building lobbies, athletic event venues, and near tourism centers. This is how Starbucks started, although success like that is rare. Several sausage cart and taco truck owners have multiple units, employing friends and relatives, usually with low overhead.

Education and Training
English, Spanish, or another language are handy, as well as the ability to read, add and subtract, and make change. Barista training at a chain coffeehouse would be instructive. A high school diploma is recommended.

Experience, Skills, and Personality Traits
Work at delis, Mexican or other ethnic restaurants, experience cooking at home for a large family, work at a chain espresso shop, or other cooking or service experience are necessary. Work for someone else in the business you want to enter to learn the intricacies of handling food or coffee, cleanliness practices, and ordering supplies.

Entering taco truck, sandwich or sausage cart, or espresso stand work requires a passion for the kind of food you will be selling and for chatting with customers. One has to not mind working alone or working long, tedious hours doing the same thing over and over, have the ability to tolerate a full range of weather, and a resourcefulness to find investors (even if family) to get started. One must hold out in hard times and bad weather and save to expand the business.

Unions and Associations
Most owners and workers of taco trucks, sausage carts, and espresso stands are extremely independent. Occasionally owners and workers network on food and supplier sources, but often an owner's family network is the "union." Staffers can join culinary unions, although turnover is high so they might not qualify for membership.

Tips for Entry
1. Check out and ask questions at established taco trucks, sandwich or sausage carts, and espresso stands—although owners may be slightly suspicious if you are too inquisitive. Ask if they could use help.
2. Work at a fast-food restaurant (sometimes called a "store") for practical food-service experience.
3. Check out job and business availability online.

PARTY PLANNER

Duties: Takes full responsibility for all plans for a party or event, usually big events. The party or event planner meets with the potential or repeat client to learn what the client has in mind; schedules the event at either the planner's facility or another facility; schedules and estimates the cost of subcontractors including caterer, photographer, videographer, rental services, flowers, and decorations, or supplies these services; gives the client a cost estimate within client's budget; oversees all stages of event from site selection and planning to cleanup and returning the site to its original condition

Alternate Title(s): Event Planner

Salary Range: $70,000 to $600,000 a year; $20 to $300 an hour

Employment Prospects: Fair

Advancement Prospects: Good

Best Geographical Location(s): Urban areas, wine country communities, wealthy suburbs with country clubs, and university towns

Prerequisites:

   Education and Training—Culinary and design courses from community, junior, or vocational col-

leges or a culinary academy; design and business management courses

   Experience—Starting at the bottom in food service and then catering and managing of large events is always handy. If one has worked at a job, one can best understand what that job's function is and how to do it. A party or event planner also needs to understand ordering, estimates and costs, event coordination, design and balance, and management.

   Special Skills and Personality Traits—A party or event planner needs to be a person who loves the excitement and pressure of organizing events, which are often fraught with cancellations and disappointments; must have artistic talent, personal or public style, and good taste.

Position Description

A Party Planner first meets with the client, who may be taking competing bids, learns what she or he has in mind, how many guests are expected, and makes cost estimates within the client's budget and coordinates the entire event. This means pulling together everything from food and flowers to furniture, decorations, music, and musicians (from mariachis to bagpipers), servers, bartenders, parking attendants, specialty coffee service, winery participation, and gift bags for guests.

The job resembles that of caterer, except that a caterer also cooks or oversees preparation of the food. In some cases, the Party Planner is, in effect, the caterer if he or she provides the food as well.

While the Party Planner has to know well every aspect of the event, including the food, she or he acts primarily as a consultant who pulls all the strings to make the party run even better than the client hopes.

For instance, a large winery might have a Party Planner, or even a staff of Party Planners, with whom a bride and her mother might make initial contact. The Party Planner will handle everything, from ceremony seating and flowers, to music, photographer, food, wedding cake, and anything else the client might think of, taking the full burden off the client—for a price, of course.

The Party Planner gets an idea of the client's dietary interests, offers a few menus with alternates according to food selections and cost, estimates the cost of food, music, entertainment, auctioneers, beverages, and the entire plan, including even valet parking. Sometimes Party Planners sketch plans that may include the layout of the site, where rented tables, stages, food and beverage service, and major imported decorative objects will go.

Some Party Planners stock warehouses of their own supplies, such as tables, color-themed tablecloths, enormous flower vases, drapes, and even risers for stages. These planners might include these in their overall cost estimate and some might itemize them, renting them to the client directly and cutting out the rental-center middleman.

Once all of this is agreed upon, the planner or the planner's lawyer draws up a contract to be signed by both the client and the planner, enumerating everyone's tangible expectations, and stipulating the total cost, required deposit (often 50 percent), and the due date of final payment. The planner will try to collect the final payment before the event, and the client might try to withhold part until after the event to make sure everything runs smoothly.

If the event is in a public place, local government permits for noise and parking may be required, so the planner might obtain these on behalf of the client. When a quasi-public event is planned for a commercial or other public building, the planner may have to coordinate nearly instant setup after the regular workday. Sometimes if the party is at a private home, the planner can have large rental equipment delivered a day before the event without an extra day's charge. Planners always have to allow for cleanup, takedown, and return of equipment, whether it is their own stock and property or rented.

The day of and during the event, the Party Planner must always be available to solve problems, adjust plans to the whims of client, find another photographer if the original one fails to show up, and generally keep everything running smoothly.

Salaries

Party Planners may earn anywhere from $60,000 to $600,000 depending on whether they own party equipment that can be rented to their client, the quality of their reputation and client base, where they are located, and whether their clients are upscale party givers or major event organizers.

Just in the role of freelance party or event decision maker for a corporate, private, or fund-raising event, a planner might charge from $50 to $200 per hour for consultation time.

Employment Prospects

Many Party Planners are self-employed and work alone as the initial person a party giver hires, or hire staffers to help depending upon the size of the events they usually coordinate. Some large corporations, hotels, and country clubs hire event planners or Party Planners, who usually coordinate in-house events to entertain employees and clients they want to impress. Many independent party or event planners are self-employed and hire friends or family members as assistants or resources, and then hire temporary staff for each event. Forming good relationships with those subcontractors is key to knowing how reliably an event will occur.

An assistant to a Party Planner might work as a secretary, answering or returning phone calls and e-mails, keeping track of inventory of party supplies, helping maintain relationships with suppliers, ordering supplies, designing invitations, writing press releases and updating Web site.

The best areas for employment are affluent suburbs, major urban or university communities, tech company centers, wine regions, and warm-weather areas where party giving goes on all the time.

Advancement Prospects

One can begin working for a party or event planner, gain more and more responsibility as one learns, and eventually start one's own business or get hired by an institution to plan its parties and events. If one works for a corporation or a winery as an event or Party Planner, one may learn enough to get hired by major event companies in the field, or progress to greater responsibility in the corporation.

Another way for an assistant Party Planner to progress in the field is to begin one's own event firm, which may mean competing with the one that taught you the business. In some big cities or even smaller communities, there is room for more than one company. To start your own, it might be wise to carve out your specialty niche, such as charity fund-raisers, silent and live auctions (complete with laptop computer bid computations and credit cards), splendiferous winery releases, or Mad Hatter tea parties.

Education and Training

Any food business experience; culinary, catering, or hospitality training at community colleges, universities with specialized programs, or culinary schools; some training in marketing and business practices, including estimating and costs; and public relations and publicity experience would all be advantageous.

Experience, Skills, and Personality Traits

Food and other catering or organizing experience are mandatory, starting with that acquired by compulsive organizers of the high school dance. Party Planners need to know food preparation and service, have experience in the food business, have creative and artistic skills, and be great communicators and motivators to coordinate people and keep everyone happily working together for the best outcome.

Just like a caterer, a Party Planner has to expect the unexpected, plan for the unplanned, and foresee the unforeseen, including a missing chef, undelivered flowers, or musicians who went to another venue. The planner must be able to think quickly of solutions to problems, and even get joy from solving last-minute changes.

If a planner works in a small community or caters to a clientele who frequent the same professional or social circles, he or she needs a wide repertoire of party plans, menus, themes, and entertainment so as to always present a new and imaginative event.

Unions and Associations

The National Association of Catering Executives (NACE, www.nace.net) offers networking, newsletters, professional tips, a job bank, certification, many chapters with live face-to-face meetings, an annual conference, and events for people in the catering and events businesses.

The International Association of Culinary Professionals (www.iacp.com) offers many of the same functions and is more oriented toward people who cook, write about cooking, photograph food, and many other disciplines that are food oriented.

Tips for Entry

1. Get some experience in food service, anywhere from a fast-food joint to busing in a restaurant to get started.
2. Look in your local yellow pages and call caterers or event planners in your community and ask for a job at the lowest level, or whatever level is appropriate for your experience. Learn at every stage and from other staffers.
3. Consider helping friends or family members put on parties, starting with a bar or bat mitzvah, birthday, or quinceañera, and moving on to weddings and other larger events.
4. Volunteer to help at local fund-raising events in your community, taking increasing responsibility with each event. All legitimate experience adds to your résumé.
5. Take your new experience to a local business that puts on events, from party or event planners to caterers, wineries, and hotels.

RESTAURANTS

RESTAURANT CHEF

CAREER PROFILE

Duties: A chef is in charge of and manages the whole kitchen in a restaurant or hotel, creates the menu, handles or directs someone else to order supplies, manages costs to meet the owner's needs and make a profit, and cooks or oversees preparation of all food.

Alternate Title(s): Executive Chef; Chef de Cuisine

Salary Range: $38,000 to $800,000

Employment Prospects: Good to excellent, following trends in location and in the U.S. economy

Best Geographical Location(s): Urban and resort areas, wealthy enclaves, tourist towns, wine regions

Prerequisites:

    Education or Training—Culinary school, vocational or culinary trade schools, apprenticeships with known or established chefs

    Experience—Working in kitchens, often from the bottom up, is best to learn every station involved;

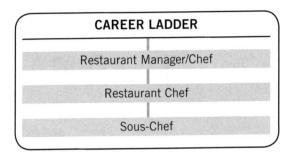

CAREER LADDER

Restaurant Manager/Chef

Restaurant Chef

Sous-Chef

any kind of business or management experience to help control costs and produce the best possible product

    Special Skills and Personality Traits—Experience comparing tastes and a refined palate for both food and wine; sense of design and artistic presentation; diplomatic skills and even-keeled personality to manage varied creative personalities and temperaments in the kitchen; experience and skills at team building

Position Description

A Restaurant Chef runs the kitchen in every way, including creating the menu, ordering, supervising expenses, and staff, and occasionally does all of the above and *is* the total staff.

It is the chef's responsibility to create a menu that keeps up with trends, shows sensitivity to the clientele's tastes and needs, provides for vegetarian and carnivorous preferences, and considers local products. Some chefs write a new menu each day, week, month, season, or year, often depending upon where they are located and the kind of restaurant.

Everything in the kitchen stems from the menu, including ordering, pricing, and creating "specials" (usually reflecting availability of fresh seasonal and local ingredients). If the chef or restaurant does not have its own vegetable garden, the chef checks daily with local growers, fishers, and other suppliers to find out what will be available in the following week to plan the menu.

The chef informs all staff of the day's or meal's menu, assigning each lead cook his or her upcoming responsibilities and sometimes showing the cook staff how to make whatever is required.

All kitchen staff arrive early in the morning to prep for lunch, or late in the morning to prep for dinner. It

is the chef's responsibility to check their time cards and make sure the vegetables, meats, fish, pasta, and everything else the kitchen will need for the day have been ordered and delivered. The chef checks each delivery to make sure the restaurant received what the bill says it did, pays in cash if necessary, files the invoices, and pays bills. The chef or sous-chef approves invoices, passes them to the bookkeeper if the restaurant has one, and follows up to make sure bills are paid. If restaurants get behind on paying, vendors will demand cash on delivery, which often means a restaurant is living day to day.

In the morning the Restaurant Chef instructs the staff on what needs to be done for the day's specials or special menu. Samples of most basic foods and specials of the day should be cooked early enough so that servers can taste and learn about ingredients; this way servers can explain and recommend each item to guests making decisions on what to order.

Once all the chopping and dicing is complete, sauces and soups have been brewing for a few hours, and customers start to stream into the dining room, the chef conducts the symphony of the kitchen. In smaller kitchens, the chef cooks part or all of the meal and checks every plate for appearance and content before it is taken from the kitchen to the customer.

A chef's artistic and design abilities are vital to creating a pleasing presentation of food on a plate, because we all taste first with our eyes, our visual sizzle. Some chefs have been known to study artistic design, and others appear to go too far by creating unnatural towers that fall over as soon as knife and fork approach.

Salaries

Chefs' salaries vary widely, with lowest earners at minimum wage in small chain restaurants in certain parts of the country, and the highest wages going to chefs who also have international television shows that take them, their recipes, and their cookbooks way beyond their home regions.

Many chefs who own their own restaurants barely get by, some struggling at first, and some forever until they close. Part of their take-home pay is feeding their families at the restaurant.

A chef's training and experience can weigh heavily into what she or he is paid. A person right out of culinary school most likely will not start at the top, but if she or he does, that person will get paid at the low end of the salary range, which may figure into why the owner would hire this person over someone more experienced.

A person with vast experience, with or without formal training, may work his or her way up, learning all the way, have a special flare for creative cooking, and become a highly valuable and well-paid chef. Salaries range from $38,000 to $800,000, depending on all the variables mentioned above, as well as product contracts, books, and television shows. New entries into the field need to know that many restaurants often pay only minimum wage or $9 to $12 per hour, with no benefits.

Employment Prospects

Restaurant jobs are available everywhere, with prospects of larger kitchens and possibly greater pay in larger cities, wine regions, resort enclaves, affluent suburbs, or in high-tech centers, all of which tend to attract people with tastes for good food. All of these places cut back in economically bad times. When the economy slumps, certain income-earning people tend to dine out less, so restaurants cut back on staff. Conversely, when the economy soars, restaurants tend to "beef up" staff, which increases opportunities.

Meanwhile, more and more people are entering culinary programs to learn the profession, so competition is increasing. Top chefs, though, are always sought and should find work fairly easily.

Advancement Prospects

Chefs move around, just as television news anchors and baseball players do. Which chef is moving where from where is hot gossip among foodies, with everyone trying to take a better job or avert boredom. Hence, there are always openings at every level to be filled by people working their way up or softening their fall down the kitchen ladder.

Education and Training

It is possible to start at the bottom of the kitchen ladder and work your way up to chef. Depending upon your background, country of origin, languages spoken, and immigration papers, you may or may not be given the traditional titles. The possibilities of working one's way up are good enough that sometimes it is worth it to take a low-level job to get your foot in the door. Consider each rung of the ladder a learning experience and work away at your passion.

Some high schools and many community and junior colleges offer educational and vocational programs in culinary arts and business, as well as apprentice programs and job placement services. Culinary schools offer intense and in-depth cooking education and experience. A local culinary program will most likely have job contacts within their geographic area. Many Web sites now offer international job opportunities as well as chef certification programs. There are also apprenticeships overseen by the U.S. Department of Labor.

Experience, Skills, and Personality Traits

The more experience you acquire at different jobs within a kitchen the greater your qualifications to be a chef in charge, since the chef has to manage everything that goes on in the kitchen, from staff scheduling, ordering, billing, menu planning, cooking, and serving and presentation. It is much easier and more efficient to oversee each of these facets if one has experienced them personally rather than just reading about them.

A chef has to have natural or developed skills that combine the use of several human abilities, including seeing, tasting, hearing, and feeling texture. Artistry for presentation of food to the public is also necessary. If a chef's palate is off-center and customers think his or her food is too salty, for example, they may not return to the restaurant, particularly if they are supposed to watch the salt in their diets.

Restaurant Chefs also need to be able to build a team and manage personnel, allowing people to develop their creative abilities within the formulas set out by the chef, while keeping control of the kitchen and inspiring people to cook their best every single time.

A chef also needs some money-management skills, excellent health and stamina, the ability to stand on one's feet for up to 16 hours a day, and an at-home partner or spouse who is either in the restaurant business or understands its rigorous physical and time demands.

A chef de cuisine is actually a chef, usually in a large restaurant or in a hotel or resort with several restaurants, who acts as chef and has responsibility for one restaurant within that establishment. Occasionally a restaurant owner will hold down a chef at the chef de cuisine level in order to make him or her work harder to pursue the chef or executive chef carrot dangling.

Unions and Associations

Chefs might gain from joining, or at least looking at, culinary professionals' Web sites for networking, conventions, shows and meetings, jobs, certification, classes, and many other resources. The American Culinary Federation (www.acfchefs.org) is a professional association of chefs, caterers, cooks, and food educators with chapters throughout the country. You can find a chapter near you by clicking on the "Chapters" link and then on your state on its Web site.

Other groups to consider include the International Association of Culinary Professionals (www.iacp.com) and the National Restaurant Association (www.nationalrestaurantassociation.org or www.restaurant.org), the latter of which boasts 60,000 business members.

Tips for Entry

1. Get some experience as a volunteer at soup kitchens, meals-on-wheels or at churches.
2. Take culinary classes at local high school, community or junior colleges, or at culinary schools.
3. Get on-the-job experience by starting at whatever level at which you can get your foot in the door.
4. Learn everything you can from those with more experience, no matter how demeaning your first job might seem. Make the most of it, master the task at hand, and work your way up the kitchen ladder.
5. Look around for your ideal restaurant, one most similar to what you would like to create or where you think you can learn the most. Walk in and ask for a job. Be ready to tell your story quickly and demonstrate what you can do.

SOUS-CHEF

Duties: Works under the chef, as assistant or second in command to the executive chef or chef de cuisine, whichever is the top chef in that kitchen. The Sous-Chef must cook in the style of the executive chef, learning his or her recipes and methods and executing them. Sous-Chefs troubleshoot where needed by order of the executive chef and run the kitchen business as delegated by executive chef.

Alternate Title(s): None

Salary Range: $25,000 to $85,000

Employment Prospects: Excellent

Advancement Prospects: Very good to excellent (with patience)

Best Geographical Location(s): Urban areas, wealthy suburbs, tech enclaves, resort and recreation areas, wine regions where there are many restaurants to go with the wine

Prerequisites:

Education or Training—Culinary education in any culinary school, with apprenticeships helpful,

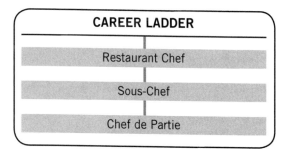

especially to progress more quickly up the kitchen ladder

Experience—Restaurant experience, from dishwashing on up to food prep; apprenticeships at any station in the kitchen, especially with recommendations and more than one year in each location

Skills and Personality Traits—Easygoing personality with ability to adapt quickly to the chef's whims, changes in menu, and cooking style, and imitate the chef's style so closely that customers will not know someone else prepared it; ability to get along with and lead others, inspiring them to do their best

Position Description

A restaurant Sous-Chef is number two in any kitchen, with responsibility to take over in the chef's absence, pass on the chef's orders, and generally assist the chef as his or her executive and boss.

The Sous-Chef needs to know how to cook all of the chef's recipes and how to teach others to cook them, even in parts at various stations. Often the Sous-Chef cooks with the chef, relays orders to other kitchen staff on behalf of the chef, and needs to be able to cook totally in the style of a particular chef. If a Sous-Chef wants to freelance, meaning add his or her own creativity, he or she must ask permission. Many Sous-Chefs or those below on the kitchen ladder have been fired for improvising on the chef's recipes.

A chef might give the Sous-Chef all responsibility for the business management of the kitchen, including ordering and purchasing according to menu demands, checking and accepting deliveries against invoices, approving time cards, training and teaching kitchen staff as they enter the kitchen or move up to a higher

job, oversee outside catering jobs, and take care of money and the closing of the restaurant in the afternoon or evening. Sometimes the Sous-Chef actually opens the restaurant at the beginning of the day.

The Sous-Chef takes over the kitchen in the absence of the chef, so he or she must be as good a cook and teacher as the chef, but still follow the chef's orders and recipes, whether they are the Sous-Chef's preferred cooking style or not.

In large restaurants or hotels with several restaurants or dining rooms, the Sous-Chef may be given responsibility to oversee those restaurants, as well as the in-house catering operation and banquets under the chef's direction.

Salaries

Sous-Chefs' salaries vary widely across the United States and Canada, from $20,000 to $70,000, depending on the kind of restaurant at which they work and its clientele, whether the restaurant is part of a chain or hotel, or an elegant stand-alone restaurant. Benefits may depend on the type of restaurant one works for.

Employment Prospects

There are thousands of Sous-Chef jobs across the United States and Canada, and there is constant turnover when a person moves on to a higher job at another restaurant or within the same establishment. Restaurants in cities, affluent suburbs, resort areas, and wine regions tend to have a more sophisticated kitchen hierarchy with more positions and more chance to advance.

Advancement Prospects

As with many businesses, sometimes the best way for a Sous-Chef to advance is to move to another restaurant where there is a chef de cuisine or chef position open. Within a restaurant or hotel kitchen, the only way for a Sous-Chef to move up to chef is for the chef to leave or move up into corporate management. Even when a Sous-Chef makes it known that he or she is interested in the departing chef or executive chef's position, a corporation might bring in someone else from another corporate-related hotel or restaurant to the chef or executive chef position.

Education and Training

A person can work his or her way up the kitchen ladder to Sous-Chef and beyond by getting all possible training at every stage and station within the kitchen. Having parents who cook or having a cultural culinary background are handy, but much can be learned in culinary programs at community and junior colleges as well as at cooking schools of all kinds. Hotel and management courses can also help.

Experience, Skills, and Personality Traits

Sous-Chefs need to be adjustable and even-tempered to deal with sometimes temperamental head chefs, while having the ability to keep his or her cool to pass down the chef's changes in plans to the rest of the kitchen staff. Some Sous-Chefs also need at least kitchen proficiency in a second language, especially Spanish, in order to communicate and translate directions from above.

Unions and Associations

Unite Here represents nearly 1 million current and former hotel and restaurant employees among others (www.unitehere.org), particularly in large hotels, amusement resorts, and gambling hotels. United Food and Commercial Workers International Union (www.ufcw.org) represent cooks and chefs in large chain grocery stores including those owned by Safeway, Albertson's, and Lucky.

In addition, Sous-Chefs might gain from joining, or at least looking at, culinary professionals' Web sites for networking, conventions, shows and meetings, jobs, certification, classes, and many other resources.

The American Culinary Federation (www.acfchefs.org) is a professional association of chefs, caterers, cooks, and food educators with chapters throughout the country. You can find a chapter near you by clicking on the "Chapters" link and then on your state on its Web site.

Other groups to consider include the International Association of Culinary Professionals (www.iacp.com) and the National Restaurant Association (www.restaurant.org.), the latter of which boasts 60,000 business members.

Tips for Entry

1. Arm yourself with degrees or certificates of completion from vocational training schools such as cooking schools, culinary academies, or community or junior college culinary programs.
2. Get experience and be willing to work your way up the kitchen ladder.
3. Offer yourself as an apprentice, even if the job pays little or nothing. Restaurant staff and owners often help find inexpensive housing for fellow workers and learners.
4. Apply for jobs at the best restaurants you can find. Having experience in fine kitchens and apprenticing with well-known chefs make for great résumés.
5. Be willing to change restaurants after you have learned all you can in order to move upward to a better position or to a better restaurant.

CHEF DE PARTIE

Duties: A Chef de Partie has responsibility for one part of food production in a kitchen and becomes a specialist in that segment of the cooking "line." The Chef de Partie oversees the line cooks who themselves may be named in their own sub-hierarchy according to the brigade system.

Alternate Title(s): Station Chef; Line Cook

Salary Range: $30,000 to $50,000

Employment Prospects: Good; cruise ships offer opportunities

Advancement Prospects: Good if one develops people management skills and learns from those above

Best Geographical Location(s): Urban areas with large hotels and restaurants, wine regions with fashionable restaurants, cruise ships, resorts

Prerequisites:

Education or Training—Often a degree from a culinary program, either public or private; English

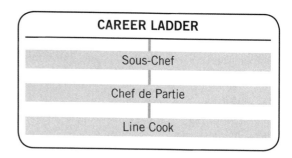

language with Spanish handy; apprenticeships offer another way to show learning

Experience—Usually two to four years' Chef de Partie or line cook experience in a restaurant, hotel, or resort

Special Skills and Personality Traits—Outgoing personality, good management skills with sensitivity to others while motivating line cooks toward high performance; ambition; adaptability

Position Description

A Chef de Partie often begins the day meeting with the executive chef, chef, or sous-chef to learn about the day's menu plans and his or her specific responsibilities. If this person is the only "line cook" he or she takes orders from these chefs higher on the kitchen ladder.

If the Chef de Partie has others on his or her staff, he or she passes on orders to individual line cooks or assistant cooks. The Chef de Partie may also need to make sure all cooks show up on time, ensure smooth and efficient operation of the line cooks and the soups and salad sections, and may supervise others down the line including garde-manger (pantry chef), saucier, poissonier (fish cook), rôtisseur (roaster), grillardin (grill chef), friturier (fry chef), entremetier (vegetable chef), tournant (roundsman), boucher (butcher), pâtissier (pastry chef), and buffet cooks.

The Chef de Partie might also be charged with requisitioning goods and checking them against receipts when they arrive, as well as maximizing production and minimizing waste of food and other resources.

Salaries

A Chef de Partie is truly a mid-level position in a restaurant kitchen, if there even is one. Fancy culinary

school graduates are lucky to enter the field at this level. Even so, the pay is low and depends upon region of the country and whether the person holds a culinary degree. The annual salary is $15,000 to $25,000, occasionally with benefits for those employed by a large corporation. Line cooks and prep people may start at minimum wage, ranging from $7 to $10 per hour, usually without benefits.

Employment Prospects

Every restaurant has high turnover in line cooks and Chefs de Partie. It is hard, hot work for little pay but it carries some dignity of a creative profession. Many immigrants work line cook jobs as one above entry level positions. The jobs of Chefs de Partie and line cooks offer two of the best prospects in kitchens or hotels.

The bigger the city or resort area, the more culinary jobs are available. Where there are larger or more elegant restaurants and hotels, there are more strata within the kitchen and more opportunities. Therefore, urban and resort areas, wine regions, gambling centers, and cruise ships offer the most jobs at every level, especially Chef de Partie and line cooks.

Advancement Prospects

Advancement prospects are good for someone who speaks English, learns quickly, shows up when expected, and works conscientiously and creatively. The best way to advance is to learn as much as possible from those around and above your position. In order to advance, be willing to leave one restaurant or hotel for another if a better job becomes available.

Education and Training

Some cruise ships, hotels, and restaurants require a chef's diploma from a culinary program, either public or private. The ability to speak English is usually required in order to translate orders from executive chefs above the Chef de Partie level to some line cooks. Spanish language would be handy in many parts of the country.

Experience, Skills, and Personality Traits

Often two to four years' experience is required for the Chef de Partie position or for line cooks. The way to gain initial experience is to start as a dishwasher or at any other job that can get you a foot in the door. Apprenticeship programs, which sometimes pay nothing, are also a good way to get vital experience, knowledge, technique, and skills.

It is handy to have an outgoing personality, good management skills, sensitivity to others, and the ability to motivate line cooks toward high performance, along with ambition and adaptability to accommodate late-changing orders from above.

Unions and Associations

Unite Here represents nearly 1 million current and former hotel and restaurant employees among others (www.unitehere.org), particularly in large hotels, amusement resorts, and gambling hotels.

In addition, a Chef de Partie might gain from joining or at least looking at culinary professionals' Web sites for networking, conventions, shows and meetings, jobs, certification, classes, and many other resources.

The American Culinary Federation (www.acfchefs.org) is a professional association of chefs, caterers, cooks, and food educators with chapters throughout the country. You can find a chapter near you by clicking on the "Chapters" link and then on your state on its Web site.

Other groups to consider include the International Association of Culinary Professionals (www.iacp.com) and the National Restaurant Association (www.nationalrestaurantassociation.org or www.restaurant.org), the latter of which boasts 60,000 business members.

Tips for Entry

1. Take cooking classes anywhere you can.
2. Take any job you can to get your foot in the door of a restaurant, even as dishwasher.
3. Aim for the restaurant or dining room you idolize and where you like the food, if you have tried it.
4. Learn cooking techniques, presentation, and kitchen diplomacy from everyone around you.
5. Improve English and Spanish language skills.
6. Learn recipes as you cook on the line to become able to teach others as line cooks.

RESTAURANT PASTRY CHEF

CAREER PROFILE

Duties: Designs and prepares desserts including cakes, sauces, pastries, custards, crème caramels, and other end-of-meal sweets in large restaurants, and bakes breads, rolls, and other items when there is no other baking staff. In larger restaurants and resorts, the pastry chef supervises other pastry staff.

Alternate Title(s): Pastry chef; Baker, Pastry Cook

Salary Range: $30,000 to $70,000 depending upon education, background, experience and region of the country. Some Restaurant Pastry Chefs are paid hourly in the $10 to $16 range for part-time work.

Employment Prospects: Good for increasing number of small, independent bakeries, excellent in urban or resort and gambling areas with lots of restaurants, hotels, and casinos that have large kitchens and restaurants

Advancement Prospects: Limited, because the pastry chef is specialized and at the top of the field. Theoretically, the better restaurants, hotels, and casinos pay better.

Best Geographical Location(s): Large cities, resort areas, casino enclaves, and wine regions where good restaurants have pastry chefs; smaller cities where small independent bakeries are cropping up; cruise ships

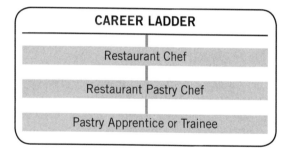

CAREER LADDER

Restaurant Chef

Restaurant Pastry Chef

Pastry Apprentice or Trainee

Prerequisites:

Education or Training—Culinary and baking classes in either a vocational cooking school, high school, community college, or junior college program, preferably with a specialty in pastry. Apprenticeships and practice at home offer great learning opportunities.

Experience—Baking experience in any bakery, or working one's way up the bakery ladder within a restaurant or hotel kitchen

Special Skills and Personality Traits—A skill for learning formulaic recipes and cooking; artistic design skills; patience and concentration; enjoyment of detail work and repetition

Position Description

A Restaurant Pastry Chef either makes or supervises other people who make all desserts daily in a restaurant or dining room, and even for all the restaurants or dining rooms in a large hotel, resort, or casino. In this case, desserts include cakes, mousses, cheesecakes, pies, custards, crème brûlées and flans, petits fours, pies, tarts and tortes, muffins, cupcakes, breads, ice creams, gelati and sorbets, puff pastries, and fabulous sauces to decorate a dessert.

The Restaurant Pastry Chef usually decides on a couple of special desserts to accompany a chef's daily menu changes and either makes them or instructs pastry cooks how to create them.

Great pastry chefs make the most of locally and sustainably grown organic fruit such as various kinds of berries, apples, pears, and stone fruits, including peaches, all of which ripen at different times in different regions of the country.

Some Restaurant Pastry Chefs and bakers make everything from scratch, while others purchase frozen or chilled balls of dough or pastry sheets, which they bake, fill, and decorate.

Pastry chefs and bakers usually begin their work days in the wee hours of the morning, which many of them find to be a peaceful time without the rest of the kitchen staff around. In fact, many bakers and pastry chefs see their operation as completely separate from the rest of the kitchen. While it is handy to have experience at every kitchen station no matter what specialty you develop, many pastry chefs and bakers have focused on their specialty from the beginning of their training. Working with a wide range of chocolates and sugars, considering percentages of cocoa and degrees of organic sugars, is a fine art in itself that needs to be learned and understood in an almost scientific approach.

In large restaurants, hotels, casinos, resorts, and on cruise ships, the restaurant pastry kitchen may have its own brigade hierarchy that includes:

- Pâtissier: The pastry chef
- Confiseur: Makes petits fours (small, iced cakes) and specialty candies
- Décorateur: Specializes in final decoration of elegant pastries and desserts as well as specialty cakes, which may appear to be meals in themselves
- Boulanger: May bake breads, cakes, breakfast pastries, muffins, and even cupcakes

Salaries

Pastry chefs in large restaurants and hotels are often highly respected for their talent and artistry, and may earn from $30,000 to $70,000, depending on where they work. In a smaller restaurant, a pastry chef might work part time, or even in a certified outside kitchen, making only $10 to $20 per hour with no benefits.

Employment Prospects

While the precise work and early morning demands of being a Restaurant Pastry Chef diminish the number of those seeking to get into the field, the top jobs in the specialty are quite competitive. Many jobs are part-time and end in the early afternoon, which allows pastry chefs to enjoy other pursuits or a second job. Large cities, destination resort areas, casino enclaves, and wine regions where good restaurants have pastry chefs are always good employment locations, as are smaller cities where small and independent bakeries are cropping up, and cruise ships, which sometimes cook daily for 3,000 passengers.

Advancement Prospects

At most, each restaurant only employs one top pastry chef. Therefore it is difficult to rise above that position unless a person wants to move up the kitchen ladder in the overall kitchen outside the pastry department.

Another way to rise as a baker or pastry chef is to move to another, better restaurant. Most chefs move around, somewhat like television news anchors.

Education and Training

Pastry chefs must be educated and trained in this specialty within the culinary profession, whether at culinary schools, community or junior colleges, or at baking specialty schools. Apprenticeships are extremely helpful, almost always expected. Through an apprenticeship, one can learn tricks and artistic techniques from more experienced pastry chefs.

A Restaurant Pastry Chef needs to know all of the basics, which are nearly impossible to learn at home in detail, including sauces, toppings, meringues, puff pastry, genoise (a kind of sponge cake), mousses, crèmes, custards of all kinds, glazes, ice creams, sorbets, and gelati.

Experience, Skills, and Personality Traits

Experience in a commercial kitchen or bakery as an apprentice or at any level is important to become a pastry chef. Innate artistic skills and enjoyment of design help a pastry chef excel. A calm personality, patience, and enjoyment of repetition and making people happy are all handy. Consistency of character, precision, and performance are all important qualities.

Unions and Associations

Union membership usually is only offered by large employers, meaning hotels, resorts, gambling casinos, and large restaurants. Unite Here represents nearly 1 million current and former hotel and restaurant employees among others (www.unitehere.org), particularly in large hotels, amusement resorts, and gambling hotels.

In addition, pastry chefs might gain from joining, or at least looking at, culinary professionals' Web sites for networking, conventions, shows and meetings, jobs, certification, classes, and many other resources.

The American Culinary Federation (www.acfchefs. org) is a professional association of chefs, caterers, cooks, and food educators with chapters throughout the country. You can find a chapter near you by clicking on the "Chapters" link and then on your state on its Web site.

Other groups to consider include the International Association of Culinary Professionals (www.iacp.com) and the National Restaurant Association (www.restaurant. org.), the latter of which boasts 60,000 business members.

Tips for Entry

1. Learn at any cooking school available close to your home and follow your taste within their program to pastries if you try making them repeatedly and passionately. Some culinary or baking programs have good contacts with restaurant or hotel chefs in the area.
2. Talk your way into an apprenticeship in the restaurant where you aspire to become part of the staff, even if you have to work for free at first. The question of how one gets experience with-

out already having some can be answered with a nonpaying apprenticeship if necessary.

3. Try to perfect your favorite dessert at home and take it to show to the pastry chef where you want to work.

4. Be willing to work at the lowest level in the bakery or pastry shop, just to get your foot in the door and learn from everyone around you.

5. Enter pastry contests, from churches to county fairs, and take any professional opportunities that arise.

6. Keep up on the latest fads in desserts, including fruit and other add-ons to sorbets, and gelati, gluten content or gluten-free, wheat-free, and flour-free foods and other trends.

GARDE-MANGER

CAREER PROFILE

Duties: Oversees the pantry of a kitchen, meaning preparation of all fresh raw vegetables, salad greens, vegetables to be cooked, cold appetizers, cold soups, pâtés, terrines, charcuterie, and tallow and ice sculpture. The Garde-Manger station may also oversee quality of ordering and inventory.

Alternate Title(s): Pantry Chef; Kitchen Steward; Pantry Supervisor

Salary Range: $10 to $15 an hour, or $15,000 to $30,000 a year, often without benefits

Employment Prospects: Excellent. There is great demand for entry-level line cooks and pantry chefs.

Advancement Prospects: Excellent for someone who speaks both English and Spanish.

Best Geographical Location(s): Anywhere in North America. Almost all restaurants need someone to perform this function, with or without the title.

Prerequisites:

Education or Training—High school, community or junior college, or other vocational cooking programs can prepare a person to become a Garde-Manger or pantry chef.

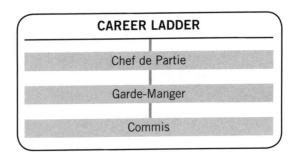

CAREER LADDER

Chef de Partie

Garde-Manger

Commis

Experience—Any kitchen experience will help. This is the kind of job one can rise to by beginning at the bottom of the kitchen ladder.

Special Skills and Personality Traits—A successful Garde-Manger must enjoy precision and detail work, take pride in his or her work, and have a good palate for balanced flavors. The person should also have genuine interest in and concern for the quality of fresh vegetables and fruit and in developing sustainable and healthful ways in which to grow foods, as well as an interest in fads in vegetables, fruits, pâtés, and charcuterie.

Position Description

The Garde-Manger, also known as the pantry chef, oversees the pantry of a kitchen, receiving and preparing of all fresh raw vegetables, salad greens, vegetables to be cooked, cold appetizers, cold soups, pâtés, terrines, charcuterie, and tallow and ice sculpture. The Garde-Manger station may also oversee quality of ordering and inventory, which requires knowing the best sources for fresh produce, including those that grow locally, organically, sustainably, and even biodynamically. Increasingly, customers want to know the sources of fresh produce.

A Garde-Manger needs to know the balances between greens, ranging from bitter to sweet and smooth to curly-scratchy, the healthful ingredients and flavors of various oils and vinegars and how they combine or affect the taste of salad greens.

The person in this position also must receive the produce, check it against invoices, check it for quality before accepting it, and prepare it for use (including washing, drying, picking, and breaking into bite-size

pieces), arrange it artfully on a plate, and take responsibility for its final presentation to the diner.

In some restaurants, the Garde-Manger is also in charge of seasonings, making cold soups, purées, and even sculptures from tallow or ice for display tables. Saving cuttings from vegetables trimmed for use in other dishes is essential to making those soups and making the best use of every vegetable that comes into the kitchen.

If the Garde-Manger is responsible for making pâtés, terrines, and charcuterie, including salumi, this person needs to know seasoning, poaching, simmering, roasting, frying, curing, drying, smoking, marinating, grinding, and puréeing, as well as guidelines for sanitation. One must know how to balance inherent and added proteins and fats. The Garde-Manger may also oversee stocks of pasta, garlic, herbs, and dried fruits in the pantry kitchen.

When the chef decides on the daily menu, the Garde-Manger may suggest complimentary salads or other accompaniments or just take orders from the chef on what he or she wants to go with their menu.

A kitchen steward's or stewardess's job may overlap with that of the Garde-Manger, but usually the kitchen steward also oversees orderliness and cleanliness of pots and all other cooking equipment, dishwashing, walk-in refrigerators, freezers, counters and other production areas, and dishes, in addition to overseeing the pantry. The kitchen steward may also supervise lower-level kitchen employees, as well as the silver cleaning and kitchen inspections, and take inventories of china, glassware and other equipment.

The job of commis is similar to that of kitchen steward or Garde-Manger, with the implication that the commis is committed to serving the chef under a mentoring relationship.

Salaries

Salaries for Garde-Manger are low, unfortunately, ranging from $10 to $15 an hour, or $15,000 to $30,000 a year, often without benefits, and depending on experience.

Employment Prospects

Employment prospects are excellent. Garde-Manger can be an entry-level position in some restaurants, and a refined science position of great pride in others. There are lots of jobs assisting the Garde-Manger, and there is also high turnover for a couple of reasons: The work is hard, and some people are not satisfied with doing a few things exceedingly well and want to move up the hierarchy. Cities and communities with high-end restaurants, hotels, casinos, and cruise ships offer the best prospects for separate jobs of this specific nature, as do fine restaurants in wine regions.

Advancement Prospects

Advancement prospects are excellent. Often dishwashers or cleaners move up to salad maker and Garde-Manger, while salad makers and Garde-Mangers learn other skills and move within a kitchen to other stations where they can learn more and move up again.

Education and Training

Any culinary classes and education, whether from high school or community college, will work well for applicants. Some Garde-Mangers have studied at full-fledged cooking schools, and this is the best job they can get to start. Others started as dishwashers or cleaners and worked their way up, gaining training along the way.

Experience, Skills, and Personality Traits

A passion for beautiful salads, fresh vegetables, charcuterie, and other responsibilities will take a person to the top of this field. English and Spanish language skills are handy. Punctuality, enjoying detail work, the ability to work alone in a chilly atmosphere, and a sense of caring are vital.

Unions and Associations

Some big cities have locals (branches) of the Hotel and Restaurant Employees and Bartenders Union. Unite Here represents nearly 1 million current and former hotel and restaurant employees among others (www.unitehere.org), particularly in large hotels, amusement resorts and gambling hotels.

Garde-Mangers, might gain from joining, or at least looking at culinary professionals' Web sites for networking, conventions, shows and meetings, jobs, certification, classes, and many other resources.

The American Culinary Federation (www.acfchefs.org) is a professional association of chefs, caterers, cooks, and food educators with chapters throughout the country. You can find a chapter near you by clicking on the link for "Chapters" and then on your state on its Web site.

Other groups to consider include the International Association of Culinary Professionals (www.iacp.com) and the National Restaurant Association (www.nationalrestaurantassociation.org or www.restaurant.org), the latter of which boasts 60,000 business members.

Tips for Entry

1. Take a beginning level culinary course in a public or private cooking or catering program to learn basic elements of cooking.
2. Get your foot in the door, whether as dishwasher, cleaner, or lettuce washer. A kitchen's pantry is a great place to learn how a restaurant kitchen works.
3. Use the opportunity to learn all you can from higher-ups, perfect your skills, and move up or to a better restaurant if you wish.

SERVER

CAREER PROFILE

Duties: Assumes all responsibilities for his or her "station," meaning the section of the dining room or tables to which he or she is assigned, including overseeing busers or assistant servers, setup of dining room uniformly to owner's or manager's specifications and style, and greeting customers when they arrive at their table to give the best possible second impression after the host seats them. A Server explains special dishes, takes orders from customers, relays them to kitchen, and serves the food unless the restaurant has food presenters or runners.

Alternate Title(s): Waitperson (formerly known as waiter and waitress)

Salary Range: Minimum wage or less to $20 an hour, plus tips, usually without benefits. Tips can range from 5 or 10 percent to 20 or 30 percent, or $5 to $100 or more, depending upon the style and level of restaurant as well as location in the country.

Employment Prospects: Excellent, with lots of room for upward mobility

Advancement Prospects: Excellent, with hard work and diplomacy. One can start as a buser and work up to server, host, maître d'hôtel, and manager, either within the same "house" or establishment or by going elsewhere for a job.

Best Geographical Location(s): Urban areas, affluent suburbs, country clubs, wine regions, cruise ships, and other vacation destinations

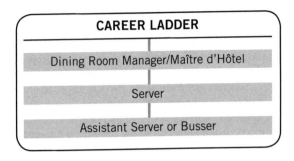

CAREER LADDER

Dining Room Manager/Maître d'Hôtel

Server

Assistant Server or Busser

Prerequisites:

Education or Training—Education can come from apprenticeships that include busing or from hotel and restaurant management schools. Knowledge of nutrition, food sources, and growing of food will be great assets.

Experience—All experience is valuable, from volunteering at senior food program centers to busing, always aiming at better quality restaurants than the previous place of employment.

Special Skills and Personality Traits—A server should believe in what he or she is doing and have genuine interest in service and making customers happy. Charm, quick thinking, comfort in apologizing, a willingness to admit errors, and real appreciation and interest in good food are assets.

Position Description

A Server has two jobs: sell the food being cooked in the kitchen, and take care of the customers to make them feel comfortable and welcome, which in turn sells more food from the kitchen. Since Servers make a base hourly pay in addition to tips based on a percentage of the total bill, the more expensive items the Server sells to the customer, the higher the tip is likely to be.

Several techniques that might increase sales and tips (gratuities) include talking customers into more courses than they planned to order, such as appetizers, salads, dessert, and coffee in addition to the main course; working with buser to flatter, flirt with, and wait on customers so they feel special; and talk customers into alcoholic beverages, including introducing the sommelier if the restaurant has one.

Most restaurants divide the dining room into sections or "stations," with a Server in charge of one station, making the Server sort of a territorial executive.

Since restaurant dining rooms are often cleared, cleaned, and reset after hours in the evening, the Server checks his or her station on arrival for a work shift to make sure everything is perfect and makes everything that way if it is not.

Depending upon the size and hierarchy of the restaurant's staff, a Server might have to fold napkins in the restaurant's prescribed style, make sure glasses are sparkling clean, and polish silverware to perfection. All dry condiment containers, such as salt and pepper shakers, sugar and sugar-substitute bowls, and flower vases must be checked, the latter for freshness of flowers and fresh water.

If some dishes are prepared at the table, a dash of flare and care are required. A Server must check to make certain any table-side carts are clean and fully equipped with fresh ingredients, such as fresh croutons and anchovies and a new wedge of cheese to be grated for Caesar salad, fresh bottles of liquor for flambé desserts, and sharp knives for meat carving.

Now that the scene is set, a Server should welcome arriving guests to their table as if she or he is honored to have the opportunity to serve and to make the occasion their best dining experience ever. A Server's greeting or presentation of themselves and the establishment where they work—from elegant restaurant to corner café—sets the mood and impacts what kind of experience the customer has and remembers, as well as how much they order and how big the tip to the Server becomes.

A good Server should be well-informed and should have tasted everything on the menu, including specials for the day. An excellent Server will be totally familiar with each item's ingredients, including gluten and meat content, where vegetables are grown and whether they are organic, where meat and poultry products are grown and what the livestock were fed, and whether seafood is from wild or farmed sources.

Servers have to answer loads of questions, which might range from what a word on the menu means to where city hall is—to whether they are single—so food knowledge and diplomacy are important.

Other kinds of important information to have at the tip of one's tongue is what rare, medium, and well-done meat means to the restaurant's chef or grill cook; whether the grilled tuna is cooked through or rare throughout; and a plethora of definitions on ethnic, organic, sustainable, or specialized menus.

For placing orders, Servers may need a variety of skills. Some Servers memorize long orders and somehow deliver the correct food to the right people; some Servers write down orders in their own shorthand or in the official code or shorthand of the restaurant; some carry computer wands into which they type code for orders; and others physically walk to computer touch screens to key in orders. All of this requires extensive knowledge and some computer skills.

Such computer programs may include details about martini flavors; how a customer likes eggs cooked (such as scrambled, over easy, or basted); how the person likes their meat prepared; regular or decaffeinated coffee; or which of various salad dressings a guest might prefer. Computer programs also help the kitchen keep a running inventory for sales and reordering records by day, week, or month, as well as records of taxes and salaries, tracking of business ups and downs, and charting of a Server's sales performance.

A Server needs to remember which order or dish goes to which diner, a seemingly small fact that, if violated, can annoy guests easily and affect whether a customer returns to the restaurant or tips the Server well or badly to make a statement.

After serving the food, the Server offers add-ons including freshly ground pepper, grated cheese, lemon, and extra sauces.

Depending on the restaurant's policy, should a customer deem the food to be unsatisfactory and tells the Server before eating half the dish, the Server should immediately remove the plate and offer to replace it with another selection, only charging the diner for one item.

A Server should never clear the plate of some diners until all guests at that table have finished eating. Language should be something like, "May I take your plate?" or "Have you finished?" rather than "Are ya' done workin' on that?"

A Server should chat enough to make guests feel at ease, but not enter into their conversation or sit down at the table. There is a delicate balance between great service and bothering the customers, which nuance is learned by experience and guidance from longer-serving colleagues.

With sensitivity to what guests have already consumed, a Server might suggest another bottle of wine, dessert, cheese selections, or coffee, all of which add to the bill and, ostensibly, the size of the tip.

Servers also help train busers or assistant waiters and can help mold that person, often new to the business, into someone who learns and serves well.

Assistant waiters, busers, and food runners all assist servers or waiters. Bussers clear tables and refill nonalcoholic beverges, food runners sometimes deliver food from the kitchen to tables, and assistant waiters basically assist servers.

Salaries

Many restaurants only pay Servers the going minimum wage or less as base pay, knowing that the Server also makes tips, and offer no benefits such as medical insurance or paid vacations. Successful Servers, who attract repeat customers and sell well, sometimes garner much higher base pay, medical benefits, retirement benefits, and vacation pay. Tips are paid either in cash or on credit card bills. There is always controversy over servers reporting cash tips as income on their tax returns. Servers should also keep track of tips charged on credit cards to make sure they get the tips they earned. Sometimes Servers have to share a percentage of their tips with busers, who are important as part of the team that provides total care of customers.

Employment Prospects

There are always abundant employment opportunities for Servers at all levels of the restaurant industry, with the premise that the better the restaurant the better the pay and tips. Restaurants with the longest-term employees should be the most attractive in which to work. If a Server has worked a long time in a restaurant or hotel, he or she must be made happy with the work conditions and compensation.

Different restaurants want Servers with differing appearances. Classic French or Italian restaurants may prefer older, established waitstaff. Hip and noisy restaurants may desire hip, young staffers.

Temporary serving jobs are popular with students, actors, musicians, and other creative people, as well as people in transitional periods between careers, and others simply intrigued with the food or beverage businesses.

Server turnover is high in some restaurants, so there are always openings. The best jobs are often where turnover is lowest. Servers stick around when work conditions, treatment of personnel, and pay are good.

A successful Server develops professional relationships with regular customers who may request seating at a particular Server's table.

Server opportunities abound at golf courses and country clubs, cruise ships, gambling centers, wine regions with good restaurants, urban areas, and affluent suburbs. "White tablecloth" restaurants offer the most elegant dining experiences, most expensive food, and ostensibly the biggest tips. When entering the field or moving to a new city, be willing to start slightly lower on the kitchen ladder and work your way up, or use the move to leave the past behind and start at a higher rung on the ladder.

Advancement Prospects

With little or no experience, people can often get jobs at the bottom of a hotel restaurant ladder, even as dishwasher, and work their way up, learning as they go. It is not unusual for a dishwasher to eventually become a fabulous Server, maître d' (maître d'hôtel) or headwaiter, chef, or executive manager. Headwaiter is now also called lead server in some establishments.

If a Server thinks she or he is not moving up fast enough, he or she might move to another restaurant with better food, better staff, and better clientele.

Waitstaffing on the floor of any restaurant varies according to how busy the restaurant is. Sometimes managers call in all Servers and some are sent home if business is slow, or managers underestimate and have to call Servers in at the last minute. Hence, work as a Server can be unpredictable and irregular.

Education and Training

Server training is available on the job and at more formal institutions. Some restaurants like first-timers because managers can mold servers in their own fashion to comply with the establishment's style and policies. Such training might range from how to dress, how to fold napkins, how to stand, walk, and speak properly, how to greet customers, hold chairs out, open napkins, address the host, suggest menu items and wine, how to work with busers and other staff, how to carve meats if necessary, or how to flame a dessert.

High school culinary programs, community colleges, and junior colleges often teach hospitality, hotel, and restaurant skills. Many of these schools teach all aspects of hotel and restaurant management, including hosting, cooking, and serving, and may include internships or externships at school or outside cafés and restaurants where students can gain on-the-job experience.

Experience, Skills, and Personality Traits

Serving in restaurants is part sales, part sensitivity, and part charm—which may be part of sales. A successful Server is usually considerate, respectful, articulate, knowledgeable about all aspects of the food she or he is serving, friendly, ambitious, energetic, and interested in detail. Fluency in the English language is usually required.

A good Server also needs a good memory for people, names, menu specials, ingredients, and a willingness to ask questions in the kitchen if he or she doesn't know the answer to a guest's question. It's also helpful if the Server is genuinely interested in food and enjoys adding touches to dishes or table-side presentations. One must never add something to a dish without the chef knowing about it, however. People get fired for such actions.

Unions and Associations

Few strong culinary unions remain, but those that do are in big cities and gambling centers, and then mostly in large hotels. United Here is one such union that represents Servers in hotels across the United States. Where they are forceful, unions have worked successfully for living wage base pay for Servers.

Tips for Entry

1. Get all the training you can, whether in school or on the job.
2. If necessary, take a job as a buser or assistant waiter/server to get your foot in the door, and ask about advancement possibilities.
3. Learn from everyone around you, by what they do right—and what they do wrong.
4. Perfect your English if it is not your first language.
5. Look for the best restaurant at which you can find a job. If you feel unsure of yourself, get a job in a lesser establishment to gain experience and learn some skills.

SOMMELIER

Duties: Tastes and orders wine for a restaurant; works with chef to plan menus and wine lists to make sure the food and wine lists are compatible; educates servers and bussers on wines, what they go with, how to pour, whether to chill or not; researches local wines to enhance sales for local wineries; recommends wines to customers

Alternate Title(s): Wine Steward; Wine Director

Salary Range: $28,000 to $100,000, sometimes with bonus and benefits

Employment Prospects: Fair, with specialized training in the right parts of the country. Some jobs are part-time and others full-time with other management responsibilities and benefits.

Advancement Prospects: Good, with good training and good reputation; moving to employers with large wine programs and wine lists, and more food compatible with wine are means to advance

Best Geographical Location(s): States and provinces where wine is popular, where wine is grown and produced, major cities with sophisticated restaurants, resorts, casinos, country clubs, and cruise ships

Prerequisites:

Education and Training—Requirements for actual sommelier status have increased in the past few

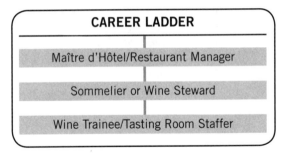

CAREER LADDER

Maître d'Hôtel/Restaurant Manager

Sommelier or Wine Steward

Wine Trainee/Tasting Room Staffer

years. Wine stewards and wine directors have less stringent standards. Several schools offer varying degrees of sommelier credentials. Visit as many wineries as possible and ask questions, and take wine courses at community or junior colleges and at some universities.

Experience—Employment at a winery, wine shop, bar, sales team, or giving wine tours are handy.

Special Skills and Personality Traits—Must love wine, have a good palate, remember wines by taste (taste or palate memory), must be devoted to wine and food. Must have deep desire to please others, good speaking and organizational skills, tact, and tendency toward precision.

Position Description

A Sommelier or wine steward organizes a restaurant's entire wine program, from tasting to pairing of wines with foods the chef might prepare according to seasonal meat, seafood, and produce availability, to ordering and keeping inventory, staying on top of local, domestic, and foreign releases, and educating waitstaff about wines and their nuances.

Some Sommeliers might manage a wine bar or general bar or several in a hotel, create innovative promotions to enhance wine sales, make sure wine is secure, reorder when necessary, keep up relationships with winemakers, keep track of and minimize glass breakage, and oversee appearance and training of wine servers.

A Sommelier must make novice wine drinkers comfortable and explain wine complexities simply, while knowing wines well enough to satisfy the most demanding customer.

Sommeliers must also be able to explain the difference between cork and plastic bottle stoppers, the wine varietals that go into each wine, the difference in vintages (year produced), and types of wine, from aperitifs and domestic or imported sparkling wines (champagne), various white, pink, and red dinner wines, and after-dinner sipping wines such as port, Madeira, and cognacs.

Often wineries are sold to large corporations, which may infuse them with money that enables them to improve, or may ruin a winery's small artisan techniques and image. A restaurant Sommelier must keep track of what is going on at which winery and which wines are best which year.

A Sommelier must also keep up on what circumstances have influenced which wine vintages from various regions to order the best and most interesting wines at the best prices to accompany the chef's cuisine and please the customers.

A Sommelier might stage events to promote the wine side of a restaurant's repertoire. Such events can include special tastings called "flights," focusing on one varietal made by several wineries, or a varietal made in separate years by the same winery. Wine and food pairing events can combine tastes of wines guests may not have access to elsewhere served with appetizers created especially to go well with those wines. A Sommelier might also invite guest lecturers such as vegetable growers and bakers to talk about what they do and how that product goes with wines.

Winemaker dinners introduce interested guests to a winemaker, who tells his or her life and winemaking stories and works with the Sommelier and chef to create a dinner guests might pay from $30 to $300 to enjoy.

If the Sommelier does not live near a wine region, wine distributors might bring the wine tasting to a Sommelier and chef to taste in their own restaurant. In this case, the Sommelier truly has to believe in his or her palate and not in sales pitches to determine a wine's compatibility with the restaurant's food.

A Sommelier needs to understand proper storage of all wines, which may vary in temperature and light, and advise the restaurant manager on building proper storage with consideration of the establishment's need for table space.

Some magazines, newspapers, organizations, and guidebooks rate restaurants by their wine lists. A few restaurants with brief menus have short wine lists, while others boast a hundred pages of cellared wines, with some bottles costing in the thousands of dollars. A Sommelier must know about and care for those rare wines and know whether to recommend them. Wine lists are sometimes more of a draw at restaurants than the food. A mistaken recommendation by a Sommelier can ruin his or her reputation, along with that of the restaurant.

There is definitely a pecking order among wine specialists in restaurants, as there is among the kitchen and service staffs. In large hotels, casinos, cruise ships, or restaurants there might be a master sommelier, head wine steward, or wine director who oversees wine stewards, wine waiters, or wine servers. This head Sommelier, and most other Sommeliers, teach waitstaff or servers about wines, and how to ask questions of and answer questions for guests.

In establishments where servers do sell wine, the Sommelier should arrange a tasting for them so they are familiar with what they recommend to customers.

Wine is a huge profit maker for restaurants, and markups are large, which is one reason some customers bring their own bottles and pay a corkage fee. The Sommelier works with management to determine the appropriate markup on wine, which the restaurant buys by the case and at a discount.

The Sommelier also decides, with the chef and management, which wines to sell by the glass. With new drunk-driving laws, more people want to sample a glass of wine, or a glass of a few different wines, without purchasing a whole bottle. Restaurants may also need to move a wine and offer it at a per-glass price, which now ranges from $3.50 to $18.50.

Sommeliers and wine directors also teach servers and other staffers about wines on the list, which wines to suggest with which foods, how to assess how expensive a wine to suggest to a particular customer, how to make the customer feel comfortable, and basic wine manners of pouring, chilling, and the order of service.

Freelance Sommeliers, who work as independent contractors or consultants for hire by individuals or organizations, can make a lot of money piecing together clients who come to rely on them for advice on building their wine collections.

Salaries

Sommelier or wine director salaries vary widely around the United States, ranging from $38,000 to $100,000. Depending upon one's individual arrangement, a Sommelier might get an annual bonus based on either wine sales or the restaurant's overall profit. If the job is full-time, the Sommelier might get benefits.

Some restaurants only hire a Sommelier on a part-time or consulting basis, in which case the Sommelier probably would not get benefits.

A freelance or personal Sommelier needs to handle his or her own health insurance, Social Security taxes, etc. since this person is a private contractor, although a freelancer can do very well adding up several prestigious clients who want to impress their friends or associates with their wine collections.

Employment Prospects

Employment prospects are fair. An increasing number of restaurants want to say they employ Sommeliers, but paying them for full-time work is another topic. There is new interest among young people to become hip Sommeliers with regional or international specialties.

Celebrity chefs with multiple restaurants that carry their names often hire Sommeliers, as might hotels with several restaurants, and casinos. Cruise ships usually have one Sommelier and several "wine waiters," who, hopefully, have learned all about the wines on the list from the Sommelier.

Big cities with sophisticated restaurants, suburbs with country clubs or elegant dining, wine regions where fine restaurants abound, and gambling centers are good places to find work. Some parts of the country are not particularly interested in wines as a food or as an accompaniment to food.

Advancement Prospects

Once one actually earns the title of Sommelier and gets hired as such, there is little room for advancement unless one moves to a grander restaurant, hotel, casino, or cruise line where one will be paid more. Sommeliers advance by four traits: exceptional palates; getting along with people; earning a reputation; and success in selling wine.

Occasionally a Sommelier or wine director might move up to manager or maître d'hôtel, although many are committed to their love of wine.

Education or Training

Sommelier training is available at a wide range of venues producing a wide range of expertise. Many community and junior colleges in wine-producing regions offer courses in wine production and wine growing and occasionally in wine pairing. Some culinary centers and culinary schools offer wine classes and low-level Sommelier courses.

The Court of Master Sommeliers is a British-founded international examining body that educates and certifies Master Sommeliers (M.S.), not to be confused with the M.S. (master of science) degree at more traditional universities. The Court of Master Sommeliers offers an introductory sommelier course, a certified Sommelier exam, an advanced Sommelier course, and a master sommelier diploma exam. The master sommelier diploma exam is the ultimate professional credential in the field. One must be of legal drinking age to enter the program.

Admission to the advanced course is through the academic admissions committee. Successful candidates have to complete the introductory course and work five years in the wine and service industry.

Topics covered on the master sommelier diploma exam include restaurant services and salesmanship, in which candidates learn about aperitifs, glassware, menu content and wine lists, decanting and serving wine, presentation, brandies and liqueurs, and answering questions with skill and diplomacy; how to speak with authority using wine knowledge, answer questions on international wine laws and global wine regions, knowledge of fortified wines, methods of spirit and liqueur distillation, knowledge of cigar production, processes of cider and beer making, and how to store all of the above products; and practical tasting, in which

candidates have to identify grape varieties, country of origin, and vintages of wines tasted.

Full membership in the Court requires passing the master sommelier diploma and receiving an invitation from the Court. Fewer than 200 candidates have attained this high goal among Sommeliers. (See www.mastersommeliers.org for more information.)

On-the-job training and tasting are also important. Learning and working with an expert sommelier can be extremely valuable, while keeping in mind that every individual's palate differs.

The Society of Wine Educators conducts programs and educates people to become a certified specialist of wine (CSW); certified wine educator (CWE); and certified specialist of spirits (CSS). (See www.societyofwineeducators.org.)

Wine Spectator School, sponsored by *Wine Spectator* magazine, conducts classes for amateurs and professionals in the wine business seeking knowledge of the industry. Topics covered include the ABCs of wine sales and service, kosher ABC's of wine tasting, world wine regions, wine and food pairing, and sensory evaluation. (see www.winespectatorschool.com.)

Many people call themselves Sommeliers with little or no training.

Experience, Skills, and Personality Traits

Sommeliers must have great taste (palate) and taste memory, understand what goes into the flavor of each wine, be able to describe it, and pair it from memory with what foods a guest has ordered.

The more wine-related experiences one has, from working at wineries or in the vineyards to washing wineglasses or apprenticing with famous Sommeliers, the better a Sommelier that person will be, and the more likely that person will get a good job.

A Sommelier should at least appear sincere, knowledgeable, genuine, interested, and sensitive to a customer's taste and budget. The person must have an organizational side that enables her or him to keep wines cellared in an orderly fashion, keep an inventory either on a list, card file, or in a computer, or else have a great memory.

Unions and Associations

The Society of Wine Educators (www.societyofwineeducators.org) offers memberships, information sharing, and an annual conference. The United States Sommelier Association is not a trade association; it is an educational program at Le Cordon Bleu College of Culinary Arts campus in Miami, Florida.

Tips for Entry

1. Visit wineshops in your area and learn all you can by reading labels, tasting if possible, asking questions of the proprietor.
2. Tour as many wineries in as many wine regions as you can. Winter is a great time to do this because winemakers are less busy and may have time to talk to you.
3. Read wine publications either in print or online. Libraries often carry these periodicals, especially in wine producing regions.
4. Attend the American Institute of Food & Wine programs around the country if possible, and read about them online (www.aiwf.org) as a way to meet people in the industry.
5. Enroll in whatever classes you can, from a local community college to the Master Court of Sommeliers, to improve your knowledge of wine.
6. Study wine lists at restaurants and choose one that represents your wine interests—this is probably where you should try for a job.
7. Be ready to accept a lower job than you would prefer in order to get your foot in the door and learn.

DINING ROOM MANAGER

Duties: Interprets and implements the owner's goals and style for the restaurant, coordinating all aspects of "the front of the house," meaning a restaurant's public area or dining room (as opposed to the kitchen); trains and supervises waitstaff; sometimes serves as sommelier when the restaurant has none

Alternate Titles: Maître d'Hôtel: Maître d'; Headwaiter; Captain; Host; Hostess

Salary Range: $30,000 to $100,000, plus occasional tips and benefits

Employment Prospects: Limited

Advancement Prospects: Limited

Best Geographical Location(s): Big cities and elegant suburbs with high-end, sophisticated restaurants; gambling centers; cruise ships

Prerequisites:

    Education or Training—The best training is to have worked every job on the way up so that you

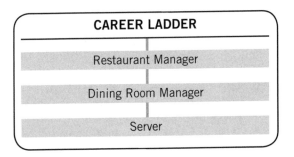

CAREER LADDER

Restaurant Manager

Dining Room Manager

Server

understand what each position entails; culinary school education from community colleges, culinary schools, or hotel and restaurant management (hospitality) schools is useful.

    Experience—Serving or management in a restaurant, private club, casino, or cruise line

    Special Skills and Personality Traits—A successful dining room manager should enjoy pleasing others and attending to their comforts, be well organized, have great people and leadership skills, and be a great team builder and coordinator.

Position Description

A Dining Room Manager translates and executes the owner's concept of what he or she wants a restaurant to be. This person runs "the front of the house" (the dining room, as opposed to kitchen or "the back of the house"), trains servers, busers, and assistant waiters or servers, oversees all matters involved in running the dining room or restaurant, sometimes greets diners and shows them to their tables when there is no host, occasionally gives a guest a better table after a subtle tip crosses hands during a handshake, and even helps to expedite service, occasionally delivering food or even clearing crumbs or dishes when a dining room is busy.

    Some managers order flowers, wine for the wine list if also acting as sommelier, and schedule staff. Some managers perform dramatic tableside service shows, such as mixing Caesar salads, serving flambé desserts, or carving meats.

    If the manager is also the sommelier, she or he will educate waitstaff on wines' compatibility with menu items, as well as the proper skills for selling and serving wine.

    Successful managers will live in or near the area, know the market, and remember customers' names.

    As a leader, the manager must inspire cooperative teamwork and make the dining room run smoothly. Happy customers tip well and return often.

    Many restaurants have cut costs by replacing this position with a host or hostess who greets guests, checks reservations, and shows customers to their tables, but earn lower salaries than the more formal positions.

Salaries

The Dining Room Manager position is usually among the few full-time jobs in a restaurant. Although they work odd hours their base pay may range from $30,000 to $100,000, plus benefits and tips, and possibly a bonus based upon wine or restaurant sales.

Employment Prospects

All sorts of restaurant manager jobs exist, in chain diners or fast food "stores" up to elegant, so-called white tablecloth restaurants. A person can work his or her way up by improving language and management skills, working well with others, and possibly moving to a better restaurant than the current place of employment.

    Big cities, affluent suburbs, resort and gambling communities, cruise ships, wine regions, or anywhere else where fine restaurants exist are good places to find work.

Advancement Prospects

One can work one's way up in every part of a restaurant operation. Dining Room Manager is a sought-after job in which people stay for several years, as long as business increases. Moving to a different or better restaurant is often a good way to advance.

Education and Training

Most community college culinary programs offer service and restaurant management courses, as do culinary schools and hotel and restaurant management schools. Until recently, the fine art of restaurant management was overlooked by schools, but the field has rapidly become a popular career destination.

Experience, Skills, and Personality Traits

A good manager should have experience at many of the dining room jobs he or she is overseeing in order to understand what staff have to do, and have knowledge of hospitality management and enjoy working with others as a team. A successful Dining Room Manager will be a person who loves to host guests, welcomes people into his or her world, and enjoys pleasing people and making them feel comfortable.

Unions and Associations

Dining room and restaurant managers fall into executive and management position categories, and are generally not members of workers' unions. Online and conference opportunities abound through the American Institute of Wine and Food (www.aiwf.org).

Tips for Entry

1. Get your foot in the door of a restaurant at the best job level you can to get experience, including with a nonprofit food service program such as meals-on-wheels.
2. Work your way up, possibly to assistant manager, to learn the field.
3. Take any local community or culinary school classes you can, particularly in restaurant management or hospitality, which is usually an early course in a college or school program.

BAKERIES AND BAKING

BAKERY MANAGER

Duties: Determines how much of which products to bake each day; orders supplies ahead of time; makes up shift schedules; hires, fires, trains, and assigns employees; often sets prices with owner; stays up to date on health department regulations and makes sure the establishment enforces all health practices. Bakery managers in large industrial bakeries become executives who lead a larger hierarchy and probably will not even touch a blob of dough.

Alternate Title(s): Head Baker; Owner

Salary Range: If paid on salary, pay ranges from $28,000 to $120,000, which may or may not include benefits.

Employment Prospects: Good

Advancement Prospects: Good

Best Geographical Location(s): Throughout North America, with higher salaries on Atlantic and Pacific coasts, in big cities, resort areas, gambling centers, and on cruise ships

Prerequisites:

Education or Training—High school or culinary school baking programs, on the job training as apprentice or floor mopper, and any nutrition, business management, or marketing courses

Experience—Any baking experience is good, including home baking from cookbooks to baking for a food bank or meals-on-wheels programs, lowest level employment in a bakery, or baking or making dessert in a restaurant.

Special Skills and Personality Traits—Get pleasure from the artistry and creativity of baking; not mind daily repetition; ability to work by formula; enjoyment of detail work; interest in producing the highest quality in both design and taste of product

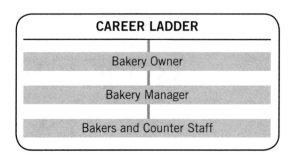

CAREER LADDER

Bakery Owner

Bakery Manager

Bakers and Counter Staff

Position Description

Local neighborhood Bakery Managers and industrial Bakery Managers have many duties in common, and many not in common. Local Bakery Managers often have to be personable and deal with the public, listen to their complaints and ideas, entertain, and change menus daily to meet customers' requests. Industrial Bakery Managers rarely deal with the public and change formulas based on giant food demand fads and trends.

A Bakery Manager or head baker is in charge of producing varying quantities and types of bread, pastries, cookies, cakes, and pies for sale to customers, whether as retail direct to customers or wholesale to grocery stores.

A local Bakery Manager must also produce enough of the above goodies to meet customers' expectations and needs, so that those who come in with expectations of buying certain items can find them fresh and in stock. Among some items, seasonality of ingredients varies the products made and sold. If blueberries or marionberries are in season in one region, or apricots in another, they certainly will show up in locally baked breakfast pastries and pies. Other variables of what is baked might include holidays, the national origin of a Bakery Manager or owner, predominant ethnicity in the neighborhood, seasons, weather, and whatever—if anything—the baker advertises. Many bakeries are so well known locally for their specialties that they don't need to advertise.

Local Bakery Managers or their employees also take special orders for everything from Easter bunnies to Star of David cookies, holiday coffee cakes, varieties of French bread, and birthday cakes.

Additionally, those favorite local bakeries make cakes, cupcakes, Danish pastries, tarts, doughnuts and breads, which may vary according to the ethnic or national origin background of the owner or Bakery Manager.

Industrial Bakery Managers need to be flexible and sensitive to major food trends to use healthful ingredients in specialized recipes, including gluten-free. Large chain food stores' bakeries may include baking sheets of cake and shipping the naked cake to the "bakery" departments of their stores where they are unstacked and restacked and decorated.

Notice that small bakeries that do have tables and chairs have few of either. The Bakery Managers or owner wants to bring customers in, but often prefers to have people make their choices, spend their money, and leave, keeping the baked goods and customer rotation rolling.

Most baking at a bakery begins the night before and goes through the night, with bread and breakfast pastries usually finished before the bakery opens in the early morning. Pastry chefs sometimes bake during the day because their products usually get consumed after lunch, through the afternoon, and into the evening.

Bakery Managers sometimes have to be there for the whole process, starting with the early shift with yeast breads that need to rise for a couple of hours before they are baked. Some basic products can be made ahead of time in large batches, and then chilled or frozen.

Bakery Managers generally end their official work day in early to mid-afternoon, and go to sleep earlier than most of us so they can get up in the wee hours to start over again.

The lives of bakers and Bakery Managers run on entirely different clock cycles than the rest of us. They often work in the dark and sleep during daylight.

Assistant bakers often make blobs of bread and pastry dough ahead of time, some of which benefit from being chilled. Assistant bakers, who might be culinary students or learners on the job, also might measure ingredients, mix doughs, clean and maintain ovens and their temperatures, make and stir custard fillings, wash or peel fruit in season, and carry trays of oven-fresh pastries out to the sales room part of the bakery, also known as "the front."

Bakers have to plan and requisition ahead to fill special orders, which can run from dozens of doughnuts to wedding cakes and holiday specialties. The Bakery Manager might call part-time bakery assistants to come in to work on special orders; these assistants may include specialists in cake decorating, who require some artistic talent.

As prices of the goods that go into bakery products, such as flour, butter, and milk increase, the more difficult the financial end of the Bakery Manager's responsibilities becomes. The Bakery Manager has to set wholesale and retail prices so that the bakery makes a profit while not overreaching beyond customers' budgets. As even Starbucks discovered, when the public's luxury income shrinks, people cut luxuries, which might include a stop for coffee and pastries.

Bakery demands often decrease in hot weather and increase in cold weather. When people are cold, they can burn off more of the calories contained in breads and pastries, and often rationalize that they get comfort from baked goods. In hotter weather, some of those same bakery specialties seem heavier and less appealing, which is when ice cream cakes swing into popularity. Even in the new dog bakeries, the canine customers seem to crave fewer "pupcakes" in the summer.

Seasonality, an overused newish food term, is important in baking. Summer fruits can and should be featured in summer pastries, along with vegetables in quiches to take home.

Bakery Managers, from local bakeries to huge industrial baking institutions, have to know customers' trends, as well as the ethnic holidays and baking traditions of their customers. Bakery staff gain this knowledge primarily from experience or by apprenticing with someone.

Bakery Managers have to hire and manage all staff, from baking assistants to cashiers, cake decorators, espresso baristas, sandwich and salad makers, busers, truck drivers, sales representatives, counter servers, and specialty bakers.

Many bakers, Bakery Managers, and bakery owners get into the business to bake and make people happy with their products, so the drudgery of actually running the business can be painful. For Bakery Managers with business backgrounds or who have taken management courses dealing with the business side is much easier.

Bakery Managers or head bakers in large restaurants or resorts often function in separate kitchens from the rest of the cooking staff, and often claim to know nothing of what goes on in the main "hot" kitchen.

Bakery jobs are available throughout the United States and Canada, with higher pay in more affluent cities and suburbs. The more diverse the urban area, the more specialty bakeries there will be, ranging from Basque to Bavarian. Every small town in America has at least one local bakery or someone who bakes at home and sells to neighbors. If you don't find one, start one.

Salaries

Bakery Managers' salaries vary greatly by region and size of bakery, with some surprises. Managers of large corporate bakeries do not make more than those at medium sized bakeries.

Bakers and Bakery Managers' median hourly wages range from about $12 to $17, and median salaries run from $29,000 at nonprofit organizations, $30,000 for the self-employed, to $75,000 in big cities. Hourly workers rarely get benefits, while salaried bakers and managers often do. Baking assistants, cashiers, busers, and espresso jockeys usually get hourly wages and no benefits.

Employment Prospects

There are lots of opportunities to work in baking and bakery management if one is willing to work odd and long hours. Bakery work and management is also an excellent opportunity for entry-level and immigrant workers. Most towns have at least one bakery or baking opportunities in a small restaurant.

Advancement Prospects

Advancement prospects are excellent. Advancement prospects for all bakery workers are tremendous, particularly for people who are willing to work long hours, have a passion for baking, and a sense for business.

A Bakery Manager who increases sales by knowing clientele, developing specialties, planning and purchasing wisely, pricing correctly for the market, and managing staff well, will attract attention from other bakeries who might want to hire that person away. If so, a Bakery Manager can earn more by moving elsewhere, or by being paid more to stay right where he or she is.

A promotion of last resort may be to start one's own bakery, where one can be the überboss and assume the manager's position or hire a Bakery Manager.

Education and Training

A Bakery Manager has to know how to bake and how to cook in general. One can gain this knowledge at community and junior colleges, culinary schools, on the job, at home from cookbooks and practice, and even at avocational cooking classes. To manage a bakery, it is important to also take some business management courses.

While it is not necessary or required, it can be smart for a potential baker to learn other aspects of cooking, unless one is thoroughly convinced that baking is her or his calling.

Often culinary students get part-time jobs in local bakeries to learn practical on-the-job training.

The baker or manager also needs to understand kinds of sugars and flours, fruits, chocolate, and the climate where he or she is working and its effect on the baking process.

Training in a baking kitchen under a master is the best education one can get.

Experience, Skills, Personality Traits

Not all bakers become Bakery Managers. A person who has worked making breads, desserts, or morning pastries, or has worked in a café or restaurant, already has experience that helps qualify him or her for working as a baker.

Baking requires the ability to follow formulas and recipes much more strictly than restaurant cooking. A baker must also enjoy repetition, making the same thing day after day and without variation except with permission from the Bakery Manager or owner. A baker must have a commitment to perfection and excellence.

Management courses from a community or culinary college will be handy in place of actual management experience. Because of their weird work hours that sometimes start at 2:00 A.M., bakers and Bakery Managers have to go home around noon or soon after, when most people are getting into their prime time at work or play.

English language and knowing the language of the bakery will be handy.

Unions and Associations

The Bakery, Confectionery, Tobacco Workers and Grain Millers Union (AFL-CIO), first organized in 1886, promotes "the material, intellectual and general welfare of all workers in the baking, confectionery, tobacco, grain milling and kindred industries" by organizing, educating, improving wages and retirement, and gives help in finding and keeping employment (see its Web site at www.bctgm.org).

Bakery Managers may be considered executives, therefore management, and thus not qualified for union membership.

Tips for Entry

1. Find a cooking school or community college baking program, which should give instruction as well as experience via internships. Many schools have good local contacts to help find jobs for learners.
2. Visit local bakeries in your neighborhood and favorite bakeries where you would like to work. Make an appointment or just show up to talk to the baker or Bakery Manager in the afternoon, or after the daily rush, to ask for an internship, apprenticeship, or a job.
3. If you have substantial experience, go ahead and ask for a managerial job.
4. Check Web sites such as craigslist.org for Bakery Manager job openings.
5. Take any job you can, including at the counter, as a cashier, or as a sweeper just to get in the door. Then tell management that you want to learn baking and work your way up. It is all possible.

BAKERY SALES MANAGER

Duties: Coordinates the sales and marketing plan for bakery manager or owner; sometimes makes sales calls, occasionally equipped with recipes, to restaurant chefs, grocery and chain stores, and even other bakeries to make an initial sales pitch; supervises Web site development, e-mail lists, mail-order catalogues; makes contact with other catalogue or online stores; oversees and schedules routes of sales and delivery staff; coordinates with the bakery manager or head baker to order and produce baked goods appropriate to public or customer demand

Alternate Title(s): Bakery Manager

Salary Range: $20,000 to $100,000 depending on experience and geographic region. Commissions can add substantially to salary, with or without benefits.

Employment Prospects: Good, although many local bakery owners think they cannot afford to employ sales managers

Advancement Prospects: Good. It is possible to talk your way into the position without experience and advance according to success, even to managerial spots.

Best Geographical Location(s): Urban areas with a big bakery audience and with headquarters for chain grocery stores. Even small-town bakers like to get their specialty breads, bagels, and pastries into grocery stores, coffee carts, restaurants, and beyond.

Prerequisites:

Education and Training—Knowledge of baking and the baking process will add to one's success,

CAREER LADDER

Bakery Manager
Bakery Sales Manager
Bakery Sales Assistant/Delivery Driver

as will management and marketing courses from community colleges. Many large bakeries will train salespeople and managers to their way of operating, particularly if the job applicant has some sales or food experience.

Experience—Any sales or marketing experience will help. Actual baking, whether at home or in a bakery, will help sell the products. The first steps and presentations to potential customers are the most difficult, so having some sales experiences in which one calls on clients, whether door-to-door or store-to-store, makes the job easier.

Special Skills and Personality Traits—Ability to speak well; get along with and enjoy people; enjoy sales and a sense of accomplishment; knowledge of baking and baked products; a passion for baked goods and the specific products one is selling; enjoy driving, calling on people you don't know, and meeting new people; a willingness to work odd hours

Position Description

Bakery Sales Manager positions vary greatly depending upon the size of a bakery and the shelf life (how long the product lasts before it spoils) of the baked goods.

Bakery Sales Managers usually develop a marketing plan considering the bakery's product line and the kinds of retailers in a geographic area (from espresso stands to large health food stores), develop sales goals and possible new products with the bakery manager, work with the production manager if there is one to schedule the entire baking, packing, and delivery process (considering seasons and holidays), and handle contracts with distributors and delivery contractors.

Bakery Sales Managers might also attend specialty food trade shows, "slow food" gatherings and other large events, and even farmers' markets, giving out samples and setting up new sales contracts.

A sales manager for a large commercial bakery calls on chain store department heads to sell cookies, breads, bread dough, doughnuts, and whatever else the bakery makes.

Some Bakery Sales Managers, or even owners, call on local grocery stores, independent coffee houses, restaurants, and carts, sell at farmers' markets, and suggest recipes when calling on local restaurants' chefs. These sales managers might also help develop the bakery's Web site, e-mail or mailing lists, take-away menus and brochures, develop sales to mail-order catalogues or produce a catalog for the bakery itself, and monitor local clientele's preferences.

Some Bakery Sales Managers also work with advertising specialists or even place advertising themselves in local newspapers, church bulletins, and on local radio stations.

Salaries

Bakery Sales Managers may be paid a base salary, plus commissions, with or without benefits, with salaries ranging from $20,000 to $100,000. Commission percentages vary widely from 10 to 40 percent and depend upon whether the salesperson also collects a monthly base salary. The higher the base salary, the lower the commission rate, unless the sales manager is known for huge successes. The lower the base salary, the higher the percentage of sales paid in commissions. And if there is no base pay, the commission should be the highest percentage possible.

If the sales manager supervises other salespeople, the manager might get a percentage of those people's sales as well. A sales manager's contract should provide for that arrangement and should also include a bonus if all sales exceed the original sales plan for the year.

Employment Prospects

Bakery Sales Managers and salespeople jobs are usually available at the ambitious small bakery, or at least at those bakeries that believe sales managers can improve their sales, and at large bakeries that serve chain stores, lots of independent groceries and coffee shops and wagons.

As with any sales job, the most successful salespeople and sales managers believe passionately in their products and know a lot about them.

Urban areas that allow for high-volume sales are always the best for any kind of sales, with sales jobs sometimes requiring sales people to relocate to better territories. Wine regions can also be good because people who like wine generally appreciate good food, including baked goods and fine breads. Many small specialty bread bakeries grow to sell to regional restaurants and grocery stores, since interest in whole-grain and multigrain boutique breads is growing.

When going into sales with large geographic territories, one should consider the need to travel, be on the road, and away from the family. If one has no immediate family, sales might be the ideal job.

Advancement Prospects

Advancement prospects are excellent, with hard work. It is possible to talk your way into a bakery sales job without experience. Loving the products helps. If you can sell yourself to the company, top staff and managers think you can probably sell their baked goods.

If a salesperson or sales manager succeeds, the company succeeds and tends to keep and sometimes reward employees who make everyone successful.

Rungs on the ladder of bakery sales include getting a better or more populated sales territory, increase in the percentage of sales commission, promotion to district manager or bakery manager depending on the size of the bakery, and moving on up the company ladder to president, depending upon the size and kind of bakery.

If a person turns down the offer of a territory in another geographic area, he or she might be passed up for promotions based on attitude.

As in many businesses, another way to move up is to take a higher job at another company or one with a greater sales territory and more salespeople under you.

Education and Training

Many companies train their own salespeople in the company's mold and often like to hire inexperienced salespeople.

A person who has come up the bakery ladder, has passion for the products, and doesn't like to be trapped in a hot kitchen might find bakery sales perfect. This person can remain close to her or his professional baking interest while having a strong role in the success of the bakery.

Community college or university courses or degrees in business or management can make a salesperson or manager more organized and successful. While bakery sales do not require any college degrees, some formal or even informal training in sales techniques can help overcome those initial fears and move up in the company.

Experience, Skills, and Personality Traits

Sales experience in any field can help a person become successful in bakery sales or as a Bakery Sales Manager. Even having a corner lemonade stand, selling coffee or burritos from a cart, or selling cookies door-to-door will contribute to experience.

Having passion for the product, possibly baking experience, and knowledge of how the product or the bakery differs from others aid a salesperson in answering potential customers' questions. It would be handy to know ingredients, sodium and gluten content, and grains included in the product, as well as sugar sources and content, when the product might best be served, and with what. Such information aids chefs and vendors know what to pair with the product.

No one can teach a person affability, but a person can learn to speak well, be friendly, outgoing, get along, close a sale (get the person to agree to purchase), and enjoy meeting new people. Honesty and reliability are qualities greatly appreciated by clients.

Unions and Associations

There are no unions for Bakery Sales Managers specifically, although there are unions for bakery sales drivers. Local chambers of commerce might provide sales and business practices seminars. Other national organizations include the American Bakers Association (www.americanbakers.org), the American Institute of Baking (www.aibonline.org), and the Retail Bakers of America (www.rbanet.com).

Tips for Entry

1. Approach your favorite bakery and talk them into letting you work there or represent them by presenting their products to local retailers.
2. Ask a bakery for a job working at the counter, which is the direct one-on-one base of bakery sales.
3. Watch local newspaper ads or online job sites for bakery sales opportunities.
4. Read newspapers to follow trends in the baking industry and local baking enterprises.
5. Attend trade shows to keep up on baking trends, new products, watch for possible jobs, and meet people who might offer jobs or information.

BREAD BAKER

Duties: Depending on the size of the bakery, the Bread Baker might actually order supplies and make the bread or, in a larger operation, might function more as an executive baker. A Bread Baker keeps track of inventory; regularly lists supplies to be ordered; oversees the bread baking process; trains and supervises assistant bakers; and works with the owner and sales staff to keep in touch with demand and develop new products. Some Bread Bakers or assistant bakers actually make the bread.

Alternate Title(s): Head Baker; Baker: Baking Assistant

Salary Range: $18,000 to $50,000

Employment Prospects: Good. There is high turnover in baking because it is hard, hot work, especially on night shifts, when most of the action takes place.

Advancement Prospects: Once in the door, a Bread Baker can slowly move up the kitchen ladder by showing dedication, hard work, passion for the product, and a willingness to learn new bread skills. One can become head baker, manager, and may even open one's own bakery.

Best Geographical Location(s): Big cities, resort areas, cruise ships, and gambling and wine regions where institutions hire in-house bakers and where independent bakeries are located

Prerequisites:

Education or Training—Must speak, read, and write the prevailing language of the bakery, be able

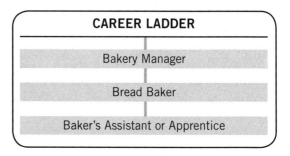

CAREER LADDER

Bakery Manager

Bread Baker

Baker's Assistant or Apprentice

to do math, be able to read and follow recipes, and have an apprentice training or baking program certificate from culinary school or community college. Some bakeries will train on the job as one works one's way up the ladder.

Experience—Some bakeries require a certain number of years' experience, particularly bakeries that create specialty breads. This experience can be gained at home, in culinary programs, or on the job as an apprentice.

Special Skills and Personality Traits—Ability to stand for hours in hot conditions; willingness to work at night; ability to speak English or the other language of the specific bakery; ability to do basic math; ability to read recipes; some artistic talent; enjoyment of both repetition and creativity. Must be strong enough to lift and push heavy carts and bags of ingredients, and operate large mixers and ovens in industrial bakeries.

Position Description

Several levels of baker fall within the hierarchy of bread baking or of any bakery kitchen, depending on the size of the bakery. If the Bread Baker is also the head baker, that person will be in charge of every phase of bread production. He or she will keep track of inventory and order supplies, oversee all bakers and bread production, maintain and create recipes, and coordinate production with the pastry chef.

Bakers and bakers' assistants work odd hours, often starting in the middle of the night, since some breads need to "rise" or involve sourdough or other starters. The head or Bread Baker usually sets the schedule for the entire baking kitchen, including extensive planning involved in dough rises, rests, second rises, forming and

baking, all on specific time schedules that consider the oven capacity of the establishment.

Various ethnic bakeries emphasize different ingredients and procedures, so even an experienced baker might need to learn something new. Organic and health bread bakeries often use organic grains and flours and add nuts, currants and raisins, sunflower seeds, pumpkin, zucchini, and other ingredients. A baker with nut allergies might have trouble in this kind of bakery.

Some Bread Bakers might also oversee production of cookies, cakes, pies, breakfast pastries, and muffins, but usually someone other than the Bread Baker handles production "on the sweet side." Baking of breakfast pastries has to be done at night as well, but cakes and afternoon pastries can be made in the morning, balancing the schedule and the oven use in the bakery.

Bread Bakers in large wholesale or discount stores or for catalogue stores generally work on one item, which can be tedious—much like automobile workers who assemble only left front doors for cars. Bread Bakers in large hotels or casinos may have to be more flexible and bake whatever is required as guest volume fluctuates.

Restaurant and hotel chefs increasingly order locally baked specialty breads because it takes the production cost out of the restaurant or hotel, it helps the local bakery, and because many local bakers create excellent breads known in the region.

The bread or head baker trains new employees in the house recipes and methods, and often has to be able to communicate in a second language to teach new employees recipes and techniques.

Some head and Bread Bakers and assistant bakers actually make bread, doing the mixing, kneading, timing and monitoring rising, forming into shapes, and baking.

Salaries

Depending on the size of the bakery, its success, and its location, a Bread Baker can make from $18,000 to $70,000 a year, often with benefits if work is full time. If the Bread Baker is also the head baker earning a base salary plus bonus based on the bakery's volume increase, he or she can earn up to $70,000.

Employment Prospects

Employment prospects are great. In every town there is a bakery of some sort, whether in a storefront or in someone's home kitchen or community center. In large cities and gambling centers bakeries abound, either as storefront shops or in-house at restaurants or casinos.

Bread Bakers trained either as apprentices or at culinary schools have great chances at jobs throughout the country, especially if they know what they are getting into, such as nighttime work and hot, noisy conditions.

Advancement Prospects

How far a Bread Baker can advance depends on the size of town or region in which he or she works or to which he or she is willing to relocate. Small-town bakeries have limited rungs on the kitchen ladder just because the staff is usually small. A Bread Baker or head baker can increase income by taking a percentage of the profits, by helping expand the bakery, or by advancing to manager, or by starting his or her own bakery.

Larger bakeries such as those in corporate grocery stores, chain bakeries and their outlets, massive bakeries that focus on supplying hotels and restaurants, and bakeries that make millions of cupcakes for every chain store in the country, all employ more people and have more strata, allowing a person to move up the ladder and achieve various levels of leadership and management.

Education and Training

Most cooking school programs in community colleges and culinary programs offer baking classes. At many schools one can "major in" or focus on baking, and it is often best to take a full range of cooking classes so that baking and its chemistry become part of what one knows in the kitchen rather than the only skill one knows. Most cooking schools also offer internships in real-life bakeries so that a learner may gain experience while studying.

Experience, Skills, and Personality Traits

Experience as a home baker, baker for nonprofit organizations, or at any position in the bread baking process will help get a job or help people know if baking should be their profession.

Bread Bakers need to enjoy repetition and find gratification in the shape and beauty of the outcome of their efforts: a scrumptious loaf of bread that will please whoever buys it.

Bread Bakers also need to be physically fit, capable of standing for hours, able to lift 50-pound bags of flour, not have allergies to nuts and seeds or gluten, understand the intermingling of flour, yeast, leavening agents or lack of same, herbs, spices, and even water.

Unions and Associations

Many urban areas have strong bakers' unions that represent employees in large hotels, restaurants, and industrial bakeries. The umbrella group is the Bakery, Confectionary, Tobacco Workers, and Grain Millers International Union of the AFL-CIO and CLC (www.bctgm.org). The union recruits members at bakeries, provides education on issues of interest to union members, works to improve pay and health and retirement benefits, monitors hours of work, helps with job placement and security, and lobbies various government agencies.

Other organizations include the Bread Bakers Guild of America for artisan bakers (www.bbga.org), the American Bakers Association (www.americanbakers.org), the American Institute of Baking, which also gives classes (www.aibonline.org), and the Retail Bakers of America (www.rbanet.com).

Tips for Entry

1. Bake at home to see if you like the process.
2. Get a job, any job, in a bakery to learn and work your way up.
3. Take baking or other cooking courses at community colleges or culinary schools.
4. Bake at home to sell to small restaurants or retail outlets in your area. Some towns and counties require a kitchen be licensed or certified for commercial baking, in which case you might use an approved church or community center kitchen to start your baking enterprise.
5. Contact any of the above Web sites for job opportunities, online classes, and career advice.

PASTRY CHEF

Duties: Pastry Chefs work with executive chefs to plan pastry dessert menus to be compatible with restaurant and hotel menus and wine lists; create new desserts in keeping with the times; hire pastry and cake decorators and baking assistants; plan quantities of each pastry or cake to be made per day; oversee ordering, storing, and inventory of ingredients; train new bakery assistants and other workers; and occasionally present creations to public.

Alternate Title(s): Pastry and Dessert Baker; Cake Baker

Salary Range: $20,000 to $60,000

Employment Prospects: Good and improving

Advancement Prospects: Good

Best Geographical Location(s): Everywhere, although positions in small towns pay substantially less than those in big cities or tourist areas

Prerequisites:

Education and Training—A baking specialty certificate or diploma from community college or culi-

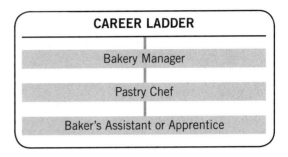

nary program in baking or pastry cook will show understanding of baking chemistry.

Experience—Any basic experience at home or at any level in a baking kitchen will increase understanding of baking chemistry and the role of sugars, fats, and other ingredients in frostings, fillings, and glazes.

Special Skills and Personality Traits—Enjoy precision and the creation of aesthetically pleasing sweets; artistic flair; physical strength to lift heavy objects and stand for long hours; ability to read recipes and formulas and calculate numbers

Position Description

In large restaurants, hotels, and resorts Pastry Chefs work with executive chefs to plan pastry dessert menus that complement the regular meal menus and sometimes work with sommeliers to coordinate wines or dessert wines with the pastries.

A pastry and cake baker, or Pastry Chef, oversees preparation of all sweet baked goods in a bakery, restaurant, hotel, or resort, especially where there is a head baker or bread baker and baking duties are divided within the kitchen.

Pastries in the Pastry Chef's domain includes everything from muffins and cupcakes to small French pastries and cakes, Danish breakfast pastries, wedding cakes, decorated cakes, candies, cookies, turnovers, pies, holiday cakes, frostings, fillings, and glazes.

Pastry and dessert baking is more formulaic than the "hot" side of a kitchen, meaning recipes and formulas must be followed exactly. Established bakeries or a baking kitchen in larger restaurants, hotels, or resorts have strict recipes, and their customers demand the goodies they especially enjoy to stay on the menu.

Occasionally a Pastry Chef will experiment with new ideas, some suggested by customers, some suggested by staff, or some from his or her own imagination or repertoire. Often when a baker creates a new item the bakery sets a plate of small samples on the counter for customers to try and comment upon.

In smaller or independent bakeries the Pastry Chef may add items to the menu to keep up with fads, and may also do everything from estimating and planning quantities needed of each pastry to keeping inventory, preparing ordering lists, finding the best suppliers at the best prices, researching new and organic ingredients, and hiring and training staff. Occasionally the Pastry Chef has the pleasure of presenting yummy creations to the public for immediate reaction, which is a most satisfying experience.

If starting a new bakery, the Pastry Chef needs to survey the potential clientele and other bakeries in the area to learn what sells and what specialty niche is not yet filled.

Within a bakery, bakers and baking assistants may specialize in cakes, breads, and morning pastries that both have to be baked at night and brought out in the early morning along with muffins, sweeter breads, and doughnuts.

Cake decorators take over after the cakes are actually baked and cooled. In some large grocery chains the cakes are baked in rounds or sheets, shipped to individual stores, and decorated by local bakery staff. Decorators usually have some artistic talent, and some ad-lib on a bakery's catalogue of designs for special occasions.

Custom cakes and pastries must be ordered at least a day or two ahead, which allows the Pastry Chef to plan, although bakery schedules usually allow for emergencies.

Local independent bakeries often sell wholesale to local restaurants, coffee wagons and counters, delicatessens, and even health spas that offer snacks to members.

Salaries

Pastry Chefs, cake decorators, and pastry assistants make between $20,000 to $70,000 a year, the median at about $25,000, with Pastry Chefs at the top of the scale. Master pastry chefs, who earn an advanced certification, can make even more.

Employment Prospects

Most towns have bakeries with pastry specialists, many of which employ family members or close friends, although there are often openings at all jobs requiring hard work during night hours. Some towns have a bakery for every thousand restaurants, while other bakeries consist of a person baking in a kitchen at home.

If a person is willing to start at the bottom of the bakery kitchen ladder, he or she can usually find a job, almost anywhere.

Of course there are more bakeries and more Pastry Chefs, and specialty and ethnic baking opportunities, in big cities. Resort and gambling centers will employ bakers and Pastry Chefs, as do cruise ship lines. Bakery and Pastry Chef jobs can be found everywhere, from chain grocery bakery departments to small town independent bakeries catering to neighbors' needs.

Advancement Prospects

It is entirely possible for a person who starts on the bottom rung to work his or her way up to Pastry Chef, particularly if that person has studied baking in a culinary or trade school.

A Pastry Chef can work her or his way up further to head baker and bakery manager if desired, or may prefer to remain in an artistic specialty.

Education and Training

No degrees are required to work in a bakery, particularly if a person is willing to start at the bottom and learn their way up. Many excellent bakers and Pastry Chefs start as apprentices, trainees, and interns.

To become a Pastry Chef one should study baking and even cooking in high school or community college culinary programs to master the chemistry of baking, including the subtleties of the wide variety of chocolates and sugars that are currently available on the world market. Pastry Chefs need to know about nutrition, health, hygiene, and sanitation regulations, operation and maintenance of machinery in the bakeshop, accounting, and how to run and market a business if they want to start their own bakery.

Experience, Skills, and Personality Traits

Enjoying sweets helps one develop interest, enjoyment, and commitment to being a Pastry Chef, Danish or cake baker, or cake decorator. Making cakes and pastries at home could show a person's passion for this field, and passion is important.

If one is not passionate and simply needs a job, the hot physical conditions might become too much to tolerate.

Having an artistic flair for color and design, as well as drawing and writing, are skills that help a person toward success.

A Pastry Chef should also enjoy precision and formula baking (an error can cause disaster), and have the physical conditioning and ability to lift heavy weights, tolerate heat, and stand for long hours. The abilities to read recipes in English and do math are also important.

Knowledge of a second language, preferably the predominant language of the kitchen, will be helpful. If the Pastry Chef's first language is English and the first language of the baking assistants is Spanish, the Pastry Chef might need to learn Spanish baking terms. If the lead baker has a language other than English as her or his first language, that person probably will need to learn English to communicate with customers and suppliers. Of course, if one's customers speak the same language as the bakers, everything works.

Unions and Associations

Many urban areas have strong bakers' unions that represent employees in large hotels, restaurants, and industrial bakeries. The umbrella group is the Bakery, Confectionary, Tobacco Workers, and Grain Millers International Union of the AFL-CIO and CLC (www.

bctgm.org). The union recruits members at bakeries, provides education on issues of interest to union members, works to improve pay and health and retirement benefits, monitors hours of work, helps with job placement and security, and lobbies various government agencies.

Other organizations include the Bread Bakers Guild of America for artisan bakers (www.bbga.org), the American Bakers Association (www.americanbakers.org), the American Institute of Baking, which also gives classes (www.aibonline.org), and the Retail Bakers of America (www.rbanet.com).

Tips for Entry

1. Visit bakeries in your town or neighborhood and approach your favorite for a job at any level if you have no experience or training.
2. Take classes in adult education at high schools, community or junior colleges, or arts institutes on baking to learn the processes and how ingredients interact. Many of these schools have job placement offices that can help with a first job.
3. Read professional baking books and bake at home to experiment or practice. Your friends and neighbors will love you.

INSTITUTIONAL FOOD

CATERING MANAGER—HOTEL, CASINO, CONVENTION CENTER, AND CRUISE SHIP

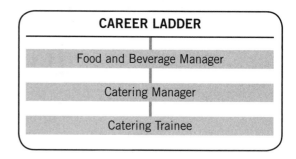

Position Description

Catering Managers of hotels, resorts, casinos, country clubs, hospitals, and universities seek and book all special events at the institution, including special conferences and the ingredients of the meals that go with them, from water to filet mignon. They look for weddings, bar and bat mitzvahs, christenings, quinceañeras, business conferences and meetings, holiday parties, workshops, balls, fund-raisers, and golf tournament meals.

Catering Managers reach out to potential clients, build professional relationships, and get involved in community good works to attract and book events at their establishment.

The Catering Manager coordinates all aspects of each event from accommodations, party arrangements, menu selections and wine pairings, to party room reservations, meeting rooms large and small, audiovisual and computer equipment, beverage service in meeting rooms, and any meals or snacks, as well as banquets and special wine tastings.

For celebrations, the Catering Manager's duties might include decoration and flower arrangements (or hiring an event planner specifically for those purposes), entertainment, working with the chef and sommelier, in-room hosted bar or no-host bar, bartenders, waiters, security, radio communications if necessary, and valet parking.

If the client lives in the town where the event will take place, the Catering Manager should invite the client or representative to tour the facility and become familiar with it. Such an exploration will guide the Catering Manager and client to decide if an outdoor tent needs to be rented, although many fine hotels and casinos now have semipermanent tents erected. The Catering Manager might even introduce the client to the executive chef and sommelier if there is one, so that the client can feel comfortable with those people.

A Catering Manager must be completely familiar, knowledgeable, and comfortable with the chef's capabilities and specialties and know everything possible about menu offerings, ingredients, gluten and sugar content of foods for special-needs diners, vegetarian and kosher options, and ethnic possibilities. The Catering Manager must ask about attendees' allergies, dietary needs, and other special requests.

Different kinds of gatherings require different food. Business meetings require coffee and breakfast pastries to keep attendees alert and awake; wedding receptions require cake and bubbly, Sweet 16 birthdays require punch and chips and salsa, and food conferences require fine foods.

The Catering Manager has to help clients work within their budget, because all extra little details and add-ons cost money, and special features add up quickly. If the Catering Manager is on commission, in addition to a base salary he or she makes money with every extra added to the event order.

After their initial meeting (if there is one), the Catering Manager communicates between the chef and the client to work out the menu and wine selections, considering any special needs requests. Then the Catering Manager makes out work orders, a contract, credit card clearances, and signatures before any arrangements actually proceed.

Some Catering Managers or their establishments give clients forms to evaluate performance and satisfaction with decor, service, and food after the event.

Salaries

Hotel, resort, and casino Catering Managers' salaries vary by size of institution and locale. The median salary is $40,000, although catering managers can make up to $90,000 with the right percentage bonuses based on sales. Those working in hospital, government, and university situations make a median of $40,000 to $51,000, according to Payscale.com.

Employment Prospects

Large and better hotel chains employ lots of Catering Managers, so they offer greater opportunity. Smaller independent hotels may have another executive who performs the Catering Manager function of soliciting and booking catering-hall business. Independent or freelance Catering Managers, who maintain contacts with chambers of commerce, businesses, and individuals, may book an event into a hotel, resort, or university site that they think best suits the event and the client's budget.

Advancement Prospects

Advancement prospects are excellent. Within hotel chains, a Catering Manager might be promoted to manager and general manager by moving up within a property, or be promoted by being sent to a new job at a larger or more elegant hotel in the same chain with the same job title. A Catering Manager might also get promoted by seeking and accepting a better job with another hotel, resort, casino, hospital, or university.

Education and Training

College level courses in hospitality management and marketing will be most helpful. Culinary school is not required, but knowledge gained in some basic cooking classes would definitely help a Catering Manager on the job.

Some hotel chains and casinos prefer to train candidates in their mold to do the job as they would like.

Experience, Skills, Personality Traits

A really good Catering Manager will love detail work, precision, and exactitude, and will also enjoy listening and matchmaking between a client's needs and the facility's capabilities and staff.

Having worked with food, sales, marketing, and tourism are important experience factors. The Catering Manager must enjoy working with people, interpreting their needs, learning about the kitchen's updates, menu changes, and trends, the wide range of price lists for everything from hotel and meeting rooms to cocktails, and the ability to instill confidence in a potential client already nervous about putting on a big event.

Unions and Associations

The American Hotel and Lodging Association (www.ahla.com) provides educational opportunities, job placement contacts, and many other benefits.

Tips for Entry

1. Attend a community college or regular hospitality or hotel management program and include some culinary courses if you can.

2. Take a job selling something, anything, to develop communication and people skills that give you and your clients confidence.
3. Find a job in any hotel or one of its restaurants (better establishments offer better opportunities) to get one foot in the door. Aim at working your way into promoting or selling events.
4. Select your favorite hotel, convention center, or university and call the general number and ask if they have a catering department, then call the general manager or catering manager and ask if they have any kind of job available.

EXECUTIVE CHEF—HOTEL, CASINO, COUNTRY CLUB, RESORT, UNIVERSITY, AND HOSPITAL

Duties: Oversees all food service in the establishment, from coffee bars to elegant restaurant and banquet rooms; creates menus; keeps up with fads; develops new menu items; may oversee garden or ask gardener to grow certain vegetables and herbs for use in the kitchens; helps interview and hire new sous-chefs, pastry chefs, pantry chefs, and other kitchen staff; oversees ordering and budget; represents hotel at local benefits for nonprofits, usually offering samples of appetizers

Alternate Title(s): Chef

Salary Range: $40,000 to $140,000 and up, with benefits, depending on size and location of establishment

Employment Prospects: Excellent

Advancement Prospects: Excellent

Best Geographical Location(s): Jobs are most easily found in big cities, wine regions, resort areas, casinos, big airports, and on cruise ship lines.

Prerequisites:

Education or Training—Advanced culinary training at a culinary school; on-the-job training working

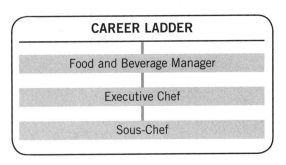

CAREER LADDER

Food and Beverage Manager

Executive Chef

Sous-Chef

up the kitchen ladder; management and marketing courses are ideal but not required

Experience—A professional lifetime of working with food, especially on a large scale. One can work one's way up from dishwasher by learning at every step. Several years as a chef also helps.

Special Skills and Personality Traits—Organizational and mathematical skills and a second language will be handy, along with refined senses of taste and smell; great physical stamina and conditioning; a strong personality with the ability to get along with others and motivate staff; creative flair and sensitivity to trends; some public relations abilities.

Position Description

A hotel, casino, country club, or resort Executive Chef oversees all food service operations and their menus within the property, which can include outdoor areas. The Executive Chef may also be the "face" of the establishment to the press and the outside world.

Large property Executive Chefs sit atop a rather pointy hierarchical pyramid, with dishwashers, floor scrubbers, and porters forming the wide base at the bottom.

In a property with several dining opportunities, from coffee shop and poolside coffee cart to fine dining and banquet rooms, the Executive Chef may supervise apprentices, and hire and supervise chefs of each venue, except possibly for the pastry chef, who most likely will bake for all facilities.

Most Executive Chefs of this sort create theme menus and promotions, develop wine tasting programs,

and create banquet menus from which customers can select dishes for their special events.

After creating menus, the Executive Chef may work with a purchasing agent to outline quantities of what needs to be ordered, order the goods, and train chefs and sous-chefs to prepare the dishes to his or her specifications so well that they can each train their subordinates, station cooks, and apprentices to do their part all the way down the kitchen ladder.

Often hotels and resorts are asked to donate food for local charity benefits, sometimes highlighting well-known chefs, so the Executive Chef plans and oversees preparation of the food to be served, and then shows up as the face of the establishment, which increases his or her familiarity in the community.

Executive Chefs often prowl the kitchens, tasting and making suggestions for improving a dish. Many chefs welcome the chance not to have to stand and cook full time after a career of doing that, while others get bored and long for the chance to flip the sauté pans—what got them into the business in the first place.

Executive Chefs of universities, where those positions exist, perform many of the same duties. Occasionally they coordinate subcontracts with local restaurants that set up concessions in a student union, plan menus for special events and meetings, seek off-campus groups to book meetings with food service as a source of income for the university, and attempt to improve food for students and faculty.

Salaries

Salaries for Executive Chefs range from $40,000 to $140,000, sometimes with commissions and usually with health benefits. The range depends upon the size of the property, the number of dining venues within the establishment, the number of outside parties attracted and meals prepared, the reputation of the Executive Chef, and that person's experience outside and inside the chain or resort.

Employment Prospects

Job prospects for Executive Chefs are excellent in good economic times when owners look ahead to growing business. In poorer economic times, owners and hotel/resort management tend to consolidate jobs, and a good managing Executive Chef who can cut costs without compromising quality will be in high demand.

Advancement Prospects

Advancement prospects are excellent. Executive Chefs of this sort advance into management within the hotel, resort, or casino, they advance within a hotel chain by getting transferred to a better property, or they get a better job with another establishment.

Education and Training

Culinary education from the best possible institution, apprenticeship with upward mobility in the old school or European system, and marketing and management courses are advised.

Experience, Skills, Personality Traits

A successful Executive Chef must have culinary training at culinary school or on-the-job training working up the kitchen ladder through a European or other apprenticeship program. Management and marketing courses are ideal but not required. Additionally, this person must have spent a professional lifetime of working with food, including several years as chef in a well-known or large restaurant. Executive abilities are mandatory.

An institutional Executive Chef must have organizational and mathematical skills; a second language will be handy; fine taste and smell skills; great physical stamina and conditioning; a strong personality with the ability to get along with others and motivate staff; a creative flair and sensitivity to trends; and some public relations abilities.

Unions and Associations

The American Culinary Federation (www.acfchefs.org), the International Association of Culinary Professionals (www.iacp.com), and the American Hotel and Lodging Association (www.ahla.com) all offer information and job opportunities for Executive Chefs.

Tips for Entry

1. If you are not yet a chef, take culinary and management courses, get the first job you can, and work your way up.
2. Ask local Executive Chefs what apprenticeship opportunities they might have.
3. If you have extensive experience as a chef, make appointments with Executive Chefs at establishments you admire near your home to ask what the employment possibilities may be, without suggesting you want their jobs.
4. Check out the above Web sites to get ideas of specific jobs available for Executive Chefs. Ask where and what each organizations' training programs might be in your area.

FOOD AND BEVERAGE MANAGER— HOTEL, CASINO, COUNTRY CLUB, RESORT, UNIVERSITY, AND HOSPITAL

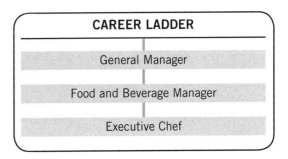
Position Description

A Food and Beverage Manager in any large hospitality business has responsibility for management of food and beverage service at every venue within the hotel, resort, casino, or even university. This person therefore oversees the business end of food and beverage service, including profits and losses, and hires and fires restaurant and bar managers, executive chefs, sommeliers, and other food and beverage staff. The Food and Beverage Manager oversees the food and beverage service for special parties, meeting rooms, wedding receptions, conferences, and even room service in hotels, resorts, and casinos.

In large hotels, resorts, and casinos, the bars, restaurants, coffee carts, sandwich stands, buffets, and catering might have individual managers, all of whom will report to the Food and Beverage Manager.

Food and Beverage Managers usually hold weekly meetings at which each submanager reports what has worked and what hasn't, assesses increases or decreases in profit and traffic, brainstorm on what can improve in which departments, and the sustainability of the entire operation, and may implement recycling and garden programs, electric carts for delivering room service and people around a large property, and even consider improvement in in-room honor bars.

One very powerful role of the Food and Beverage Manager might be evaluations of various managers who have bonus or commission sections in their contracts to augment their salary or hourly pay rates based on increased business, increased profits, new ideas and long-range planning, and their ability to train and manage staff.

When there is a Food and Beverage Manager, that person might work with the business's general manager or manager to think up and promote special events to attract attention, publicity, and business.

Occasionally theme nights are planned way ahead to coordinate food service and decor throughout the business.

Food and Beverage Managers constantly make rounds (as doctors do) and rarely sit in their offices. Cell phones have increased communication with these folks, who are always visiting the food and beverage outlets within the property, sometimes altering their route to surprise managers and staff.

During these rounds, managers and staff can relate their concerns and needs, while Food and Beverage Managers tell them of guest complaints (and hopefully compliments) and mechanical and other problems to be fixed, and establish the best communication possible to make the entire facility run as close to perfectly as possible.

The Food and Beverage Manager position epitomizes hospitality management's hierarchical pyramid, in which he or she oversees the managers of the food and beverage departments and reports to the institution's general manager.

Salaries

There has not been much movement in Food and Beverage Manager salaries in recent times. Depending upon the size and location of the hotel, casino, country club, resort, or university, one might make anywhere from $40,000 to $120,000, which is a wide range. Benefits, bonuses, and commissions are often added to salaries. Obviously F&B managers of small hotels in small towns will make less, while those working in large hotels or resorts in large cities or gambling centers will earn larger salaries.

Employment Prospects

High-end resorts and hotels seem to continue to do well during economically difficult times, and Food and Beverage Managers are often in demand as business managers who can get the most out of submanagers, who can cut costs and enhance profits, without sacrificing quality. In good economic times, F&B managers have the luxury of working with managers to enhance products and services.

Advancement Prospects

Advancement prospects for Food and Beverage Managers are excellent. A person can move up to general manager and president, or move sideways within a chain operation to a new job at a better facility with the same or better title and salary.

Education and Training

Hotel and hospitality management courses, culinary and wine program education, as well classes in human relations, marketing, and business management will help, especially when combined with practical experience.

Some people work their way up to Food and Beverage Manager all the way from dishwasher, by learning everything possible from people around them along the way up the bar or kitchen ladders.

Experience, Skills, and Personality Traits

Many Food and Beverage Managers have worked their way up through either the food, wine, or bar side of an establishment, learning all there is to know as they go. Some have been executive chefs, others have been bar managers, and yet others have taught at cooking schools. This managerial job takes them out of the kitchen and out from behind the bar, which may or may not please them after they get some experience.

The more experience with the food and beverage products and management at every level that a person has, the better and more successful he or she will be as a Food and Beverage Manager.

An F&B manager must be able to get along with others, cajole others into being excellent managers of their own departments without intimidating them, love to achieve excellence, enjoy pleasing others, and be willing to work odd hours when important parties and events come up.

Unions and Associations

The American Culinary Federation (www.acfchefs. org), the International Association of Culinary Professionals (www.iacp.com), and the American Hotel and Lodging Association (www.ahla.com) all offer information and job opportunities for Food and Beverage Managers.

Food and Beverage Managers might also join local service clubs, culinary societies, and national and international organizations such as the International Association of Culinary Professionals (www. iacp.org), the American Institute of Wine and Food (www.globalchefs.com), La Chaîne de Rôtisseurs (www. chaineus.org), or Women Chefs and Restaurateurs (www.womenchefs.org).

Tips for Entry

1. Take any job in a large operation restaurant or bar and learn all you can.
2. Take courses at a local community or junior college in cooking and restaurant management,

hotel management, hospitality, and human resources, and be sure to ask specifically if there is a culinary or hospitality management program. Many college or culinary school programs have job placement and internship programs.

3. Ask a Food and Beverage Manager if you might be able to work with her or him as an intern or apprentice, even for free.

4. Learn everything you can about all levels in every department of food and beverage service.

CORPORATE OR INSTITUTIONAL CHEF

Duties: A Corporate or Institutional Chef plans all meals and menus, often with sensitivity to the ethnic interests of employees, patients, inmates, or visiting diners; orders ingredients; hires and fires staff; manages the budget; tries to vary the offerings; and runs the entire food operation.

Alternate Title(s): Executive Chef; Managing Chef; Chef

Salary Range: $38,000 to $120,000 depending upon type of institution or corporation

Employment Prospects: Good

Advancement Prospects: Good

Best Geographical Location(s): Urban areas, high-tech centers, and business centers, mostly on Pacific and Atlantic coasts. Prisons, hospitals, and universities exist throughout the United States.

Prerequisites:

Education or Training—Cooking and management classes at a community or junior college or at a cooking school are the best preparation. Working

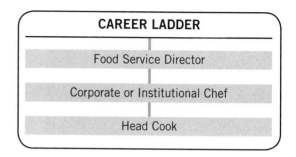

CAREER LADDER

Food Service Director

Corporate or Institutional Chef

Head Cook

one's way up the kitchen ladder from the bottom is also an excellent way to learn.

Experience—Any commercial cooking experience, particularly high-volume cooking. Ethnic cooking might also be handy.

Special Skills and Personality Traits—Taking joy in pleasing others with food, ability to be sensitive to "clients'" tastes, good organizational skills, good business management skills, and some knowledge of whatever second language might be the first language of cooking staff will be helpful.

Position Description

Whether cooking for a Silicon Valley high-tech campus or for a state prison, a hospital, a convalescent home, or a team of race car drivers, the Corporate or Institutional Chef has to vary menus, consider food allergies and ethnic customs, and whether clients are vegetarian or vegan while planning and preparing all meals at the institution.

In this case, *institution* obviously means a variety of entities, and not just those whose residents are confined to cells.

Some Corporate or Institutional Chefs oversee on-site vegetable gardens that produce either part of or all of the kitchen's vegetables and herbs.

High-tech companies often hire well-known chefs to create fabulous and varied foods to please or even entice employees, along with child care, gyms, and yoga sessions. These corporate chefs sometimes have to cook meals that reflect four or five different national origins, both for employees from those countries and for the culinary interest of other staffers.

Prisons, too, hire chefs trained in top culinary schools, as might a hospital, an airline, or a railroad, if only as consultants. Some hospitals believe that good food helps the healing process by helping to make patients happier, even if they have to mash potatoes with peas to get the patient to eat. Hospital diets range from liquid and bland to puréed, diabetic, gluten-free, low-sodium, low-fat, and vegetarian. Some hospitals price cafeteria food to attract the community to dine on healthy food inexpensively, occasionally making a slight profit for the hospital.

Convalescent hospitals and retirement homes face different challenges and need to deal with senior digestive systems and temperaments. Many chefs love working in this atmosphere, cooking to please their elders, and going home without the concerns that come with running a restaurant business.

University chefs need to cook or order ready-cooked food or coordinate concession stands that meet the dietary expectations of students, many of whom have grown up with microwaved burritos.

School cooks and district chefs generally don't cook much anymore and often heat food prepared elsewhere. They do plan menus of what is cooked on-site, and increasingly strive to eliminate foods loaded with trans fats and sugar in favor of proteins and whole grains. Some school and school district head cooks and chefs oversee kitchen gardens to supply the cafeterias with fresh vegetables.

Each Corporate or Institutional Chef usually has total responsibility for hiring and training kitchen staff, which usually includes at least two shifts depending upon the institution.

Some institutional kitchens produce a few thousand meals a day, and therefore offer enormous numbers of entry-level jobs, all under the Corporate or Institutional Chef. Such a chef has to divide the kitchen into several subdepartments, all of it extremely well organized and similar to a large restaurant or hotel kitchen operation.

Those subdepartments might include bakery, early-morning prep, salad or pantry (also known as cold prep), hot food, desserts, service (if cafeteria style), and delivery to rooms if in a prison, hospital, or convalescent home.

The Corporate or Institutional Chef might vary the menu to pique clients' culinary interest, or may repeat a daily menu week after week. The chef may oversee teaching cooks how to prepare new food items, meet with heads of departments to discuss recipes, and educate new employees on how the business works, including sanitation and cleanliness standards and laws, sustainability factors such as recycling grease into fuel, and using alternative detergents.

An institutional chef also oversees the kitchen budget as if he or she were running any other department of the corporation or institution, figuring the costs of food, dietary planning, labor costs (and what you get for what you pay), per-person meal costs including dietary restrictions, cost control, and ordering and receiving.

Sometimes institutional or corporate food service is brought in by companies on contract to provide food, whether in a hotel, prison, university, airline, or school. In such cases, the chef or head cook will oversee service staff and secondary preparation (reheating) of the food and some ordering of fresh items, but little actual cooking.

Work hours for Corporate or Institutional Chefs are usually shorter and more reasonable than in restaurants, with most work done in the early morning through mid-afternoon. Many Corporate or Institutional Chefs' jobs carry benefits, union representation, and long-standing employees.

Salaries

A Corporate or Institutional Chef's salary might range from $38,000 in some school districts to $120,000 for a giant high-tech corporation, with benefits, and with hours much better than the late nights often required in restaurants.

Employment Prospects

Employment prospects are good. Each institution only has one top chef. But there are loads of cooking jobs across the board in this category, from universities with fraternities and sororities and private and public schools, to hospitals, convalescent homes, all kinds of camps, growing residential care facilities, country clubs, and even railroads.

There are many entry-level corporate and institutional cooking jobs available to new immigrants and others with nearly no experience. One can learn and move up the kitchen ladder fairly easily.

Advancement Prospects

Because of the ideal hours and benefits, and often the sense of doing good, Corporate or Institutional Chefs tend to stay put and do not engage in "musical chefs" the way many restaurant chefs do, the latter often on the move to find a better job. Basically, those looking for corporate and institutional jobs are not the kind of people who want to be star chefs on television.

Many Corporate or Institutional Chefs seek security and seniority, both of which rarely exist in restaurants. Advancement usually comes in the form of moving to a larger or more exciting corporation or institution, and occasionally into general management.

It is possible to work one's way up from dishwasher to chef in these institutions, but only if one is proficient in English (unless the institution is owned by people whose first language is other than English).

Education and Training

Corporate or Institutional Chefs need management training as well as culinary training. Community and junior colleges often offer more real-life management courses than do sophisticated culinary schools.

Experience, Skills, and Personality Traits

Many low-level institutional and corporate cooks are recent immigrants with few English language skills. A Corporate or Institutional Chef must speak some of the language of employees, while possibly teaching them kitchen English.

Experience cooking for a food delivery program such as meals-on-wheels, a church, large restaurant, or even summer camp where one can get experience cooking for lots of people will be helpful.

A Corporate or Institutional Chef has to have a cool temperament, great managerial and human resources skills, be able to juggle duties, and be sure to show up early in the morning.

Unions and Associations

The American Culinary Federation (www.acfchefs.org), the International Association of Culinary Professionals (www.iacp.org), and the American Institute of Wine and Food (www.globalchefs.com) have local meetings, national conventions, and job referral pages on their Web sites.

The National Association of College and University Food Service (www.nacufs.org) offers everything from online meal planning courses to job placement, indus-try gossip, and news. The American Society of Hospital Food Service Administrators offers classes, books, and general support resources (www.ashfsa.org).

Tips for Entry

1. Volunteer at a food delivery program like meals-on-wheels, a soup kitchen, a church, a school, or a camp to try this kind of cooking for lots of people, where your duties might be narrow and specialized.
2. Check out community and junior college culinary and hospitality programs for those with a class in volume cooking.
3. Volunteer or get a paying internship at the best corporate or institutional kitchen in your area, whether it is a corporate cafeteria, convalescent home, or university food court.

INSTITUTIONAL HEAD COOK

CAREER PROFILE

Duties: Serves as the on-the-ground lead cook and in front of the stove supervisor who oversees all stations and station cooks in the kitchen, trains all new staff, learns all stations and their daily menus, fills in when someone fails to show up, manages sanitation and health conditions, schedules workers, and coordinates menu production

Alternate Title(s): Head Cook; Kitchen Supervisor; Kitchen Manager; Chef Tournant

Salary Range: $28,000 to $45,000, usually with benefits

Employment Prospects: Excellent

Advancement Prospects: Fair

Best Geographical Location(s): Always better in large cities, gambling centers and resort areas, but similar positions are available everywhere

Prerequisites:

Education and Training—Courses at community colleges, culinary schools, and vocational institutions, combined with experience. Specific training for position often comes from working one's way up the kitchen ladder, but management classes might help.

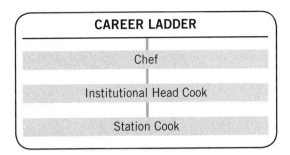

CAREER LADDER

Chef

Institutional Head Cook

Station Cook

Experience—Experience managing people in a kitchen is mandatory, along with enough cooking experience to know what ingredients go into menu items and a mastery of what work each cooking station requires.

Special Skills and Personality Traits—Enjoyment of managing others with tact; enjoyment of creativity and detail work; enjoyment of good food and pleasing others; an ability to make station cooks work as a team; the additional language of kitchen employees may be necessary

Position Description

In a prison, hospital, business campus dining room or cafeteria, university, school, country club, convalescent home, or retirement home, the head cook may or may not be a certified chef, but oversees and supervises all of the institution's cooks and has to know how to perform the functions of every cooking station on the line. The head cook must be so familiar with recipes and menus that he or she can step in anywhere at any time and substitute for someone who doesn't show up. Those stations may range from salad (or pantry), cold foods, bakery, sauces, hot food, tray lines in cafeterias, and desserts.

As kitchen manager or head cook, she or he reports to a food service director, who does not cook but runs the budget and business end that includes menu planning and sometimes ordering. The food service director might also hire and fire staff, or that may also be done by the kitchen manager or head cook.

Generally the head cook or kitchen manager orders and receives food and supplies to be used to cook the menus, checking what shows up against invoices and

delivery slips to make sure everything ordered is there. This person also coordinates food storage to make sure nothing spoils or is wasted, rotating back of shelf items to front of shelf, considering temperature required for proper storage.

The Institutional Head Cook or kitchen manager also has the responsibility for managing costs, calls meetings of staff under him or her to bring everyone up to date on company or institutional rules and changes and menu plans for the week, and represents the kitchen staff at meetings with staff above him or her, including reporting to the chef or executive chef if there is one.

Head cooks or kitchen managers should be so involved that they teach cooking recipes to the staff, taste large dishes before they go out to the public, and ensure the priority of sanitation practices, including washing cutting boards, chopping blocks, knives, and bowls after use and before reuse. This person also often also takes responsibility for getting people to maintain and fix machinery, mixers, ovens, air conditioners, and even toasters.

Basically, the kitchen manager or head cook coordinates everything in the institutional kitchen, wherever it is.

Salaries

Institutional Head Cook pay varies widely according to location, size, reputation, and elegance of the institution. Generally salaries range from $28,000 to $45,000, often with benefits and vacation.

Employment Prospects

Employment prospects are excellent. There are loads of jobs available in all sorts of institutions, from prisons and hospitals to universities, residential care homes, country clubs, gambling casinos, resorts, and some hotels and spas. Once one is a kitchen manager or head cook, it is relatively easy to move to a better institution once one has experience.

Advancement Prospects

Many head cooks stay with one employer because they like the work and the security of where they are. If one wants to move up within the institution, he or she needs to constantly study and learn, improve cooking skills, learn foreign languages, and possibly advance to chef or executive chef.

If a head cook wants better pay without additional qualifications, he or she should look for a better paying job at a more prestigious institution.

Education and Training

Culinary programs at community and junior colleges and cooking schools provide the basics of cooking and management. A person who aspires to being an Institutional Head Cook or kitchen manager will need to take every possible cooking class he or she can find, because he or she will need to know everything there is about a kitchen and how to run one.

Learning on the job is also an excellent way to progress, even if one starts cooking at one station and moves around to learn and cook at other stations. The head cook to whom a line cook reports may help a promising staff member attend school while still working at the institution.

An immigrant worker would be smart to take English classes as well, while an English speaking head cook would be smart to learn the prevailing second language of the kitchen.

Experience, Skills, and Personality Traits

An Institutional Head Cook or kitchen manager must like change and excitement, for overseeing such a kitchen is loaded with unpredictables, such as staff not showing up, while the menus can be repetitive week to week.

This person must enjoy preparation of food to please other people, sometimes in large numbers. He or she must also like people, work well with others, have the ability to motivate people to work together as a team and fill in for one another, and at the same time not mind repetition, depending on what sort of institutional kitchen it is.

A head cook or kitchen manager should also have second-language abilities and make an effort to learn the native language of kitchen staff, as well as make an effort to teach staff kitchen English a little at a time.

Unions and Associations

Only a few cities have strong culinary unions anymore, and in some cases one can join when hired. Gambling areas have strong culinary and hotel worker unions, as do some large cities.

Otherwise, all sorts of information, job placement, classes, and even recipes can be found from the International Association of Culinary Professionals and local affiliates (www.iacp.com) and the American Culinary Federation (www.adfchefs.org).

Tips for Entry

1. Take any job you can in a large kitchen to get your foot in the door and learn everything you can on the way up the kitchen ladder, moving from one cooking station to another.
2. Take cooking and management classes at a local community or junior college either before or while working to learn as much as possible about every aspect of cooking in a restaurant or institutional kitchen.
3. Phone or visit food service or food and beverage departments of local hospitals, convalescent hospitals, retirement homes, hotels, and even prisons and ask for an entry-level job.
4. If English is your second language, learn all the English you can. It will be useful forever.

COMMUNITY AND SOCIAL SERVICE

EXECUTIVE DIRECTOR, COMMUNITY FOOD BANK

Duties: Coordinates all facets of the food bank, including obtaining and securing a location to receive, store, and pack food; coordinates volunteers; solicits or procures supplies, including delivery bags and food as necessary; coordinates storage and rotation of foods; hires paid staff if any; raises funds for program from private donors, foundations, and local service clubs such as Rotary, Kiwanis, and Lions clubs; oversees fund-raiser benefit events and the budget; writes, edits, or gets someone else to do the newsletter, either online or in print; writes and sends out press releases and pleas for assistance; puts together the annual report; meets with a board of directors to keep it up to date and get guidance for and take advantage of their contacts to solve problems; and strives to identify and define who needs the food bank's services

Alternate Title(s): Food Bank Manager

Salary Range: $40,000 to $70,000, sometimes with benefits; volunteers unpaid

Employment Prospects: Limited

Advancement Prospects: Fair

Best Geographical Location(s): Large cities or specific depressed communities where people need help either due to age, health problems, or lack of employment

Prerequisites:

Education or Training—Education in the culinary arts, marketing, and food management; an M.A. in

CAREER LADDER

Board of Directors or Government Agency/Commission

Executive Director, Community Food Bank

Deputy Director or Development Director

organizational development or management may be advantageous. Often a person who has worked for nonprofits has a leg up for the job.

Experience—Volunteer community service in nonprofits that serve those who need help; work in grocery stores; experience in public speaking, event planning, fund-raising, and experience getting people to work together are important.

Special Skills and Personality Traits—Special qualities that can come in handy include a good and even temperament, enjoyment of working with people and helping them help one another, enjoyment of sometimes dirty work in depressing locations, and acceptance of the joy of feeding people who need help.

Position Description

Food banks exist because we have thousands of people in the United States who don't have enough food, cannot get to grocery stores in their neighborhoods (in some neighborhoods in inner cities there aren't any grocery stores), or simply need our help and are perhaps homeless.

Food banks are everywhere, some formal and some informal. Big cities may have several official formal food banks where food is gathered, sorted, stored, and packed into bags for distribution to those who need it, and who may line up to get their bags filled. Some food banks are unofficial and informal and are located in a large room or the kitchen of a church.

The food bank collects, stores, packs, and passes out packaged foods, and occasionally fresh produce, to those who need it, usually as a nonprofit organization.

Most community food banks have boards of directors made up of an assortment of leaders who have contacts in many parts of a community so as to raise as much interest, money, and donations of food for the cause as possible. Some food banks offer nutrition education, although most clients are usually interested in just having enough to eat, period.

A Community Food Bank Executive Director finds the best structure and location possible if one does not already exist, and may even relocate to a building closer to the center of where clients might live. Paid or not, the executive director coordinates food and financial donations, "hires" volunteers and workers and coordinates their schedules, arranges storage and rotation of foods on the shelves, and oversees nutritious packing of foods for the needy and the distribution of food.

The executive director must also keep outreach and relationships with prominent community members, members of service clubs such as the Rotary, Kiwanis, and Lions clubs, puts on or oversees fund-raising events and budget, writes press releases, meets with the board of directors and relays outcome with staff and head volunteers, and often writes an annual report.

Depending upon the size of the food bank and the community it serves, it may have no paid staff members or a few, which might include a general manager, warehouse or storage manager, truck drivers or volunteer deliverers, and even someone who keeps track of inventory and is capable of logging it into a computer.

Food bank executive directors coordinate fundraising and grant writing, and keep contact with large organizations that help fund community food banks such as Second Harvest, which officially renamed itself Feeding America in September 2008 (www.feedingamerica.org). Feeding America supports food banks nationwide, partially with chef's dinners held in restaurants across the United States.

The executive director also generally is responsible for publicity and speaking to service clubs, and churches, and other community groups to keep the community aware of what their food bank needs and what it has accomplished, and for writing a newsletter, which can be sent online to many supporters to save trees and money that would otherwise be spent on paper and postage.

On the education level, the executive director helps coordinate the staff and employees, keeps them jollied up and working well together, and actively seeks chances to explain the food bank to community groups to help them understand how they might help those in need.

Most counties and states have food bank associations from which executive directors can get information, advice, and ideas from others trying to feed the hungry.

Salaries

Some food bank executive directors work for free as volunteers, while others that manage large food banks in large cities must be paid. Salaries depend upon how much money the surrounding community gives to the food bank, how many other paid staff are required, the director's experience and education (including management and human resources courses taken), and the director's finesse at such a sensitive job. Salaries usually range from $40,000 to $70,000, with or without benefits.

Employment Prospects

Employment is limited. Many rural food banks are run by volunteers.

Advancement Prospects

The position of executive director is usually at the top of the pyramid in a food bank program and there is no higher office to attain. If an executive director wants to manage a more sophisticated or popular program and earn more money, he or she will have to move to a larger food bank, probably in a more urban area, to achieve that goal.

If a community food bank Executive Director seems to hit a glass ceiling, he or she could work in related agencies such as meals-on-wheels, halfway houses, family service organizations, and, in some counties, in meal and nutrition programs.

Education and Training

A good Community Food Bank Executive Director should have education in nutrition, human resources management, organizational planning or development, and possibly even certificates or a master's degree in social work, psychology, and business management.

Experience, Skills, and Personality Traits

All relevant experience, including volunteering at a food bank or meals-on-wheels program, social work with organizations, event planning, public speaking, social and professional contacts, and fund-raising skills will be helpful.

A good personality, a sense of humor, and enjoyment in helping others are mandatory. A good candidate will enjoy and be skilled at team building, creating new ideas and approaches to food and money donations, and must be caring and dedicated to those less fortunate.

Unions and Associations

The Association of Fundraising Professionals has workshops, conferences, certification, and loads of tips on how to do one's job better, as well as a Web site with all of the latest pertinent news (www.afpnet.org).

Tips for Entry

1. Volunteer to help at a local food bank, Red Cross operation, or meals-on-wheels, where there are

all sorts of opportunities to find out if you like the work. You can pick up food, stack or rotate food on shelves, plan and coordinate fund-raising events, keep records on the office computer, or whatever you enjoy. After you learn that job and prove you can do it well, ask the executive director for a job at any level, including sweeping the floor, which is an important job.

2. Contact head fund-raiser (or development director) of an existing food bank or volunteer food program and ask if there are any jobs available. Take any job to get your foot in the door. Fund-raisers are always important.

3. Work your way up within a food bank, even starting as a volunteer, and if you don't get the executive director job get a letter of recommendation from the existing one and from a couple of well-known members of the board of directors and apply for a job at a neighboring food bank.

4. Start your own food bank if there isn't one. Get nonprofit status or latch onto and existing nonprofit organization to get started.

PREPARED MEALS
PROGRAM MANAGER

CAREER PROFILE

Duties: A Prepared Meals Program Manager organizes food preparation and delivery to housebound people; gets funding for programs and food purchases; coordinates staffing of paid and volunteer workers; develops menus with balanced diets; runs a food production facility that meets local health standards; coordinates cooking, packaging, and delivery of meals to those in need; and often feeds volunteer or hired staff and drivers. Advance preparation for food distribution during disasters should also be part of the job.

Alternate Title(s): Program Director; President of the Board of Directors, Nonprofit Organization

Salary Range: Volunteer ($0) to $50,000

Employment Prospects: Limited

Advancement Prospects: Limited

Best Geographical Location(s): Medical treatment centers; also, most cities and towns have food delivery programs; areas with large senior citizen populations, which may include those with mild weather and cultural attractions

Prerequisites:

Education and Training—Culinary programs that include management at a community or junior col-

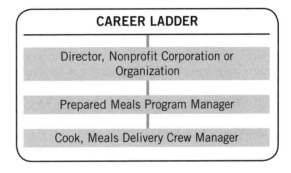

CAREER LADDER

Director, Nonprofit Corporation or Organization

Prepared Meals Program Manager

Cook, Meals Delivery Crew Manager

lege would be helpful, but passion for helping others will go a long way

Experience—Experience cooking for large groups, mathematical skills to enlarge recipes, fund-raising capabilities, and organizational experience, particularly with nonprofits, are all advised

Special Skills and Personality Traits—Passion for helping people, tolerance of different kinds of people, possibly a second language pertinent to the community; a talent for talking grocery stores and other contributors into donating food, and for talking local farmers into growing extra vegetables for the program's meals will take an applicant a long way.

Position Description

Meals-on-wheels and county and church programs deliver food to people who cannot leave their homes because of age or medical conditions. Either paid staff or volunteers or a combination of the two get donated food or purchase the food, prepare it, package it in hot trays or bags, and deliver it to housebound clients.

A new role for Prepared Meals Program Manager should include advance planning and preparation for food distribution during disasters, whether natural or created.

The manager of a prepared meals distribution program organizes or coordinates the entire operation, including raising money, setting and complying with the budget, establishing relationships with farmers, bakers, and grocers to get good deals or donations of food or money, or works with county officials in their

food distribution efforts. He or she must also make sure health practices are always up to date and performed well enough to pass unannounced government inspections. There must be one person on-site at all times who is versed and certified in safe food practices.

The program needs a home, and the manager has to find a certified kitchen, either in a county building, church, senior center, part-time restaurant, or other facility where workers can prepare and assemble the meals to be distributed. He or she has to attract paid staff or volunteers and coordinate their schedules, and develop and comply with a budget, whether it comes from a government agency, grants, or from community donations.

Rent, food costs, refrigerators and freezers, disposable hot tray inserts, paper bags, liability insurance, and any salaries all must be figured into the budget. In some cases, and if the manager has good relations with local farmers and bakers, those people will occasionally grow and bake extra food for the distribution program.

Recipes must be tested, tried, and modified to stretch ingredients for a large volume of clients, occasionally with sensitivity for special diets.

Some programs deliver a hot meal and a bag lunch weekdays to a client's home, while others make burritos twice a week or deliver meals to central locations twice a week, depending on need and availability of financial and food support.

Either the program manager or director or a person whom they designate will coordinate drivers who actually take food to the clients and select especially sensitive drivers who have time to chat with recipients on some routes. The food deliverer may be the only visit or conversation the client has, and this person can become extremely important to the client's well-being, happiness, and healing.

Some program managers or directors write and send out press releases, either print or e-mail newsletters to program supporters, and hold fund-raiser events and even thank-you dinners for supporters and volunteers.

Salaries

Many delivered meal programs are run by passionate volunteers or by staff generally underpaid and willing to work for less than they would earn "on the outside" because of their dedication to serving other people.

A locally prominent board of directors might raise funds to pay an excellent executive chef and organizer, but it is unlikely that they will be paid according to their experience or talent. Most Prepared Meals Program Managers or directors are paid from $15,000 to $50,000.

Employment Prospects

Many leaders of food delivery organizations set up the program and stay with the organization for years, so there is little attrition. Few people leave these jobs except from burnout or the actual need to earn more money.

Some communities may have more than one program, such as at a senior center, YMCA or YWCA, meals-on-wheels programs, or church or local government programs, so there may be more opportunities in some areas.

Many available leadership positions in prepared meals programs go to people already involved in the program because boards of directors know that the person is dedicated to what he or she is doing. Get your foot in the door to get in that line.

Advancement Prospects

A Prepared Meals Program Manager position is the top of the kitchen ladder in these programs, so in order to advance in this field one probably needs to move to a larger program in the same or another city to earn more money or prestige.

Education and Training

Culinary programs that include management at a community or junior college would be helpful, but passion for helping others will go a long way. One can learn about cooking for large numbers of people and organizing nonprofit programs on the job by volunteering to get started, even if just one day or evening a week.

Experience, Skills, and Personality Traits

Cooking for large groups, mathematical skills to enlarge recipes, fund-raising capabilities, organizational experience (particularly with nonprofits), and the ability to motivate and coordinate passionate people are mandatory personality traits for Prepared Meals Program Managers.

A person in this job must be able to bond with community members and service clubs, convince people to join the cause of serving others, raise money comfortably, and attract volunteers. The manager or director must also be able to select volunteers and food servers or deliverers who are sensitive enough to understand the value of spending time with clients or food recipients.

The manager or director must share the passion and dedication for serving those in need, as well as attract supporters who will help support the program financially. A good manager's dedication will pass on to those who volunteer or give in other ways.

Unions and Associations

While there is no association of managers of prepared meals program managers, the meals-on-wheels umbrella group, the Meals on Wheels Association of America, offers resource information on how to set up a program to serve nutritious meals to seniors, the homebound, the disabled, the frail, or to-at-risk individuals, and how to be prepared for emergencies, and features a newsletter and an annual conference (go to www.mowaa.org).

Formerly known as America's Second Harvest, Feeding America (www.feedingamerica.org) is another helpful organization, made up primarily of restaurant chefs whose mission is to provide food to Americans living with hunger.

Tips for Entry

1. To get your foot in the door or to get experience in a prepared meals program, volunteer at a local church, senior center or meals-on-wheels program to get experience from the ground up ordering, shopping, cooking, packing, developing large quantity recipes, and delivering meals for those less fortunate. You can even start volunteering one morning a week or month to find out if this kind of work is for you before you look for managerial positions.

2. Attend fund-raisers or presentations through service clubs (Rotary, Kiwanis, Lions, and others) by prepared meals activists to find out if the concept evokes your passions, and if so then volunteer. Make yourself vital to the program.

RESTAURANT FOOD RUNNERS OR DISPATCHERS

CAREER PROFILE

Duties: A Restaurant Food Runner or Dispatcher establishes links with both restaurants and social service food delivery groups. This person or a designated driver picks up food from restaurants and other commercial food purveyors and leftovers from big parties and distributes it to food distribution programs, which in turn give it to those in need.

Alternate Title(s): Food Distribution Manager. (This definition of food runner is different from a food runner in a fine restaurant whose main role is to deliver and present food from the kitchen to the customer.)

Salary Range: $0 as volunteer to $18,000 for half-time work, with some unusual time demands. Occasionally one can collect "mileage" expenses in times of high gasoline prices.

Employment Prospects: Limited to low

Advancement Prospects: Low to limited

Best Geographical Location(s): Any town with food distribution programs of leftovers from kindhearted restaurateurs and people with hunger needs

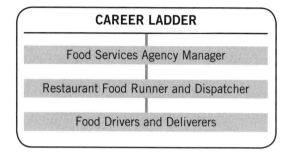

CAREER LADDER

Food Services Agency Manager

Restaurant Food Runner and Dispatcher

Food Drivers and Deliverers

Prerequisites:

Education or Training—Possibly a valid driver's license

Experience—Anyone who shops at grocery stores, delivers anything or anyone on time including children, and has the desire to help can do this job.

Special Skills and Personality Traits—Anyone who is a good driver, is passionate and motivated to help others, likes to hang around restaurant kitchens or back doors, is cheerful and can get along with others, and is a good motivator of food donors will be popular in this job.

Position Description

The manager of a restaurant runner program may be a freelancer, work for one of the local restaurants that donate food, or work as either a volunteer or staff member of one of the food distribution nonprofit organizations.

Such a person may have to raise his or her own funding for liability insurance and fuel and keep in good communication with donor restaurants and recipient charities.

This person or a designated driver picks up food from restaurants, caterers, event planners, and other commercial food purveyors and leftovers from big parties and brings it to food distribution programs, which in turn give it to those in need. While restaurants cannot always predict how much extra food they will have unless they purposely cook extra to give away (and some do), food runners try to estimate what will be available and work as a communication and physical liaison between the restaurants, caterers, and event

planners and the churches, senior centers, community organizations, and meals-on-wheels programs.

Food runners pick up cooked food that is ready to serve or food picked fresh at local farms and carry it to the delivering organization, which may have to store it properly overnight and reheat or cook it the next day. This contrasts with food banks where uncooked food is received and stored, and either cooked or bagged for distribution to clients who then take it home and cook it.

Contributing restaurants do most business on weekends, so a runner may have to do his or her rounds on weekends and have arranged proper storage that can be accessed at odd weekend or Monday hours. Cell phones and computers can help tremendously for the food runner dispatchers to keep in touch constantly with which establishments have excess food and with which nonprofit organizations' clients are most needy at the moment.

Some runners and dispatchers need to be sensitive to some restaurateurs' and catering chefs' desires to deliver food directly to the nonprofit so they can better appreciate their good deed and see that the food actually goes to the right place and is cared for properly.

Many food distribution nonprofits have direct relationships with restaurants, caterers, and event planners who may deliver food directly to the organization or have a designated volunteer or staffer who regularly delivers food on the way home. The organizations may also have staffers or volunteers who especially like to visit certain restaurants to pick up extra food.

A food runner might have special relationships with local caterers who can call them as soon as a party is over to alert them to come get the excess food, which means food runners have to be motivated to run after food at odd hours. Some catering chefs might enjoy delivering leftovers to the food-service organization themselves, but that is rare.

Salaries

Many Food Runners or Dispatchers are volunteers, and those that are paid are greatly underpaid, so one must be extremely dedicated to the work.

Managers of nonprofit food banks and food delivery organizations often raise funds for their salaries, rent, power bills, and other necessities, usually without thinking about paying a food runner or collector. For food runners that are paid, $18,000 to $25,000 is the national pay average, but such salaries are rare except in super urban areas.

Employment Prospects

Rarely do Food Runners or Dispatchers leave their jobs, unless they go on to become the manager of a nonprofit food distribution organization. Most people in these positions love what they do and are dedicated to this form of contributing to society.

If you get involved with one of these entities and see that a food runner or dispatcher would make operations run more efficiently or successfully, suggest that you create the position and fill it. Your next step might be to survey restaurants to find out if they will contribute if they do not already.

Advancement Prospects

Advancement for a Food Runner or Dispatcher is limited, although one can move up to manager or get invitations to work at larger food banks or food distribution organizations.

Education and Training

Neither education nor training is required, but a valid driver's license and liability insurance are necessary for those who need to drive.

Experience, Skills, and Personality Traits

Some experience volunteering for nonprofits, along with passion, compassion, patience, dedication, and a good personality to keep up relations with restaurants, chefs, and caterers will be most helpful.

Unions and Associations

Local communities sometimes have small organizations of their nonprofits, and United Way groups may offer advice and expertise.

Tips for Entry

1. If your community already has a food runner system, volunteer, learn the ropes and routes, and work your way into a job.
2. If there is no food runner program, talk to food programs, caterers, and restaurant owners and find out if they would contribute to nonprofit food delivery organizations if you set up a pickup and delivery program.

FARMING

FARMER

Duties: A Farmer grows herbs, vegetables, and edible flowers, and raises animals for home consumption or for sale, either through distributors, co-ops, or farmers' markets. Some Farmers grow food on their own property, some lease from other property owners, and others grow for the owner. Some small Farmers grow extra for food distribution organizations that serve the needy. Farming may also include aquaculture, or fish farming.

Alternate Title(s): Grower

Salary Range: $30,000 to $80,000 and more for corporate farmers

Employment Prospects: Good, especially for self-starters in nonurban areas

Advancement Prospects: Limited

Best Geographical Location(s): Almost anywhere with dirt and water, although some crops grow better in some states and almost everything grows well in California

Prerequisites:

    Education or Training—Apprentice on a farm, ask questions at nurseries, take farming and business classes at a community college or university, join Future Farmers of America in high school or 4-H if

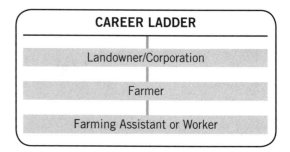

younger, and get an agriculture-related degree at a four-year university.

    Experience—Work for someone else, talk to as many Farmers—large and small—as possible before making the professional plunge, and visit farmers' markets to ask questions of farmer/vendors and the market manager.

    Special Skills and Personality Traits—Whether farming in your backyard or working for someone else, a Farmer has to respect and enjoy growing food for himself or herself or for others. One must have passion for working with dirt, growing and nurturing plants from almost nothing, improving people's lives, and working alone and communing with nature.

Position Description

Conscientious Farmers may be the new rock stars of the food industry. Opportunity abounds for farming a backyard or acreage, or even growing your own vegetables in pots on a balcony or terrace. There is money to be made and money to be saved.

Farmers grow crops and raise animals for food or clothing. Small Farmers usually grow for local consumption, which saves energy and costs for long distance transportation, and sell from farm stands or community-supported agriculture organizations (CSAs), to local grocery stores or at farmers' markets. Many small Farmers travel on a farmers' market circuit, earning hundreds of dollars in cash at each stop.

Farmers find the best sources for seeds, and have to decide when to plant, fertilize (if at all), and harvest, and how to sell their crops. Many pursue organic or biodynamic seeds and farming practices.

Other Farmers look for good animals and machinery to buy, learn new technology, and keep up on new farming methods. Many Farmers now need to master computer programs that might tell them when to pick grapes, tomatoes, or corn or keep track of their inventory and employees. All Farmers have to take care of tools, machinery, barns, and greenhouses.

On small organic farms, seeds and plants are often put in the ground by workers' hands, while on large corporate farms machines plant and harvest crops. Spraying for pests is optional.

Crop Farmers grow fruits and vegetables, herbs, some grains, and harvest, pack, store, and ship or deliver them.

Animal Farmers grow and nurture livestock including chickens and turkeys, geese, sheep, goats, cows, water buffalo, and other animals and even breed and slaughter them and possibly sell milk to dairies and cheese makers.

Horticultural Farmers grow flowers for home and food decoration as well as shrubs and sod grass that arrives in rolls.

Some aquaculture Farmers raise fish and shellfish, without antibiotics and harmful substances that can contaminate wild fish. Generally, aquaculture Farmers care for their ponds and floating nets in ocean or river waters, stock their ponds, feed the fish, and eventually ship them to wholesalers or sell a few off the dock.

Farmers need to work long hours every day with few vacations and some danger. Plants and animals don't take vacations from needing care, while female buffalo, dairy cows, sheep, and goats need to be milked every day. When crops are dormant or sold, Farmers repair machinery, paint the barn, order seeds, and occasionally work at other jobs.

Suburban to rural areas are, of course, the best locales for starting a farm, working for another Farmer, or growing herbs for sale. With a trend toward "living" roof gardens, enterprising souls might start big-city vegetable gardens on office building roofs or window ledges, either to eat and give away produce to friends, to sell to other tenants or for use in the company cafeteria. It is important to check with building officials to make sure the roof can withstand the weight of both dirt and water or that it is safe to put objects on the window ledge.

Some big and little cities have community gardens where you can lease a plot and grow your own produce, either for personal consumption or for sale. For most vegetables, light exposure and protection from winter weather are important, so a south-facing plot might produce the most vegetables.

Planting and working in vineyards is also considered farming, so getting on-the-ground experience in a vineyard or orchard would help someone decide whether to get into the field. In some locales, fruit or olive trees have been planted between vineyard rows to increase productivity and income.

Some self-starters have been able to begin their "farms" by growing herbs in pots on a porch, expanding to the backyard, and then leasing more land from a neighbor while selling herbs to local restaurants and their branches. Others rent a plot at a community garden and begin by selling what they grow on-site or at farmers' markets.

New urban Farmers, whether on corporate rooftops or in vacant lots, are the new wave for feeding staff or whole neighborhoods.

Salaries

Farmers generally are independent and self-employed, so do not receive traditional salaries and live on the profit they make and the food they grow. Independent small Farmers, whether they own or lease land, make around $50,000, although large corporate Farmers can make millions of dollars, including farm subsidies from the U.S. government, which some collect without growing anything. Farm employees make from $18,000 to $40,000.

Many veterans returning from Iraq have ventured into working at small farms to help their recovery and do something positive and productive.

One can also help to start one or several school gardens, coordinate curriculm and growing programs, and organize farmers markets at schools where children and the community can purchase vegetables.

Employment Prospects

Good, especially for self-starters who grow at home or on small plots of land. Anyone willing to work really hard outdoors can work in the farming industry for themselves or for someone else.

Advancement Prospects

Either one works on someone else's farm or starts his or her own; there isn't much room for advancement in either place. One could learn by working on another person's farm, save money, and lease or purchase one's own small plot.

There is room for advancement when a Farmer hires many workers and promotes experienced individuals to manage or supervise a crew of employees as foreman or manager. Moving to a bigger farm may yield higher pay and more responsibilities. Those who save their money and invest or expand farms create their own higher jobs.

Education and Training

Many high school adult education programs and community colleges offer courses in basic farming, agriculture, and viticulture. Any library or bookstore will have gardening books, so try to get one that has information localized to your region.

Experience, Skills, and Personality Traits

Growing vegetables or herbs on your balcony or in your backyard can be valuable experience to help you decide how interested you might be in larger scale growing or farming.

One needs to be fearless and curious and ask questions at nurseries and of Farmers, winegrowers, and the sources where one might want to sell produce.

A Farmer also has to be able to entertain himself or herself among the rows of plants or animals and be happy with nature rather than surrounded by people. In fact, people who prefer communicating with plants and animals to mingling with lots of people might be especially good at farming.

Farming is hard work, especially on organic or biodynamic farms where things are sometimes done in old-fashioned ways. On larger corporate or industrial farms, sophisticated machines and computer programs make the work less backbreaking. Many plows are now equipped with closed-in cabs that have air conditioning, Wi-Fi, and music, quite unlike older, dusty, windswept tractors.

Unions and Associations

Most counties have farm or farmers' organizations, and some Farmers even belong to their local chamber of commerce. Dairy farmers may join the American Dairy Association (www.dairyinfo.com) or the Milk Industry Foundation (www.idfa.org).

Nationally, the American Farm Bureau claims to be "the voice of agriculture" and has bureaus in most counties (www.fb.org). The National Farmers Union makes similar claims (www.nfu.org). Both organizations offer political, health, and agricultural news, and both offer insurance.

Growing Power is a nonprofit that promotes community-based farming to help foster nutrition, education, and community (www.growingpower.org).

Tips for Entry

1. If you are still in high school, join your local Future Farmers of America (www.ffa.org), or 4-H (www.4-h.org) if even younger.
2. Grow some vegetables, work at a community garden, rent a plot somewhere and start growing.
3. Take a high school adult education or community college class in basic agriculture, farming, and viticulture, as well as courses in math, biology, dairy science, horticulture, crop and fruit science, fisheries biology, and hatchery management. Study bookkeeping, marketing, economics, and learn how to use a computer. One can also study these subjects gradually, so it is not necessary to take all of these classes at once.
4. Get a job at any low level helping someone already in the farming business.
5. Help a farming vendor at a farmers' market and learn the retail side of farming at the most basic person-to-person level.
6. Work for a CSA (community supported agriculture) organization.

COMMUNITY-SUPPORTED AGRICULTURE (CSA) MANAGER

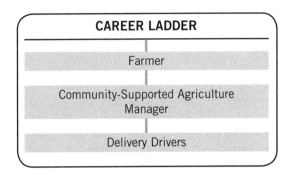

Position Description

For centuries Americans grew their own food and traded or bartered with neighbors, meaning most people had access to a variety of fresh food or preserved foods put away for the winter. Then we trended toward high-tech corporate farming to produce more for less at almost any health cost. Currently, consumers seem to be returning to the basics of touching the dirt or at least purchasing from someone who does. Hence, home farming and community-supported agriculture (CSAs) have become a worldwide movement.

Community-supported agriculture involves "subscription" sponsorship by which customers pay in advance for the vegetables and eggs they will receive in the future, and thereby sponsor the farmer and help him or her finance everything from seeds and feed to water. By buying into a CSA, members become shareholders or subscribers, sometimes help with farming or harvest, and may even help deliver the produce.

CSA Managers coordinate the farming, collect sponsors', shareholders', or members' money, grow the food,

supervise picking and packing, and deliver the farm-fresh food directly to the doorstep of the subscriber or consumer.

They also work to retain members or shareholders by sending out newsletters, recipes, educating them about expectations and crop rotations, hold social events and potlucks, get young people involved, focus on the best vegetables to grow in the area, provide flowers, eggs, honey, and baked goods, and survey their members and supporters.

Each CSA Manager or farmer should decide on modes of distribution, which might include using on-farm pickup, selling at farmers' markets, using an off-site distribution center, delivering to homes, and deciding whether to deliver once or twice a week.

CSAs may include a farmer, a membership coordinator, and a driver, with the goal of linking farmers and consumers for pickup or direct delivery of fresh organic produce.

One may organize a CSA without being a grower. He or she will pick up food products (vegetables, eggs, or flowers) from farmers, pack them for delivery in a warehouse or garage, and then deliver them to customers or subscribers.

CSAs are usually organized by farmers interested in creative and unconventional marketing and distribution ideas, groups of consumers who find a local farmer or farmers interested in a ready market, several farmers who collaborate to sell together without a middleman distributor, or by church groups, schools, and other community groups who bond together for this purpose.

A CSA Manager or farmer first meets with friendly people to explain the CSA concept and become members or supporters who commit to paying $400 to $700 a year for home delivery of fresh, usually organic vegetables, flowers, and eggs, sometimes paying for the whole year in advance, other times paying monthly. By paying in advance, CSA members share in the risk that the crops will succeed, and many subscribers believe in their investments in pure and sustainably grown agriculture.

Most CSAs have a core group that serves as a board of guidance and helps make decisions with the farmer, works to enlarge the group membership, sometimes shares in the work, and discusses membership or shareholder dues or prices, crop selection, distribution, volunteer activities and food fairs, e-mail lists and newsletters, and special events such as harvest celebrations.

The CSA Manager or farmer then uses these advance funds to buy seed, new tools, fuel, and feed for the next season's crop or herd. The CSA Manager or farmer develops a business plan and a budget that reflects real production costs and a fair salary to the farmer, the costs of land and equipment, labor costs, and insurance.

The CSA Manager or farmer develops a delivery route that consumes the least vehicle fuel and makes the most of the trip to deliver vegetables, fruits, flowers, nuts, and eggs and determines how frequently he or she can deliver to each subscriber.

Additionally, the CSA Manager or farmer avoids having to deal with marketing to big chain grocers and can deal directly with consumers. He or she may also consider branching out and including other farmers' products.

Salaries

Salaries come from membership, and range from $30,000 to $120,000, depending upon how many of the duties the CSA Manager assumes, and whether he or she is the only employee or if just one among several employees.

Employment Prospects

Job prospects are limited, with possible opportunities in assisting the farmer or driving, but there is lots of opportunity to start a CSA in most communities, especially when people are trying to limit their own auto fuel consumption. The best locations for employment include big cities and suburban or commuter communities near nutrition and food-aware areas.

Advancement Prospects

Advancement prospects are limited, but there are as many opportunities to start your own CSA in almost every community in North America, and even start a network of CSAs from which one might earn commissions.

Education and Training

While a person could certainly start a CSA without farming or marketing experience, it would be smart to take marketing, business, culinary, and agriculture classes to improve his or her chances of success.

The best training would include spending time growing vegetables and fruit sustainably or working for someone who does, working with a nonprofit organization that delivers food, knowing people in your community and their culinary interests, and whether the community can financially afford the cost of delivered organic foods that result from investing in a farmer and his or her farm.

Experience, Skills, and Personality Traits

A CSA Manager needs passionate commitment to or interest in sustainably grown food and sharing it with others. This person also needs a personality that can convince others to be interested in and commit to support the community farm, and charm them into putting up money to become a member or shareholder.

A CSA farmer should have farming experience, or at least experience growing food in a garden, and a CSA Manager should have organizational skills and some management and marketing experience.

CSA farmers also have to be able to financially and emotionally withstand bad crop seasons, poor harvests, bad weather, or pests' banquets.

Unions and Associations

Nationally, the American Farm Bureau claims to be "the voice of agriculture" and has bureaus in most counties (www.fb.org). The National Farmers Union makes similar claims (www.nfu.org). Both organizations offer political, health, and agricultural news, and both offer insurance. The Biodynamic Farming and Gardening

Association offers information on CSAs and sustainable and biodynamic farming and gardening (www.biodynamics.com).

Other excellent sources of information include farmer John Peterson's Web site, at www.angelicorganics.com, and Local Harvest's www.localharvest.org.csa.

Tips for Entry

1. Grow vegetables in pots on your balcony or in your garden to learn all you can.
2. Study agriculture or horticulture either at a community or junior college, adult school, or university to learn the conventional/industrial science of growing food. (Some argue that "back to basics" sustainable farming is the real "conventional farming," and that corporate farming should be called "industrial farming.")
3. Attend your local farmers' markets to meet sustainable growers and ask if you might apprentice or work with them to learn how they do things.
4. Find a location to grow on a larger basis and get your hands and feet dirty.
5. Find a local CSA and offer to drive, pack orders, till rows, pick vegetables, or do any job that might be available.

FARMERS' MARKET MANAGER

CAREER PROFILE

Duties: Secures an indoor or outdoor location for marketplace, makes rental arrangements with landlords (which may include local government agencies), finds vendors, sets a financial system with vendors, collects fees, advertises the market to the community, oversees cleanup, thinks up and coordinates special events and school visits, settles disputes among vendors and neighboring businesses, and deals with the board of directors if one exists

Alternate Title(s): Farmers' Market Director; President; Coordinator

Salary Range: $18,000 to $80,000

Employment Prospects: Limited. There is usually only one manger per farmers' market. If there is no farmers' market in your area, start one.

Advancement Prospects: Limited

Best Geographical Location(s): Suburban cities on the East and West coasts where healthy food awareness is strong, urban areas where farm food can be brought in by vendors, or any town in America offer prospects.

Prerequisites:

Education or Training—Bookkeeping courses, knowledge of nutritional food balances to get a full range represented, human resources familiarity

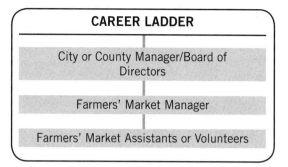

CAREER LADDER

City or County Manager/Board of Directors

Farmers' Market Manager

Farmers' Market Assistants or Volunteers

Experience—Management experience; working for another farmers' market or any retail operation is great training for managing a farmers' market, especially if you have worked with lots of varied personalities passionate about their work. Other sales or marketing experience will be useful.

Special Skills—Persuasiveness, diplomacy, tact, patience, ability to help people work together, knowledge of farming and compatible foods, contacts with and appreciation for arts and crafts that might complement food vendors

Position Description

A Farmers' Market Manager has to find a venue that is attractive, suitable, well located, and available and get permission of either a landlord or a city or county government to use a street or public property. The Farmers' Market Manager also must find appropriate vendors that grow and offer a variety of foods that balance nutritionally to offer consumers the widest range of healthy foods possible.

Some farmers' markets have boards of directors who hire managers and decide if the market will sell only organic foods or not, which often creates a problem because many small farmers grow organically but do not get certified because of the expensive and complicated government application process.

Another critical decision to be made is whether the market will allow only local (say, in a five-mile radius) growers and vendors or allow others from farther away. Sometimes and in some climates, farmers' markets

would close if they could not include vendors from outside the close geographic area.

Many Farmers' Market Managers include artists, woodworkers, egg ranchers, jewelry makers, seamstresses, pie bakers, and preserve cooks in their market lineups to augment offerings and make more money, especially during holiday periods.

Some managers collect only set table or booth fees, while others take a percentage of each vendor's sales, which requires honesty in a situation where records of each sale are rarely kept.

The Farmers' Market Manager has to oversee cleanup and put the venue back to the way, or better than, it was when they arrived. The manager also puts on special events such as zucchini races, Halloween costume contests for children, musical performances, visits by school classes, and just about any other fun community event to attract and involve locals.

Salaries

Farmers' Market Managers make between $18,000 to $80,000 a year. Those managers who are independent and manage a single weekly farmers' market earn at the lowest rate since their income derives from vendors and not from a well-financed nonprofit foundation. Obviously their income increases if they can hold more than one market a week, which some do particularly during summer when crops are at their most bountiful.

Managers of large urban markets are paid higher salaries that sometimes come from market profits and sometimes from the nonprofit foundations that run some markets. Some Farmers' Market Managers are paid by a board of directors, sometimes by the local government, and sometimes as a percentage of the vendors' take on a particular day.

Employment Prospects

Employment prospects are good. Farmers' markets always need help, and turnover is great in some markets although rare in others. Boards of directors get in disagreements with managers, and may look for new staff. Managers who basically run their own farmers' markets stay for a long time. One can offer to help or to substitute for vendors who may be sick or absent for some reason. If there is no farmers' market in your area, start one.

Advancement Prospects

The only way for independent Farmers' Market Managers to advance is to add new markets to their repertoire, thereby multiplying their income. Some entrepreneurial managers attempt to run several markets in one county or multiple counties with varying success, collecting a percentage of vendors' revenues at each one.

Education and Training

Courses in management and human resources might be helpful, although personal experience at retail sales or growing vegetables, even on your patio or in your garden, will make managing a farmers' market easier. Bookkeeping and knowledge of nutrition, organic farming, and food balances will be valuable.

Experience, Skills, and Personality Traits

Working at other farmers' markets or for another creative retail operation is excellent training in dealing with the proud, individualistic personalities that turn up selling their pride and joy: the vegetables and eggs they have grown, and the knit caps, preserves, benches, and jewelry they have made. Diplomacy, patience, persuasiveness, ability to help people work together, knowledge of farming and food, and appreciation for arts and crafts will help managers tremendously.

Unions and Associations

Most states and some regions have their own farmers' market associations. The North American Farmers' Direct Marketing Association offered a national convention for sharing ideas until it spun into the Farmers' Market Coalition. The coalition is an information center and an advocate for North American family farms; it promotes farmers' markets and facilitates networking among farmers and farmers' market managers (see www.farmersmarketcoalition.org and www.familyfarms.com for more information).

Tips for Entry

1. Volunteer to work for a vendor or for a Farmers' Market Manager in your community and learn all you can.
2. Work at farming or growing to understand the business from the ground up.
3. Take marketing, human resources, and management courses at a local community college, as well as any agriculture marketing courses you can.

SCHOOL GARDEN FARMER OR DIRECTOR

Duties: A School Garden Director manages garden coordinators at schools within a school district and conducts any commercial sale of products, while a School Garden Farmer supervises learning programs and planting connected with the garden. The School Garden Director may also be responsible for raising funds for the program.

Alternate Title(s): Edible Schoolyard Gardener; School Garden Coordinator; School Garden Farmer; School Garden Director; School Garden Supervisor; School Garden Teacher

Salary Range: $0 to $30,000

Employment Prospects: Good

Advancement Prospects: Excellent, within limits

Best Geographical Location(s): Suburbs or rural areas where schools have space for gardens. But even urban schools can create school vegetable gardens by building boxes, bringing in dirt, and using lunch fruit and vegetable scraps to collect compost for fertilizer.

Prerequisites:

Education and Training—Some education training and experience with students, experience working in vegetable gardens or interest in learning about gardening, good English skills and a second language are helpful.

Experience—To guide a school garden project, one needs a couple of years working with vegetable gardens, experience working at a farmers' market, nursery work, and some teaching experience.

Special Skills and Personality Traits—Good organizing skills; love of the outdoors; love of teaching children; diplomacy to deal with school officials, parents, teachers, and students; passion for nutritious dietary habits; and an ability to create and nurture contacts and friendships with local farmers who can give advice and guidance

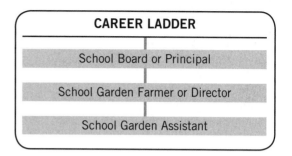

CAREER LADDER

School Board or Principal

School Garden Farmer or Director

School Garden Assistant

Position Description

School Garden Directors and Farmers work together to coordinate development and management of school vegetable gardens, as well as teaching students about how to garden and the value of raising food from the ground up.

The garden director first works with the school district to help the staff and school board understand the importance of teaching children how to grow food, particularly where students believe carrots grow in cellophane bags and milk grows in plastic-coated paper cartons. This person has to find financial support for the gardens, either from school officials or from outside sources such as local farmers or foundations, with the hope that eventually the gardens will pay for themselves with sales of garden products to local restaurants after school needs are met, sales to students and parents to take home and often has to report finances to the school district officials.

The School Garden Farmer may be a teacher at the school or a paid outsider with expertise in vegetable growing who actually supervises teaching students about growing food and takes responsibility for the gardening practice itself and finding and coordinating garden volunteers.

All of these jobs focus on guiding students through propagation and seed collection, planting, cultivation, irrigation, discussion of the value of organic gardening and eating, and maintenance of the garden, including helping to structure teaching plans on the benefits and methods of serious gardening.

The garden director also should create good communication with the school community and general community as well as garden volunteers, create events around the garden such as celebrations of planting and harvest, and attract and coordinate visits with and from the media.

Salaries

School Garden Directors and Farmers may have widely ranging salaries. In some cases, a volunteer will oversee the program or an individual garden, ranging from garden club members to master gardeners.

In some schools and school districts a teacher might receive a stipend to oversee the edible school garden, or a school district might fund a director, a coordinator, or even individual school farmers.

Hence, pay might range from $0 or $1,200 to $30,000, which might also depend upon whether the edible school garden is farmed for a season or year round. Members of the school community or surrounding residents might care for the garden during school vacations and reap the benefits—and the vegetables—which they might consider enough payment for their work.

Employment Prospects

School vegetable gardens are increasingly popular throughout North America as both teaching tools and sources of healthy food for students. Many school districts are considering school vegetable gardens but most have not yet developed them. This leaves lots of prospects for garden entrepreneurs.

More and more schools are considering or planting school vegetable gardens for both educational and kitchen use. If your school or school district does not yet have a school garden, propose one to school officials and go through the steps recommended above, basically creating your own job. Such opportunities can develop into good jobs for garden entrepreneurs. There is also the possibility of working for a percentage of profits from a production garden.

Advancement Prospects

A School Garden Director or Farmer can start with one garden at one school and increase his or her responsibility and salary by developing gardens at more schools and for more school districts. This person can move up further to coordinating school vegetable gardens in a whole school district, or at school districts throughout one county or more. A person could also specialize in developing learning gardens at private schools, charter schools, and for home school networks, or coordinate school gardens in several school districts.

Education and Training

While no particular education or training is required for School Garden Directors and Farmers, some education and horticulture courses, experience with students, experience working vegetable gardens even on a home scale are important. English and a second language could be helpful.

Experience, Skills, and Personality Traits

Experience growing vegetables, working in a farmers' market, nursery work, some teaching experience, or experience working with children will be handy. Love of the outdoors, a passion for teaching students the value of good food and where it comes from, enjoyment of solitary work, and a willingness to get dirty will be valuable. Organizational and diplomatic skills and abilities to create and nurture contacts and friendships with local farmers, potential donors, and customers will also lead to success.

Unions and Associations

A primary source of information and support is the Chez Panisse Foundation, created by Alice Waters, owner of Chez Panisse Restaurant in Berkeley, California. Waters and her foundation started the Edible Schoolyard movement (www.chezpanissefoundation.org).

Tips for Entry

1. Volunteer or get an entry-level job, even if it is just watering plants, at a local nursery and learn about plants and vegetables.
2. Take beginning courses in farming or horticulture at a local community college.
3. Volunteer to work at an existing school garden or for a local organic farmer who uses labor-intensive practices.
4. Become friendly with school administrators, teachers, and parent-teacher organizations.
5. Propose a new school garden where one is needed.
6. Web sites with information include the School Garden Start-Up Guide (celosangeles.ucdavis.edu/garden/articles/school_startup_guide.html); the Edible Schoolyard (www.edibleschoolyard.org/howto.html); California School Garden Network (www.csgn.org); School Garden Registry (www.kidsgardening.com/school); and Canada's Office of Urban Agriculture (www.cityfarmer.org/schgard15.html).

GOVERNMENT AGRICULTURAL ADVISER

Duties: Help local small and large farmers or growers by giving advice on how to grow healthy crops, how to develop their crops into useful food or other products, provide information on government regulations and how to package and market products safely, as well as which trade shows might be a good place to display or sell their products. The roles of state and county ag departments and marketing advisers vary by state and county.

Alternate Title(s): Government Ag Adviser

Salary Range: $70,000 to $135,000

Employment Prospects: Limited at the state level, because not all states offer this position, but most counties have agricultural commissioners or the equivalent.

Advancement Prospects: Limited

Best Geographical Location(s): Agricultural states that offer the position, or in ag counties throughout the country. State agricultural advisers of any kind are often headquartered in the state capital, although in larger states they sometimes have satellite offices in the heart of farm country or in a big city where the state has other offices. Regional product associations are usually located where the products are grown, and county agricultural offices usually are in the county seats.

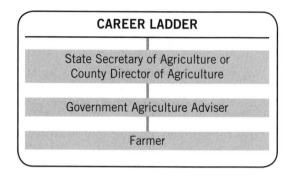

CAREER LADDER

State Secretary of Agriculture or County Director of Agriculture

Government Agriculture Adviser

Farmer

Prerequisites:

Education or Training—A college degree in agriculture, agricultural marketing or management, marketing, or communications would be advantageous.

Experience—Get marketing experience, agricultural or farming experience, or try food-related marketing.

Special Skills and Personality Traits—One needs the ability to keep up with the latest requirements and technologies of food product production, a deep curiosity and passion for agriculture and agricultural products for both business and consumers, organizational skills to coordinate information, an ability to get along with a wide range of people, and a deep commitment to promoting agricultural businesses.

Position Description

Some state agriculture departments give advice to farmers and growers on regulations and product development, and facilitate exposure and sale of those products abroad. In a few states where there is a state agricultural marketing adviser, that person may actually travel around the world to market his or her state's products.

County agricultural advisers may be able to give more direct advice to local farmers since they tend to have more knowledge of local agricultural products and growing conditions.

Such government advisers sometimes offer expertise on what are called value-added products, meaning side products to be made from the food farmers grow, beyond selling their vegetables or fruits directly. Exam-

ples include apple butter or juice from apples, almond butter and almond milk from almonds, wreaths made from pruned grape vines, vinegars, olive oil, wines, jams and preserves from berry crops, or lavender cream from lavender.

Once the Government Agricultural Adviser gives the farmer or grower advice on regulations, the adviser might lead the grower or farmer to people and companies that process the foods into jarred products, ranging from jams to tomato sauce. Every step along the way to make value-added products creates business, and hopefully jobs and wealth, as well as taxes that would go into county and state government coffers.

Agricultural marketing advisers can also supply trade show contacts and schedules, dates when appropriate reports are due to state agriculture departments, how to get licensed and what the required licenses are for food, beverage, and condiment processors and packagers, and how to buy into county or state advertising publications or advertisements planned for magazines, newspapers, or online.

The state or county marketing adviser can give tips on what business help is available from the government agency, give general advice short of improving specific products, and sometimes supply sample press releases from other companies without writing them for an individual farmer or processor.

At large trade shows state agriculture marketing advisers may give favored placement to that year's newcomer products, producers, and growers, so these new businesses have to be able to make enough of their product to offer ample samples to entice retailers or restaurants to order their goodies. While sometimes expensive to attend, trade shows can offer great opportunities to learn about what other people are making, how they do it, how they market in person or online, and whether they sell wholesale or discounted online.

In some states, the agricultural marketing adviser might promote a cluster of new businesses in local or regional newspapers and radio shows, or can be a great resource for mountains of publications and Web sites with information about what quantities to plant and what food processors, packagers, designers, graphic artists, marketers and test marketers, and consultants are available for employ.

Salaries
Salaries for Government Agricultural Advisers can range from $70,000 to $135,000.

Employment Prospects
Prospects are limited because not all states have Government Agricultural Advisers, although many counties do have someone who performs this function. Often there are several local or state jobs in the agricultural field, which may include secretarial assistants, computer professionals, inspectors, and specialty crop advisers.

Local product associations that range from lettuce and eggs to nuts and poultry perform similar functions. Private county, state, and national farm bureaus also promote agricultural products, sometimes better than the government agencies do.

Advancement Prospects
Advancement is limited within state government strictures, through which one usually moves up slowly through the grade levels. There is more opportunity to advance within county agricultural agencies or local product organizations. An entrepreneurial marketer could put together a group of local product organizations to represent and increase his or her income with each added group.

Education and Training
A college degree in agriculture, agricultural marketing or management, marketing, or communications would be advantageous, along with background or courses in nutrition, dietetics, and food science.

Experience, Skills, and Personality Traits
One can enter the job ladder in a state agricultural marketing department as a secretarial assistant without a whole lot of experience, at lower salaries than a marketer. One can learn and work up the ladder once there.

Tact, passion for agriculture and its potential products, a strong desire to help people and give them information to better themselves, an ability to get along with growers, farmers, and retailers, and a great collection of contacts and e-mail lists accumulated from venturing out into the farmland and trade shows are all helpful.

Unions and Associations
The Grocery Manufacturers and Food Producers Association (www.fpa-food.org) offers information on employment possibilities, public requirements, regulations, and communication. The National Association for the Specialty Food Trade (www.specialtyfood.com) puts on several Fancy Food Shows every year in several locations around the United States.

Tips for Entry
1. Take any courses you can at a local community, junior, or state college in agriculture, agriculture production, organizational development, marketing, or communication.
2. Take any entry-level job in a state or county department of agriculture to get your foot in the door and learn. Aim for the marketing office if that is your interest.
3. Find a way to attend a Fancy Food Show to see the vast array of products offered, ask producers lots of questions, and try to find and meet a state agriculture marketing adviser.

SPECIALTY FOOD PRODUCTS

CHEESE MAKER

Duties: A Cheese Maker keeps up on latest milk products, orders and purchases milk, supervises production of cheese from delivery through wrapping and shipping, watches over product quality, trains Cheese Makers and apprentices, and occasionally markets cheeses.

Alternate Title(s): Head Cheese Maker; Production Manager; Assistant Cheese Maker; Cheese Maker Apprentice

Salary Range: Minimum wage to $50,000

Employment Prospects: Limited

Advancement Prospects: Limited

Best Geographical Location(s): Agricultural areas where cows, sheep, goats, and buffalo live

Prerequisites:

Education or Training—No experience or training is required to get foot in the door and start as an apprentice; a food chemistry degree or experience could help in large operations, but education and training requirements vary by position.

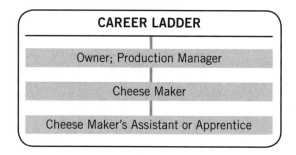

CAREER LADDER

Owner; Production Manager

Cheese Maker

Cheese Maker's Assistant or Apprentice

Experience—Food production experience in any field will be helpful, but working one's way up in cheese making is even better to learn all the steps in production.

Special Skills and Personality Traits—One should have a love of making food and creating edibles, have some scientific knowledge, a love for working indoors, the strength to lift heavy weights, an ability to work in damp conditions, skill at learning, managing, and teaching others to make cheese.

Position Description

There are at least three levels of Cheese Maker in any cheese producing operation, with responsibilities that vary according to the size of the plant or business. More and more artisinal cheese businesses are popping up throughout the United States and Canada.

In the few remaining union cheese making businesses, there are basically three to four positions including apprentice, assistant cheese maker, head cheese maker, and the rare master cheese maker or consultant. Nonunion commercial shops also have Cheese Maker helpers, computer specialists, and categories of assembly line jobs.

In large industrial cheese making operations there are rarely any unions, but there are lots of computer-run steps and many minimum wage workers.

The Cheese Maker or head cheese maker oversees all steps in cheese making from finding and purchasing the best milk nearby to delivery, cheese production, control of texture and appearance, packaging, and shelf life. The head cheese maker also hires, fires, and trains all cheese making personnel. The better the staff works together, likes the job, and gets along, the better will be the cheese it produces.

Myths abound about the origin of cheese 7,500 years ago. Credit generally goes to an Arab nomad or a Greek farmer, both of whom apparently saved milk in animal tissue pouches, resulting in the animal's rennin causing the separation of curds and whey, resulting in cheese.

Workers along the line participate in receiving milk, cooking it, pasteurization and separation of butter fat, mixing ingredients (sometimes by hand, sometimes by giant computerized mixers), tests milk, adds rennet, allows milk to coagulate into curds, separates curds to release whey, works to achieve desired firmness and texture, drains the whey, adds spices or coloring, presses curd into shapes, and wraps and places cheese on shelves to age. Aging is longer for dry cheeses such as Asiago and Parmesan, and shorter for fresh cheeses, including mozzarella.

The Cheese Maker also oversees important humidity and temperature controls in refrigerated rooms or in natural or constituted caves. Duration of minimum aging of various cheeses is regulated by government agencies.

Cheese making is both a repetitive and creative process, with each batch of milk and cheese product slightly different.

Some Cheese Makers raise their own sheep, goats, buffalo, or cows, which gives the Cheese Maker control of every facet of cheese making from what the animal eats and produces to what is done with the milk.

Salaries

Cheese Makers who work for someone else's company in a union shop often start as an apprentice for about $15 an hour or $31,000 per year and work their way up through assistant cheese maker, cheese maker 1, head cheese maker, and even consulting master cheese maker. Top salary is about $48,000. Union shops pay all benefits; nonunion shops often pay no benefits.

For a Cheese Maker in his or her own operation, pay varies according to marketing and sales success.

Employment Prospects

Employment prospects are limited, because cheese making plants are limited in number. More and more artisinal cheese making businesses are cropping up throughout the country, although many of those employ few people and are nonunion.

Large cheese making plants, which are mostly nonunion, hire employees to watch machines in computer-run operations or to line up labels, or inspect finished products.

Advancement Prospects

If one considers all levels of cheese making employees to be "Cheese Makers," there are lots of advancement prospects. A person may begin as a technician with no knowledge of cheese making, learn, and work his or her way up, but it takes several years. A full-fledged Cheese Maker has little prospect of advancing, because he or she is already at the top of the cheese ladder. One could advance by moving to a better cheese company or to a larger one, if that is one's interest.

Education and Training

Many large cheese companies require a college degree in food chemistry or food technology and preferably some experience in cheese making or related dairy industry field. Food and culinary courses at a junior or community college, or even in a culinary school, will be helpful, from food sciences to marketing. A few cheese making schools exist around North America.

Experience, Skills, and Personality Traits

A love of good cheese will definitely help one to become a successful Cheese Maker. A calm, low-blood pressure personality that doesn't mind repetition works well. A curiosity about food and cheese trends around the world, an interest in food science and chemistry, an ability to teach apprentices, perfectionist inclinations, and some experience in all steps of making cheese will help a person become a superior Cheese Maker. A working knowledge of English and Spanish would be useful.

Unions and Associations

The American Cheese Society (www.cheesesociety. org) is an organization of small cheese producers who focus on artisanal, handcrafted specialty or farmstead cheeses, often made organically from milk produced by organically raised animals. The American Cheese Society welcomes Cheese Makers, distributors, retailers, academics, writers, chefs, dairies, and cheese fans and offers a job bank, national festivals, cheese competitions, and definitions of American cheese styles.

The Teamsters Union (www.teamsters.org) represents about 35,000 Cheese Maker employees.

Tips for Entry

1. Check out both the American Cheese Society and Teamsters Web sites to learn as much as possible.
2. Through their Web sites, or even your local telephone book, find the cheese making facility nearest to where you live.
3. Go to that Cheese Maker, buy some cheese, take it home, and get an idea of what styles of cheeses they make.
4. Go back to the Cheese Makers, volunteer to clean up, sell retail at the counter if they have one, clean up after the animals if they raise their own, offer to sell at farmers' markets, or do anything that seems to need to be done to ingratiate yourself and learn.
5. Check out nearby cheese making programs at community colleges, culinary schools, or cheese making schools.
6. Contact your county farm bureau or county farm adviser to learn about local areas where cows, sheep, goats, and buffalo are raised and offer to work for those farmers.
7. Get a job in the cheese department at a local grocery store to learn what cheeses they offer and where the cheeses are made.

SAUSAGE OR HAM PRODUCER

CAREER PROFILE

Duties: A Sausage or Ham Producer procures the best meats, makes sausages or ham, and hires helpers, develops recipes, cures, smokes, and markets all meat products, and takes responsibility for health permits and sanitation.

Alternate Title(s): Charcutier; Salumi Producer

Salary Range: $25,000 to $60,000

Employment Prospects: Fair to moderate, with more opportunity in large sausage and ham production plants than in the growing subindustry of small artisanal salumi craftspeople and producers

Advancement Prospects: Good

Best Geographical Location(s): Areas near where pigs, sheep, and cattle are raised, food fan centers, and ethnic communities where sausages and ham are part of traditional diets. People from nationalities and ethnicities accustomed to eating sausages, such as German, Swiss, Austrian, Polish, eastern European, Irish, and Jewish immigrants, have long traditions of eating sausages so cities where they live are good places to produce sausages; boutique gourmet sausages are also becoming popular in several big cities and wine regions.

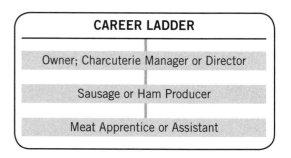

CAREER LADDER

Owner; Charcuterie Manager or Director

Sausage or Ham Producer

Meat Apprentice or Assistant

Prerequisites:

Education or Training—Education at a culinary school where there are meat processing and production courses; training on the job in butchering, recipe development, and marketing; or courses in growing animals in an agricultural school or program

Experience—Recipe development, work with meats, or any food preparation experience would come in handy.

Special Skills and Personality Traits—Liking pork products comes in handy, as does the ability to stand chilly work conditions, interests in recipe development and creativity, some tolerance of repetition, and physical strength for lifting.

Position Description

Companies that produce sausages, salumi (sausage or cured meat), and ham range from enormous factories to practically cottage industries. Pork sausages traditionally made use of pork trimmings, fat, some fillers, salt, and occasionally preservatives packed into a casing. Turkey, duck, chicken, beef, veal, and lamb are also used to make sausage, and fillers might include soy flour or dried milk solids to stretch or give body to the contents. The longer sausages are dried, the firmer they become. A sausage with a larger diameter will remain moist longer than one that is smaller, so smaller sausages can dry faster.

Salumi is an Italian word that means (usually) hand salted and cured cuts of meat or sausages made mostly from pork. These include various salami from lamb or pork, coppa (spicy cured pork shoulder), cappicola, lomo, lardo, Speck, chorizo, mortadella, salametto, bresaola (air-dried beef), prosciutto, culatello, sopressata (dried pork sausage), chorizo, benita, guanciale, jamon Serrano, and pancetta.

Charcuterie, a French word, also includes pork specialties such as pâtés, rillettes, and galantines. *Affettati* in Italian means approximately the same thing as charcuterie and includes ham.

Salame is a cured sausage that is usually made of ground pork, lamb, turkey or chicken. *Salami* is more than one salame. Salumi includes salami and other products.

Artisan salumi makers believe the best salumi, sausages, charcuterie, and ham come from the best raised animals, hopefully raised in open space, and nurtured and fed hormone-free food on sustainably managed land and that the same standards should apply to pigs, cattle, lambs, turkeys, goats, sheep, and chickens. Large computerized sausage manufacturers may seek other ingredients.

Sausage producers, whether making charcuterie, salumi, or bologna, must understand and be capable selecting the finest animals for the money and of butchering those animals to use every part to eliminate waste.

Hence, some not-so-appetizing trim parts of those animals go into sausages, leading to the trite saying that "There are two things you don't want to watch being made: sausages and laws."

The sausage producer, whether in a small artisanal salumi factory or in a giant midwestern ham or sausage processor, must make sure the entire operation keeps the most clean and sanitary conditions possible to prevent contamination of vulnerable ingredients.

The U.S. Department of Agriculture and Food Inspection Service have regulations and most states and counties have strict licensing requirements that dictate what materials sinks, counters, and processing machines as well as floors and floor coverings must be made of, regulations that also aim at health and sanitation. These requirements include hairnets and some gloves for workers, as well as white coats and occasionally boots worn over or instead of personal shoes.

Curing meats began when people discovered that salt preserved meat so it could be consumed long after an animal's slaughter, using animal parts that could not be used in other ways. The meat, organs, and even blood are ground, spiced, and encased. One needs a meat grinder, which vary tremendously in size, a meat thermometer, and some spices, with the finished product only as good as the ingredients.

The sausage producer must know the desired ratio of lean meat to fat and salt, which vary according to what type of sausage he or she is making. This person must also consider whether to use sodium nitrate to inhibit development of *Clostridium botulinum* or botulism, a deadly toxin, in addition to additions of herbs and spices such as peppercorns, cloves, nutmeg, cinnamon, ginger, basil, mustard seed, allspice, coriander, cilantro, thyme, marjoram, parsley, chives, garlic, and even some fruit bits.

Some sausage producers may have to butcher animals themselves to get just the ingredients they want and must know what to do with the finer cuts of meat, whether selling directly to consumers, retailers, or restaurants.

After curing, ham and sausages can last a long time without spoiling. Many home sausage makers in cold climates simply hang their homemade sausages from their basement or cellar rafters.

Like a composer, a sausage producer must know historic recipes in order to improvise and develop new sausage recipes and understand ingredients, techniques such as grinding, mixing, brining, smoking, and salting, and their scientific and culinary affects on the meat, fat, and other ingredients in the sausage. A Sausage or Ham Producer must also understand and enforce federal and local food safety guidelines and follow guidelines in labeling sausages.

In large plants a sausage producer has to operate large mixing machines and dump ingredients into the machine vats. In a small sausage or ham processing plant, the "big cheese" or sausage producer might be the only employee or may supervise others. In a large plant, union or nonunion and often immigrant workers work at one or a few tasks in the process on assembly lines and are required to comply with all health and cleanliness codes.

Someone has to hose down and clean workspaces and floors with antiseptics, eliminate contaminated air, and wear gloves and uniforms to keep dirt or germs from their street clothes from getting into the mix. The sausage maker trains all staff on how to make sausages and keep the plant cleaned properly.

In small sausage and ham producing companies, sometimes the sausage producer also has to handle public relations and marketing as well as sales calls on retailers or wholesalers and distributors. Distributors often require that a producer be able to make a minimum quantity so that the distributor can assure retailers that they can have a constant fresh supply. Often it is difficult for a new or small producer to meet those quotas.

Web site and mail order catalogues can be productive sources of orders and give a glimpse into seasonal or holiday demand directly from consumers. Sausages become more popular for breakfast around Easter and Christmas, hams become more desirable before Easter, Thanksgiving, Christmas, and New Year's, corned beef hits its demand peak in March around St. Patrick's Day, and then sausages zoom up in popularity during summer grilling season.

Salaries

A few large sausage and ham producing plants pay no more than minimum wage, and some have been closed down for mistreating employees, particularly non-English speaking new immigrants. Union shops pay more. A sausage producer with either a culinary or college degree may earn from $30,000 to $58,000 in rare cases. Sausage production owners earn whatever is left after paying for supplies, equipment, utilities, packaging, marketing, and salaries or wages, which may range from $35,000 to $100,000.

Employment Prospects

Fair to moderate, with more opportunity in large sausage and ham production plants than in the growing subindustry of small artisanal salumi craftspeople and producers. Artisanal sausages are creeping into supermarket coolers, with more and more interest growing in healthier, lower fat, and preservative-free products. Small producers are cropping up throughout the country, while most big producers are headquartered near stockyards.

Advancement Prospects

If one starts one's own sausage factory, advancement prospects are unlimited, although one is already at the top—maybe even at the bottom at the same time.

A person who enters the sausage or ham business with a college or culinary degree or meat product or butchering skills and experience should advance after being on the job and learning specifics of sausage making or ham treatments.

If a person gets a job making sausage products without any pertinent education or skills, he or she can still learn on the job, work different parts of the process by working each step, and rise up the kitchen ladder based on newly acquired technical skills.

Computer skills will help one advance rapidly.

Education and Training

Several courses of study can be handy in the sausage and ham businesses. Agricultural and culinary schools offer courses in meat science, processing, charcuterie, flavor, texture, balance, and lean-to-fat meat content.

Experience, Skills, and Personality Traits

A successful Sausage Producer should love sausage and have a palate for good sausage or friends, associates, or employees who have good flavor palates and creative recipe imaginations.

Sausage making can be repetitious and scientific, so one must be able to stand tedium and have the ability to follow recipes or formulas. One must also be strong and physically fit to lift and move quantities of meat, fat, and spices, or have the ability to operate machinery that mixes ingredients.

Computer skills will be most helpful to calculate and set measurements and machinery in large ham and sausage plants.

Unions and Associations

The United Food and Commercial Workers Union (www.ufcw.org) represents poultry workers, meat cutters, and packagers, sausage producers, ham smokers, and workers who make hot dogs, bacon, and sausage and process chicken. The International Association of Culinary professionals might also be helpful (see www.iacp.com).

Tips for Entry

1. Take classes in a high school, community college, or cooking school in meat and meat cutting, sausage making, terrines, pâtés, and charcuterie to learn the process and find out if you like it.
2. Get a job as an apprentice in a local sausage factory after visiting, making a tour, and observing. Be sure to notice the smell and decide if you like it or if it bothers you.
3. Get your foot in the door, learn all you can of every part of the sausage making or ham smoking processes, work your way up, and then start your own sausage factory.

CONDIMENTS AND DRESSING MAKER

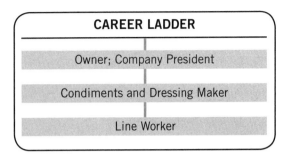

Position Description

Condiments and Dressing Makers make jams, jellies, mustards, salsas, pasta sauces, salad dressings, fruit and simple sugar syrups, vinegars, and chutneys. They have to develop recipes, design or get others to design packaging (meaning jars or bottles and labels), and develop or contract with a commercial kitchen for the production, warehousing, and distribution of their products.

Some Condiments and Dressing Makers develop successful businesses to produce and distribute other people's recipes or formulas and put those people's label on the product as if they had made it. Subsequently the producer might also handle warehousing and distribution to retailers and restaurants for the client. This way Joe Blow's Diner can sell its chocolate sauce with its own label, produced elsewhere under someone else's commercial kitchen license and certified health standards, without having to go to the expense of setting up its own bottling equipment.

Many Condiments and Dressing Makers start with a bright idea, often developed while working in a restaurant or even in their home kitchen or garage.

Condiments and Dressing Makers range from at-home jam makers who grow their own organic fruit, boil up a potful in their own kitchens or garages, and sell jams at farmers' markets in some geographic areas, to enormous corporate businesses with famous brand names that procure ingredients from all over the world and sell their products all over the world.

A Condiments and Dressing Maker has to develop, buy, or rent machinery or buy time on someone else's equipment to make full batches and standardize quality and formulas. One has to consider smooth versus chunky, thick versus thin, hot fill versus cold fill, container opening size, and foaming tendencies. If one is going to sell commercially, one needs to make enough product to enable distributors to keep shelves stocked, which may mean one line that produces 35 to 60 bottles per minute. Major companies such as Heinz, Nestlé, and ConAgra can produce hundreds and thousands of bottles per minute.

Ingredients need to be received, logged in with delivery and expiration dates clearly marked and noted, and used appropriately to avoid spoilage or waste.

After products are made, they need to be packaged, labeled, and sold, possibly beginning at farmers' markets and eventually in supermarkets. A Condiments and Dressing Maker needs to design or hire a designer to make a marketable label that sells the product inside the jar or bottle, have the labels printed, and find the right distributor or salesperson.

There are so many small Condiments and Dressing Makers, or people with ideas who have others produce for them, that space on specialty food market and supermarket shelves is quite competitive, and one might have to pay—or have their distributor pay—for good placement.

Many kinds of insurance and local permits are required, so one must consult local government officials for proper licensing.

Salaries

Condiments and Dressing Makers make from minimum wage or about $15,000 on production lines to $60,000 for a manager and $150,000 as owners or managers when business is good.

Employment Prospects

Almost every community has someone making sauces and condiments out of a home or on an assembly line, and many people try to start their own companies every year. Since small manufacturers often do "private label" bottling and packaging, meaning altering formulas and recipes or not according to someone's taste and putting different labels on the jars or bottles, one can develop a product without actually owning a production plant.

Learners can work for someone else's business and find out how recipes are developed, how ingredients are prepared, how they are bottled or packaged, how they are marketed and distributed, and learn enough to start their own business.

Or a person may well enjoy the work so much that he or she stays on, looking forward to the scents encountered each day at work.

Some plant work varies by growing season, so work may not be full-time.

Advancement Prospects

Excellent if one is ambitious and learns at every step along the assembly line, assuming the company succeeds. You can move up within a company or move to a higher position at a company where owners and managers have heard of your abilities.

Education and Training

Some line workers speak little English, have little education, and have little training, although they often have a strong desire to learn and succeed. Any cooking courses, especially food technology or food chemistry, will be most helpful. It's also easy to learn sauce making from the bottom up and become a manager. Bilingual skills would help.

Experience, Skills, and Personality Traits

Whether a line worker, manager, or owner, a Condiments and Dressing Maker must love the products, have a strong interest in perfection and a taste for good food, and understand how the whole operation and production system works.

The Condiments and Dressing Maker trains new employees and sometimes teaches them English and new skills within the plant, needs a good sense of humor, should not mind repetitious work, should be a good organizer, and should be open to new ideas and recipes whether they come from his or her own mind or from someone else. An extra element of intuition helps producers know what sauces, dressings, and condiments will please customers of the moment and sell well.

Unions and Associations

Condiments and Dressing Makers might profit from membership in the Association for Dressings and Sauces (www.dressings-sauces.org), which holds meetings and provides information on science, marketing, promotion, suppliers, and other resources.

Food technologists will gain from the Institute of Food Technologists (www.ift.org). The entire company might join the National Association for the Specialty Food Trade (www.specialtyfood.com), which puts on annual Fancy Food Shows in New York and San Francisco.

A manager might want to join the Association of Food Industries (www.afi.mytradeassociation.org) and any culinary employee is welcomed into the International Association of Culinary Professionals (www.iacp.com).

Tips for Entry

1. To work for someone else, take any job you can just to get your foot in the door. You can rise rapidly if you speak good English and learn fast.

2. Take any culinary, sauce and condiment, or food technology classes that may be offered at a local high school, community college, or culinary school.

3. Talk to career advisers at such a school and ask what realistic job placement services they offer, perhaps even before you enroll.

4. Get yourself into a specialty food show or the annual Fancy Food Shows in San Francisco or New York to observe, taste a wide range of products, and meet as many managers, producers, and owners as you can. Get their business cards, give some out yourself, and follow up with phone calls and e-mails.

5. Contact your county farm adviser or agriculture officer to find out where local small food companies are and as much about them as possible. These experts can also give you advice on what you need to do to meet local requirements to set up a new business.

FOOD AND FLAVOR CHEMIST

Duties: A Food and Flavor Chemist studies and focuses on the science and chemistry of foods, how to improve flavors and content, and how foods interact and deteriorate. Food and Flavor Chemists participate in developing recipes or formulas, as well as processing, preserving, and packaging.

Alternate Title(s): Food Technologist; Food Scientist; Flavorist; Flavor Chemist

Salary Range: $21,000 to $105,000

Employment Prospects: Excellent

Advancement Prospects: Excellent

Best Geographical Location(s): The best geographic areas to find work as a Food and Flavor Chemist is near a research university, wherever the federal government's U.S. Food and Drug Administration (FDA) is researching food science, or where there are large commercial producers of food products. The U.S. East Coast, midwest, and California offer the most jobs.

Prerequisites:

Education and Training—A college degree in chemistry, biochemistry, biology, food science, or chemical engineering, a master's degree in food science or a Ph.D. are required to do detailed research

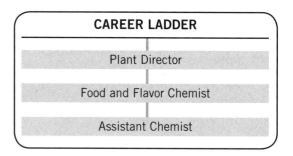

or to teach. The Society of Flavor Chemists also offers a flavorist training, and the Institute of Food Technologists oversees 50 schools with food science programs.

Experience—Any chemistry experience, particularly with processing companies, ingredient supply companies, baking and confectionary companies, retail food chains, or with dairy, meat, fish, fruit, and vegetable companies

Special Skills and Personality Traits—See food chemistry as art, be creative and curious, relatively outgoing and competitive, motivated, have excellent senses of smell and taste and have good odor and taste memories, work well under pressure, and enjoy precision and note taking

Position Description

Food and Flavor Chemists focus on the science and chemistry of foods, how to improve flavors and content to make the food taste the way the public expects it to, and study how foods interact and deteriorate. Food and Flavor Chemists participate in developing recipes or formulas, processing, preserving, and packaging, thereby "improving" foods and flavors chemically. They also study the processes of canning, freezing, heat processing, packaging, and appearance, taste, aroma, and freshness, as well as analyze, develop, and inject vitamins, preservatives, and minerals into food.

Often a potential Food and Flavor Chemist starts as a lab assistant under a more experienced person, maintain tasting notebooks while learning the characteristics of flavor materials individually and as they affect one another. Next comes an apprenticeship, an interview, and eventually certification as a flavorist by the Society of Flavor Chemists (www.flavorchemist.org).

Some Food and Flavor Chemists use their knowledge of how ingredients function and interact to work for companies that produce everything from fillers and thickeners to stabilizers and flavors for more efficient production and more appealing products.

Food and Flavor Chemists also study the properties of proteins, fats, starches and carbohydrates, additives, and flavor components, using both natural and artificial ingredients, sometimes to replace flavor removed by reducing fat or sugar.

Many Food and Flavor Chemists work in labs set up like a combination of kitchen and chemistry lab and equipped with the tools of both the culinary and chemistry fields, whether working for the government, for companies, or for universities.

Food and Flavor Chemists also work to lengthen the shelf life of food products, develop and improve packaging and storage methods, work with production plant engineers, make food product samples for testing, and make sure products meet government health standards.

Some examples of what chemists do include figuring out how to give cereals artificial flavors and colors and making corn chips taste like salsa when there are no fruit or other vegetables involved in the product, or how to put fiber back into cereals.

Salaries

Most Food and Flavor Chemists earn from $21,000 to $105,000, depending upon how long they have been researching. Starting salaries often do not reflect the investment made in advanced education. During economic contractions, food processing companies have shifted the research work to their suppliers, meaning food ingredient supply companies.

Employment Prospects

Prospects are excellent, if one is willing to go where the work is. During hard economic times, fewer new food products are created, but as soon as people have money to spend employment possibilities increase again. According to chip route delivery people, demand for chips and beer increase as cheap entertainment during difficult economic circumstances.

Food trends keep Food and Flavor Chemists busy looking for ways to reduce fat and trans fat content, add healthy coloring, or add coloring and flavors to appeal to the public to sell more of a product.

Advancement Prospects

With the appropriate university degrees, Food and Flavor Chemists can become supervisors, inspectors, regulators, marketing, sales, or even start their own research, testing, or food processing companies.

Education and Training

A college degree in chemistry, biochemistry, biology, food science, or chemical engineering, a master's degree in food science or a Ph.D. to do detailed research or to teach are required. The Society of Flavor Chemists also offers a flavorist training, and the Institute of Food Technologists oversees 50 schools with food science programs.

Experience, Skills, and Personality Traits

Chemistry experience is necessary, particularly with processing companies, ingredient supply companies, baking and confectionary companies, retail food chains, or with dairy, meat, fish, fruit, and vegetable companies. To succeed as a Food and Flavor Chemist it helps to see food chemistry as art, be creative and curious, relatively outgoing and competitive, motivated, have excellent senses of smell and taste, have a good odor and taste memories, work well under pressure, and enjoy precision and note taking.

Unions and Associations

The Society of Flavor Chemists (www.flavorchemist.org) works to advance the field by encouraging the exchange of ideas and personal contacts, and sponsors meetings, lectures, and symposia. It also sponsors a fellowship through the Institute of Food Technologists. The Institute of Food Technologists (www.ift.org) conducts meetings and exchanges information, job possibilities, training, and many other professional functions.

Tips for Entry

1. Enroll in any food science courses you can at a high school extension, community college, university, or culinary school.
2. Get a bachelor's degree in food science, biology, or chemistry.
3. Be willing to work at the lowest level in the food chemistry industry and to move wherever the jobs are.
4. Learn all you can and work your way up in a field of expertise.

BEVERAGES

WINEMAKER

Duties: Tests or tastes grapes in vineyard and decides when they should be picked; oversees the crushing of the grapes (the crush) and stages of fermentation and aging; schedules and perhaps does bottling, storage, and release of wines; oversees wine-making staff; sometimes pours at public events to promote wines. Other jobs in the wine-making field include bottling line worker, labeler, and quality control worker.

Alternate Title(s): Enologist; Vintner

Salary Range: $50,000 to $200,000, depending on region, size of winery, and experience

Employment Prospects: Limited, although there are new wineries every week

Advancement Prospects: Limited

Best Geographical Location(s): California, Oregon, Washington, British Columbia, and New York. Most states now produce wine, so there are jobs everywhere.

Prerequisites:

　Education and Training—A degree in enology or chemistry from one of the specialized university

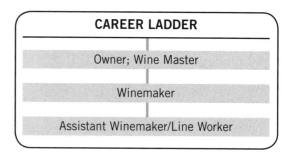

CAREER LADDER

Owner; Wine Master

Winemaker

Assistant Winemaker/Line Worker

programs, or focused courses at community and junior colleges. A few Winemakers have worked their way up from "cellar rat."

　Experience—Home wine making and experience at every level of the wine making process make the best Winemakers.

　Special Skills and Personality Traits—Excellent sense of taste and smell, ability to solve problems and manage people, ability to make accurate scientific observations, good communication and interpersonal skills, and possibly the abilities to fix machines and equipment and raise money from investors

Position Description

The Winemaker position varies depending upon the size of the winery, many of which start as a one-person operation or, to the other extreme, a corporate winery that makes millions of cases (each case holds 12 bottles) per year.

In a small or boutique winery (defined as less than 5,000 cases), the Winemaker may be hired by the owner or may *be* the owner. If a Winemaker is the owner, he or she is the chief cook and bottle washer, in fact. The position includes working with the vineyards from which the winery buys grapes, or working with the viticulturalist who oversees the winery's vineyards. In some cases, the Winemaker is also the winegrower, whose whole family participates in pruning, picking, crushing, aging, bottling, marketing, and distribution.

The Winemaker may purchase grapes from others, buy "juice" from growers or those with a "crush pad," or from wineries that cannot sell their grapes or juice. If one buys the juice and blends it to create his or her own wine, this person might be a *négociant,* rather than a

Winemaker, since négociants are not actually performing all of a Winemaker's functions.

Those functions include communicating with winegrowers (viticulturists) on what they are growing; whether they use organic, sustainable, or biodynamic growing methods; how their crops look for the harvest season including how the weather has affected the yield (with global climate change a strong factor possibly affecting vines that need frost as well as those that require hotter seasons where climates have leveled out); and what is the best harvest time for the grapes. Some growers and Winemakers can decide by walking into the vineyard and eating a few grapes, while others scientifically test the pH, sugar, and acidity in a grape and even run the statistics through a computer program to make their decision.

In a small winery the Winemaker supervises the crush and pressing of the grapes (no bare feet usually) and the settling of juice from pulp and the fermentation process, decides whether to use a gravity filtering process to remove solids, monitors the quality of the wine, places filtered (or unfiltered) wine in wooden casks, imported or domestic oak barrels, or in metal tanks, and decides when to move from one container to another.

The Winemaker makes plans for bottling and may even bottle the wine himself or herself, or he or she may supervise cellar personnel ("cellar rats") who perform all these functions. In a large winery a supervisor will oversee the bottling line, which can process from five to hundreds of bottles of wine per minute.

The Winemaker also may oversee or monitor vineyard and winery maintenance during the winter, confer with sales and marketing staff to make sure the type, varietal, style, and quality of the wines will match market demand, possibly oversee local, domestic, and export wine sales, select and train cellar staff, and even give tours and conduct tastings during which guests learn how to make wines and what their qualities might be.

Depending on the region of the country and microclimates within that region, pinot noir grapes may be picked first, followed by various white varietal grapes, then cabernet sauvignon and other reds. In geographic areas where wineries and vineyards abound, such as the Sonoma and Napa valleys, the September night air carries a heady aroma of wine essence from the grape crush.

In a large winery, the Winemaker may oversee several assistant winemakers who specialize in certain varietal wines, in addition to supervising large crews of cleaners, bottlers, label affixers, quality inspectors, packers, and even teamsters who cart cases of wine around a facility and onto delivery trucks.

Some Winemakers eventually become celebrities in certain circles and work hard to travel and promote their wines, occasionally even calling on distributors and retail stores and restaurants.

A Winemaker may become a senior winemaker, or a master of wine, who has passed a rigorous course and testing process (see www.mastersofwine.org for more information).

Salaries

Winemakers' salaries vary by size of the winery, region of the country, and the Winemaker's length of involvement in the wine industry. Wineries in California and New York pay best, with Winemaker pay in hugely popular cult wineries ranking up with the largest corporate-conglomerate salary. Median pay ranges from about $50,000 to $200,000, averaging far less than the romantic and glamorous image of the job might lead one to believe.

Employment Prospects

Most wineries employ only one Winemaker, although large operations hire several Winemakers, chemists,

and microbiologists. New wineries constantly open up new jobs at every level of the wine-making process.

Advancement Prospects

If a Winemaker owns the winery where he or she works, that person already holds the top position. Otherwise, Winemakers seem to move from winery to winery, much like television news anchors, sometimes motivated by higher pay, the prospect of having more control over the entire process, or the hope of working for a more exciting, innovative, or higher quality winery.

People working in various segments of the winemaking process always have the opportunity to learn, study, and move up within the ranks.

Education and Training

A college degree in enology from a specialized university program or a degree in chemistry or microbiology is usually required. Some community colleges in geographic areas where wine grapes are grown and wine is made offer excellent and practical courses that are helpful in both home and commercial wine making. One can also learn as a sort of apprentice to an accomplished Winemaker or wine master and work one's way up the wine ladder. The title of wine master or master of wine is also synonymous with sommelier (see www.mastersofwine.org).

Experience, Skills, and Personality Traits

A Winemaker must have on-the-job dirty-hands-on experience in wine making to attain the position because the experience becomes the knowledge. This person must have excellent senses of smell and taste, the ability to assess chemical problems and analyze and solve those situations, and have good communication and interpersonal skills.

A Winemaker must also know wine varietals, climate influences, and how to produce and identify classic wine styles. Depending on the size of the operation or the number of employees, he or she should also know how to fix pertinent machinery and know whom to call to fix a water main break; it may take mechanical talents to keep the machinery going.

The Winemaker should have organization and motivational skills to keep people and operations running smoothly and happily.

Unions and Associations

Many Winemakers belong to local winery associations in each wine region, such as the Sonoma Valley Vintners & Growers Alliance. Winery workers might belong to the Brewery, Winery & Distillery Workers union. The American Society for Enology and Viticulture, or

ASEV (www.asev.org), serves enologists, viticulturists, and wine and grape producers and researchers. An outgrowth of the University of California and California Winemakers, ASEV's membership includes professionals from wineries, vineyards, academic institutions, and wine organizations. ASEV conducts a scholarship program and symposia and publishes a newsletter.

Tips for Entry

1. Find a home Winemaker in your community and ask if you can hang out, learn, and help.
2. Look up your local winery association, talk to local Winemakers and ask if you can apprentice.
3. Take any job at a winery, from sweeping and hosing down to serving as cashier in the tasting room, just to get a foot in the door.
4. Take courses in enology, business, or viticulture at a community college to find out how much you are really interested.
5. Get a job—any job—in a retail wineshop to learn about varietals and regional wines from all over the world.
6. Enroll in a major wine program at a university with a specialty major in wine making, enology, marketing, or viticulture.

WINERY CELLAR MASTER

Duties: The cellar master supervises the actually making of wine at a winery, as well as keeping all production equipment in good shape and managing the entire plant operation and staff. A cellar supervisor manages the aging of wine.

Alternate Title(s): Production Manager; Assistant Winemaker

Salary Range: $40,000 to $50,000

Employment Prospects: Good

Advancement Prospects: Good

Best Geographical Location(s): California, Oregon, Washington, British Columbia, New York. Most states now produce wine, so there are jobs everywhere.

Prerequisites:

Education or Training—A high school diploma; community college courses in chemistry, science, math, and reading and writing in English will all be helpful. Vocational training or training on repairing

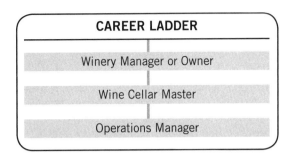

CAREER LADDER

Winery Manager or Owner

Wine Cellar Master

Operations Manager

and running large equipment, as well as computer skills, give an advantage.

Experience—Any experience in a winery, from the bottom up, is most valuable, as well as hands-on experience in food production or other bottling experience.

Special Skills and Personality Traits—Ability to evaluate practical and technical problems, make decisions, and act quickly, as well as openness to consulting others. Both physical strength and love for operational details will bode well.

Position Description

In a small winery, the owner might perform all functions of winemaker, Winery Cellar Master, and general cleanup and bottling crew. In a larger winery, with more tiers of functions and employees, the cellar master runs the winery mechanics while the winemaker oversees the winemaking itself. The cellar master's duties might vary according to which duties the winemaker wants to delegate to the cellar master.

In preparation for receiving grapes at harvest time, the cellar master makes sure all receptacles, vats, tanks, and barrels are in perfect shape, clean and free of outside matter. The cellar master and crew wash out all tanks and barrels; some have switched to steam cleaning, which saves about two-thirds of the water consumption per barrel. Other wintertime duties include making all mechanical repairs and checking all sanitary regulations and preparations to be ready to go when the grapes come in.

When the grapes arrive, work becomes extremely intense, sometimes affording workers little sleep. Once the crush begins, timing is important. The cellar master supervises the transportation and unloading of grapes, oversees the actual crush and pumping of juice and

residue, and generally manages this whole part of the winemaking cycle.

As the wine develops in tanks and barrels the winemaker makes decisions about how much oxygen should be allowed to affect the juice, and the cellar master carries out the winemaker's orders. Meanwhile, the cellar master makes sure the crew thoroughly cleans and repairs delivery and crush equipment.

The winemaker makes decisions about blending of varietals, filtering, and other quality challenges, and the cellar master executes the winemaker's orders and gets the work done, either personally or by overseeing a crew.

The Winery Cellar Master directs and manages the maintenance and use of bottling equipment, whether on-site or at another plant. If on-site, the cellar master makes sure all hoses and piping are in good condition and clean in order to move wine from barrels and tanks and into the bottling line.

Cellar masters actively train new crew members, often including an assistant cellar master.

In a small boutique winery, friends and family may put corks in the full bottles and affix labels by hand. In a large winery, computerized assembly line equipment does the bottle washing and sanitizing, corks the bottles, sticks on labels and places bottles in shipping boxes under the supervision of the winemaker or cellar master. Bottling line workers constantly inspect every step of the process, and the cellar master or other supervisor inspects the bottling line.

Salaries

Winery Cellar Masters make somewhere between $40,000 to $50,000, depending on the size and quality of the winery, their experience, and their skill. Some cellar masters only work seasonally, while others work year-round.

Employment Prospects

With wineries opening and being sold throughout North America, Winery Cellar Master jobs open up all the time, although some employees stay forever at one winery.

Advancement Prospects

A cellar master can progress up the winery ladder into almost any department since this person knows wine production inside out. Hence, advancement prospects for assistant cellar masters are also good. A cellar master might advance as well by moving to a better or larger winery where he or she might gain more respect and higher pay.

Education and Training

A general, practical education that includes math, science, computers, and some mechanical training are necessary. English language is a must, but Spanish may come in handy. Some vocational courses in equipment and mechanics would also be useful. On-the-job training and learning from those who know more from practical experience is another key to success.

Experience, Skills, and Personality Traits

One can work one's way up to cellar master even by starting at the very bottom of the winery ladder, whether by pruning vines, hosing down tanks, or shoveling dirt. The more winery or food processing experience that involves machines the better.

A cellar master has to have talent and skills to work with machinery, be able to tolerate damp conditions, have person-to-person management skills and the ability to motivate others, and a personality that thrives on stress. This person must also like the smell of wine, love precision, and be passionate about winemaking and his or her particular winery.

Unions and Associations

Few wineries are unionized but in those that are, workers may belong to the Winery, Distillery and Allied Workers division of the United Food and Commercial Workers International (www.ufcw.org).

Most wine regions or counties where wine is grown and produced have local trade associations.

Tips for Entry

1. Volunteer to work crush or take any low-level job in a tasting room or anywhere else in the process just to get your foot in the door.
2. Take pertinent classes at local high school adult programs, community college, junior college, or university with math, science, biology, chemistry, or just technical and mechanical courses to prepare you for work in a winery.
3. Visit wineries, ask questions, talk with the staff, and learn anything you can, including about potential job openings.

WINERY CHEMIST

CAREER PROFILE

Duties: A Winery Chemist may test grapes in the vineyard to determine the perfect time for harvest, tests the juice during the crush and in the tanks and barrels, and sometimes does high-tech chemical analysis on grapes, water, and other materials to tweak the wine as it ferments.

Alternate Title(s): Wine Analyst; Lab Manager

Salary Range: $35,000 to $60,000 if full-time

Employment Prospects: Limited

Advancement Prospects: Fair

Best Geographical Location(s): California, Oregon, Washington, and other wine growing and producing areas

Prerequisites:

Education or Training—Often a bachelor's degree in chemistry, food chemistry, biochemistry, or biology is required. On-the-job training adds to one's qualifications.

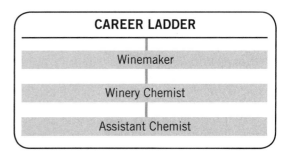

CAREER LADDER

Winemaker

Winery Chemist

Assistant Chemist

Experience—Sometimes one to five years' wine, food, or environmental lab experience are required.

Special Skills and Personality Traits—A Winery Chemist must be passionate about scientific research and methods, get a thrill out of solving chemical, scent, and flavor problems, not mind damp conditions or chemicals in the air while enjoying repetition and working alone.

Position Description

Some wineries have a Winery Chemist who may analyze the grapes on the vine to determine if the sugar content, acidity, alkalinity, and total acid are at peak level for picking and starting the wine-making process. At some other wineries, the owner or winemaker simply goes into the vineyard and tastes the grapes. One method is scientific, the other is more artistic and dependent upon the taster's palate.

Where a chemist performs these functions, that person watches the sugar rise, acid fall, and pH levels increase. Most large wineries, and many small wineries as well, post all of this information on specialized computer programs that tell the chemist and winemaker when the perfect harvest moment is expected or arrives. All of these factors will vary according to the grape varietal and kind of wine it will be used to create. Timing is crucial.

The Winery Chemist keeps testing for sugar, acid, and pH throughout the process as the wine ferments. The chemist and winemaker examine the wine several times a day to check the sugar in bottling tanks, in storage, and in bottles, as well as how the wine holds up to cold and heat to make sure it is stabilized before it leaves

the winery in bottles. The chemist tests for malolactic bacteria, foreign matter, and percentage of alcohol and monitors quality control. The chemist also operates and maintains laboratory equipment, interprets data, and reports on his or her findings.

In one extreme case, one California firm uses computer programs to analyze the chemicals that give wine its taste, aroma, and texture and tells winemakers how to alter their wines to attain high scores by critics. Most wineries shun such analysis in favor of the art of wine making and wine growing, with some returning to organic and even biodynamic growing and wine-making practices.

Some Winery Chemists occasionally help with special winery tours to explain the wine-making process to visitors.

Salaries

Winery Chemists' salaries in western wine regions are higher than throughout the rest of the country, and usually range from $35,000 to $60,000 if working full time. Many wineries hire chemists only when needed, so their pay at each winery might be much lower, in the $20,000 to $35,000 range.

Employment Prospects

Employment prospects for full-time Winery Chemists are limited. Often in a small winery the winemaker or cellar master performs the chemist's functions, which eliminates the job. The wineries that employ full-time chemists also have assistant chemists, some of whom work seasonally. Most job opportunities are in large wineries, most of which are well known.

Advancement Prospects

A Winery Chemist might move up to assistant winemaker or winemaker, either through formal classes or on-the-job learning. Another way to advance is to move to a larger, better, or higher-paying winery.

Education and Training

Often a bachelor's degree in chemistry, food chemistry, biochemistry, or biology is required. On-the-job training adds to one's qualifications. One can also learn the narrow field of wine chemistry at community colleges with winemaking courses or in an enology program at a university.

Experience, Skills, and Personality Traits

Some of the larger and more mechanical wineries require one to five years of wine, food, or environmental lab experience. A Winery Chemist must have knowledge of pertinent computer programs or have the aptitude to learn them quickly.

A Winery Chemist must be passionate about scientific research and methods, get a thrill out of solving chemical, scent, and flavor problems, not mind damp conditions or chemicals in the air, enjoy repetition, scientific accuracy, keeping meticulous records, and working alone.

Unions and Associations

Few wineries are unionized but among those that are, workers may belong to the Winery, Distillery and Allied Workers division of the United Food and Commercial Workers International (www.ufcw.org).

The American Society for Enology and Viticulture (www.asev.org) publishes a newsletter, hosts a wine and grape symposium, and grants scholarships to students.

Tips for Entry

1. Take any job you can in the lab, including hosing down the floor, to get your foot in the door.
2. Take any job at all in the winery, including in the tasting room or office.
3. Take classes at a local high school adult program, at a community or junior college, or at universities in biology, chemistry, viticulture, wine making, or any science to prepare yourself.
4. If there is a food processing plant but no winery in your area, get a job there as a chemist or biologist to see how you like the field. If you are still passionate about wine chemistry, move to a geographic area where there are many wineries to increase your potential job possibilities.
5. Check out various agencies and Web sites that specialize in winery jobs, such as www.winejobs.com, www.boltstaffing.com, or www.napasonomajobs.com.

WINERY PUBLICIST

Duties: Works with winery staff and executives to market and publicize the winery, pitches "free" stories to television and radio stations, magazines, and newspapers, and occasionally writes advertising copy. Some publicists also organize publicity-oriented winery events to create press-worthy publicity, travel to promote the winery's products, and represent the winery at trade shows and tastings.

Alternate Title(s): Winery Marketing Director; Advertising Promotions Director or Coordinator; P.R. (Public Relations) Coordinator

Salary Range: $30,000 to $80,000

Employment Prospects: Limited to good

Advancement Prospects: Good

Best Geographical Location(s) for Position: Major wine-producing regions, although there are now wineries in every state

Prerequisites:

Education or Training—A college degree in marketing, advertising, communications, graphic design, English, journalism, or writing will be helpful. Marketing or writing for any company,

especially in the food and wine industries, will provide training.

Experience—Press release writing, journalism experience, or writing advertising copy; word processing experience (meaning writing on a computer); public speaking experience, event planning, and some knowledge of the wine industry and wine varietals should help.

Special Skills and Personality Traits—Passion for the wine industry and a winery's product are essential, along with the ability to shuffle priorities as needed; great social and verbal skills, writing skills, and computer skills including MS Word, Excel, PowerPoint, Outlook, and Publisher.

Position Description

A Winery Publicist's duties vary widely from staging wine-tasting events to writing press releases, leading groups of visitors on tours, consultation on label, logo, or image design, or traveling around the country introducing a winery's wines at trade shows or winemaker dinners, a popular method of reaching wine aficionados.

A Winery Publicist creates the winery's image or "brand" and decides how to appeal and sell to various audiences, keeping in mind that the winery must stand out compared to thousands of others. To do this, the publicist works with the winemaker, winery owner, and webmaster to interpret and maximize their wine's qualities and appeals through labels, brochures, postcards, press releases, online and print newsletters, and social media and advertising copy for both the winery's Web site and print ads. The publicist also designs, writes, assembles, and distributes press kits, and develops relationships with wine writers.

Winery Publicists send out press releases via e-mail and printed snail mail to announce new organic or sus-

tainability standards, new winemakers or other significant staff or ownership changes, early or late harvests, new wine releases, awards and medals won, events such as big public holiday celebrations or small exclusive winemaker dinners, and even the acquisition or death of the winery's pet dog.

A Winery Publicist might decide or execute someone else's decision to put on a party or press conference to announce an important development. The publicist should be in on every step of the event's organization in order to create the proper image, sales, and news coverage, from invitations, publicity, and decor to what food should be served with the winery's wines. The publicist might even serve as host of the event, or he or she could easily take a behind-the-scenes functioning position to highlight the winemaker or owner.

If the winery does not have an event planner or hospitality director or hire a contractor, the publicist might make all arrangements for events, from selecting decorations to hiring a caterer, ordering rental equipment, and hiring musicians, and afterward publicizing the event and who attended.

Some publicists connect with industry trade associations, appellation or county vintners' associations, local chambers of commerce, and serve as liaison for and even demonstrator of the winery's products at local events to promote tourism. Some even join the local tourist board or association to represent the winery or themselves.

At some wineries, the publicist also coordinates the wine club membership, by which those who pay to join receive an agreed-upon number of bottles per month or quarter from the winery. Working with the sales manager, the publicist might also write and produce the winery's online and printed catalogues and sale announcements.

Winery Publicists might also put together gift baskets for VIP presents or for sale and oversee printing the winery's image and logos on everything from wineglasses to tote bags to baseball caps to sweatshirts and corkscrews.

The most successful Winery Publicist will be one who has worked other jobs within the winery and who writes press releases so well for specific purposes that a journalist, editor, or news reader does not need to do anything for it to be ready to print or read.

Salaries

Winery Publicists can make from $30,000 to $80,000 or more depending upon the size of the winery, its budget, its location, and its popularity. A publicist with an excellent reputation for "making" wineries may earn more to put a new winery "on the map" or rescue an older one that is in trouble. Some publicists have arrangements by which they make commissions from wine sold at specific events. Health and other benefits vary by winery.

Some Winery Publicists work for agencies in wine regions that handle several winery accounts.

Employment Prospects

Only one or two people, if any, work as publicists in each winery. One can always start one's own publicity company and start by publicizing a winery or two for free just to get started and gain a positive reputation.

Advancement Prospects

A publicist's role might expand as the winery grows, whereas some winery owners may think a publicist has done so well and made them so famous that they don't need the publicist anymore.

Publicists can move up in management, especially if they have trained in many aspects of the business, or move to a larger winery where the position pays more.

Education and Training

A college degree in marketing, advertising, communications, graphic design, English, journalism, or writing will be helpful. Marketing or writing for any company, especially in the food and wine industries, will provide training.

One can also learn these specific fields in community and state colleges, as well as earn degrees in hospitality or tourism with an emphasis in publicity.

Experience, Skills, and Personality Traits

Public relations and advertising experience in any field will be helpful, as might be teaching experience, because a publicist basically teaches the public and media about a product. A good publicist should be able to envision questions the public or media will have and answer them. Passion about the wine and winery, a love for creating fun or interesting events and media products, availability for working odd hours at events, and general enjoyment of working with the public will be helpful. Computer skills are a must.

Unions and Associations

Local tourism bureaus, state and local winery and vintners' associations, advertising and media clubs, local food and wine groups, and chambers of commerce provide the best networking opportunities for publicists.

Tips for Entry

1. Take any courses available in adult education, community or junior colleges, or state universities to learn how to write, publicize, or otherwise communicate.
2. Take classes in winery management or even science classes to learn how the business works.
3. Ask a winery publicist if you can work as an assistant or even as an intern to learn the job.
4. Get an internship at a local newspaper to learn how to write real news stories, thereby picking up the format and content editors really want.
5. Take computer classes so that you know how Web sites are constructed and managed.
6. Work in a winery tasting room or at any other job in a winery to learn all you can and get experience by volunteering to help the person in charge of publicity. Work your way up from there.

WINERY SALES MANAGER

CAREER PROFILE

Duties: Recruits, hires, trains, and manages sales representative team and its support staff; develops sales and pricing program; coordinates and supervises regional sales directors and staff; represents the winery at trade shows and tastings; sometimes thinks up, develops, and oversees special tasting events at the winery; works to retain sales outlets and develop new ones. May alternatively work for a wine or liquor distributor to sell or "carry" certain wine labels to outside retail clients

Alternative Title(s): Marketing Director; Wine Sales Representative; Marketing Specialist

Salary Range: $30,000 to $110,000, with outside commissions and commissions from tasting room sales

Employment Prospects: Fair to moderate

Advancement Prospects: Good to excellent

Best Geographical Location(s): Either in wine-producing regions if working at the winery or in big cities where distributors are located and lots of wine is consumed; a good deal of travel may be included

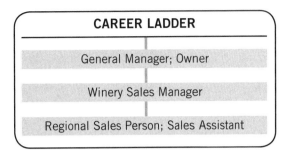

CAREER LADDER

General Manager; Owner

Winery Sales Manager

Regional Sales Person; Sales Assistant

Prerequisites:

Education and Training—College degree, preferably a bachelor's degree in sales and marketing, business, or communications

Experience—Two to five years' wine sales experience, although sales experience in other fields, especially food and beverages, is useful

Special Skills and Personality Traits—Good computer skills; leads by example and hard work; able to be a self-starter with good goals, a good communicator, and a motivator; negotiation skills; works well with a team; good writing skills; driver's license; able to pass drug screening test; enjoy travel and enjoy people and wine

Position Description

A Winery Sales Manager directs sales, and may also serve as marketing director at a winery, combining sales and promotion of the winery and its wines. This person develops a marketing plan by figuring out the winery's target market, which depends on the wine itself, its price, and how much of the wine will be produced, as well as where and how to market and distribute the wine, and submits the plan to the winery manager or owner (which could be the same person).

The plan and its execution will include the size and geographic territories of salespeople, sales goals by region and sales from the winery's tasting room, all based on what is available. Marketing plans need to be more aggressive in difficult economic times.

A large winery's sales manager usually hires, trains, and manages his or her team of "sales reps" who each have responsibility for a certain geographic territory. The sales manager may promote the wines throughout the country, while a distributor actually represents the winery's wines to large chain grocery, liquor, and big

box stores. If the winery has regional sales directors or reps, the sales manager will coordinate and motivate the reps to sell more and more wine, sometimes motivated on a higher sales commission for the sales manager, and make sure the sales reps know how to get the best shelf placement for the wines.

The Winery Sales Manager might organize sales trips featuring the winemaker to impress buyers and potential customers, bring those customers and sales reps to the winery for more intimate sales pitches, organize those events from winemaker lunches and dinners to luxurious stays at local inns, or organize winemaker dinners featuring local chefs who produce food best paired with each of the winery's wines served at the meal.

A Winery Sales Manager may represent the winery at trade shows and tastings; sometimes thinks up, develops, and oversees special tasting events at the winery; and works to retain sales outlets and develop new ones.

It might also be the sales manager's duty to enter wines in judging contests, show or pour tastes of the wine at the medal awards event, and generally cozy up to wine writers.

A wine sales manager may alternatively work for a wine or liquor distributor to sell or "carry" certain wine labels to outside retail clients.

In a small winery, the sales manager might also be the tasting room manager and event planner, oversee shipping and public relations, and personally travel throughout the country to sell the wine to buyers, sometimes accompanied by the winery owner or winemaker.

Generally, the Winery Sales Manager becomes an ambassador for the winery.

Salaries

Sales managers usually earn a base salary plus commission on sales, which may mean a commission on *all* sales, from the tasting room to major contracts with national outlets and big box chain stores. Earnings range from $30,000 to $110,000 and may run higher, depending on one's individual arrangement. Generally, the higher one's base pay, the smaller is the percentage or sales one can earn on commission; commission often ranges from 15 percent to 40 percent. In difficult economic times, the base pay may be lower and the commission percentage higher.

Employment Prospects

There seems to always be opportunity in sales for sales representatives, but not everyone can be the Winery Sales Manager. At most, there is one per winery. A sales rep who knows local restaurant clientele and has developed other solid contacts can always find a job selling wine.

Advancement Prospects

Good sales representatives always have the possibility of advancing to sales manager. Really good sales managers can work their way into winery management. They can earn more by moving to a similar level winery with better sales, higher price points, and more potential, or to a larger winery with greater sales.

Education and Training

Currently many serious wineries prefer salespeople and sales managers with a college degree, preferably a bachelor's degree in sales and marketing, business, or communications. Some of the finer points of sales techniques can only be learned on the job.

Experience, Skills, and Personality Traits

All sales experience is valuable, particularly experience in the fine food and beverage industries. A winery sales representative or manager must have a good taste palate and a passion for the wine in order to be able to discuss the wine's finer qualities. Of course sales techniques, solid knowledge of the wine and what it pairs best with, and concern for the customer's pleasure and buyer's success in selling the wine are important.

A successful Winery Sales Manager must also be able to communicate with and lead others on the team, have good writing and computer skills, a valid driver's license, a passion for travel, and the ability to pass a drug screening test.

A winery sales rep or manager should also have the physical strength to lift a case of wine (about 40 pounds) and have an interest in precise reporting and record keeping.

Unions and Associations

Since there are no unions for Winery Sales Managers, the best associations he or she can make are with local or regional winery and vintner associations, restaurant associations, and chambers of commerce. Donation of wines for charity and nonprofit fund-raisers and tastings is a great way to make friends, although such requests can become so great that the cost outweighs the benefits. But goodwill and good relations can hardly be replaced.

Tips for Entry

1. Get a job, any job, in a wineshop to learn all you can about wines, what goes into them, and where they come from. You will also meet people who are in the wine business.
2. Take marketing, sales, communications, and even computer courses at adult classes held in local high schools, community or junior college, or at a university.
3. Talk your way into an internship at a local winery or wineshop, possibly with the winery's sales manager, while you get your bachelor's degree or simply to gain winery sales experience. Some schools may give credit for on-the-job experience earned while attending their program.

WINE CLUB DIRECTOR

Duties: Develops memberships; determines wines to be included in monthly or quarterly shipments, what financial levels of membership (investment) might be, and what members get for those levels of membership; keeps extensive e-mail lists; designs e-mails and mailers to membership; keeps track of all orders received and shipments to members; with the winemaker and winery owner or manager, plans other offerings to members

Alternate Title(s): Wine Club Manager; Sales Manager; Mail-Order Manager; Online Sales Manager

Salary Range: $30,000 to $80,000, depending upon size of club and winery and commission rate

Employment Prospects: Good

Advancement Prospects: Good

Best Geographical Location(s): Wherever wineries are located, which is now throughout the United States

Prerequisites:

Education or Training—Marketing, sales, and communications courses or a college degree in

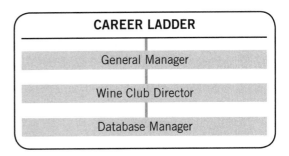

CAREER LADDER

General Manager

Wine Club Director

Database Manager

these fields will be helpful. On-the-job or self-taught online marketing are useful.

Experience—Any tasting room experience, online marketing, and knowledge of the winery's wines and clientele are important to understand target markets.

Special Skills and Personality Traits—Computer skills, including Excel or other spreadsheet software; great communication skills to convince customers to become wine club members and "own a piece" of the winery's future; a fun-loving and enthusiastic personality; and enough charm to woo people into a financial commitment

Position Description

A Wine Club Director develops private lists of wine fans who know and truly enjoy a winery's wines, works to expand that list and develop memberships, determines the wines to be included in monthly or quarterly shipments, what financial levels of membership (investment) might be and what members get for those levels of membership, keeps extensive e-mail lists, designs e-mails and mailers to membership, keeps track of all orders received and shipments to members, and, with the winemaker and winery owner or manager, plans other offerings to members.

Winery wine clubs are among a winery's most profitable efforts for these reasons: the winery is guaranteed certain sales, depending upon the number of wine club members; and there are no middle people, such as sales reps or distributors, so the winery makes all of the profit between its cost of making a bottle of wine and the retail price.

Wine club members benefit if they live far from their favorites wineries; they get to purchase wines at a slight discount that might not be available to nonmembers or outside the winery's tasting room; and they can

plan their wine budgets. Residents of several states cannot purchase via wine clubs because their state governments prohibit shipment of wine into their states, either for religious reasons, to try to prevent minors from purchasing, or to protect their own wine industry.

Small wineries use the wine club membership to enlarge their production, because they can use the projected or real income to develop and process wine and packaging. A small winery might have an employee or tasting room manager run the wine club until it gets large enough to require a full-time director.

When the Wine Club Director and the winemaker or owner meet to choose the wines to be shipped periodically, they consider wines that haven't sold well, "library wines" (fine wines saved for a long time), and new releases. Then the Wine Club Director creates a print mailer and e-mail to send to club members, collects members' payments by credit card, registers the orders, oversees shipping, prepares a sales report for higher-ups, and generally is the jolly communicator between the winery and winemaker and the club member.

The Wine Club Director also has to make sure the wines included in the shipment are the best they have to offer and will make the member proud to serve and happy to consume. A wine club is sometimes only as good as its last shipment, and the wine club director or manager gets much of the praise as well as blame.

Wine Club Directors occasionally set up special winemaker dinners, often catered by a local restaurant or caterer, to treat wine club members to special wines and foods as an extra benefit to membership. Other wine club member events can range from a Mexican Independence Day celebration to an annual Italian festival.

Salaries

Wine Club Director salaries usually start with base pay and add on commission for sales. Salaries range from $30,000 to $80,000 depending upon size of the club, the winery, and the commission rate, the last of which is negotiable. If the job is only part-time, the person might also work in another part of the winery such as the tasting room and earn more for that posting.

Employment Prospects

There is always room for wine marketers, because most (but not all) wineries want to sell more wine. The greatest opportunity is to find a winery that does not have a wine club and create one for it. One can also move from an existing job within a winery to creating or enhancing a wine club.

Advancement Prospects

If a person works for a winery that has no wine club, the potential to rise to Wine Club Director is great, with some initiative and computer skills. A Wine Club Director can advance within the winery by doing exceedingly well, increasing winery sales tremendously, and making himself or herself valuable. Such a person could work up the ladder to sales manager and even president of the winery, or move to a larger volume winery or to one that pays a higher rate of commission.

Education and Training

Marketing, sales, communications, desktop publishing, database courses, or a college degree in these fields will be helpful. Most of the pertinent classes are also avail-able at community and junior colleges. On-the-job or self-taught online marketing can work.

Experience, Skills, and Personality Traits

Any tasting room or marketing experience, online marketing, and knowledge of the winery's wines and clientele are important to understand target markets.

One should have good computer skills, including spreadsheet software, great communication skills to convince customers to become wine club members and "own a piece" of the winery's future, be fun-loving and enthusiastic, and have enough charm to woo people into a financial commitment.

A Wine Club Director should also have good writing and design skills to be able to develop a brochure, mailing, or e-mail that will instantly make the reader want to join the club or order wine. Enjoying people and having good verbal skills will help the Wine Club Manager deal with potential or complaining customers on the phone.

Unions and Associations

While there are no real unions or associations of Wine Club Directors, socializing in the winery's community always helps, whether by joining a chamber of commerce or a local winery or vintners' association or volunteering to pour your winery's wine at local charity and nonprofit events. Get to know other Wine Club Directors in the area, from whom one can learn plenty.

Tips for Entry

1. Take all pertinent courses at local community or junior colleges.
2. Visit local wineries and ask about their wine clubs, how they are run, and how they increase membership. Then compare notes and ask to intern with the Wine Club Manager.
3. Get a job in the winery's tasting room, either pouring and/or selling wine, to get to know the wines and the clientele and therefore the target market.
4. If the winery doesn't have a wine club, offer to create and build one. Wine clubs are among a winery's best sources of income and ways to develop new and loyal customers.

WINERY TASTING ROOM MANAGER

Duties: Manages the winery's tasting room and staff, oversees purchase of all non-wine merchandise, trains tour guides and tasting room personnel, and helps the sales manager and events people to promote, organize, and put on public events that attract people to the winery

Alternate Title(s): Hospitality Manager; Director of Retail Sales; Wine Educator

Salary Range: $15,000 to $60,000 plus commissions

Employment Prospects: Limited to fair

Advancement Prospects: Good

Best Geographical Location(s) for Position: Wine producing regions throughout the United States, keeping in mind that there now are wineries in every state

Prerequisites:

Education or Training—Some wineries require a college degree for tasting room managers, or practical experience in wine-making and the specific winery, or courses in marketing and communications.

Experience—Sales experience in any field, preferably in food or wine industries, or any time spent training and motivating staff

Special Skills and Personality Traits—Great communication and computer skills, a passion for wine and the winery where one works, great leadership qualities, skills to motivate people and build a team, an outgoing personality, ability to lift 40 pounds and stand around for hours at a time. Wineries often hire either attractive young men and women or retirees who can and want to work part time.

Position Description

A Winery Tasting Room Manager runs a winery's tasting room, which usually is its showcase to the public where visitors gain an impression of the winery, its wines, and the people who put their heart and soul into the wine. Visitors often travel from one tasting room to another sipping, comparing wine, and hopefully purchasing bottles of their favorites.

The tasting room manager assembles the best team possible to basically seduce the guest into tasting and purchasing wine, often including attractive young people or knowledgeable seniors who work part time.

Most sales in a tasting room are retail, and the winery makes all of the profit since there are no middle people such as wholesalers and distributors.

A tasting room manager helps marketing or other executives lure people to the tasting room, organizes special events such as winemakers' dinners, special festivals, barrel tastings, and any other event that will attract visitors who will buy wine.

The tasting room manager selects and trains all staff as the "face" of the winery to the public. His or her success, and pay, hinge on how well tasting room staff do, because everyone is on commission, including the manager.

The manager makes sure the pouring and sales staff in the tasting room truly knows what goes into each wine, can describe it, and can refer visitors to other local attractions including restaurants.

No job is too small for a successful Winery Tasting Room Manager, who, especially at a small winery, might occasionally have to wash wineglasses, wipe the counter, sweep the floor, or even clean the bathrooms. At the other end of the spectrum, a tasting room manager may also become a roving ambassador for the winery, pouring wine at charity or culinary events that gain excellent public exposure for the winery. A tasting room manager's hours may be irregular and include weekends and some evenings.

Winery Tasting Room Managers also set the staff's work schedule, salaries, wine discounts, decide whether staff members get a free bottle of wine with their paycheck if they meet or pass their quotas, and decide how many full- or part-time employees the tasting room should employ. Currently in major wine regions the trend is to employ as few full-timers and as many part-timers as possible to avoid paying health and other benefits to staff.

Salaries

A Winery Tasting Room Manager's salary ranges from $15,000 to $60,000 plus commissions on everything sold in the tasting room, from bottle stoppers to wine. Therefore it is in the manager's best interest to hire and keep happy the best sales staff possible, because he or she will probably make a commission on what they sell, as will the staff making the actual sale.

Employment Prospects

At most there is only one tasting room manager in each winery, although there are more and more wineries popping up throughout the country. In tiny boutique wineries the tasting room manager may be the spouse of the winemaker. Passion for the specific wines or for the wine industry may help one get started working in a tasting room.

Advancement Prospects

A successful Winery Tasting Room Manager has every opportunity to work up to sales manager, public relations manager, and even president of a winery. Or one can move to a larger winery with a larger base pay, better commissions and wine discounts, more tasting room staff and sales, and therefore more commissions. One can start as a clerk in a tasting room and work up to tasting room manager and beyond.

Education and Training

Many tasting rooms require a college degree, preferably in marketing or sales, communications, or hospitality. Some wineries require a college degree for tasting room managers, courses or practical experience in winemaking or the specific winery, or marketing and communications courses. Winery Tasting Room Managers must have a full knowledge of viticulture, the winery's wine-making process, its varietals and specialties, the winery's history, and the region's history.

Experience, Skills, and Personality Traits

Sales experience in any field, preferably in food or wine industries, or any time spent training and motivating staff help. Working one's way up the winery ladder, performing as many jobs in production as possible, can equip a tasting room manager with valuable knowledge.

Great face-to-face social, communication, and people skills, computer skills, a passion for wine and the winery where one works, great leadership qualities, motivational and team-building skills, an outgoing personality, and the ability to lift 40 pounds and stand on one's feet for hours at a time make the best tasting room manager candidate.

Unions and Associations

Local and regional wine, culinary, and restaurant associations provide excellent networking possibilities in a field where there is no union representation. Such mingling and exposure helps to make the winery more familiar and popular with potential customers and members of the food and wine communities.

Tips for Entry

1. Take some basic classes in wine-making and marketing at a local community college to bring yourself up to speed.
2. Visit tasting rooms and talk to tasting room staff to find the style of winery and wine that you like most.
3. Offer to volunteer or intern in the tasting room to get experience and learn about the winery's history and specialties.
4. Visit wineshops or even the wine department of a supermarket to figure out which wineries' wines you like.
5. If you don't live near a wine region, take a trip to a nearby wine region and spend some time learning as much as you can.
6. Take a job, any job, at a winery, learn on the job, and work your way up. The more you know the better.

VINEYARD MANAGER

CAREER PROFILE

Duties: Directs growing, cultivation, and maintenance of vineyards; turns a conventional vineyard into a sustainable or organic one as desired; coordinates with the winemaker and owners to schedule care of vines; oversees the vineyard crew and consultants; monitors water usage or dry farming; keeps up heavy equipment; schedules appropriate sampling or analysis of grape nutrients; estimates crop yield; maintains records; leads crew safety meetings; and coordinates with winery operations

Alternate Title(s): Viticulturist

Salary Range: $35,000 to $90,000 with benefits

Employment Prospects: Limited

Advancement Prospects: Good

Best Geographical Location(s): Wine producing regions throughout the United States, particularly on the West Coast

Prerequisites:

Education and Training—A bachelor's degree in viticulture is often required, along with knowledge of sustainable, organic, and conventional (chemical) farming practices, according to the winery's guidelines.

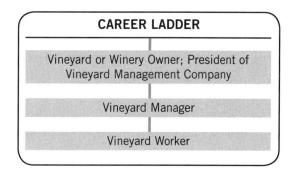

CAREER LADDER

Vineyard or Winery Owner; President of Vineyard Management Company

Vineyard Manager

Vineyard Worker

Experience—Most wineries or vineyard management companies require a few years of experience for a vineyard manager, although some start as pruners and pickers or perform other hands-on jobs, knowledge of which is vital.

Special Skills and Personality Traits—Fluency in English, Spanish, or other language; a love of working with other people as well as a love of the outdoors; and an appreciation for the art and craft of vineyard pruning, planting, grafting, and thinning will be handy, as will willingness to work long and odd hours seasonally.

Position Description

A Vineyard Manager directs vine purchases, planting, growing, cultivation, and maintenance of vineyards and may turn a conventional vineyard into a sustainable or organic one as desired. Wine can only be as good as the grapes that go into it.

The Vineyard Manager coordinates with winemaker and owners to schedule the care of vines; oversees the vineyard crew and consultants; monitors water usage or dry farming; oversees maintenance of all tractors and other heavy equipment; schedules appropriate sampling or analysis of grape nutrients; estimates crop yield; maintains records; leads crew safety meetings; and coordinates with winery operations.

Some of the detailed work the Vineyard Manager oversees includes pruning, planting, grafting, spraying (if used), hedging, leafing, thinning, management of cover crops planted to provide natural fertilization or bug prevention, and netting to prevent birds and deer from devouring the grapes.

Vineyard Managers also oversee all seasonal crews and work in the vineyard, teaching the workers the particular vineyard's standards and practice (which is where Spanish language abilities are often handy), stay up to date on the latest science and research in viticulture, attend seminars and sometimes speak at them to share information and learn, maintain a computer database, and help the wine-making team as requested.

Salaries

Salaries for Vineyard Managers usually range from $35,000 to $90,000 with benefits, depending upon the size of the winery and its vineyards and whether one works directly for the winery or vineyard or for a vineyard management company. The latter usually pays $10 to $15 an hour based on seasonal work.

Employment Prospects

Vineyard management job availability is fair, because some wineries hire only one Vineyard Manager, others hire assistant vineyard managers who may oversee one of many vineyards, and vineyard workers often move from one vineyard to another from south to north because of the weather.

Advancement Prospects

Vineyard Managers and assistant vineyard managers are extremely important to any winery. Good vineyard management means good grapes, which means good wine. A good Vineyard Manager can move up into other parts of a winery's management team or to a winery with more vineyards to earn more money and get a promotion.

One can also "advance" by starting a vineyard management company that employs vineyard workers and manages vineyards for several wineries or growers. Many wineries purchase grapes from vineyards owned by others and do not have vineyard managers.

Education and Training

A bachelor's degree in viticulture is often required, along with knowledge of sustainable, organic, and conventional (chemical) farming practices, according to the winery's guidelines. Often one should also be fluent in Spanish to communicate with some vineyard workers. It is also possible to learn on the job as a vineyard worker and rise to Vineyard Manager. Sometimes a Vineyard Manager also needs a state pesticide applicator license if such substances are used in the vineyard.

Experience, Skills, and Personality Traits

Most wineries or vineyard management companies require a few years of experience for a Vineyard Manager. Fluency in Spanish and English, love of working with other people, as well as a love of the outdoors and an appreciation for the art and craft of vineyard pruning, planting, grafting, and thinning will be handy, as will the willingness to work long and odd hours seasonally. A Vineyard Manager must be able to motivate a crew outside and get along with the inside staff and winery team as well.

Unions and Associations

There are no real unions for Vineyard Managers, although the United Farm Workers (www.ufw.org) represents some vineyard workers. Local vintners' and vineyard growers' associations offer great networking, seminars, contacts, and support.

Tips for Entry

1. Study viticulture at a community or junior college or at a four-year university.
2. Get any job available working in a small winery's vineyard to learn all you can or apprentice with an established viticulturist.
3. Get any job in a winery to get your foot in the door and slowly work your way toward the vineyard and toward your goal. The more you know the better.

BEER BREWER

Duties: Oversees making of beer and the fermentation process; supervises brewery workers, maintenance, and quality control; supervises bottling and labeling of beer once it is produced

Alternate Title(s): Brewmaster; Head Brewer

Salary Range: $27,000 to $130,000

Employment Prospects: Good

Advancement Prospects: Good

Best Geographical Location(s): Throughout the United States, especially where barley and hops are grown and breweries operate

Prerequisites:

Education or Training—A knowledge of beer styles and vocabulary, beer chemistry, and ingredients; knowledge of what goes into mass-produced beers as well as microbrews; a bachelor's degree in microbiology, chemistry, biochemistry, or related sciences or even marketing are sometimes required.

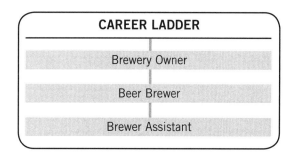

CAREER LADDER

Brewery Owner

Beer Brewer

Brewer Assistant

Experience—At least three years' on-the-job experience in brewing are required to ascend to brewer or brewmaster, whether in a microbrewery or in a large industrial brewery. Many jobs are available lower down the brewery ladder.

Special Skills and Personality Traits—Ability to taste lots of beer; self-motivation; good communication and team building skills, enjoyment of solving problems and multitasking; good computer skills; and enjoyment of working indoors. Spanish language skills could be necessary in a large brewery.

Position Description

The Beer Brewer or master brewer's duties vary by the size of the brewery. Generally, a brewer oversees the making of beer and the fermentation process, supervises brewery workers, maintenance, and quality control, and supervises the bottling and labeling of beer once it is produced. In a small brewery, the brewer might do everything, even sweep and hose down the floor. In a large brewery, the brewer or master brewer is more of a manager with beer-making knowledge and skills.

Most commonly, a brewer coordinates all the activities of the actual brewing process, leads a culturally and linguistically diverse team, hires and trains staff to perform each function of beer making and bottling, schedules beer making with sales and marketing, develops recipes for new beers, learns old beer recipes, and manages the ordering of all supplies.

The brewer also trains bartenders if beer is served or sold at the brewery, orders kegs and taps, and organizes cleaning schedules. On the fun and more public end of the process, the brewer represents the brewery at tastings, clubs, and conferences and often appears in the media.

There are many other jobs available in a brewery from line worker to heavy-equipment driver, as well as jobs in warehousing, marketing, administration, finance, and human resources.

Salaries

Brewers and brewery workers make between $27,000 to $130,000, depending upon the size of the brewery and size of the crew they supervise, or whether the brewer is also the owner with only one or a few aides. Large breweries employ many minimum wage workers, while the brewer or brewmaster in the same establishment can earn much more.

Employment Prospects

Employment prospects are good if you live near a large brewery. Microbreweries come and go as the economy ebbs and flows. Many of the country's largest breweries have production plants throughout the United States.

Advancement Prospects

Brewery workers can rise from the bottom of the barrel to the top by hard work, good language skills, and fast learning. Beer Brewers and brewmasters are at the top of the barrel already, so they can advance by moving into management spots such as marketing and executive positions, by moving to a larger brewery, or by moving to a small brewery with big ambitions (and money).

Education and Training

A knowledge of beer styles and vocabulary, English and possibly Spanish, beer chemistry, and ingredients; knowledge of beer history and of what goes into mass-produced beers as well as into microbrews; a bachelor's degree in microbiology, chemistry, biochemistry, or related sciences, and marketing experience are sometimes required.

Experience, Skills, and Personality Traits

A beer specialist or worker needs at least three years of on-the-job experience in brewing to ascend to Beer Brewer or brewmaster, whether in a microbrewery or in a large industrial brewery. Many jobs are available lower down the brewery ladder, and all require the ability to take directions and be patient.

A brewer or good brewery employee must have the ability to taste lots of beer, have a passionate dedication to beer, be self-motivated and a multitasker, have good communication and team building skills, enjoy solving problems, have good computer skills, and enjoy working indoors. Spanish language skills could be necessary in a large brewery.

In a small brewery the brewer also might need to enjoy showing off his or her passion for beer and beer knowledge with customers who come to a tasting bar to sample the products.

Unions and Associations

The International Brotherhood of Teamsters represents most beer and soft-drink workers, particularly at the large corporate breweries, and provides training opportunities, pay negotiations, and representation, hosts blogs, and runs giant conventions where members can express their concerns (www.teamster.org). Home brewers can legally make up to 200 gallons of beer a year for private consumption and can find networking and lots of information through the American Homebrewers Association (www.beertown.org). The Beer Institute is not really an association but its site offers lots of information and links (www.beerinstitute.org). The North American Brewers Association offers information, a beer fest, competition, and awards (www.northamericanbrewers.org). The American Brewers Guild has craft brewers' apprenticeships, classes in brewing science and engineering, employment services and financial aid (www.abgbrew.com). The Master Brewers Association of the Americas (www.mbaa.com) offers abundant information, regional seminars, and advice for brewers of all size establishments.

Tips for Entry

1. If you are passionate about beer, try making beer at home. Many states allow the sale of home brewing kits.
2. Read all you can about making beer.
3. Take beer classes at community or junior colleges.
4. Get a job in a brewpub or brewery, even if it is cleaning kegs and equipment, learn all you can, and work your way up the beer ladder.

RETAIL AND WHOLESALE FOODS AND GROCERIES

SPECIALTY FOOD STORE BUYER/ MANAGER

CAREER PROFILE

Duties: Orders, inventories, oversees displays of imported and specialty food products, either for a department within a large grocery store or for the whole store if its entire stock is gourmet and specialty foods; hires, trains, and schedules other gourmet department managers or specialists (such as a cheese buyer); circulates in community to make inventory known and to enlarge customer base; listens to and receives customers' special requests and determines if they would be popular; occasionally demonstrates products; and may help develop a mail-order or online catalog and business

Alternate Title(s): Gourmet Food Buyer; Organic Foods Buyer

Salary Range: $34,000 to $110,000

Employment Prospects: Limited but increasing

Advancement Prospects: Excellent

Best Geographical Location(s): East and West coasts where there is a large customer base of people either from different countries or who consider themselves to be gourmands and gourmets and people who like to cook and serve fine and exotic foods

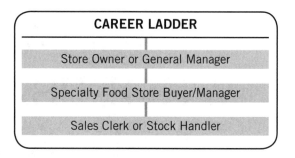

CAREER LADDER

Store Owner or General Manager

Specialty Food Store Buyer/Manager

Sales Clerk or Stock Handler

Prerequisites:

Education and Training—Business management, culinary, food chemistry, or marketing courses from community or junior colleges, or any food and cooking courses from culinary schools, or a strong ethnic culinary background

Experience—Any retail sales experience, particularly in food, including stocking shelves or cooking

Special Skills and Personality Traits—Enjoy good foods and discovering new products; have a love of cooking and helping people learn about foods or find them products they read about or miss from home; can prioritize tasks; can work well with others; have a good personality to receive suggestions and become friendly with customers with varied tastes to keep them coming back

Position Description

A specialty food buyer for a large grocery store or chain and the buyer/manager of a small specialty, ethnic, or gourmet food store have similar duties. As Americans broaden their outlooks and look to foods from their ancestors' homelands or simply look to try new tastes, more specialty food stores crop up, and supermarkets, sensing this trend, employ more people with knowledge of specialty foods to buy for this market niche. As consumers become more aware of good food and food that is good for them, stores or organic markets hire specialty buyers who know the local organic food growers and sources to meet the public demand.

More Americans are looking for whole grains, organic vegetables, fresh wild fish, arborio or organic basmati rice, specialty organic beans, triple-cream bries, specialty processed meats, pastas, and herbs and spices from around the world. As economic times change and people are less likely to drive miles to find a special food item, more stores are searching for and stocking foreign foods to meet customers' requests.

Even though many of these delicacies are available online or by catalog, thousands of home cooks want to purchase something they find in a recipe, and they need it "now." Hence, specialty food stores and specialty food departments in broader appeal stores grow constantly.

Neighborhoods where residents of particular national or ethnic origins live often have distinct specialty food stores that offer "foods from home," including canned sauces, dried spices, and even cookies or biscuits.

Specialty Food Store Buyers and Managers usually have a goal to attract and cater to both the residents of the neighborhood and to attract food fans from outside the area who might come to purchase special ingredients. Hence, a buyer or manager will need to speak English as well as the language of the neighborhood.

Specialty Food Buyers and Managers in large general grocery stores often try to purchase items that will meet the needs of foodies who want to cook new foods as well as for people for whom the foods are native. They have to keep up on what is available and fashionable and even stay ahead of the trends so they are equipped when a fad hits. To do this, they may receive many specialty food distributors who call on them in the store, or attend enormous Fancy Food Shows or other specialty food shows on both coasts and occasionally in Chicago.

Many specialty food departments and buyers offer sample tables where customers can try new tastes, usually with a good supply available and a coupon on the display table for easy purchase.

The Specialty Food Store Buyer or Manager orders everything in the specialty department, but might have separate assistant buyers for subspecialties of coffee and tea, rice, cheeses, Asian foods, and various Latino or Middle Eastern foods.

This person is also in charge of arranging appealing and clean displays of specialty foods and sample tables; hiring, training, scheduling, and firing of staff; setting up a catalog or online sales; getting the department's goods into the store's ads; creating awareness in the community of what products the store offers with easy recipes; and getting to know the customers and listening to requests and comments to better serve their needs.

A Specialty Food Store Buyer or Manager has to make sure inventory moves and is always fresh and of high quality and complies with state health and safety codes, and may even cut and wrap cheese, rotate stock, and keep a spoilage log.

Salaries

Specialty Food Store Buyers' and Managers' salaries vary and range from $34,000 to $110,000, depending upon the size of the store, its location, whether the person receives commissions or straight salary, or is an owner. These amounts may include benefits and bonuses, or those may be paid on top of a salary.

Employment Prospects

Specialty Food Store Buyer and Manager jobs constantly increase throughout North America.

Advancement Prospects

If the Specialty Food Buyer is also the manager and owner, the person is probably at the top of their ladder. If one starts as an assistant buyer or clerk, there are lots of rungs up the ladder to climb. If a person is a specialty food buyer in a chain grocery store, the person can climb to regional or national buyer. One can also move up by going to work at another grocery, either a smaller and more specialized store or a larger chain store group. The more one learns, the more one is likely to advance.

Education and Training

Business management, culinary, food chemistry, or marketing courses from community or junior colleges or any food and cooking courses from culinary schools will be helpful. Knowing sources and visiting local farms and suppliers or traveling to a specific specialty food's country of origin will produce enjoyable and productive knowledge.

Experience, Skills, and Personality Traits

Any retail sales experience, particularly in food, including stocking shelves or cooking, is beneficial. A Specialty Food Store Buyer/Manager should enjoy good foods and discovering new products; should have a love of cooking and helping people learn about foods or finding them products they miss from home or read about; have a good personality to take suggestions; and become friendly with customers to keep them coming back.

A specialty food buyer should be able to lift up to 40 pounds and speak English as well as the language of the specialty food store, whether Korean, or Italian, or whatever it may be. Good computer skills are a must.

Unions and Associations

Small specialty food stores usually are not unionized, and a Specialty Food Store Buyer or Manager in a large grocery store may be categorized as management. If a person remains in a worker-level job instead of becoming an executive, he or she may join the United Food and Commercial Workers International Union (www.ufcw.org), which represents retail store workers, meatpacking, poultry, food processing, and food manufacturing workers in insurance and compensation negotiations.

Getting to know people in the community who buy various ethnic foods might help a buyer understand the food's uses, traditions, role in society, and even recipes, while drawing more locals to the store or place of business.

Tips for Entry

1. Take any job in any size grocery store you can get, whether it is an ethnic market down at the

corner or wrapping cheese in a cold back room of a gourmet grocery store.

2. Talk your way into a pass to a fancy or gourmet food show and collect contact and product information, sampling as many nibbles as possible and asking sales representatives if they are sold in your area.

3. Go to the store where specialty products are sold and talk your way into a job—any job—while explaining that you want to learn.

4. Take any specialty food classes offered at nearby adult education programs (often held in local high schools), community colleges, or cooking schools to learn about everything from locally grown and cured olives or sausages to chocolate and any ethnic foods.

SUPERMARKET MANAGER

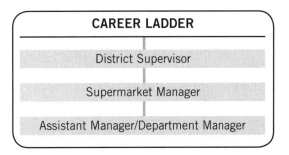

Position Description

A Supermarket Manager runs the entire store and ultimately orders all foods and supplies, sometimes via the head office, and occasionally is allowed to stock local products such as local authors' books or local organic growers' fruits and vegetables.

The manager hires, trains, fires, lays off, and disciplines employees; gets involved in the community with local public relations, and sometimes joins service organizations such as Kiwanis, Rotary, Lions, or Soroptimist clubs. In a pinch he or she fills in checking and bagging customers' purchases. The manager also works out payment for product placement and works with and juggles distributors for shelf space and special displays; oversees compliance with health and safety regulations; and coordinates advertising if it is a small enough store or chain.

Often a supermarket's central office does most of the ordering because it can get better deals by ordering in

bulk for many stores. Individual supermarket managers have some leeway depending upon the store, its location, and the size of the supermarket chain operation. At the other end of the process, the manager is also responsible for all computerized inventories and spreadsheets that track sales successes, failures, and occasionally trigger automatic reorders.

Supermarket Managers can make decisions on the test stocking of specialty items that may have been requested by several customers and then have to keep track of how well that item sells. For instance, a particular brand of tea that a cluster of customers request may be put on the tea shelves for a few weeks to see how it does. It has to pay its way in occupying shelf space and will be removed it if doesn't sell as well as a product that could also take that space.

Local vendors may have to show evidence to the manager of product liability insurance, organic certification, and the ability to produce in adequate quantities to fill potential demand, whether dealing with local tomatoes, locally grown and produced wine, or a locally produced and bottled pasta sauce.

Supermarket Managers also coordinate all staffing, walking the tightrope between having enough checkers and clerks on hand to satisfy customers' timing needs and having too many workers around when business is slow. They will also want to get stocking done so there will not be hand trucks and stacks of cans in the aisle during rush hour.

More managers are hiring part-time workers at minimum wage and in nonunion jobs to avoid paying benefits and making long-term employment commitments, thus ostensibly cutting costs.

Many entry-level employees need to be trained in sanitation, customer service, bagging techniques, language skills, and even pronunciation of some products' names. The manager is responsible for all of these tasks and for keeping track of which employees are working up to expectations. Through this process, the manager can determine which employees are worthy of promotion; some of these may even work their way up the grocery ladder to manager one day.

New employees too young to sell alcohol work as baggers until they learn the procedures, and can move up to checker when they have worked for several months and are "of age," which varies by state.

A Supermarket Manager also coordinates all department managers but is ultimately responsible for product freshness and appearance of the store, as well as the store's operating budget and keeping up on developments in competitive stores.

Managers also have to stay up-to-date on new products through catalogues, e-mailed advertisements, social media, trade magazines, and online newsletters.

Managers now also make arrangements and coordinate concessions, such as rental and percentage deals with national coffee and juice chains and banks that take space within the store to offer their products.

Besides the store's bottom line, a grocery store becomes a local marketplace, historically and currently regarded as a place of social contact and conversation. Thus, how the Supermarket manager conveys his or her and the chain's personality through personal conversations and the attitude the supermarket's staff display is all-important.

Salaries

Supermarket Manager salaries vary according to the size of the store or chain of stores, the city in which it is located, his or her experience, skills, and academic degrees. Generally average salaries range from $45,000

to $80,000, more if the manager makes commissions or has a special bonus arrangement.

Managers usually receive full benefits, but fewer and fewer new supermarket employees get any benefits as they are hired part-time at minimum wage or slightly higher hourly pay.

Employment Prospects

There is great turnover in the grocery supermarket business, especially with large box stores getting into the grocery field. Managers move around in a sort of musical chairs, so there are lots of opportunities.

Advancement Prospects

Advancement prospects in the supermarket management business are tremendous, although recently they have become more limited—especially if a local supermarket's business declines because a new box store with a grocery department moves into the neighborhood.

One usually has to start at the very bottom, work hard, learn, and work one's way up the grocery store ladder. Some union member department managers choose to remain in those jobs rather than move to upper management in order to retain union protection, benefits, and seniority.

A person with the best possibilities for advancement will have experience from the warehouse or bagging stations and above as well as a degree in sales and marketing, business management, human resources, psychology, computer science, or even real estate. One can move up into corporate management and into departments of real estate, advertising, human resources, purchasing, computer science, or even overall management.

Education and Training

A high school education is acceptable, especially for part-time entry-level work, but advancement possibilities improve with a college degree with sales and marketing, business, human resources, and computer science, combined with on-the-job training to work one's way up the grocery ladder. High school students can also start working as baggers, shelf stockers, or deli workers.

In-store training is available at every level, so how much one takes advantage of what is offered can mean the difference between doing well and not.

Experience, Skills, and Personality Traits

A few years' experience in the grocery business at as many kinds of jobs as possible are mandatory, with store management elsewhere extremely helpful and almost crucial to rise to Supermarket Manager. If a person has worked at another supermarket at any level, he or she will probably start near the bottom and advance faster than other employees. During tough economic times, when some middle management union staffers were out of jobs because the supermarket where they worked closed, those employees have had to take lower-level jobs at other stores just to retain their jobs and benefits, all through union negotiations.

An excellent Supermarket Manager needs the ability to build team spirit and encourage initiative and decision making; have an even temperament and be able to jolly up employees and customers; good communication skills at every level and computer skills; the ability to multitask, juggling many grocery store problems at once and yet have the entire store and staff look calm, organized, and appealing at showtime when the doors open.

Unions and Associations

Supermarket Managers are management and do not have a union. The United Food and Commercial Workers International Union (www.ufcw.org) represents many supermarket and grocery store workers up to the management level. Big box stores often have no union representation.

Tips for Entry

1. Take any job in a small or large grocery store to get your foot in the door, whether it is bagging, sweeping, unpacking boxes and shelving goods, or making deli sandwiches. Many supermarket and grocery employees get a great deal of satisfaction from dealing with food and people.
2. Check out the full range of grocery stores in your area, from tiny corner stores and specialty food stores to chain supermarkets and box stores.
3. Get a job in any of them to get started.
4. Take classes in business management, computer science, communications, and human resources at a high school adult education program, community or junior colleges, or at a nearby university to improve your chances for getting a job and advancing within the supermarket system.

RESTAURANT SUPPLY BUYER

CAREER PROFILE

Duties: Selects all products and equipment to be sold by traveling salespeople and through print and online catalogs and e-mail solicitations; constantly researches new products and those available by all producers; anticipates what culinary clients might want or need; negotiates deals on large orders; sometimes hires and trains company sales team, educating members on product benefits; attends trade shows to represent company; keeps up on competition and new products

Alternate Title(s): Merchandise Manager, Merchandise Director; Purchasing Agent

Salary Range: $35,000 to $100,000

Employment Prospects: Good

Advancement Prospects: Good

Best Geographical Location(s): All large cities where there are lots of restaurants

Prerequisites:

Education or Training—There are few academic requirements to purchase equipment beyond familiarity with the equipment, its functions, and benefits,

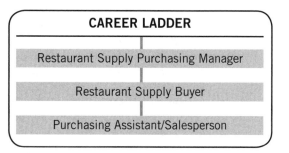

CAREER LADDER

Restaurant Supply Purchasing Manager

Restaurant Supply Buyer

Purchasing Assistant/Salesperson

and new food preparation technologies. On-the-job sales training is important. A bachelor's degree in marketing or business will help.

Experience—Sales, buying, or purchasing experience will be valuable, as will culinary or food preparation experience

Special Skills and Personality Traits—Passion for cooking equipment; compulsive curiosity about cooking and kitchen equipment and latest inventions and trends; the ability to enjoy and travel to trade shows; and computer skills such as the MS Word, Excel, and Outlook applications

Position Description

The Restaurant Supply Buyer selects all products and equipment to be sold by traveling salespeople and through print and online catalogs and e-mail solicitations helps create the equipment marketing company's image by determining how up-to-date its equipment and presentations are.

Salespeople for kitchen equipment and gadget producers seem to hound a Restaurant Supply Buyer because such a buyer is the key to an enormous restaurant market door. How the sales company builds its catalog, how it deals with potential or current customers, and how much it sells totally affects the producer's success. If the Restaurant Supply Buyer for the distribution and sales company likes an item, he or she might buy it as well as help with co-op advertising and give it favorable positioning in print or online catalogs.

A Restaurant Supply Buyer aggressively and constantly researches new products and those available from all producers and, in fact, hears constantly from producers' representatives anxious to update and remind the buyer of their products' virtues and advantages.

Experienced Restaurant Supply Buyers know the language of the industry, know how to read sales pitches they receive, know whether certain equipment will comply with government regulations in various states, tour equipment production plants to make sure the plants are clean and that the producer can keep up production if the buyer's company creates demand, know how volume discounts work for both seller and buyer, and keep current on price levels and discounts.

The buyer also sometimes tours restaurant kitchens to find out what chefs want in order to anticipate what culinary clients might want or need and tries to acquire the best products for the money that are appropriate for their clientele or potential customers.

The buyer negotiates deals on large orders and then figures out how to market the products to his company's customers, and works to minimize transportation costs and maximize rebate opportunities.

Sometimes the Restaurant Supply Buyer actually hires and trains the company sales team once he or she has selected the products, educates the team on product benefits and intricacies and potential "special buys," and keeps sales staff abreast of what chefs seek to keep up with trends.

A Restaurant Supply Buyer attends trade shows to represent the company he or she owns or for which she or he works, and keeps up on competition and new developments and products while making new contacts. If there are new food products, ranging from nuts to dried fruits, the buyer might set up tastings to find out if the producer can provide fresh products as well as educate salespeople on the attractions and benefits of those foods. In this case the buyer may help arrange demonstrations for the vendor.

Local government agricultural advisers and buyers occasionally suggest producers create new "value-added" products, such as jams or condiments from excess berries or tomatoes.

The 3,000-member National Association for the Specialty Food Trade (www.specialtyfood.com) puts on what it calls Fancy Food Shows each summer in New York City and each winter in San Francisco. The association also produces an excellent magazine and Web site loaded with information, and both efforts signal the next trend in equipment and food products.

Any Restaurant Supply Buyer also has to read the financial pages of major American newspapers to keep up on restaurant or supply company mergers, buyouts, bankruptcies, spin-off companies, layoffs, and closings.

Salaries

A Restaurant Supply Buyer for a distribution company usually earns between $35,000 and $100,000, sometimes including benefits, stock, or profit sharing.

Employment Prospects

Prospects are good since nationwide restaurant supply companies need buyers throughout the company and smaller companies are scattered around the country. Both kinds of companies may employ several buyers or purchasers, although in tough economic times restaurants, like everyone else, cut back on new purchases, so new hires may be harder to find than in good economic times.

Advancement Prospects

A buyer who starts out at any level in a restaurant supply company can move up in purchasing or any part of management if he or she is constantly open to new information and learns at every step of the way. One can learn the business in a small local or regional company and work one's way into a larger company with larger responsibility, pay, and stock options.

Education and Training

While no specific education is required to be a Restaurant Supply Buyer, a degree or at least classes in sales, marketing, culinary or food production, and the restaurant business will be advantageous. For higher-paid buyer jobs, a bachelor's degree in business or economics or a combination with strong sales experience in the field are best.

Experience, Skills, and Personality Traits

A Restaurant Supply Buyer ideally should have a good five years of recent experience in purchasing kitchen equipment and products. Computer skills working with applications such as MS Excel, Word, and Outlook may be required. Sales, buying, or purchasing experience will be valuable, as will culinary or food preparation experience, a passion for cooking equipment, compulsive curiosity about cooking and kitchen equipment and the latest inventions and trends, and an ability to enjoy and travel to trade shows.

Unions and Associations

While there are no unions of Restaurant Supply Buyers, there are several useful associations, including the Association of Food Industries (www.afi.mytradassociation.org), the Snack Food Association (www.sfa.org), the Food Processing Supplies Association (www.iafis.org), and the Prepared Foods Association (www.preparedfoods.com), all of which provide newsletters, magazines, seminars, and conventions.

Tips for Entry

1. Learn all you can about food, cooking, kitchen equipment, and ingredients.
2. Take business courses at a local community or junior college in business, marketing, or computer programs.
3. Ask at local restaurants who their equipment suppliers are and arrange to meet someone from the company. Get to know that person, tag along with him or her, and learn what the job entails.
4. Try for a job assisting an experienced buyer and work your way up.

RESTAURANT SUPPLY SALESPERSON

CAREER PROFILE

Duties: Calls on chefs and hotel and restaurant purchasing agents, taking samples or brochures about new equipment or exotic or improved food products; goes to company briefings on new product lines; keeps up awareness of new products and watches out for what chefs say they might find interesting; attends trade shows to know what the competition offers; keeps track of orders; relays orders via phone or e-mail; may even work solely on Internet sales

Alternate Title(s): Sales Rep; Supplier

Salary Range: $51,000 to $230,000, based on rate of commissions

Employment Prospects: Good, for entrepreneurs

Advancement Prospects: Good

Best Geographical Location(s): Any urban area with lots of restaurants, rural counties with diners and coffee shops, and even from home where one can sell online without leaving the house

Prerequisites:

Education or Training—Culinary, business, computer program training, and marketing courses at any level will help.

CAREER LADDER

Restaurant Supply District Manager

Restaurant Supply Salesperson

Restaurant Supply Sales Assistant

Experience—Sales experience of any kind is good, especially selling to restaurants, or cooking in restaurants so one might know from the inside what chefs might need. Many companies prefer to train salespeople in that business' sales methods.

Special Skills and Personality Traits—Passion for the food business, joy from helping others improve their business, lack of fear of approaching people cold, an optimistic outlook, and the ability to take a "no" answer and turn it to a "yes"

Position Description

A Restaurant Supply Salesperson first calls on prospective clients—meaning chefs—to get acquainted and hopefully develop good working relationships. Relationships, even friendships, are extremely important in sales, particularly to restaurant chefs, school head cooks or dietitians, institution chefs, and hotel and casino chefs. One sale to a client is good, but a salesperson's success relies on repeat business.

Chefs and others in the business also shop online for everything from slicers, single burners, and biodegradable flatware to nuts and apricots, sometimes to save money and sometimes even to avoid contact with a salesperson.

A salesperson visits chefs "door-to-door" to establish a relationship, which may be followed up in person, by telephone, or by e-mail, or simply by the chef logging onto a Web site and ordering directly. Hence, a first impression of trust and the efficient presentation of the catalog could determine whether a chef goes to that salesperson's particular Web site or that of another distributor.

In communicating with a chef or food director, the more knowledge a salesperson has of how a professional kitchen works and how restaurants are run, the more successful he or she will be.

Salespeople attend in-person or virtual company meetings to introduce new products the company represents, with product salespeople or sales reps presenting their products and their virtues. Tasting new nut mixtures or condiments might be a part of the job. Salespeople can actually have some say in whether a product will sell and whether it is ordered and put in the catalog.

Sometimes a salesperson will arrange for a lease of kitchen equipment with the option to purchase it, particularly if the owner is a promising new chef with some backing. In rare cases, particularly with a famous chef, equipment companies will install equipment for free just for the advertising and association—the company will get publicity through the chef's fame or media exposure.

If a product is accepted to be sold, the distribution company will either order a good supply or act as a paper processor, relaying orders directly to the manufacturer. Occasionally an equipment manufacturer or food packager takes orders in advance and produces according to the orders received.

A Restaurant Supply Salesperson has to be familiar with food crops and sources to know if and why a product is or is not included in the company's product line and should be able to explain this to a chef. The chef may want to know if a food product is organic or sustainably grown, and its country of origin.

While a restaurant supply company may carry around 50 to 100 products, a Restaurant Supply Salesperson may call on 50 to 100 clients, some monthly and some weekly or even twice a week.

Many restaurants have little storage and chefs often want products as fresh as possible, so they may want to order daily, twice a week, or weekly, which also keeps waste low. In some cases the restaurants get billed weekly or monthly or are on a cash-on-delivery basis with the supplier. The salesperson sometimes works with the company's credit manager to work out payment schedules that get the company paid while not offending or strapping the restaurant—all of it a delicate balance. It is, of course, in the best interest of the salesperson to keep the restaurant open and viable, help it work out a pay schedule, and keep it ordering products, all of which means more commissions to the credit of the salesperson.

Salespeople who sell restaurant equipment also need to have relationships with chefs and purchasing agents and keep them informed of their latest and greatest products. The salesperson also needs to know a client's restaurant's kitchen in order to recommend new appliances or gadgets appropriate for the chef's style of cooking and presentation.

Salespeople often work by geographic territory, possibly in a few counties or states; or may deal solely with an online catalog and Internet sales.

Many Restaurant Supply Salespeople are trained on the job by more experienced salespeople and eventually will mentor up-and-coming sellers themselves.

Salaries

When a Restaurant Supply Salesperson first starts on the job, he or she is paid a living wage to get started, which is sometimes withdrawn as the person's com-

missions start rolling in. Once a person has worked his or her own territory for a few years, he or she can earn from $51,000 to $230,000, based on the rate of commissions and the kind and level of restaurants with which the person deals. Once a salesperson is known and trusted by chefs and purchasing officials, he or she can almost reorder for these clients automatically—but that is after many years of very hard work and travel.

Employment Prospects

There are many national and regional food and restaurant supply companies, although some regional ones have either been gobbled up by larger corporations or have gone out of business recently. An entrepenuer can start a supply company, gathering a catalog of local producers to represent.

Advancement Prospects

Advancement prospects are excellent once one is in the company's sales force. As a salesperson, if one does well one might rise to district supervisor over several salespeople. A supervisor may receive a salary and/or a percentage of the salespeople's sales as a motivator to get them selling more.

Education and Training

Culinary, business, computer program training, and marketing courses at any level will help. One might try the other end of the sales spectrum first as a purchaser of restaurant supplies for a distribution company or for a restaurant or group of restaurants or hotel.

Experience, Skills, and Personality Traits

Sales experience of any kind is good, especially selling to restaurants or cooking in restaurants so one might know from the inside what chefs might need. Many companies prefer to train salespeople in that business' sales methods. To fully understand chefs' needs, experience in cooking in a commercial kitchen would be the best source of knowledge and a foundation for good working communication.

Passion for the food business, joy from helping others improve their business, lack of fear of approaching people cold, an optimistic outlook, and the ability to take a "no" answer and turn it to a "yes" are all needed traits.

Most Restaurant Supply Salespeople enter a restaurant via the kitchen's back door, and usually interrupt whatever people are concentrating on. This person needs to be sensitive to the kitchen's rhythm, have a gift in hand, share a little trade gossip (salespeople and delivery people are full of gossip about what's going on in all the restaurants), and perhaps know each kitchen's timing. Any salesperson needs to know how to say just enough and when it's time to "fold 'em and close 'em."

Unions and Associations

While there are no trade unions for Restaurant Supply Salespeople, there are several trade associations. These include the Commercial Food Equipment Service Association (www.cfesa.com), the Foodservice Consultants Society International (www.fcsi.org), the Manufacturers' Agents for the Food Service Industry (www.mafsi.org), the North American Food Equipment Manufacturers (www.nafem.org), the National Association of Wholesaler-Distributors (www.naw.org), and the National Restaurant Association (www.restaurant. org). Most have newsletters, conventions, and lots of information resources.

Tips for Entry

1. Learn all you can about food, ingredients, the chemistry of food, kitchen appliances, and other equipment. The more you know about the cooking field, the more you know about chefs' needs and priorities.
2. Take classes in sales management, marketing, inventory, and computer programs.
3. Track down a Restaurant Supply Salesperson, possibly by asking local chefs or restaurant owners who calls on them, and hanging around.
4. Ask that restaurant Supply Salesperson if you can ride with or apprentice with him or her, while trying to get a job at the best hotel or restaurant in your area.
5. Get an apprenticeship or job at any level in purchasing for a restaurant, hotel, hospital, school district, large country club, casino, or resort.

COOKWARE AND EQUIPMENT

COOKWARE STORE BUYER

Duties: Meets with salespeople to come to the store and schedules their visits, scours catalogues in print and online, attends trade shows to find the latest trends in public needs or desires, watches inventory and Web site and keeps track of what sells and doesn't, reorders or stops orders, often organizes seasonal promotions, and works with webmaster to coordinate online specials

Alternate Title(s): Purchaser; Purchasing Manager

Salary Range: $40,000 to $100,000

Employment Prospects: Good in good economic times, more difficult in bad economic times

Advancement Prospects: Good

Best Geographical Location(s): Throughout North America, wherever cookware is sold, whether in small local groceries, local kitchenware shops, or at central buying offices for large retail chain stores

Prerequisites:

    Education or Training—General education, particularly with courses in culinary arts, business,

CAREER LADDER

Owner/Purchasing Manager

Cookware Store Buyer

Assistant Buyer/Clerk

spreadsheets, management, marketing, and design will help

Experience—Retail sales experience, particularly in the food or cooking fields, or being a home cook helps one understand what cooks will look for, as well as trends in the business and the timing of orders to meet holiday shopping.

Special Skills and Personality Traits—Passion for cooking equipment and home cooking, interest in new culinary trends, the gift of gab, the ability to turn a "no" answer into a "yes," the freedom and willingness to travel, and great computer skills either to develop a Web site or process orders

Position Description

A Cookware Store Buyer can often get tremendous vicarious pleasure out of buying tons of cookware with someone else's money—unless, of course, the buyer is also the store owner.

The buyer schedules visits and meets with salespeople who come to the store, listens to their sales pitches, decides what to order, and eventually receives the items and checks delivery slips with carton contents. Cookware inventory might include pots and pans of iron or clay or metal; kitchen utensils of all kinds, from easy-grip varieties to some made of new materials; cookbooks; dish towels, aprons, placemats, and tablecloths; mixers, from reproductions of classics to modern design; bakeware; casseroles; celebrity name–brand pans and utensils, and glassware.

A Cookware Store Buyer has to know the store's clientele and consider their needs and desires when ordering. Television cooking stars' products may sell in some parts of the country and not in others, while reproductions of old-fashioned cast-iron goods

may sell to cooks of one economic bracket but not another.

Cookware buyers scour wholesalers' and manufacturers' Web sites, catalogues, and e-mails, and go to gift and houseware trade shows a few times a year. The largest show buyers go to is the International Housewares Show in Chicago (www.housewares.org) in January, at which 25,000 buyers from 100 countries may order and 2,000 exhibitors from 30 countries sell their best goods. What you see there are samples of equipment, and the manufacturers take orders and produce the goods based on orders taken.

If buyers represent a large store or chain of cookware shops, salespeople will call on them to show off new items and find out when seasonal discounts or deeper "recession discounts" are planned.

Seasons to consider and for which special products are made, bought, and sold include Christmas, spring, summer and fall. Christmas kitchen gifts are popular, followed by sales that clear inventory for spring, and pre-wedding orders complete with bridal registries in which prospective brides list gifts they would like for guests to give them as wedding presents. Summer sells lots of outdoor cookware from barbecues to plastic and biodegradable utensils, plates and cups, and picnic baskets. Stores and their buyers progress through Mothers's Day and Father's Day, graduation time, tourist gifts for family and friends back home, or perhaps wineglasses if the shop is in a wine region visited by tourists.

Buyers might also attend the Fancy Food Shows in San Francisco and New York if their stores carry oils and vinegars, pasta and pasta sauces, chocolate in various forms or coffee (see www.specialtyfood.com).

Many buyers prefer face-to-face contact, making choices of what products to carry. They bear a lot of responsibility for their decisions, since the store owner will rely on them to order what customers will buy.

Buyers also get caught up in a lot of office paper work on their computers to check inventory, what has sold and what has not. Stores with shorter lines of credit or less cash on hand may have to order more frequently on a cash-on-delivery basis.

A Cookware Store Buyer often organizes seasonal promotions and displays and works with the store's webmaster to coordinate online specials to make sure there is enough inventory to fill orders as they come in. The buyer also orders all cookbooks and other books sold in the store, which means he or she also has to follow the latest and best-selling cookbooks and trends and possibly order books either at gift shows or at large book shows.

Salaries

Cookware Store Buyers are usually salaried shop employees who work without commission but get health benefits. Occasionally buyers are freelancers and have to put together a string of shops to make a living, in which case they would not get benefits. While it is not called commission, many buyers receive a bonus at the end of the year based on a store's sales and profits. Salaries range from $40,000 to $100,000, depending on the size of the store or the number of stores in a chain for which he or she is buying. Bonuses vary vastly, meaning they will be lower in hard times and higher in good times, and depending on percentages of profits or sales agreed upon.

Employment Prospects

Employment prospects are good in good economic times and more difficult in bad economic times. In small stores, the owner may double as buyer and manager. Chain cookware shops and other large chains hire central buyers, with each local branch staff having some input on what the local market might purchase.

Advancement Prospects

Once you get a job in a cookware shop and learn everything you can, you can work your way into the buyer position. After you do a good job at that, in some places you can progress to store manager or join a larger store or chain of stores to have greater buying or purchasing responsibility and a better title and salary. A cookware buyer in a large business may progress to general purchasing manager.

Education and Training

A college degree of some sort, even in liberal arts, particularly with courses in culinary arts, business, spreadsheets, management, marketing, and design will help.

Experience, Skills, and Personality Traits

Any retail sales experience, particularly in the food or cooking fields, or being a home cook helps one to understand what cooks will look for, as well as cooking trends and the timing of orders to anticipate trends and holiday shopping. Occasionally people who have sold kitchenware for manufacturers or distributors switch to the retail buying side in order to travel less.

A great Cookware Store Buyer needs to have passion for cooking equipment and home cooking, an interest in new culinary trends, the ability to turn a "no" answer into a "yes," the freedom and willingness to travel, great computer skills either to develop a Web site or process orders, terrific energy and enthusiasm, and quick-thinking artistic and design skills to plan and create store displays and promotions.

Unions and Associations

Cookware Store Buyers do not have a union or trade association, although they might find the Web site of the International Housewares Association (www.housewares.org) and its trade show helpful both for goods and for networking.

Locally, a Cookware Store Buyer might join local culinary societies, a local chamber of commerce, wine or winery clubs or associations, and even local service clubs to find other people interested in cookware and in food and wine.

Tips for Entry

1. Get a job, any job, in a cookware shop in your community, or work in the cookware

department of a large store in your area just to begin to learn what is available and how the buyer functions.

2. Attend the housewares show in Chicago or the Fancy Food Shows in New York or San Francisco to see (and possibly be overwhelmed) by what is available and to meet cookware buyers and cookware store owners. Take a peek at the order forms they use, and even take one to study the language of cookware ordering.

3. Collect some product catalogues to familiarize yourself with what supplies different manufacturers, wholesalers, and distributors offer.

4. Research every cooking utensil or piece of equipment you can on the Web to learn as much as possible.

COOKWARE STORE MANAGER

Position Description

Most people who have a home have a basic pot, pan, coffeemaker, and some cooking utensils, which are basic kitchen needs. A Cookware Store Manager has to convince home cooks that they want or need lots of other pots, pans, utensils, and other gadgets in all shapes, colors, and degrees of usefulness.

A Cookware Store Manager has to try to increase sales of kitchenware to customers through clever window and store displays of merchandise, cooking demonstrations, special promotions, advertising, publicity, and purchasing.

The manager might also be the owner, and has responsibility for attracting knowledgeable employees and hiring, training, scheduling, evaluating, and firing of staff, from people who unwrap goods from shipping boxes and stack them safely in the back storage area to salespeople and clerks.

The manager will either serve as the store's buyer or purchaser or oversee the person who performs that function. He or she might also be in charge of whoever selects in-store or window displays, as well as managing purchases and display and layout for the company's online store if it has one. If the store doesn't have one, a manager might oversee the development of a Web site to increase sales.

In a stand-alone cookware or kitchenware store, the manager probably is the first person there in the morning before the store opens and the last one to leave at night. He or she opens the doors, turns on the lights, makes sure everything is dusted, and that computers or cash registers are turned on and functioning, and checks to see that all staff are on time and in place.

While some store managers love to be on the floor greeting customers, using personality and personal connection to help sales, they also have lots of office work to perform, such as keeping up with inventory, sales, profit and loss, making sure bills are paid, coordinating ads in newspapers, on Web sites, and even on local radio or television stations, handling job interviews and other human resources tasks, and coaching staff to please customers.

Cookware and kitchenware store managers have to plan for seasonal purchases, which seem to be gift-giving times such as Easter, Mother's Day in May, Father's Day in June, barbecue equipment in summer, fall preparation for the December holidays of Hanukkah and Christmas, and several postholiday sales. In tough economic times they also have to get creative to lure potential and even regular customers to part with their money for the latest fad or gift.

Cookware stores, like many retail operations, have to gear their stock to their customers, from designer table linens to straw placemats and iron skillets to Cuisinart coffeepots.

When new products come in, which usually is frequently, the manager teaches the staff what there is to know about the new implement or gadget because the more they know the better they can sell. Anyone can sell what he or she loves better, so salespeople that love to cook and cook well, respect the process, and get excited over a new mandoline (slicer) or ergonomic can opener are employees managers look for.

A Cookware Store Manager succeeds if the rest of the team does well and succeeds. If salespeople work on commission, they earn the most if they sell well, and the manager, undoubtedly on commission, also profits by their success. The manager has to keep track of financial success or lack of same, how each salesperson does, and therefore how the whole store does.

If the cookware or kitchenware store is a department within a large store, many of the same circumstances apply. The manager has to report to higher-up managers, as would be required of a manager of a store in a chain of cookware shops.

Salaries

Many cookware or kitchenware store managers work on straight salary, while others work on salary plus commission. In the latter case, the manager makes more money if the sales staff does well, so it benefits the manager to teach and help the staff. Salaries usually range form $35,000 to $80,000, with benefits and commissions negotiated in advance.

Employment Prospects

Especially in hard economic times, cookware shop owners might want to take over managerial duties themselves and not fill the position if a manager leaves. In many independent shops, the owner is the manager. Chain stores such as Sur la Table, Williams-Sonoma, and Crate and Barrel have managers for each branch, and a department store might have a manager for its cookware shop.

Advancement Prospects

If one starts as a clerk or salesperson in a cookware or kitchenware store, one can work up the kitchen ladder to manager, albeit slowly. People who get into the kitchenware business usually love it and stay.

If one works in a chain of cookware stores, one may do well and progress to department or headquarters buyer and into upper management of the chain. In the kitchenware department of a large store, one may progress to floor manager and general manager, and even up the ladder to store manager.

Education and Training

Courses in cooking, business management, marketing, public relations, design and display, and human resources will all be helpful.

Experience, Skills, and Personality Traits

Any retail experience or cooking experience, a deep interest in entertainment of guests, or window display and marketing experience will help. A successful Cookware Store Manager should enjoy food and cooking, have a passion for making people happy, be good at finding the right salespeople and motivating them, and have good computer skills.

Unions and Associations

There are no unions for Cookware Store Managers, although employees may belong to the United Food and Commercial Workers (www.ufcw.org), which was made up from a combination of the Retail Clerks Union and Amalgamated Meat Cutters Union. Local food and wine associations and chambers of commerce are open to membership by managers of local kitchenware stores.

Tips for Entry

1. Take courses in business, cooking, marketing, design, and computers, most of which are available at local community colleges.
2. Find all the cookware or kitchenware stores or departments in your area and learn all you can from visiting them.
3. Ask for any kind of job in the cookware shop or in the cookware or demonstration department of a larger store or grocery store.
4. Be willing to take a temporary job during seasonal sales and do the best job the employers ever saw, gaining respect and possibly a full-time job for yourself.

MAIL-ORDER CATALOG DESIGNER

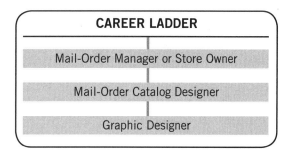

Position Description

Catalog designers are in demand for both print and online catalogs because more people are distance shopping, either by fingering through a print catalog or browsing a Web site or online catalog. Once a customer starts to order from print catalogs, some of which are the size of magazines or even paperback books, he or she becomes inundated with piles of them in advance of holiday shopping.

Even in the time of online shopping and expensive business, paper, and printing costs, mail-order catalogs still provide sales for large companies. Some companies publish catalogs monthly, quarterly, or annually, with periodic special-occasion and season-specific short catalogs.

Food growers, food producers and processors, kitchenware stores, and manufacturers and retail stores all create and send out catalogs at holiday times, from Easter to the Fourth of July to Halloween to Christmas and Hanukkah.

A Mail-Order Catalog Designer or editor works with the company's buyer, manager, and marketing staff to coordinate design to meet the appropriate seasonal needs and to get potential customers' attention in an irresistible way. They have to synchronize delivery dates, warehouse inventory, and product availability before the item can safely be placed in a catalog.

All items to go in the catalog have to be sorted, photographed, written about, and assigned a coordinated catalog or purchase number and price, with sale prices marked where needed.

Catalog design includes clustering items on the page or in the overall layout to appeal to purchasers of the items nearby so that customers will purchase more than they need or intended to—all part of merchandizing psychology. Food products get placed next to pans or salad bowls, and chocolate sauces appear next to baking pans or ice cream machines.

The catalog designer works with whoever is his or her supervisor, either a mail-order manager or even a store owner, along with the photographer, copywriter, and tech staff who probably lay out the catalog with special publishing software. Mock-ups or galleys have to be proofread and carefully inspected by several people to make sure copy and photos are all correct and attached to the proper item and in the right order.

Catalog Designers often begin to work on the next catalog as soon as the current one goes to press.

Salaries

A full-time Mail-Order Catalog Designer can earn from $50,000 to $100,000, with benefits. A freelance designer can work for several catalog operations and make a lot more or a lot less. Several food product businesses, like other businesses, recently dismissed full-time employees and now hire freelancers to save salaries and avoid paying benefits. Many of those laid-off designers now earn more as freelancers, charging between $50 and $150 per hour, depending upon their location and experience.

Designers can make more if they also do the company's Web site catalog.

Employment Prospects

Employment prospects, specifically in the cookware and fine foods mail-order catalog field, depend on how many companies survive and continue to publish catalogs.

Companies have to weigh how catalog sales will help them when retail store sales decrease and, in good economic times, how catalog sales will help them to supplement sales, always considering how the cost of fuel influences customers' driving and purchasing habits.

Advancement Prospects

Once a graphic artist has a job designing mail-order catalogs, his or her advancement depends upon the size of the company, whether it is one independent storefront whether items in the catalog sell well, represents a large chain of stores.

A successful Mail-Order Catalog Designer could move up in the kitchenware or cookware business to editor of the catalog, marketing director, manager, and even president of the company in the right situation. On the other hand, in a small family-owned business, the top spots may be held by family members.

One can always move to a larger operation to get a designer job with more financial gain, or propose to a smaller store that it expand its online presence and sales and thereby its market share.

Education and Training

Courses at community or junior colleges in advertising, communications, marketing, design, computer skills, color, and graphics will be helpful. Classes or a degree from an art or design school should lead to even greater opportunity.

Experience, Skills, and Personality Traits

Any experience in print production, design, copywriting, editing, and Web design will be helpful. Experience working in magazine publishing, newspaper advertising layout, for advertising agencies, or in the design and production of brochures and fliers will be valuable, particularly if you have good computer design skills.

One needs to enjoy minute detail work and space relationships, have organizational skills, enjoy concentrating on a project, and have the ability to get along with and motivate a team working on the same project with the same goals.

Unions and Associations

While there are no specific unions for kitchenware or other catalog designers, local or regional advertising clubs, wine associations, online blog groups, and even chambers of commerce all have designers as members with whom one can communicate, share experiences, and network.

Tips for Entry

1. Visit Web sites of food and cookware production companies and check out their design and marketing ideas.
2. Visit kitchenware stores and departments to get a good feeling of what is old and what is new and which "old" items are "new" again.
3. Ask to meet with the store's owner, manager or marketing director and find out what you might do to help. Even take a job as a sales clerk to get your foot in the door and work your way into design.
4. Contact existing mail-order cookware companies and ask for a job, any job.
5. Go to any pertinent trade shows, from the Fancy Food Shows to packaging and book shows, talk to staff at booths that interest you, and ask if they do mail-order or online catalog sales. If they do, offer to help. If they don't, offer to create catalogs for them.

KITCHEN DESIGNER

Duties: Works with homeowners, architects, real estate "flippers" (people who buy houses inexpensively, fix them up, and sell them for a profit) and contractors to redesign or design a remodel of an older kitchen or design a new home or restaurant kitchen; keeps up to date on all kitchen fashion fads, new appliances, and accessories, countertop surfaces, flooring, cabinets, window boxes, usable recycled materials, windows and lighting, and oversees installation of everything he or she has designed and ordered

Alternate Title(s): Kitchen Architect; Kitchen and Bath Designer; Interior Designer; Kitchen Planner

Salary Range: $57,000 to $200,000

Employment Prospects: Good

Advancement Prospects: Good

Best Geographical Location(s): Western and southern states, particularly in wealthy communities or wealthy, upscale neighborhoods

Prerequisites:

Education or Training—Interior design, general design, architecture, drafting, and cooking courses; any design experience and cooking expe-

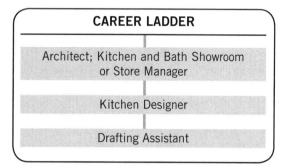

rience to know firsthand what new appliances can accomplish

Experience—Work in a design firm, especially in kitchen design; sales of kitchen appliances or cabinetry; cooking experience; work for a Kitchen Designer or showroom; work for cabinet shop or construction business

Special Skills and Personality Traits—An interior designer's innate or learned ability to remember shapes and spaces; color memory; a passion for constantly learning and remembering new products; good negotiation and mediation skills to act as a go-between between client and subcontractors and keep things calm between the principals

Position Description

Many homeowners, developers, and investors believe that the best investment one can make in a house or condominium is to remodel the kitchen and the bathroom. Fads come and go as to what is the best countertop, flooring, stove, or other appliances, ranging from Formica to slate, linoleum to earthen tile, professional gas range to countertop electric burners. Kitchen Designers have to know what the latest is from the standpoints of fashion and utility, and how to blend those interests with the goals of the customer. Window quality and fashions also come and go, as does every other major ingredient of a kitchen, and companies even come and go. A kitchen designer actually has to work hard to evaluate quality, availability, and reliability of products and their manufacturers.

Kitchen Designers do all sorts of work, from remodeling a condominium or apartment kitchen or planning one with original architects and contractors to helping new homeowners, caterers, and even restaurant owners and managers.

Any interior designer or kitchen specialist has to be able to listen to the client's desires, needs, goals, and budget, which can take several conversations or visits, and interpret those in order to come up with a proposal. Some clients may want an expensive up-to-date kitchen with all the latest and finest appliances, while others may want to create a new look as inexpensively as possible. Some clients may or may not cook but want it to look as if they do. In both cases, those who want to create an image will know what they want, and real cooks will usually know as well. All of these people will have ideas and need advice and individual recommendations.

The designer carefully measures the kitchen space, taking into consideration which of the existing cabinets and appliances will stay in place or be moved, and draw out a floor plan for the new design.

The Kitchen Designer and client might visit showrooms of appliance manufacturers or sales representatives at design centers to view products of various suppliers, especially those recommended by the designer, including energy-saving stoves and ovens, hoods, fans, refrigerators and freezers, and water saving sinks, faucets, compactors, and composters. Color combinations and all this information can become confusing to a client, so the Kitchen Designer has to target those showrooms and brochures most in line with the client's tastes and needs.

Next the Kitchen Designer draws another floor plan, this time with the client's selected materials and appliances in place. The plan can be a pencil sketch, an architectural drawing, or a computer-generated layout.

The client will want to know a realistic cost estimate of the work, appliances, cabinets, and flooring that they have decided upon, so the designer has to make a detailed estimate of all costs, which always change. The Kitchen Designer has to figure in the price of the hard goods as well as time and labor estimates from subcontractors, craftspeople, and installers, as well as the designer's own charges for design services and running around.

Designers keep up to date by reading trade magazines, snooping at other designers' kitchens on house tours, perusing all the brochures and catalogs they receive from manufacturers or suppliers, touring the finest producers in North America and Europe, and going to trade shows.

Some kitchen and bath designers specialize in rooms for visually or physically disabled clients, some of whom have service dogs that can help with kitchen and bathroom activities, or for short or tall customers.

All interior or Kitchen Designers have big card files, Rolodex organizers, or online address books of their favorite subcontractors and suppliers. As travel agents are said to be only as good as their last trip, Kitchen Designers are only as good as their last kitchen.

Salaries

Kitchen Designers tend to work independently, or for a housing developer, a design firm or showroom, or a kitchen or interior design firm.

Independent designers may work for a set fee per job or for quoted services, while some designers also collect a commission or kickback from manufacturers or wholesalers. If they work for a set fee that includes all subcontracted work, they can get in trouble if a sub's estimate is under reality and the designer has to take the difference out of his or her own fee. Good kitchen and bath designers with good estimating skills can easily earn $57,000 to $200,000 a year, with earning potential greatest in big cities, on the West Coast and in the South.

Kitchen Designers who work for design firms, retail showrooms or housing developers earn slightly more modestly in the $57,000 to $100,000 range.

Employment Prospects

Employment prospects are good for freelance independent Kitchen Designers, but the person has to have a circle of friends and contacts who have the income to afford kitchen makeovers. If a designer works in a showroom or for a retail store, he or she may work on a fixed salary or strictly on commission.

Occasionally there are openings even in big box stores that may employ a kitchen designer to advise do-it-yourself customers. New housing developers, when they are building, often hire full-time Kitchen Designers, who are always working on the next development project.

Advancement Prospects

Happy clients can influence a Kitchen Designer's rise in popularity, reputation, and success. If a designer works for a large firm, he or she can start in sales and move up to lead designer and potentially go out on his or her own as an independent kitchen designer.

Some Kitchen Designers who specialize in high-end restaurants work up to owning and developing new restaurants with varied success rates.

Education and Training

Community or junior college courses and even a degree in design, architecture, and business management from a university would be ideal. Some culinary schools offer design courses, and the National Kitchen and Bath Association (www.nkba.org) offers a certificate instruction program for designers.

Training as a formal or informal apprentice to an accomplished designer or architect will contribute to one's abilities as a Kitchen Designer.

Cooking classes will also help a potential designer understand how appliances work and which ones will actually deliver what a client wants.

Experience, Skills, and Personality Traits

Good experience may include work for a design firm, especially in kitchen design; sales of kitchen appliances or cabinetry; cooking experience; work for a Kitchen

Designer or showroom; and work for a cabinet shop or construction business.

A kitchen and bathroom designer, or any interior designer, needs a good memory of color, spatial relationships, fabrics and other materials, and knowledge of the products available and the best subcontractor to deal with each installation.

A person needs to be able to get along with anyone and everyone on the job, from clients to workers, and not be bothered by people's idiosyncrasies, which the designer will definitely encounter along the design and remodel process. The designer will also need to be able to keep confidences, because clients will tell a kitchen and interior designer all sorts of intimate details of their lives, whether he she needs to know them or not.

A Kitchen Designer must have great passion for constantly learning and recalling new products; good negotiation and mediation skills as a go-between from client to subcontractors, and be able to keep things calm between the principals, even in their own home. A certain degree of voyeurism might come in handy in checking out other designers' latest efforts. A designer may also need to be able to sublimate his or her own taste for that of the client.

Unions and Associations

Three national and international trade associations offer networking, education, job placement, conferences, trade shows, and other helpful services: the National Kitchen and Bath Association (www.nkba.org), the American Society of Interior Designers (www.asid.org), and the International Interior Design Association (www.iida. com).

Tips for Entry

1. Take high school or community college courses in art, design, drafting, and culinary classes.
2. Hang out at a local cabinetmaker's workshop, get a job in a cookware or kitchenware shop or department, or work in a restaurant kitchen to learn and experience what a client might need.
3. Scoop up brochures and kitchen design magazines and research online to learn all you can.
4. Offer to work as an apprentice for a cabinetmaker, flooring expert, interior designer or Kitchen Designer, for a wholesaler of kitchen supplies, or in a design showroom to get experience and learn.
5. Make yourself valuable by becoming expert in some part of the field.

CULINARY
TOURISM

CULINARY TOURISM AND AGRITOURISM DIRECTOR

Duties: Researches interesting organic, "green," or biodynamic farms; farm stands; dairies and cheese makers; restaurants; organic pastry shops and bakeries; farm-made fruit jams and pie stands; a pretzel or gourmet sausage vendors or factories; cooking schools; cookbook and kitchenware stores; wineries; breweries; distilleries; food and wine festivals; and farms where guests can stay and participate in the farming experience; and organizes tours by subject matter or by tourists' tastes and wishes

Alternate Title(s): Culinary Guide; Gourmet Guide; Tour Leader

Salary Range: $20,000 to $80,000

Employment Prospects: Limited

Advancement Prospects: Fair

Best Geographical Location(s): Anywhere in the United States or Canada, particularly where there are small farms and wineries nearby and an abundance of food and wine fans or tourists

Prerequisites:

Education or Training—Courses in hospitality, agriculture, enology, cooking, "green" travel, farm-ing, marketing, and business management might help, along with any training in organization

Experience—Little specifically since culinary and agritourism are relatively newly formal fields, although any cooking, farming, baking, or wine-making experience help make a good tour guide

Special Skills and Personality Traits—Organizational skills, knowledge of what is available in both culinary and agritourism in your area, passion for food, wine, and beer, and an affable, pleasant personality that gets along with people and gets fun out of organizing and making people happy, as well as has an ability to converse with and develop friendships with farm bureaus, farmers, and other growers

CAREER LADDER

Company Owner

Culinary Tourism and Agritourism Director

Farm Tour Manager

Position Description

The positions of Culinary Tourism Director and Agritourism Director are slightly different. A Culinary Tourism Director researches and organizes tours depending upon the tastes and interests of their guests, including interesting organic or biodynamic farms, farm stands, dairies and cheese makers, restaurants, organic pastry shops and bakeries, farm-made fruit jams and pie stands, pretzel or gourmet sausage vendors or factories, cooking schools, cookbook and kitchenware stores, food and wine festivals, wineries, breweries, and distilleries.

An Agritourism Director might do all of the above as well as find small and interesting farms where guests can stay overnight for a week or longer to experience farm life, farmwork, harvesting, and cooking.

Both directors have many responsibilities, including making themselves aware of all of the food and beverage opportunities in their area or in other countries where they may specialize in travel.

For instance, if a group of travelers wants to visit all of the artisan cheese makers in a country, the tour director needs to have relationships with those cheese makers, managers, or owners, set up a tour schedule that suits host and guests and makes logistical sense, organize transportation and rest stops that may include a meal at a specialty restaurant, plan an animal milking experience if one affords itself, possibly provide shipping services for any goods purchased by guests who don't want to carry loads of food back to their homes, and arrange hotel, air and ground transportation (with insurance), and transfers.

A successful Agritourism Director develops a network of specialty farms in their area with guesthouses or cabins that provide meals, welcome guests as a way to supplement farm income, and share some of their lives and farm secrets. This tour director will also usually arrange all transportation and possibly coordinate a succession of farm stays for some guests, often with each stop offering a different kind of farm experience.

Salaries

Most Culinary Tourism and Agritourism Directors create and run their own businesses, so their pay often relates to how hard and cleverly they work and organize. A director will charge a set fee for a tour that will include payments required by the host and, in some cases, charge or accept a commission on goods purchased by members of the tour group. Average take-home earnings usually range from $20,000 to $80,000.

Employment Prospects

While most tour directors and guides are self-starters, more and more county, state, and provincial governments are developing culinary tourism and agritourism departments. If there isn't one in your area and there should be, create it or approach government officials and propose that they let you start an office of culinary tourism or agritourism.

Advancement Prospects

One can develop a network of culinary tourism or agritourism companies in various regions or develop a salaried job with a county office, local visitors' bureau, or tourism office.

Education and Training

Courses in hospitality, agriculture, enology, cooking, marketing, and business management might help, as will training in organic or "green" farming and travel practices.

Experience, Skills, and Personality Traits

Any cooking, farming, baking, or winemaking experience help make a good culinary tour or agritour guide, and a love of being outdoors is helpful. It also helps to have great organizational skills, knowledge of what is available in both culinary tourism and agritourism in your area, a deep passion for food, wine, and beer and an affable, pleasant personality that gets along with people and gets fun out of organizing and making people happy.

Unions and Associations

The International Culinary Tourism Association was created in 2001 by Erik Wolf and now links programs worldwide, as well as sells his products to instruct people on how to be tour directors and benefit from his organization. Otherwise, there is no union that covers culinary tourism and agritourism. Travel agent organizations that might be helpful include Specialty Travel Agents Association (www.specialtytravelagents.com) for agents that specialize in green and sustainable tourism; American Society of Travel Agents (www.asta.org); and the National Association of Travel Agents (www.nacta.com). The American Institute of Wine and Food (www.globalchefs.com) and Women for WineSense (www.womenforwinesense.org) might also be helpful.

Tips for Entry

1. Educate yourself on all the finest farm, food, and wine destinations and food and wine festivals in your area.
2. Take a few courses in hospitality, tourism management, and cooking at a high school adult education program, community college, cooking school, or junior college.
3. Go to your local city hall, visitors' bureau, or tourism office and find out what programs exist and if they might help you create one.
4. Ask at your local visitors' bureau or tourism office about jobs or volunteer opportunities.

FARM TOUR MANAGER

CAREER PROFILE

Duties: A Farm Tour Manager finds local farms and food producers who are willing to participate in farm tours or agritourism to help inform people of the advantages of locally grown food; finds schools, teachers, and parents interested in facilitating school trips to local farms; develops a business plan and proposals for alternative tours; finds funding for the tours or charges for tours to pay expenses; and publicizes tours and creates events to attract visitors to local farms.

Alternate Title(s): Agritourism Manager, Agritourism Guide

Salary Range: $20,000 to $70,000

Employment Prospects: Good

Advancement Prospects: Limited

Best Geographical Location(s): Try suburbs with small or large farms and semirural counties close to urban areas where food and wine quality are important considerations. Even big cities have neighborhood farmers' markets with produce brought in from farms somewhat close.

Prerequisites:

Education or Training—Courses in tourism, communications, and agricultural management would be handy, along with a valid driver's license and automobile insurance

Experience—Agricultural, food management, nursery work, and teaching experience can be handy but are not required.

Special Skills and Personality Traits—One needs diplomacy, charm, and persuasiveness to lure in farmers to participate; good organizing skills and the ability to entertain tourists; entrepreneurial skills to devise and take advantage of city dwellers' curiosity about fresh and healthy food; and an ability to communicate with both farmers and tourists, who may be very different kinds of people.

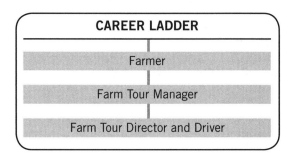

CAREER LADDER

Farmer

Farm Tour Manager

Farm Tour Director and Driver

Position Description

A Farm Tour Manager gets to know and reaches out to local working farmers to find those who are willing to have visitors—or at least might listen to the concept of having visitors—and educate these tourists about local sustainable farming, perhaps even sell them some fruit, vegetables, or eggs.

The Farm Tour Manager gathers a group of local farmers and sets out to coordinate a sensible tour that respects each grower's schedule and tries to mesh those with a potential tour schedule, some of which could include other activities. The tour might also include overnight farm stays where visitors can actually participate in farmwork, or dine on the farmer's cooking.

Local farmers might be interested in helping to educate people about healthful and tasty food, sell some of their products, and get some work and income from agritourists' visits.

Farm Tour Managers also develop good working relationships with schools and teachers to guide school students to farms, which is important to suburban communities, and even more important to students in urban areas who may think lettuce grows in cellophane bags and milk and juice grow in cartons. Teaching experience or passion for farming and working with children helps greatly with this group. The wonderment in the children's eyes may be a lifetime reward for the tour manager and the farmer.

Farm Tour Managers should develop a business plan for their tourism business, including targeting markets and groups they want to entice to learn by touring local farms. Visitors may take home all kinds of vegetables pulled straight out of the ground, juices, fruit right off the trees, preserves, books, eggs, and even pies.

Commercial agritourism lives primarily on fees paid by tourists to visit the farms and occasionally even enjoy a meal cooked on the farm and made up of products from the farm. Farm Tour Managers often seek community subsidies of some sort, possibly from school districts, local farmers, farmers' markets, a community foundation, or a county farm bureau.

Somehow the Farm Tour Manager's expenses need to be covered as well as his or her wages, unless he or she conducts farm tours for the fun of it without financial concerns. A manager's costs might include automobile and fuel, salary, telephone and cell phone, computer, and liability insurance, which may cover both passengers in his or her car and injury on the tours.

Farm Tour Managers need to think up fun gimmicks and help farmers conduct them, such as Halloween pumpkin sales and costume contests, visits to u-pick farms, corn mazes, and zucchini races. The managers also take responsibility for the publicity of tours and special events in local newspapers and on local radio and television stations, newsletters online or in print, and even occasional signage.

Salaries

Since most Farm Tour Managers basically create their own jobs, no salaries are guaranteed. People in this position have to raise money to pay themselves, so the better they do in organizing support, the more they earn. Salaries may range from $20,000 to $70,000.

Employment Prospects

Imaginative people with passion for local farming and educating people about the value of growing and purchasing food locally can create a position for themselves with some entrepreneurial dedication. Occasionally there is turnover in this relatively new profession.

Advancement Prospects

Moving up in the Farm Tour Manager business usually happens in a few ways. The manager moves to a larger organization with more farms, vehicles, and tourists; the manager enlarges his or her "stable" of farms and vehicles; or the manager adds more tours, vehicles, staff, and regions in an entrepreneurial fashion to expand the operation into other geographic areas or to more farms, leaving openings at various rungs on the ladder. Basically, create your own tour, expand your tour, or expand the geographic regions to be toured.

Education and Training

There is no specific educational requirement for being a Farm Tour Manager, but courses in tourism management, communications, organizational development, and agricultural management could be helpful.

Experience, Skills, and Personality Traits

Passion for farming, for good clean food, and for education are primary personality traits necessary to be a successful Farm Tour Manager. One must have the diplomatic and organizational skills to make farmers, parents, school districts, and teachers want to be part of a farm tourism program, and be able to convince each party that there is great benefit to them as well as to the community. Teaching experience, volunteering in a local visitors' bureau, and some farming or selling at a farmers' market all could be helpful.

Unions and Associations

Most states have agritourism associations. The Farmers' Market Coalition (formerly the North American Farmers' Direct Marketing Association) promotes and advocates for farmer's markets across the country (www.farmersmarketcoalition.org or www.familyfarms.org).

Tips for Entry

1. Volunteer at your local tourism office or bureau.
2. Volunteer or get a job with a vendor at a local farmers' market and get to know the growers and farmers in the area.
3. Get to know family farmers in your county and establish relationships with them.
4. Investigate business license and insurance policy needs to start your own farm tour company.
5. Get to know teachers at every school level, as well as culinary and agricultural program directors.

PUBLICITY, PUBLIC RELATIONS, AND MARKETING

RESTAURANT OR HOTEL PUBLICIST/PR DIRECTOR

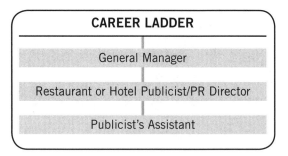

Position Description

Some restaurants and hotels have full-time publicists or public relations directors, while others retain freelance publicists who may have several other clients, and still others have owners or managers who try to do their public relations efforts themselves.

The Restaurant or Hotel Publicist or Public Relations Director has responsibility for creating the property's public image through "free media" such as editorial stories in local newspapers, magazines, online bloggers, and Web sites. Some PR directors also manage advertising copy, design, and placement.

While a publicist works to get positive image stories into local newspapers and food and travel magazines, his or her job also includes keeping bad or negative stories, such as a bad banquet meal or dirty sheets, out of the same media. Some restaurants and hotels want famous guests' names publicized, while others prefer to keep them quiet to keep those celebrities coming back without fear of crowds.

A publicist develops a vast network of media contacts from local food, wine, and "society" editors to full-time and freelance wine and food magazine writers, restaurant reviewers, bloggers, and Tweeters. To do this, the publicist invites these people to meals and special events at the restaurant or hotel or takes them out elsewhere, sends them bottles of wine or gift cards for overnight stays, supplies passes to a cooking demonstration or class, and carefully dribbles out little newsy tidbits to to give each writer a particular "exclusive."

The publicist also circulates in the community at other hotel, resort, winery, or restaurant events, possibly joins local service clubs, and the local chamber of commerce, chats up the attendees, and creates contacts and a friendly image for the restaurant, hotel, or resort he or she represents.

One of a publicist's goals is to lure parties and meetings of these community groups and leaders to their restaurant or hotel to host special guests or even nonprofit groups' benefit events, which can mean big sales of food and wine. The more guests the publicist invites, and the more community and media guests are pleased with the food or accommodations, the more a "buzz" builds around town or even around the world through current media that include Facebook and Twitter.

Smart publicists also look for other "free media," such as giving away a room for two for a few nights as a prize on a popular television quiz show or hugely popular Web site, or donating a room or dining experience as a local big charity auction "lot" or prize, resulting in widespread publicity worth far more than the cost of the meal or hotel stay itself.

A publicist often works with a hotel or resort's general manager or with a restaurant owner or manager to plan publicity-driven promotional events, story placement, and even advertising to coordinate with events and themes.

The publicist might also send out massive e-mails (e-blasts) to all customers, suppliers, potential customers, prominent entertainment characters and local characters, civic officials, and leaders of local nonprofits to announce upcoming events, new menus, and even include a recipe or two. Tweeting, or twittering, through the Twitter site is also a good way to reach focused "friends" or customers.

The publicist might also write the company's printed or online newsletter and contribute to the corporation's publications, whether another print or online newsletter or magazine. He or she also writes specific press releases touting new menus, new accommodations, even new hotel sheets or decor, special events, and new managers or chefs, all requiring competence in computer desktop publishing.

Often the publicist acts as a sort of communicator among employees or departments, smoothing over ripples and making everyone happy with optimistic and positive programs and attitude.

Salaries

Whether an owner of a single restaurant or large hotel hires a full-time publicist depends on the community where the property is located, what can be accomplished by a local publicist, and the size of the restaurant, resort, or hotel. Salaries range from $30,000 to $120,000, depending on all those variables in addition to the publicist's experience, technical skills, event planning skills, and other attributes.

PR people can also do well as freelance publicists, representing several clients that don't compete with one another in the restaurant, resort, and hotel fields.

Employment Prospects

Progressive restaurants, small and large chain hotels, historic inns, and other specialty properties most likely will hire publicists or public relations directors. The community of highly professional PR people in these categories is made up of accomplished publicists, many of whom know each other in a region of the United States or Canada, network often, and even inform one another of job opportunities.

Advancement Prospects

Restaurant owners who expand to more than one restaurant always need publicity; growing hotel chains need consistent public relations directors; and both opportunities can lead to a greater role and higher salary for the publicist. Some owners cut publicists and advertising in tough economic times while in the same situation others get aggressive and hire more public relations staff to gain a rung on the hospitality ladder.

A publicist can advance within a company by taking on more responsibility or by moving to a larger or more desperate restaurant or resort or hotel chain that will pay more. Or the person can create his or her own agency and take on several clients in the same field.

One danger for Restaurant or Hotel Publicists or Public Relations Directors is that occasionally they do such a good job and make the entity so successful that the business owner thinks they no longer need a PR person because they "got there on their own merits."

Education and Training

One usually needs a bachelor's degree in writing, copywriting, journalism, graphic arts, digital photography, communications, or marketing to succeed in the PR business. On-the-job training is often the best way to learn specifics and develop professional press releases.

Experience, Skills, and Personality Traits

Experience that will help a good publicist includes working for any public relations or advertising agency or similar department for any business; working at a restaurant or hotel to gain familiarity with demands and needs of the job; working for a newspaper, radio or television station; or even being a super Web worker who knows how to manipulate the Internet.

One needs a deep love and passion for the restaurant or hotel business, an understanding of what goes into making those businesses work, a willingness to work odd hours, an enjoyment of making professional friends and connections, and have design skills, accurate writing skills, and the ability to work with others.

A publicist also needs the nerve to pleasantly tell a client hard news, such as that the food isn't good, certain functions of a hotel aren't delivering or working, or that the biggest convention of the year was canceled because of the mayor's position on something.

Unions/Associations

No publicist or PR director unions exist, but the National Restaurant Association (www.restaurant.org), the American Institute of Wine and Food (www.globalchefs.com), and Women for WineSense (www.womenforwinesense.org) offers lots of publicity guidelines.

Local advertising or press clubs, media associations, chambers of commerce, and restaurant and wine associations can be helpful in the market local to the business.

Tips for Entry

1. Take classes in writing, communications, marketing, and business, and learn computer skills and publishing programs at a community or junior college or university if available.

2. Ask the college's counseling department for job placement recommendations.

3. Online sources offer guidelines to writing press releases and how to succeed at public relations work. Enroll in an online or in-person seminar at writing press releases.

4. Introduce yourself to publicists for restaurants, wineries, resorts, casinos, hotels, and cruise lines, and ask if they know of any entry-level jobs in the field or if they need an assistant.

5. Attend any seminars on public relations given by nonprofit groups, local newspapers, or online, where you will also find job lists.

HOTEL OR RESORT SALES MANAGER

CAREER PROFILE

Duties: Works to attract (or "sell") bookings for meetings, weddings, holiday parties, and other events by individuals and groups, including hotel or resort dining rooms, banquet rooms, restaurants, and hotel rooms to event attendees; entertains local business and social leaders; joins and circulates in service clubs and chambers of commerce; establishes contacts with travel agents, restaurant owners, PR people, and event planners; negotiates rates for both hotel rooms and catering events

Alternate Title(s): Marketing Director; Manager

Salary Range: $56,000 to $110,000, plus potential commission

Employment Prospects: Fair

Advancement Prospects: Fair

Best Geographical Location(s): Resort and gambling areas; big cities that attract lots of tourists; wine regions; cruise lines

Prerequisites:

Education or Training—Courses in marketing, business management, communications, and hospitality will help

CAREER LADDER

Director of Sales; Manager

Hotel or Resort Sales Manager

Assistant Sales Manager; Assistant

Experience—Any sales experience will help, as will working at almost any job in a hotel, resort, or restaurant

Special Skills and Personality Traits—Ability to get along with and charm others; ability to close a deal; a love of detail work and pleasing others; passionate knowledge of the hotel, resort, or restaurant; good negotiation skills

Position Description

A Hotel or Resort Sales Manager may be the public "face" of the hotel or resort to the local public and to potential guests in nearby cities.

The sales manager's goal is to book, or "sell," rooms, parties, banquets, and other events to build up the entity's business, sometimes working on commission. He or she may also oversee the scheduling of such events to avoid conflicts.

To reach this goal, Hotel or Resort Sales Managers schmooze and develop relationships with local leaders including chambers of commerce members, service clubs, council members, leading citizens and socialites, country club leaders, travel agents, wine tour operators, culinary tourism directors, and certain restaurant owners and managers. Occasionally a new Hotel or Resort Sales Manager will make a cold call to someone he or she does not know, and subtly invite the person to lunch, dinner, or to some special event.

After establishing this contact, the sales manager has to balance frequency of contact between being useful and driving the prospective client nuts, the latter ending in a negative response. The sales manager follows up with e-mails, bulletins, online or print newsletters, invitations to special events, a gift of a bottle of wine, and occasional phone calls.

Besides joining a chamber of commerce, a sales manager should attend chamber monthly "mixers" or "after hours" parties, which usually rotate among business members, and even host one of these well-attended events to impress the community with what his or her property has to offer.

If the sales manager joins a local or international service club, such as the Kiwanis or Rotary, he or she should show up at weekly meetings, make friends, join a subcommittee, and become known as reliable and generous by showing up for community work projects.

A good sales manager will become friendly with local visitors' bureaus or tourism associations, travel agents, hotel and resort managers outside of the area who can make referrals, winery owners, and culinary tourism directors who also can refer clients. If the sales manager has a special interest in food, restaurants, and cooking, he or she might also join the American Institute of Wine and Food (www.globalchefs.com), Women for Wine-Sense (www.womenforwinesense.org), or local culinary, wine, and wine growers' societies or associations.

The Hotel or Resort Sales Manager might also help the marketing director organize cooking classes or a series of cooking classes in the hotel or resort and offer package deals of the classes, including a room, meals, recipes, and even a cookbook from the celebrity chef who leads the class or from the resident chef.

Salaries

Many Hotel or Resort Sales Managers receive a base salary plus commission pay. Often sales managers and their superiors work out how the commission will be paid as part of an employment contract. If the sales manager is a good negotiator, his or her salary will remain steady in months or quarters when sales (business brought in) does not meet the agreed-upon goals. In good months or quarters when sales exceed the goals, the sales manager will receive a percentage of the sales over the base. Hence, salaries can fluctuate. Salaries range from about $56,000 to $110,000, plus potential commission.

Employment Prospects

Sales managers are the top of the heap in resorts and hotels, and have worked their way up probably serving in sales several other places. Sometimes a resort or hotel chain will send an employee at one of their properties to another to take the sales manager position. While a new sales manager may not have local community contacts, he or she arrives with a set of portable skills and the ability to quickly ingratiate himself or herself into the community.

Advancement Prospects

A lower-level salesperson within a resort, casino, or hotel chain can certainly work his or her way up the ladder to sales manager. A single-property sales manager can advance to general sales manager for a region or entire chain of hotels and resorts, or leave to join another, possibly larger, chain of hotels or resorts with a better reputation, and for a better job title and pay level.

Education and Training

While there is rarely a required degree for sales work, a solid background in marketing, business management, communications, and hospitality will help.

Experience, Special Skills, and Personality Traits

Any sales experience will help, as will working at almost any job in a hotel, resort, or restaurant along with the ability to get along with and charm others, and close a deal, have a love for detail work and pleasing others, a passionate knowledge of the hotel, resort or restaurant, and good negotiation skills.

Unions and Associations

Hotel or Resort Sales Manager jobs are usually considered "management" and not union eligible. Visitors' bureaus, tourism offices, and culinary societies can provide networking and helpful information.

Tips for Entry

1. Take courses in sales, business, and marketing.
2. Get some experience in sales—selling almost anything. Overcoming fear in that first ice-breaking sales pitch is most valuable.
3. Talk your way into a sales job at a hotel or resort and offer to work as the right-hand person to the sales manager, and then learn all you can from him or her.
4. Take any job in a hotel or resort with the goal of learning all you can about the business and work your way up.
5. Draw on any and all sales experience in your background when applying for a sales job in a hotel or resort, including selling Girl Scout cookies, running lemonade stands, selling raffle tickets, clerking in wine tasting rooms, hawking newspapers, or anything else.

DESTINATION MANAGEMENT COMPANY ACCOUNT MANAGER

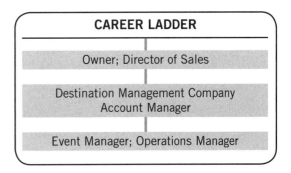
Position Description

Account managers for destination management companies (or DMCs) organize and design special events and special-event tours from airline reservations and transfers to ground transportation (limousines, buses, vans, or even off-road vehicles) and decor at a special events venue.

At the hotel or resort end of the arrangements, the destination account manager works to bring in out-of-town clients who might bring groups to the hotel or resort as the focal point of their business, conference, retreat, or special interest tour.

Destination management companies organize and schedule the entire tour from the home office, making frequent trips to the destinations to check on and learn about new or trendy opportunities, from new cooking school classes and winemaker visits to exotic animal collections and historic attractions. They also coordinate hotel rooms, catering, transportation, and other demands of the clients.

Some clients might want a themed tour or event, ranging from racetracks, golf, or organic vegetable farming to history, art, music, spas, wine, brewpubs, or fishing.

The DMC Account Manager makes all meal reservations and other arrangements, from catered events at a winery to box lunches for hikes, always considering vegetarian alternatives, and banquets at hotels, resorts, or restaurants.

Usually either the in-house account manager or the DMC Account Manager or both greet the traveling group on arrival to facilitate all transfers, safe luggage movement and storage, and any special needs of the guests. The account manager stays close throughout the trip to troubleshoot and make sure everything runs smoothly.

The account manager follows up with clients after the trip to measure satisfaction, keep up-to-date on tourism trends, and coordinate and send all pertinent invoices.

Such an account manager is judged mostly by his or her last trip or tour—they all have to be perfect.

Salaries

Salaries range from $60,000 to $150,000, and sometimes involve commissions based on sales.

Employment Prospects

There are few management companies and they are quite specialized, both in kind of tours and regions they cover, although they have an international network. Since these kinds of personalized tours and services are fairly expensive, the customer base is relatively small but affluent. Some of such clientele cut back in hard economic times, while others remain untouched financially.

Some resorts and hotels employ either in-house Destination Management Company Account Managers or work with freelancers.

Advancement Prospects

An account manager can rise to regional manager or national manager, can work toward salary or commission increases, move to another larger and more successful company, or start his or her own company to advance.

Education and Training

Hospitality or culinary, communications, or marketing classes will bring great advantage, as will a thorough knowledge of the geographic area where one wants to organize tours. One can teach oneself by traveling a lot and noticing organization details and how they can be improved.

Experience, Skills, and Personality Traits

A successful account manager will have comprehensive knowledge of the tour area from sports activities to cultural events, restaurants, wineries, and other special attractions of the location. Any work in hotels or resorts, travel agencies, events planning, or in the culinary world will be most helpful. An account manager should enjoy precise and exacting detail work; love the challenge of pleasing demanding and occasionally high-maintenance clients; have the ability to get along with anyone and everyone; be creative; have the ability to respond pleasantly and quickly to plan changes; be friendly; and have a cool head.

Unions and Associations

Both the Meeting Professionals International group (www.mpiweb.org) and the Professional Convention Management Association (www.pcma.org) offer loads of online and personal networking, learning opportunities, and conferences in desirable locations around the world.

For the food and wine aspects of these tours, one should get involved in local culinary societies and winery, vintner, or winegrower, associations to learn and get to know as many people as possible involved in the restaurant and wine businesses in the area. National organizations include the American Institute of Wine and Food (www.aiwf.org) and the International Association of Culinary Professionals (www.iacp.com), both of which offer networking, conferences, and all sorts of learning opportunities.

Both of these organizations can give information on how to "green" your tour; both to use less energy to travel and to visit the latest local "green business efforts," which may include an interesting winery, art gallery, or stadium.

Tips for Entry

1. Contact a local hotel and ask their public relations person or manager if and which destination management company they use, or if they hire in-house account managers.
2. Look online for destination management companies to see if there are any near where you live or in places where you might like to live and work.
3. Get a job in a hotel or resort and work your way into sales, a position that could put you in contact with destination management companies that could eventually hire you.

COOKING SCHOOLS, VOCATIONAL TRAINING, AND ACADEMIES

COOKING SCHOOL DIRECTOR

Duties: Schedules all cooking classes; sets standards and screens applicants; hires, trains, and schedules staff and volunteers; oversees writing and design of promotional brochures or Web sites; schedules publication of class catalog both in print and online

Alternate Title(s): Cooking School Manager; General Manager

Salary Range: $25,000 to $80,000

Employment Prospects: Limited

Advancement Prospects: Limited

Best Geographical Location(s): Urban areas where there are lots of good restaurants, wineries nearby, and culinary schools or art schools with culinary departments

Prerequisites:

Education and Training—Culinary training, high school diploma or associate's degree from a community or junior college in business, management, communications, or human resources

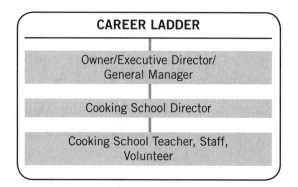

CAREER LADDER

Owner/Executive Director/ General Manager

Cooking School Director

Cooking School Teacher, Staff, Volunteer

Experience—Cooking instruction at any level, work in any business, or responsible positions in other fields all can help

Special Skills and Personality Traits—Diplomacy, good team building skills, tendency toward perfectionism, interest in details of organization, love of teaching, passion for food and cooking, and a natural ability to teach

Position Description

A Cooking School Director assesses the school's audience in its region and what target market audience it can address and attract from outside the immediate community. Sometimes that research is based on which classes people attend and which they ignore.

The Cooking School Director procures the finest teachers possible; schedules classes; designs and publishes the school's brochure, pamphlet, print catalog, or online catalog with text, calendar, and class schedule; and assigns teachers to classes closest to their fields of specialty.

The manager or director sets a budget that has to include equipment and ingredient supplies for classes; teachers' pay; utilities, insurance, rent or property taxes, and any other expenses. On the plus side, the director also projects income from students' fees, catered events held at the cooking facility, and any rental of certified kitchen to canners or other aspiring food producers.

The director may also handle registration and decide which classes have enough students to proceed and which do not, obtains recipes ahead of time from instructors and organizes or directs shopping for

ingredients, has copies of recipes printed for handouts to class attendees, and finds and coordinates volunteers.

The manager or director will also schedule in-class assistants for the instructor, who usually will be either staff or experienced volunteers as sort of backup singers to the star chef soloist. For hands-on classes, the manager oversees several tables of learners, assistants, and instructors, makes sure guests are using implements safely, and sees that each student understands what to do and how to accomplish it.

If the class includes tastes, samples, or an entire meal, the director or manager coordinates assistants, servers, and volunteers who set up all flatware and dinnerware for the number of guests attending, serve all of the courses, and help clean up afterward.

If the class is large, the manager/director might also arrange for angled overhead mirrors and well-placed video screens and cameras so that all guests can view the goings-on in the kitchen.

Cooking schools range from corporate burger chains that have "cooking schools or universities" for their future employees, to high school, community, and junior colleges, and private culinary school programs.

Instructors may include local chefs and specialists in baking, chocolate, or Italian cuisine to local or regional television show hosts or even nationally famous cooking personalities. Many just focus on good local cooks, and some of those good cooks teach people in their homes, restaurants, grocery stores, cookware shops, resorts, and even on cruise ships. Others teach to an in-person class with other learners watching online at home.

Some cooking schools cater to professional cooks or aspiring professional cooks, while others specialize in teaching home cooks, with classes growing as people prefer to cook at home instead of dining out. Many second-career people are looking for a new vocation and try cooking in a "casual" cooking school atmosphere and progress to a more professional school.

A director or manager keeps up to date on cooking trends and what latest fads might interest students, while balancing the teaching schedule with classics and basics classes everyone can use at home or in a restaurant.

Local cooking instructors or chefs with followings usually make friends with the Cooking School Manager or director so that they are high on the quarterly or annual list of classes, and they often work with the director to develop classes guests might like.

Well-organized cookbook authors and their publishers and publicists will want to fit into the school's schedule soon after their book comes out so they can sell them to the students and sign the books after class. It is the manager's or director's responsibility to keep up relationships with the cookbook publicists to make sure the school gets on an author's itinerary, which is planned several months in advance.

Directors and managers also stay in touch with other cooking schools in other geographic areas so that they can all get a broader view of methods and scheduling plans of chefs and authors who are touring. School directors and managers often share this kind of information—as long as they are not in competition with one another.

Many directors and managers are also chefs and teach cooking classes in their own cooking schools, and then plan others' courses way ahead of time to allow for printing and mailing of the quarterly, half-yearly, or yearly schedule. Many also review or plan ahead during their own "vacations" or downtime in their culinary season.

Salaries

Cooking School Directors or managers sometimes are also the owners of the establishment, in which case they pay themselves after other expenses are paid. Those who work for an owner get paid from $25,000 to $80,000 after the school builds its studentry and does well.

Employment Prospects

Job openings for Cooking School Directors managers are limited, but one can start teaching friends to cook in one's own kitchen and eventually expand to opening a cooking school in a storefront, elegant resort, art school, or other private institution. As more Americans seek jobs in the food industry, more cooking school leadership posts should open.

Advancement Prospects

One can move up within a cooking school or within a business or institution in which the cooking school is located. A Cooking School Director can also move to an academic program, to larger corporation's school to make more money, or just by building the program where he or she is into the best cooking school anywhere.

Education and Training

There is no strict education requirement to run a cooking school, but a sound culinary training in a high school or an associate's degree from a community or junior college will help, especially if you take business, management, communications, and human resources courses. One might also serve as an assistant or "apprentice" to a cooking school manager or director.

Work to obtain a certificate from the International Association of Culinary Professionals (www.iacp.com) as well.

Experience, Skills, and Personality Traits

Cooking or cooking instruction at any level, work in any business, or responsible positions in other fields all can help. Nurturing teaching skills, whether innate or learned, and some knowledge of psychology go a long way.

One must know food, some food chemistry, how foods interact, food history, and what is available fresh, organic, and locally.

Diplomacy, good team building skills, perfectionist tendencies, interest in details of organization, love of teaching, a passion for food and cooking, and a natural ability to teach and lead others would be ideal.

Unions and Associations

The International Association of Culinary Professionals (www.iacp.com) offers networking, conferences, certification, and annual vocational and avocational awards of excellence for various culinary achievements, including cooking schools.

The James Beard Foundation (www.jamesbeard.org) operates James Beard House, where rising chefs cook fund-raising dinners for the foundation. James Beard House gives cooking demonstrations, master's classes for professional chefs, and operates other programs, including an esteemed awards program.

Local culinary associations, or even loosely connected chefs' e-mail lists, offer educational programs, educational wine tasting, and valuable local networking.

Tips for Entry

1. Learn to cook as well as you can.
2. Work in a restaurant or cooking school, starting with any job available and learn all you can.
3. Give small classes, even starting with your family, in your own home kitchen.
4. Volunteer at a cooking school as a class or kitchen assistant.
5. Work your way into a paying job by learning and making yourself valuable.
6. Tour other cooking schools and look for jobs.

COOKING TEACHER

CAREER PROFILE

Duties: Cooking teachers plan classes, write outlines and recipes, demonstrate cooking techniques, share secret tips, explain ingredients, their relationships, and the sources of ingredients, and tell learners about the effects of refrigeration and heat from different sources on the ingredients. Duties vary by whether the cooking teacher works at a high school, community college, cooking school, "cooking school" for a corporate food chain, or teaches in a winery, bakery, or at his or her home or at someone else's home.

Alternate Title(s): Cooking Instructor; Cooking Demonstrator; Owner; Chef

Salary Range: $500 to $5,000 freelance per class for cooking schools, up to $60,000 in public schools

Employment Prospects: Fair to good

Advancement Prospects: Good

Best Geographical Location(s): Big cities where good food is valued, wine regions, resort areas, or where you live

Prerequisites:

    Education or Training—Culinary courses at any level, from high school or art school program to self-

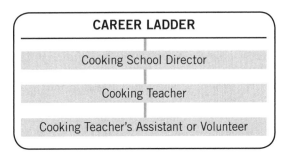

taught; culinary schools or any teaching training or certificate; some knowledge of food chemistry

    Experience—Home cooking, cooking in restaurants or hotels, and any teaching experience will help—even at-home cooking classes

    Special Skills and Personality Traits—An ability to teach and share knowledge and insights with others and organize a lesson plan with recipes; a sense of humor; ability to entertain; a love of detail work; a love of minutiae of ingredients; and perhaps a specialty in a food category

Position Description

A Cooking Teacher's job description varies according to the kind of school or situation in which he or she teaches. A high school Cooking Teacher deals with teenagers with varying degrees of interest and commitment. A teacher at an upscale elegant cooking school or in his or her own home kitchen works with somewhat affluent adult home chefs who are there because they are willing to spend lots of money specifically to learn techniques their friends may not know.

A Cooking Teacher assesses his or her target market or audience and their interests and plans a program or class at the technical level appropriate for the group. The teacher selects a theme and sets a menu with recipes as a class plan. Sometimes the teacher rewrites and adapts recipes according to what ingredients are available in a geographic area.

All teachers need to have the ability to entertain in order to hold their students' attention, making sure they have a good time and want to come back again. When teaching a particular class for the first time, teachers

might rehearse in front of friends or family. If they are repeating a class in a new venue, they must look over the recipes and make sure their commentary applies to the new location.

Some cooking classes present an entire menu, from cold or hot soup to dessert, and usually include five or six recipes along with techniques for boning, foaming, or kneading, for example. Other ingredient-specific classes may teach nine ways to prepare chocolate, with recipes included. Recipes have to be precise and include readily available ingredients or learners will be disappointed.

If a Cooking Teacher does offer a class with exotic ingredients, he or she might have to bring those contents and any imported utensils or clay pots that she or he will need, along with retail or online sources where learners can get the ingredients and implements either in their city or by shopping online. If that person teaches frequently at the cooking school, the institution might keep the supplies on hand, or the teacher can give good warning to a local grocery store so that it can order the ingredients knowing demand will increase due to the class.

At many finer cooking schools, assistants or volunteers prepare the *mise en place,* meaning they measure and weigh all ingredients and place them in little bowls or in quantities suitable for chopping on cutting boards for the instructor, or with knives for each table if it is a hands-on class.

The Cooking Teacher arrives at least an hour or two ahead of the class to check on preparations and make sure everything is there that he or she will need, including his or her own cookbooks if the instructor wants to sell or sign them. Ingredients and implements should be lined up in the order in which the teacher will use them according to the menu.

Recipe copies should be passed out to students as they arrive, along with any other information such as the instructor's e-mail address and Web site.

Assistants and volunteers should help pass out tastes of each item on the menu once it is cooked or prepared so that learners get an idea of what it should taste like when they try to make it at home.

Teachers often invite students to speak out and ask questions, but the instructor needs to control the rhythm of conversation and not talk too much or allow one learner to take over the room. As groups get busy making the menu's recipes in a hands-on class, an ambiance that resembles chaos or pandemonium appears to take over, with different learners capable of understanding or following directions at different rates. Everything should come together with the help of trained volunteers and assistants and the instructor.

Some of the tasting goes on as each recipe is completed. In a large class, the cooking school kitchen staff might prepare the dishes in another kitchen and serve a meal of the recipes all at once at the end of the class, perhaps with a glass of local wine. This is when students and the Cooking Teacher get to know one another better and the teacher has the chance to further impress learners and encourage them to come back for their next class or purchase his or her books.

Salaries

Fees collected by cooking schools for individual classes vary by the fame and reputation of the cooking teacher, the cost of the ingredients, how much staff help is required as a backup, whether the class is a large room demonstration or a small hands-on class, and the popularity of the subject. Television chefs get the largest pay, while a new cooking instructor might be at the low end of the pay scale, ranging from $500 to $5,000 per class for cooking schools and up to $60,000 annually in public schools.

Employment Prospects

Anyone who has cooking expertise, particularly with food from a different culture or country or with bread or chocolate, can become a cooking teacher, often starting in one's own home and eventually formalizing the instruction at a cooking school or restaurant.

If one has a good reputation for sharing culinary knowledge, local cooking schools—which are always looking for fun teachers to fill their schedules and attract new students—will be interested. High school adult education programs also look for new instructors, as do community and junior colleges.

Cooking schools flourish and expand in good economic times because learners have extra money to spend, but schools often have to limit programs in bad economic times when students cut spending on their own pleasures.

Advancement Prospects

Advancement as a Cooking Teacher comes as one attracts a following, more students enroll, and the cooking school can charge a higher fee for the class, after which the school can pay the teacher more. A cooking school teacher can move up to culinary director or cooking school general manager or director. There are relatively few cooking school directors or general managers, and possibly just one of each at a cooking school.

Popular cooking school teachers also get requests to teach in homes and at other teaching venues, and some even develop a sort of circuit as traveling cooking teachers, especially if their written work appears in magazines or if they write cookbooks.

Education and Training

A good Cooking Teacher needs to know basic cooking techniques from experience or education. Some teachers do very well having taught themselves or learning from family members, while others learn from structured classes or watching cooking shows on television. (TV cooking shows, however, teach about as much kitchen reality as TV "cop" shows teach about police beat reality—they both primarily entertain.)

Culinary courses at any level, from high school or art school programs to culinary schools or any teaching training or certificate, and some knowledge of food chemistry will definitely help.

Experience, Skills, and Personality Traits

Home cooking, cooking in restaurants or hotels, and any teaching experience will help. Even at-home cooking classes or teaching your children will contribute to your ability to teach. Basically a person needs to be passionate about sharing knowledge and insights with others, have a sense of humor and patience since not all students learn at the same rate, enjoy jollying people up and entertaining, love detail work, love minutiae of ingredients, and occasionally have a specialty in a food category. A really good cooking teacher will constantly look for new trends and ingredients in their specialties, whether that means availability of Moroccan spices or handmade chocolate or tortillas.

Unions and Associations

The only unions for Cooking Teachers are in public schools, which are more general teachers' unions or associations. Most cooking school teachers in private cooking schools work on a per-class contract or agreement basis.

Started in 1978 as the Association of Cooking Schools to promote the interests of cooking schools and cooking teachers, the International Association of Culinary Professionals (www.iacp.com) now includes 3,000 members in 45 countries and offers certification, newsletters, e-mail bulletins, networking, and annual conferences.

Tips for Entry

1. Watch all the cooking shows on television that you can, especially Julia Child reruns. You are bound to learn something.
2. Find whatever classes at any level available in your area and take the classes. Check with school principals, culinary program directors, food editors, and want ads to find other classes.
3. Practice teaching cooking in your own home for friends and relatives.
4. Videotape, or record in any video form, yourself teaching others to cook.
5. Write a résumé that includes all of your cooking experience, culinary travel, and cultural cooking interests and influences.
6. Send a DVD or other videography of you teaching along with your résumé to local cooking schools to open the door for you.
7. Call or follow up.
8. Volunteer at a local cooking school to assist in-house chefs with prep, events, or visiting teachers.

COOKING TEACHER ASSISTANT

CAREER PROFILE

Duties: Prepares (preps), chops, minces, and measures foods for teachers to use in class recipes, assists the cooking teacher during class and gets anything needed, helps serve food the teacher has prepared during class, and helps to clean up after the class and return space to look as if no one had been there

Alternate Title(s): Volunteer; Assistant

Salary Range: $0 to $15 per hour

Employment Prospects: Lots for free; limited for pay

Advancement Prospects: Good

Best Geographical Location(s): Big cities where good food is valued, wine regions, resort areas, or anywhere you live, with larger cooking schools needing more assistants for more teachers

Prerequisites:

Education or Training—Knowledge about cooking techniques, meaning all of the basics such as knife skills, blending and puréeing, measuring with exactitude, and knowledge of all equipment a cooking teacher will use

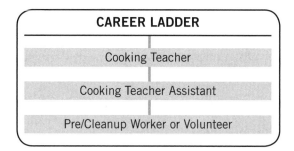

CAREER LADDER

Cooking Teacher

Cooking Teacher Assistant

Pre/Cleanup Worker or Volunteer

Experience—Lots of home cooking; learning at or attending a variety of cooking classes to see what you need to know; teaching at any level; restaurant experience handy but certainly not necessary

Special Skills and Personality Traits—Patience with sometimes demanding cooking instructors; resilience and the ability to take criticism; ability to take orders and follow directions precisely without correcting instructor or talking back; a general desire to please and learn

Position Description

Cooking Teacher Assistants are the heroines and heroes of cooking classes because they perform or coordinate all of the work that has to be finished before the class starts to make it run smoothly.

For the class to run well, all of the prep work has to be done ahead of time by someone. That person is usually a cooking teacher's assistant, many of whom are volunteers who show up to learn, sometimes from famous chefs who are teaching. So the assistant either does or oversees others who chop, mince, weigh, and measure ingredients specified in recipes and put them in small containers, all of which collectively are called *mise en place* and are ready to combine in the order required by the recipe and the teacher. The assistant sets up trays of *mise en place* for hands-on classes so that each learning table has its own set for students to use while making the recipes.

An assistant must do everything in the order the cooking teacher wants it and not question or argue, even if the assistant is an accomplished cook and is right. The teacher is the director or the general, and the assistant is just that, who follows the teacher's orders

and instructions. If an assistant has questions, he or she should ask them before the class, and even run through the recipe, checking ingredients, before the class starts.

Before a class starts, the assistant, who may work repeatedly with a teacher or even be requested by a teacher, makes sure the counters are perfectly clean, that everything is available in the proper order and quantities, and that there is water or other preferred beverage available to the teacher. Some cooking teachers even ask a trusted assistant to shop for certain ingredients for them.

Often teacher assistants serve samples of each recipe or whole meals to students after they have cooked or after the teacher performs his or her demonstration.

Assistants remove all equipment as it is used, wash it elsewhere, and have all utensils and cooking equipment returned to cabinets before the class leaves. Assistants often get extra, more personal conversation with cooking teachers, which is definitely one of the perks of volunteering or working in this role.

If the teacher has cookbooks to be purchased and signed, the assistant sometimes helps collect money or record credit cards and helps maintain the signing line.

Salaries

Many Cooking Teacher Assistants are volunteers who work for the sheer joy of getting experience or getting close to famous chefs, but some hope to gain experience to eventually qualify as a teacher themselves. If a cooking teacher assistant is paid, the hourly pay usually ranges from minimum wage to $15, and some work in the school office as well if they are lucky.

Employment Prospects

While Cooking Teacher Assistant jobs are much sought after for the experience, there are loads of unpaid opportunities for volunteers. Sometimes the "pay" consists of free cooking classes, meaning an assistant gets to attend another class without paying.

Some cooking teachers have their own assistants who travel with them and either assist them for a class or oversee local cooking school teacher assistants and their prep work.

Advancement Prospects

Being a Cooking Teacher Assistant is great groundwork for working one's way up the kitchen ladder because you learn many techniques, what they require, how to treat people, and how to balance entertainment with information.

Many assistants work up to giving their own classes as they, too, develop followings. They also can become so useful to a particular teacher that he or she may hire them to be their personal or full-time assistant.

A Cooking Teacher Assistant may also work in the school office, become more useful, work up to culinary director of the school and even manager or general manager.

Education and Training

While basic cooking technique knowledge is about all that is required of Cooking Teacher Assistants, one should have good knife skills, know blending and puréeing, measuring with exactitude, and understand all equipment a cooking teacher will use. The training one receives assisting an accomplished cooking teacher is great training in itself.

Experience, Skills, and Personality Traits

One can become a Cooking Teacher Assistant with just home cooking experience, by learning at or attending a variety of cooking classes to see what you need to know, and teaching at any level. Even restaurant experience can be handy but is certainly not necessary.

Patience with sometimes demanding cooking instructors, resilience and the ability to take criticism, an ability to take orders and follow directions precisely without correcting the instructor or talking back, the sense to ask questions before the class starts, and a general desire to please and learn are the most important traits for an assistant, but he or she also needs to know basic knife skills and some culinary terms.

Unions and Associations

There are no unions for Cooking Teacher Assistants, but local culinary or cuisine societies and even wine groups offer excellent networking opportunities. The International Association of Culinary Professionals (www.iacp.com) offers all sorts of information, provides eventual certification, hosts conferences, and e-mails newsletters.

Tips for Entry

1. Take a few classes in adult education programs at high schools, community or junior colleges, private cooking schools, and even at your ideal cooking school where you would like to assist, and learn by observation how a cooking class and an instructor work and what is required.
2. Volunteer to assist at any level at a private cooking school in your area, even for no pay.
3. Become familiar with the good or popular teachers and try to become one of their assistants so you can learn even more about the combination of education and entertainment.
4. Find independent or private cooking teachers through your local or regional newspapers and offer to assist them.

TRAVELING COOKING TEACHER

CAREER PROFILE

Duties: Creates a series of cooking classes to give throughout a region or around the country, or gives a similar class at distant locations where attendees would not overlap; plans the series and sells the classes, appealing to different markets, target audiences, and locales; pitches the classes to cooking schools, restaurants, and wineries; writes or rewrites recipes; takes along his or her own special utensils and cookware as needed; demonstrates pertinent cooking techniques; informs the school or other host what ingredients will be needed and may even purchase them; and teaches how to cook a full menu or individual recipes to those who attend the class, whether home cooks or professionals; signs and sells cookbooks

Alternate Title(s): Guest Chef; Guest Cooking Teacher; Visiting Teacher; Chef

Salary Range: $500 to $5,000 per class, plus possible book sales

Employment Prospects: Limited

Advancement Prospects: Good

Best Geographical Location(s): Anywhere in the country, particularly big cities where there are good

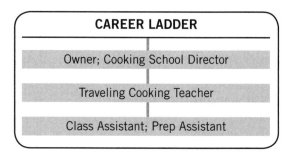

CAREER LADDER

Owner; Cooking School Director

Traveling Cooking Teacher

Class Assistant; Prep Assistant

restaurants and demand for good food, as well as wine regions

Prerequisites:

Education or Training—Either self-taught, culinary education, or extraordinary cooking skills

Experience—Home cooking classes, cooking experience in field teaching, real-life cultural experience in a culinary specialty such as exotic cuisines or bread baking; requirements vary by school

Special Skills and Personality Traits—Expertise in your field; ability to get along with and motivate people; ability to entertain and teach; humor; timing; patience with people less knowledgeable who really want to learn; a passion for sharing culinary skills and knowledge

Position Description

Traveling Cooking Teachers, if they are lucky, try to plan their travel and cooking school itineraries a year in advance or even further, partly because cooking schools' catalogs and calendars are printed and posted up to three months ahead. A few super-popular chefs and TV chefs have agents who do the booking for them.

Traveling Cooking Teachers starting out may begin by getting to know directors or managers of local or area cooking schools, and arranging one class at a time. If that class works well, it is wise for the teacher to book another one for the future, and build on the first success to go to another school not too far away and pitch a class there.

The teacher designs the teaching syllabus, which may include the menu, recipes, a list of ingredients, and online and local sources to buy special ingredients. The last item may require special attention to find local markets that carry required spices and grains or good substitutes.

Traveling Cooking Teachers often set up a tour based on their most recently published cookbook or when they

are testing recipes for their next cookbook. The tour itinerary should consider logical and economical travel patterns and air or train fares, as well as the instructor's health and well-being. Therefore, the trip must make sense in terms of energy, publicity, and money earned.

When the tour is planned, the teacher creates or reviews existing printed materials and handouts, either to be reproduced by the cooking school or by the teacher and distributed to the students or e-mailed to each student. The teacher has to review each packet ahead of time to make sure the contents make sense for each audience and that the ingredients or alternatives are available locally or online.

A Traveling Cooking Teacher will tell each cooking school what equipment and ingredients he or she will need, and either the school's assistants or the cooking teacher will do the actual shopping. The instructor might bring or ship ahead his or her own set of knives and other equipment that might be unique to his or her cuisine or menu.

Popular traveling teachers might arrange for a full day or two- to three-day classes in one location, or sometimes two in one day, thereby limiting travel and being able to charge more per class or for more classes.

TV chefs often bring their own assistant, or the cooking school provides an assistant for the visiting teacher or chef.

All the prep is done before the class by assistants who chop, mince, and weigh all ingredients, with equal setups for each of the student workstations in a hands-on class. Learners receive the syllabus as they enter the teaching kitchen or room and are informed whether they will be tasting each recipe as they go or have a complete meal at the end of the demonstration.

Either the teacher or the cooking school management might arrange for interviews on local radio or television or with a local food editor, which can result in even greater publicity and exposure beyond the school's immediate audience.

Salaries

Traveling Cooking Teachers can put together a slim living, usually on a per-class contract basis with each school. Cooking classes serve to gain public exposure and publicity for aspiring cooking teachers, and those with current or upcoming books to sell.

Often a school will reimburse teachers for the costs of printouts if they do them themselves. Pay may range from around $300 and $500 up to $2,000 per three-hour class. Famous television chefs command $10,000 and more per class. Some schools pay for teachers' overnight accommodations and other expenses, and a few have inn rooms on-site.

Employment Prospects

The hundreds of cooking schools in North America and around the world always have their eyes and ears open for new instructor talent to spice up their schedules to attract more students or keep regulars coming back. Cooking teachers often start with at-home classes, and when they successfully branch out, cooking school managers will often tell others at other cooking schools about instructors who do a good job.

Advancement Prospects

Advancement for traveling cooking teachers often means gaining popularity, charging higher fees, writing magazine articles or cookbooks, and even starting a television show.

Education and Training

A Traveling Cooking Teacher can be self-taught, have a culinary education, or have extraordinary cooking skills and the ability to entertain and bring in repeat students to be successful. An interesting or unusual specialty such as Thai, Mexican, or North African helps as well, as does expertise in certain techniques in baking, chocolate, vegetarian cuisine, or other ethnic cuisines.

Experience, Skills, and Personality Traits

Taking home cooking classes, having cooking experience in your specific field, teaching others at home, garnering real-life cultural experience in a culinary specialty such as exotic cuisines or bread baking are useful; requirements vary by school. Expertise in your field; the ability to get along with and motivate people; the ability to entertain and teach; humor; timing; patience with people less knowledgeable who really want to learn; and a passion for sharing culinary skills and knowledge will all encourage cooking school managers to hire a Traveling Cooking Teacher.

Unions and Associations

In the absence of an actual union of traveling cooking school teachers, the International Association of Culinary Professions (IACP) provides the most information. Started in 1978 as the Association of Cooking Schools to promote interests of cooking schools and cooking teachers, the IACP (www.iacp.com) now includes 3,000 members in 45 countries and offers certification, newsletters, e-mail bulletins, networking, and annual conferences.

Tips for Entry

1. Try teaching friends or family in your home first.
2. Set up free classes in other people's homes as a sort of warm-up for actually charging.
3. Ask people who attend to spread the word to their friends everywhere to build some demand for your teaching services.
4. Join the IACP and make use of its online "Education" section, which provides a list of cooking schools by city.
5. Volunteer to cook, demonstrate, or teach at any and all nonprofit charity events and festivals to make your talents, food, and personality better known and to create demand for your teaching abilities.
6. If you travel for other purposes, look in your destination's local yellow pages for cooking schools, visit whatever schools are available and ask for the manager or director, introduce yourself, present your card or brochure that includes praiseful remarks by attendees and cooking school managers, and ask to be considered to teach there in the future. Follow up the following week with a phone call to nail down a date.

FOOD-SERVICE MANAGEMENT TEACHER

CAREER PROFILE

Duties: Teaches skills of restaurant or institutional food management such as production costs, menu pricing, and budgeting; facility maintenance and sanitation; inventory and ordering; pertinent computer programs; human resources management and staff scheduling; institutional food planning, preparation, and new trends; and sometimes coordinates internships

Alternate Title(s): Instructor; Assistant Professor; Professor; Culinary Arts Teacher

Salary Range: $35,000 to $60,000

Employment Prospects: Good

Advancement Prospects: Good

Best Geographical Location(s): Throughout the United States, wherever there are community and junior colleges and wherever culinary or vocational schools are

Prerequisites:

Education or Training—College bachelor's degree preferred; sometimes master's degree; culinary certification through a culinary academy or the International Association of Culinary Professionals; highly

CAREER LADDER

Vocational, College, or University Director or Department Head

Food-Service Management Teacher

Foods Teaching Assistant/Computer Science Teaching Assistant

visible work experience and background in food service may substitute for degrees

Experience—Teaching food service at a high school or in adult education classes; professional food service management and cooking experience

Special Skills and Personality Traits—Excellent teaching and communication skills, both oral and written; a passion for sharing food and food service management knowledge; patience with slower or less committed learners; an ability to entertain, be flexible, and enjoy detail work

Position Description

Food-service management instructors teach a practical, slightly less romantic side of the food service business. They teach in a few high school programs, adult schools at high schools run sometimes by nearby junior colleges, community colleges, junior colleges, culinary schools, and even hotel and hospitality schools.

Food-Service Management Teachers have students who may have never cooked a meal, some who have taken culinary courses in high school, community college, or elsewhere, and some who have great aspirations and cooking experience.

These teachers have to prepare their students for the careers they want, such as running cafés or restaurants, feeding whole camps or high-tech company employees, and generally improving their culinary and management skills to run food service departments of everything from delis to department stores.

Those students who take food service management classes sometimes have to be told basics, such as the fact that they have to show up on time, clean and sober (in more ways than one), in their uniform if there is one, looking and acting professional and interested.

Food-Service Management Teachers teach everything from knife skills and how to make sauces to customer relations and good service; how to make sure facilities are clean and sanitary; inventory and ordering procedures including computer programs that help with these tasks; seating chart computer programs; how to work with the chef to create appropriate menus with proper pricing; how to hire, train, schedule, and fire workers; how to supervise assistant managers; how to manage banquet and catering operations; cashiering and ordering by computer and processing paperwork and bookkeeping; how to set up internships for students at restaurants and hotels; and help cook or clean when needed—meaning "no job too small."

Sometimes Food-Service Management Teachers also oversee hands-on programs that include cooking in or for a school cafeteria, café, or snack bar. On the cooking side, and according to a well-organized lesson plan (cleared with superiors), practical skills taught include a how to poach eggs and make hollandaise sauce for eggs Benedict, sandwich making, filling short orders, deli salad and sandwich making, and working with butters, vegetables, potatoes, rice, legumes, meats, poultry, fish, and shellfish. The program assumes students have never cooked before. Learners even make ice cream, gelati, sorbets, tarts, cakes, and maybe even profiteroles (cream puffs).

The Food-Service Management Teacher also needs to know French culinary and kitchen hierarchy terms as well as French cooking terms while mastering early level classic methods, sauces, and even theory.

The Food-Service Management Teacher even needs to know how to teach dining room and kitchen renovation and decor; marketing; and even some basic equipment mechanics.

Salaries

Salaries vary according to how long one has been teaching and at what level of school, from high school to university hotel and management programs. They range from $35,000 to $70,000.

Employment Prospects

Job prospects are good throughout the country, because more and more people want to enter the food-service business, even in tough economic times, and therefore there is a demand for schools to keep and even expand their culinary programs and hire more Food-Service Management Teachers.

Advancement Prospects

As with teachers in any institution, there is always the opportunity to move up to department head or chair, and even into school, college, or university administration. How far you can go rests on your college degrees, work experience in the kitchen (and in what kitchens), seniority, and reputation as a teacher. You can also move up the culinary education ladder by moving to another school where you get a better title and more responsibility and pay.

Education and Training

High schools and adult schools usually accept a college or university bachelor's degree as a prerequisite, while some community colleges, junior colleges, and universities require bachelor's and master's degrees,

and hotel and hospitality schools require more specific certification. On the culinary side, culinary certification through a culinary academy or the International Association of Culinary Professionals (IACP), or highly visible work experience and background in food service may substitute for degrees.

Experience, Skills, and Personality Traits

The best teacher of vocations is a person who has worked that business and has real-life experience. It is much easier to teach from experience, and easier to relate real information to students if one has actually done the job, with all of its glories and pitfalls. Working in hotels, restaurants, nursing homes, school cafeterias, Little League hot dog stands, as a counter clerk, or for an active catering company all are great preparation for teaching food-service management.

One has to know human resources law and practices, cooking techniques and skills, use of a wide range of equipment, safety and sanitation regulations and methods, and business and restaurant menu planning and accounting, and have huge amounts of sensitivity to students.

A Food-Service Management Teacher has to be alert to when certain students "don't get it" or are falling behind, because not everyone is equally good at all facets of the class or classes. A teacher cannot assume that all students have had the same home or public culinary experience, some having grown up on frozen burritos while others help family members cook every day or go out weekly to restaurants.

A Food-Service Management Teacher needs excellent teaching and communication skills, both oral and written; a passion for sharing food and food-service management knowledge; patience with slower or less committed learners; the ability to entertain, be flexible, and enjoy detail work; and the derivation of pleasure from seeing happy and prepared students graduating.

Unions and Associations

The International Council on Hotel, Restaurant and Institutional Education (www.chrie.org) helps food service and hospitality teachers at high schools, community colleges, certificate programs, universities, graduate students, industry professionals, and food service leaders in all sorts of industries.

Local teachers and culinary associations as well as connections to food economists, food historians, and food chemists can be helpful, as are the American Culinary Federation (www.acfchefs.org), the National Restaurant Association (www.restaurant.org), and the IACP (www.iacp.com).

Tips for Entry

1. Get any experience you can as a cook at any level to have some real-life experience.
2. Depending on your age, check out high school, community and junior college, and university programs, and take courses at the one closest to you that will help you accomplish what you want to do.
3. Before enrolling, ask about job placement services.
4. Get the degrees or certification you need to teach.
5. Be willing to start as an assistant teacher or teaching assistant to work your way up.
6. Prepare a résumé with photos showing your experience, or even make a Web site or personal blog that demonstrates what you have done.
7. Search job Web sites for Food Service Management Teacher job openings.

VOCATIONAL CULINARY SCHOOL DIRECTOR

Position Description

A Vocational Culinary School Director basically runs the culinary program. The director often works with a board of directors of the program that advises and provides contacts that may lead to financial support and interesting guest instructors for the program.

The director also selects faculty when there are openings, trains new faculty in the ways of the particular vocational school, supervises all instructors and their guest chefs, and fires people when necessary or even possible, which is rare given current law. The director helps instructors develop curriculum and lesson plans, balancing classes and expertise so that students have the opportunity to get a full range of culinary experiences and knowledge.

The director needs thorough knowledge of business management, both to teach it and to run the finances of

the department, which is important because of equipment needed in classrooms such as computers and software, stoves, mixers, "walk-in" refrigerators, and even spoons. He or she also needs to be able to teach food service management including calculation of all costs, menu pricing, and purchasing.

The director observes and evaluates teachers throughout the year, with the goal of making sure students learn what they need to, occasionally guiding the instructor to teach better and more effectively. Directors hire instructors to teach specialities such as nutrition, service management, food and beverage management, baking and pastry, charcuterie and butchering, and food presentation.

As is true for many teachers and directors, both academic and vocational, a Vocational Culinary School Director has to get teachers to plan way ahead, develop their curricula, and list or requisition any equipment and nonperishable ingredients needed. He or she has to order a new stove in time to get it delivered and installed if the old one broke down and can't be repaired, and has to make requests of the dean or school officials for replacement of parts or new equipment.

The director has to estimate student enrollment accurately and hire or lay off enough instructors to teach the number of students who show up, while estimating the cost of hiring these people, paying for the functions they will perform, and getting supplies into classrooms that are correct for the classes that will take place in that room. To make all this happen, the director has to submit a budget to the dean and to other higher-ups and even argue in its favor, particularly if her or she is asking for more money or if enrollment has decreased in the culinary school.

The director administers the entire culinary program including hiring, training, firing, and supervising culinary teaching staff; may design a culinary program facility within larger vocational school; selects, orders, and maintains equipment; reviews all teachers' lesson plans; observes teachers and results to make sure learners get what they need; manages the department budget; and occasionally teaches a class.

The director reads magazines and online publications to keep up to date on the industry, all facets of culinary education and training programs, trends in vocational training and professional cooking, and goals of newcomers to the food industry.

Directors also try to go to trade shows, professional and food conferences, and local seminars to stay up to date. They also do all they can to keep informed about the culinary job market and new skills required, and attend hospitality and restaurant conferences and meetings.

Vocational Culinary School Directors also try to keep in touch with local restaurateurs, managers, chefs, hotel personnel, and winery owners and winemakers to get good advice and recommendations, as well as to help develop a job placement network for graduating students. Local food, wine, and hospitality industry managers can also offer advice and counseling to students.

Salaries

Salaries for Vocational Culinary School Directors are often set by state standards, as are advancement steps and salary increases, if one teaches at a state-run community or junior college or university. Generally, salaries range from $40,000 to $70,000.

Employment Prospects

As more and more people turn to culinary jobs for employment, whether as a first career, reentry into the job market, or as a career change, there is greater and greater need for people to teach them how to function in the culinary and hospitality businesses. Each school needs a director, and may need assistant directors as the school adds departments or specialties to the curriculum. There are online opportunities as well as opportunities at high schools, community and junior colleges, cooking schools, and even new cooking school programs at art schools that are spreading nationwide.

Advancement Prospects

One can move up within a vocational program possibly from director to dean or into the school's administration. A Vocational Culinary School Director can also get "promoted" by taking a better job at another school with more potential.

Education and Training

Community and junior colleges and universities require a bachelor's degree. Vocational schools may consider practical experience in the food and hospitality industries to be just as valuable. Community or junior colleges expect some teacher training or a teaching credential, while culinary academy certification, human resources training, marketing experience or classes, and experience in professional cooking or teaching cooking classes are all valuable. Some schools may hire a locally well-known hotel or restaurant chef with loads of practical experience and knowledge to share.

Experience, Skills, and Personality Traits

A director should have three to five years' teaching and supervisory experience, human resource management, budget management, and professional cooking and food management experience from working a hot dog stand to running a cafeteria at an industrial plant. Teaching, hospitality, and cooking experience help a director understand the teachers they will direct and will help if the director is required to teach as well.

One must have the ability to manage personalities and relationships as well as jealousies and ambitions; have leadership and team building skills; understand academic budgets and state financing cutbacks; have a passion for teaching high school and post–high school students as well as learners looking for a new career or change of career; and have a great level of understanding for people looking for a job category in which they can gain employment.

It is also important to have contacts and relationships with hotels and restaurants in the area to help arrange apprenticeships for serious students.

Unions and Associations

Started in 1978 as the Association of Cooking Schools to promote the interests of cooking schools and cooking teachers, the International Association of Culinary Professionals (www.iacp.com) now includes 3,000 members in 45 countries and offers certification, newsletters, e-mail bulletins, networking, and annual conferences.

Many cooking and vocational culinary schools belong to the International Council on Hotel, Restaurant and Institutional Education (www.chrie.org), including food-service and hospitality teachers at high schools, community colleges, certificate programs, universities, graduate students, industry professionals, and food service leaders in all sorts of industries.

Local teachers and culinary associations, food economists, food historians, and food chemists can be helpful to know, as are the American Culinary Federation (www.acfchefs.org) and the National Restaurant Association (www.restaurant.org).

Tips for Entry

1. If you don't have cooking experience, volunteer at a local meals-on-wheels program or soup kitchen to learn the ropes.
2. Enroll in community or junior college culinary or hospitality courses including teaching vocational programs.
3. Get involved with local culinary and wine associations to meet people and keep up on local trends. Join professional organizations and keep up with their online or print publications, such as the International Council on Hotel, Restaurant and Institutional Education (www.chrie.org), the American Culinary Federation (www.acfchefs.org), the National Restaurant Association (www.restaurant.org), and the International Association of Culinary Professionals (www.iacp.com).
4. Check teaching and director job opportunities at all of the above Web sites.
5. Learn all you can about budgets and funding, sources of funding, and curriculum development, possibly by joining your school's curriculum development committee.

APPRENTICE PROGRAM CHEF

CAREER PROFILE

Duties: Oversees chef trainees in a three-year or 6,000-hour apprenticeship program working in restaurant or hotel kitchens following study in any vocational culinary training program and particularly through the American Culinary Federation, which awards a certified culinarian degree; the U.S. Department of Labor coordinates some programs and awards journeyman chef certification through its Bureau of Apprenticeship and Training

Alternate Title(s): Apprentice Chair; Apprentice Director; Chef-Teacher

Salary Range: $32,000 to $50,000

Employment Prospects: Limited

Advancement Prospects: Limited

Best Geographical Location(s): Wherever there are community or junior college culinary programs, particularly in big cities with big hotels, big kitchens, and large staffs, including banquets and catering

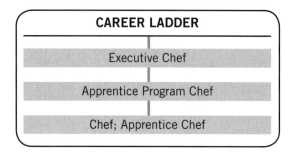

CAREER LADDER

Executive Chef

Apprentice Program Chef

Chef; Apprentice Chef

Prerequisites:

Education or Training—Top-level culinary training and some teaching training combine for this important job

Experience—Cooking in a variety of situations, preferably from small to large kitchens to provide a broad range of knowledge to the apprentice, as well as any teaching experience or learning from good and bad features of their own apprenticeships

Special Skills and Personality Traits—Patience, good English language skills, a passion for teaching others and a willingness to share cooking secrets

Position Description

Serious cooking apprenticeships are extremely important parts of a chef's training because they take the would-be chef from the theory of the classroom to the real-life hands-on work in the kitchen.

An Apprentice Program Chef guides the chef candidate through a rigorous three-year or 6,000-hour experience and should be certified as an apprentice supervisor. In small restaurants in small towns, a chef, owner, or head chef might take on a local apprentice as a student helper. Upon completion of the apprenticeship and classes, an apprentice may receive an associate of applied science degree in hospitality management from some learning institutions.

Some of the top television chefs in the United States have apprenticed in the world's most famous restaurants, often "apprenticing" themselves to world-famous chefs for free and paying their own living expenses just to be able to learn in the shadow of a great chef.

An Apprentice Program Chef in a restaurant or hotel kitchen is supposed to follow guidelines and requirements set by the American Culinary Federation (www.

acfchefs.org), which is registered with the U. S. Department of Labor.

If a culinary student is lucky, his or her vocational program director will pair him or her with the most suitable restaurant or hotel kitchen and arrange for the apprenticeship introduction.

The Apprentice Program Chef, and possibly some of his or her assistants, interviews the chef candidates, sometimes gives written or live cooking tests, and decides which aspiring chef(s) get accepted.

Once a candidate is accepted as an apprentice, he or she works with the Apprentice Program Chef to organize a work schedule, occasionally integrated into a classroom schedule elsewhere. Often the apprentice's first six months are probationary, so they can also be the hardest, because an Apprentice Program Chef might purposely make that period the toughest just to test the candidate's mettle.

The chef and candidate work together to make sure the apprentice gets to work all stations and come out of the experience as well trained as possible. This means work at the soup station, making sauces, salads, meats, fish, poultry, game, and vegetables, baking, making desserts, and butchering, which may include making charcuterie or salumi. The program chef will also make sure the apprentice learns about recipe development, presentation, budgets, purchasing, how to work as a team, and how to supervise parts or all of a kitchen crew. An apprentice might even learn or master skills such as ice carving and tallow sculpting, cake decorating, and the artistry of garnishing and food display.

While Apprentice Program Chefs may have more than one apprentice under their culinary wings, apprentices come in handy because they enter the kitchen having been through some academic or vocational culinary courses and higher up the culinary knowledge ladder than an entry-level employee. If you become an apprentice you may also "earn while you learn" on the job.

Apprentice Program Chefs may also have the job of executive chef or head chef and therefore already be really busy. Apprentices need to work with sensitivity to pressures on their supervisor and his or her other responsibilities.

Many Apprentice Program Chefs or directors generously fill out the full culinary picture for aspiring chefs by using their contacts to arrange field trips to local organic or biodynamic farms or vineyards, cheese makers, fishing centers, artisan bakeries, and wineries. Chef directors might also encourage apprentices to enter cooking and baking contests for the experience, and possibly a chance to experience early public success.

Salaries

An Apprentice Program Chef or chef-teacher may get paid for supervising apprentices in addition to their executive chef or sous-chef salary, totaling more than any other kitchen employee. The pay for running the apprentice program may range from $32,000 to $48,000, even if that is the chef's only job.

Employment Prospects

Most communities with restaurants and large hotels have apprentice programs, or could do so through the American Culinary Federation's many chapters. Each hotel or restaurant has the opportunity to provide an Apprentice Program Chef to help with students or graduates in local high school, adult school, community or junior college, or culinary school apprentice programs.

Advancement Prospects

Apprentice Program Chefs might find that they enjoy working with learners more than cooking and can get an exciting job teaching full time at a culinary school. Within a hotel or restaurant chain, one could rise to supervise all apprentice programs within the hotel or restaurant group.

Education and Training

Chef training comes from culinary schools, community and junior colleges, art institutes, and actually working in restaurants in as many varied positions as possible. An apprentice director should have top-level culinary training and some teaching training, which may include the American Culinary Federation's certificate.

Experience, Skills, and Personality Traits

Cooking experience from a variety of situations, preferably from small to large kitchens, provides Apprentice Program Chefs a broad range of knowledge to impart to apprentices, as will teaching experience or good and bad features of their own apprenticeships.

A successful apprenticeship director should have good English language skills, perhaps speak Spanish, have a passion for teaching others, and have a willingness to share cooking secrets with those much less informed.

Unions and Associations

Some cities have culinary workers unions, particularly in large hotels. Some food-savvy communities have local culinary societies, which are mostly made up of food fans rather than food workers.

The American Culinary Federation (www.acfchefs.org), the National Restaurant Association (www.restaurant.org), and the International Association of Culinary Professionals (www.iacp.com) offer networking, learning programs, online newsletters, job pages, conferences, and some local chapters for personal interaction.

Tips for Entry

1. Contact local culinary programs at high schools, community or junior colleges, culinary schools, or universities to find out if they have or need apprentice programs and offer to take on a student or to organize an apprenticeship.
2. If you are employed as a chef in a restaurant or hotel and there is no apprenticeship program, suggest to the owners or managers that you create and supervise one through the American Culinary Federation's certification program.
3. If you already work in a kitchen where there is an Apprentice Program Chef or director, offer to help and perhaps take on learners in addition to the one(s) he or she already teaches.

CULINARY ACADEMY INSTRUCTOR

CAREER PROFILE

Duties: Teaches professional culinary skills and business management to prepare students for internships, work, and management of restaurants and catering companies; helps with internship and job placement

Alternate Title(s): Cooking School Teacher; Culinary Arts Teacher; Chef

Salary Range: $45,000 to $80,000 for full time

Employment Prospects: Limited but improving

Advancement Prospects: Good

Best Geographical Location(s): Wherever there are culinary academies or full-time cooking schools, with numbers growing and branching out to art institutes across the United States

Prerequisites:

Education or Training—Associate's or bachelor's degree in hospitality or related field; training in specialty field

Experience—Two to seven years' on-the-job cooking experience, some teaching experience, professional cooking experience in a variety of skills or stations

Special Skills and Personality Traits—Excellent verbal and written communication skills, great conflict resolution skills, ability to build teamwork, computer skills, a love and passion for food and teaching, patience with beginners (or anyone else)

CAREER LADDER

Culinary Academy Director or Dean

Culinary Academy Instructor

Academy Chef/Learner

Position Description

Culinary Academy Instructors or teachers work either full time or part time and teach learners both techniques and real-life skills to become chefs in restaurants and other settings. It is hoped that a group of instructors with varied specialties will combine to give the students a full picture and experience of what it is like to cook in a high-pressured and hot kitchen.

Most cooking schools teach students all facets of the professional kitchen, including salads and pantry, garde-manger, stocks and soups, sauces, butchering, meats, poultry, fish and shellfish, dairy and eggs, bread and pastry, and the processeses of sautéing, roasting, and braising. Often students spend a few weeks on each topic and learn by both reading and doing.

Sanitation, health regulations, kitchen safety, tools and equipment, ordering and inventory, menu pricing, and the computer programs that go with these subjects are usually taught in a classroom—as are business management skills, if one is lucky.

The executive chef or director of the academy has to make sure all necessary courses are put in the curriculum and supervises the teachers, while the school's administrators often stick to hiring and firing staff.

Some instructors teach full time, although more and more schools are hiring part-time chef instructors to teach their own specialties. For instance, a baking program within a culinary school might hire instructors to teach how to make artisan breads, baked goods and pastry, advanced patisserie and display cakes, sugar work, plated desserts, and chocolate, confections, and centerpieces.

Most culinary schools include internships in restaurants or large hotel kitchens as part of their required curriculum, so an instructor who comes to a program with good contacts among the area's best chefs can be a real asset to the culinary academy.

Many culinary schools have a café of some sort where students can begin to cook for the public as soon as they have learned basic skills, with beginning students cooking breakfast or lunch, more advanced students doing dinner, baking students making breads, and pastry students making desserts and pastries.

While cooking instructors need to be somewhat patient with beginners, cooking schools and kitchens run by strict rules and standards, many of which are dictated by the chef or teacher. The instructor enforces rules with the threat of expulsion; these rules include cleanliness, showing up on time clean and sober and excited to work hard, and not smoking.

As with music or visual arts, students need to learn the basics before launching into cooking or even creating recipes. One has to learn proper knife skills, which are much more involved than carving the Thanksgiving turkey, and eventually even acquire one's own set of knives or tools.

Since a kitchen's hierarchy dictates that the chef is always right, Culinary Academy Instructors have to teach that point while also trying to actually *be* right. An important kitchen principle that students need to learn is that they must follow the instructor's orders without questioning or arguing. The next chef/instructor might teach just the opposite, but the student has to follow that person's orders as well while in that class and be able to work either way.

A Culinary Academy Instructor might apply to the school he or she thinks is the best one around, as culinary students will look for the school with the best reputation for internship and job placements, with graduates working at the finest restaurants and hotels.

After all the training, a culinary academy instructor might help with actual job placement at restaurants and hotels appropriate for the graduate's skills.

Salaries

Some culinary academy instructors make between $45,000 and $80,000 for full-time, year-round teaching. Many "part time" positions in specialties pay $500 to $20,000, depending upon the commitment (whether the course is a few hours or a month), the instructor or chef's experience and reputation, what advanced degrees or certifications the chef has, or whether the chef hosts a television show.

Employment Prospects

As more and more people look to food careers as entry-level occupations or as reentry professions and some cooking schools close, more cooking schools pop up, even at art institutes around the country. Some culinary schools are adding campuses and new programs. All of these schools need highly skilled professionals to teach.

Advancement Prospects

Restaurant chefs and culinary instructors play a kitchen version of musical chairs. Chefs and instructors move to better opportunities all the time, which leaves openings for others or for new instructors with sophisticated training. Instructors can move up to become directors

and managers of the school, and even a national director in a chain of cooking schools or at a chain of art institutes with culinary programs.

Education and Training

Culinary Academy Instructors get their jobs mostly based on their level of chef skills, expertise, and experience. It is handy to have an applied science degree or bachelor's degree in hospitality or a related field, a chef's certificate, and training in a field of specialty. Skills in kitchen management and teaching experience in a classroom setting all contribute to one's chance of being hired to teach in a culinary school. Some specialty programs require a bachelor's degree in hospitality or a certificate from an accredited culinary program.

Experience, Skills, and Personality Traits

Some schools expect two to seven years of on-the-job cooking experience, some teaching experience, as much professional cooking experience as possible in a variety of skills or stations, as well as great skills at working with others and motivating learners.

An instructor should have excellent verbal and written communication skills, great conflict resolution skills, the ability to build and teach teamwork, computer skills, a love and passion for food and teaching, and patience with beginners or anyone else.

Unions and Associations

Some individual instructors as well as cooking schools and culinary academies belong to the International Council on Hotel, Restaurant and Institutional Education (www.chrie.org) and to the International Association of Culinary Professionals (www.iacp.com).

Tips for Entry

1. Start by giving a cooking class in your home kitchen to find out how you like teaching others and being ultra-organized.
2. Make sure you have the credentials listed above, from professional cooking experience to degrees or certification.
3. Use your connections at the culinary academy or program you attended and work your way into assisting an instructor or teaching there yourself.
4. If you are a chef, teach a class or two at a local cooking school and build a following of food fans while perfecting your teaching and entertaining skills.

NUTRITION AND DIETETICS

NUTRITION COUNSELOR, UNIVERSITY OR SCHOOL DISTRICT

Duties: Creates and disseminates a nutrition program that includes best-eating practices and current health information for high school, college, and university students, as well as staff and faculty; works with a team of medical doctors, nutritionists, psychiatrists, nurses, psychologists, and school cooks to make healthy foods available on campus and to steer people to those healthy selections; teaches students of nutrition, culinary science, and others to educate their peers; produces e-mail and print campus newsletters full of good nutrition advice; teaches nutrition classes; continues his or her education for constant updates to keep certification/registration; provides nutritional counseling

Alternate Title(s): Registered Dietitian; Nutritionist

Salary Range: $30,000 to $55,000

Employment Prospects: Good

Advancement Prospects: Fair

Best Geographical Location(s): Throughout the United States; wherever there are high schools, colleges, and universities of all levels

Prerequisites:

Education or Training—At least a bachelor's degree in nutrition and dietetics, public health nutrition, food and nutrition, or health science, followed by an internship overseen by the American Dietetic

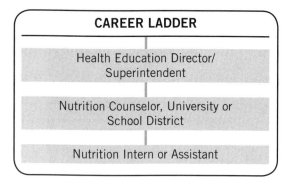

CAREER LADDER

Health Education Director/ Superintendent

Nutrition Counselor, University or School District

Nutrition Intern or Assistant

Association; state registration; continuing education to keep up license or registration; computer science knowledge

Experience—Customer service, an internship that gives exposure to all facets of nutrition counseling, and cooking or food service

Special Skills and Personality Traits—Ability to communicate with students and adults; realistic knowledge of food fads; sensitivity to touchiness of needs for counseling such as fitness and weight; a passion for helping others; fascination with minutiae of food science; knowledge of at least English and Spanish languages in some regions; computer skills; willingness to follow school protocols; willingness to keep up to date on the latest developments by reading online and print publications

Position Description

A university or high school Nutrition Counselor has lots of responsibilities, including newly recommended ones. Traditionally, the Nutrition Counselor gives out information in person or on paper flyers about proper eating habits and how nutrition can help intellectual and physical success. In order to do this, he or she works with doctors, nurses, school cooks, psychiatrists and psychologists, staff and students to let people know what a balanced healthy diet is and how it can be helpful. Now Nutrition Counselors also have to communicate through Web sites, e-mail, and even Twitter.

Nutrition Counselors help students, staff, and faculty with all sorts of special needs that can be addressed with nutrition, including stress, illness, hangovers,

disabilities, and uniquely American weight problems. More Americans are overweight than ever before, with incorrect eating and lack of exercise thought to be the culprits responsible.

Other health problems faced by college and university students include anorexia, bulimia, depression and other neuroses, bipolar problems, AIDS/HIV, various forms of cancer, high blood pressure, and high cholesterol—the last two may have genetic causes but are more likely due to bad nutrition. Staff and faculty often have some of the same problems, sometimes due to eating unhealthy food on campus for years, even though most school districts, colleges, and universities are taking some steps toward offering healthier foods.

A college or university nutrition counselor is responsible for educating students informally about nutrition, and perhaps formally in a nutrition, health science, or fitness class.

While too few students ever take advantage of the information Nutrition Counselors provide, they could get important facts on eating disorders, exam and breakup stress, concerns about sexually transmitted diseases, and classic first-semester weight gains.

Nutrition Counselors have several education roles: teaching in classes; disseminating information through various media; deputizing students to learn about nutrition and have them make presentations in classes, dorm rooms, and other venues; and counseling by personal appointment.

The Nutrition Counselor might also evaluate a student's current diet, make recommendations of eating style changes, explain how food can affect wellness, energy, and mental clarity, demonstrate healthy cooking, make home visits and take clients or students on grocery store shopping trips to show them what foods to buy and what foods to avoid.

Students who might be interested in nutrition and food's influences on physical and behavioral health include those who want to be nutritionists, food chemists, doctors, public health officials or researchers, and even chefs. All of these learners stand the chance of making great spokespeople for good nutrition.

Since a school or university Nutrition Counselor is also a dietitian, he or she may also advise on the school's food production, steering the kitchen staff toward offering healthy alternatives to french fries, pizza, and pastry. In schools where salad bars and pasta bars have been installed, many students have actually migrated to healthier foods and, therefore, toward health.

Often school teams working on health, nutrition, and fitness include the school district dietitian or nutritionist, a representative of a physical education program, school cooks, and parents.

A nutrition team scans publications in the field and sends out links or copies of potentially interesting articles to faculty members, staff, student leaders, student offices, and students in the field. Interesting topics might include easy vegetarian cooking, healthy frozen and microwavable foods, and easy ethnic recipes. Nutrition's role in stopping flu and colds from spreading and information on eating disorders are popular flyer or brochure topics.

The Nutrition Counselor often writes and arranges for printing and distribution of materials or for posting them on the department's or school's Web site, bulletin boards, and kiosks. In the case of a sudden epidemic, the dietitian or nutritionist might have a role in whatever statement of advice goes out to students, staff, and faculty.

Some dietitians have motivated school districts and universities to incorporate organic foods into their meal plans, plant vegetable gardens on the institution's property, and teach students the value of organic foods and how to grow them, even in some dormitory window boxes.

When schools can afford to send them out, or when they go on their own time, a nutrition counselor may spread the nutrition word out into the larger community by going to health fairs, farmers' markets, showing videos and DVDs at surrounding schools, and speaking to local service clubs such as Kiwanis, Rotary, Lions, and Soroptimists, as well as breakfast clubs.

Finally, a Nutrition Counselor continues his or her education for constant updates to keep certification or registration, toward which teaching outside classes or even lecturing in cruise ships might count.

Salaries

Salaries for full-time nutrition counselors or school dietitians range from $30,000 to $55,000 a year, depending upon the nutritionist's experience and tenure and the depth and breadth of his or her responsibilities.

Employment Prospects

High school, college, and university nutrition and dietetics programs, as well as culinary programs, are growing in interest among students who are looking for careers that are "safe" in a volatile economy. In tough times school districts tend to hire one nutritionist or dietitian for the whole district, and cooks and head cooks at the individual school level, and colleges cut back in all departments. Bottom line: good job prospects in good times. Nutrition Counselors tend to stay in their positions for a long time.

Advancement Prospects

Advancement for a university Nutrition Counselor might mean more teaching and climbing up the academic ladder, advancement in school administration, or moving to a larger institution where the pay may be greater. Pay increases may come if a Nutrition Counselor gets advanced degrees in nutrition or related fields such as counseling and education.

Education and Training

Most colleges and universities require at least a bachelor's degree in nutrition and dietetics, public health nutrition, food and nutrition, or health science, followed by an internship overseen by the American Dietetic Association. A Nutrition Counselor must be a registered dietitian (R.D.), have state registration or certification, and keep abreast of advancements and new developments. Many Nutrition Counselors get advanced degrees and take computer classes outside of work or from their department's resident technical expert.

Experience, Skills, and Personality Traits

Nutrition Counselors are required to do internships and have a broad range of experience in the field. They must have excellent customer service skills and be extremely sensitive to college and university students living away from home for the first time and wanting to be independent, but recognizing they need help.

A Nutrition Counselor needs the ability to communicate with students and adults in ways each feels comfortable, have a realistic knowledge of food fads and peer pressures both to eat bad food and to stay thin; sensitivity to the touchiness of needs for counseling such as fitness and weight; a passion for helping others; fascination with the minutiae of food science; knowledge of at least English and often Spanish languages; computer skills; and a willingness to follow school protocols.

Dietitians and Nutrition Counselors combine psychology with a knowledge of food, health, and fitness to provide emotional support for people in need of help.

Unions and Associations

The American Dietetic Association (ADA; www. eatright.org) is the most prominent and productive group of dietitians and nutritionists. The ADA provides accreditation and certification, coordinates undergraduate and dietetic internship programs, facilitates networking and online and face-to-face multidisciplinary continuing education, hosts an online career center with job placements, publishes online and print periodicals, and holds conferences to help students and seasoned nutritionists and dietitians.

The American Association of Nutritional Consultants (www.aanc.net) offers information and memberships without accreditation.

Tips for Entry

1. If you are in high school or community or junior college, consult a counselor and ask for guidance toward classes that will lead you to being a nutritionist or dietitian.
2. Ask the same counselor what community colleges, junior colleges, or universities have the best programs in health education, public health, and nutrition and dietetics.
3. Check out scholarships via the American Dietetic Association either in your state or nationally, for educational materials, good schools, scholarship possibilities, and eventual job placement through its online career center.
4. If you are already studying at a university with a nutrition program or a public health program with dietetics or nutrition within it, get to know the leaders of the department who can lead you to good internships and possible employment.

DIETITIAN, RETIREMENT RESIDENCE

CAREER PROFILE

Duties: Works with residence cook/chef and food-service director to plan nutritious, interesting, and enticing meals for retirement residence assisted-living and independent-living clients and residents; helps plan nutritious meals or substitutes for nursing care residents; oversees food service operation at all levels; hires and trains head chef, cooks, dining room manager; responsible for meeting all health codes and public health requirements for food service at facility

Alternate Title(s): Food-Service Director or Coordinator; Director of Dining Services; Nutritionist; Convalescent Home Dietitian; Management Dietitian

Salary Range: $26,000 to $70,000

Employment Prospects: Good

Advancement Prospects: Good

Best Geographical Location(s): Almost anywhere in the United States or Canada

Prerequisites:

Education or Training—Bachelor's degree in food science, food-service systems management, or nutrition from an accredited university with some business or food-management courses; registered dietitian status

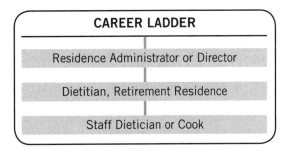

CAREER LADDER

Residence Administrator or Director

Dietitian, Retirement Residence

Staff Dietician or Cook

Experience—Any food-service or restaurant experience or management, particularly in an institutional setting and especially in hospital and nursing facilities (although food service at corporate offices would also be useful)

Special Skills and Personality Traits—Passion for good food and food science and for taking a role in clients' wellness and health through appropriate food; concern for residents and their well-being; diplomatic skills to coordinate multiple dietary requirements and staff at all levels; good organizational and motivational skills to manage full range of food service staff

Position Description

Retirement residences range from small independent-living residences to large and expensive complexes where residents purchase their "home," usually while healthy, and look forward to several levels of medical care and assistance as they age. Many of these facilities provide small kitchens in individual rooms, offer group dining in a dining room, and provide food service when necessary in their in-house care facilities, often until the end of life.

At these residences, the registered dietitian is responsible for dining room service for healthy residents as well as those with individual dietary needs, from no-salt to no-gluten to low-cholesterol regimens.

At the same time, many healthy residents want to eat as well as they used to cook or better, and like the ambiance of being in a nice and comfortable restaurant or resort. Healthy residents have choices of cooking for themselves or eating snacks in their rooms, or enjoying three meals a day in the "restaurantlike" dining room, which means the dietitian has to be able to basically run a restaurant at that level. A maître d' greets residents and seats them at the same tables for each meal, where they join friends and even play cards after meals. Some residential dining rooms have a buffet that includes all sorts of comfort foods from mashed potatoes to gelatin in addition to a daily menu. In some areas, there is a trend toward using seasonally grown local produce for healthier ingredients. Some dietitians have motivated hospitals and retirement residences to incorporate organic foods into their meal plans and even to plant vegetable gardens on the institution's property.

Dietitians work closely with the chef to produce healthful holiday meals to suit all religions and ethnicities and change the menu seasonally, and even weekly, depending upon what is available and according to what their clients might expect.

The Retirement Residence Dietitian also works with the chef to plan theme parties to entertain residents, with the food following the theme within some dietary constraints. Residents also hold private parties and celebrations, from bridge parties to anniversaries, and hire the entire food staff to cater the event. Residents are charged separately for special events, which can be a good source of income for the residence when Medicare cuts and insurance payments, coupled with rising prices, cause food budget tightening.

As residents age they usually require more care, which may be handled in their rooms, or they may be moved to an assisted-living section of the retirement residence. At this level, the dietitian has a more clinical or scientific role in planning individual nutrition and intake of essential nutrients, while residents also usually want "regular" foods and meals.

The dietitian and food-service department often redecorate the dining room to spruce up appearances and cheer up residents. They also have the responsibility to meet or exceed local and federal public health regulations with up-to-date kitchen equipment, menus, portions, grease vents, and even refrigerator temperatures, and be ready at any time for health inspectors' surprise visits.

The next higher level of health care within the residence requires more intense nursing care and nutritional control by a clinical nutritionist helping plan residents' intake. The final level of care may mean residents spend their time in wheelchairs, hospital beds, and even needing help feeding themselves, with food following doctors' specific dietary orders that consider each patient's dietary needs and abilities to digest and absorb. The dietitian, chef, and food-service staff must provide what the doctor orders in an appealing way if possible.

The Retirement Residence Dietitian still hires and fires staff, works to motivate the food-service team, and keeps track of some menu planning and ordering.

Salaries

Salaries vary by size and elegance of the retirement residence, its number of residents and range of care offered, which determine the range of menus and kinds of meals to be offered. Salaries range from $28,000 to $55,000 for a fairly "normal" or medium-sized residence with about 250 live-in clients.

Employment Prospects

As American boomers age, with possibly unprecedented wealth and inestimable needs for care, the retirement residence concept is growing. Facilities are cropping up under the sponsorship of all sorts of organizations, from churches and service clubs to university alumni associations. With difficult economic prospects, some hotels and unsold condominium developments could be converted to retirement residences, which would expand the need for Retirement Residence Dietitians.

Advancement Prospects

A Retirement Residence Dietitian can rise within an institution's management hierarchy, progress to functioning as dietitian for a whole chain of retirement residences, move to a larger or more elegant home to get a better title and pay, or strike out on his or her own as a freelance dietitian consultant with several client residences.

Education and Training

A dietitian or food service director of a retirement residence should have a bachelor's degree in food science or nutrition from an accredited university with some business or food-management courses and have registered dietitian status through the American Dietetic Association (www.eatright.org). Others need a master of business administration degree, or training as a chef.

Experience, Skills, and Personality Traits

Any food service or restaurant experience or management, especially in institutional settings such as hospitals and nursing facilities, possibly including food service at corporate offices, would be handy. One also needs to understand and work with the physiological changes in senior citizens' tasting abilities while searching for substitutes to provide flavor within dietary limitations.

Such a food-service director needs to have great empathy for our aging population, both as a group and for individuals, some of whom may miss their "usual" foods and families. He or she also needs to be almost obsessively attentive to detail, food science, and cleanliness according to regulations.

A good Retirement Residence Dietitian needs a passion for good food and food science and for taking a role in clients' wellness and health through appropriate food; have genuine concern for residents and their well-being; have diplomatic skills to coordinate multiple dietary requirements and staff at all levels; have good organizational and motivational skills to build a real team of food service staff.

Unions and Associations

The American Dietetic Association (www.eatright.org) is the nations most prominent and productive group of dietitians and nutritionists. ADA provides accreditation and certification, coordinates undergraduate and dietetic internship programs, encourages networking, sponsors online and face-to-face multidisciplinary continuing education, hosts an online career center with job placements, publishes online and print periodicals, and holds conferences to help students and seasoned nutritionists and dietitians.

The American Association of Nutritional Consultants (www.aanc.net) offers information and memberships without accreditation. Its membership includes personal trainers.

Tips for Entry

1. If you are studying the culinary arts, you might consider becoming a Retirement Residence Dietitian or nutritionist, because many chefs get great pleasure out of making people happy with food when, in some instances, they don't have a whole lot of joy in their lives; or other chefs simply like to please lots of people and contribute toward their health.

2. Work toward a nutrition or dietetics degree through an accredited college or university or the American Dietetic Association.

3. Talk to a counselor at a school that has good nutrition or dietetics departments.

4. Volunteer or work part time at a retirement residence to find out if you like it.

FOOD-SERVICE-COMPANY DIETITIAN

Duties: Plans, runs, and markets food-service management to health care facilities, retirement residences, some school districts, prisons, airlines, corporate cafeterias, chain restaurants, and some hospitals; supervises services of food; advises on hiring, training, and firing; supervises dietetian interns; helps develop new menus of nutritious and popular foods; supervises nutrition service staff including kitchen staff, delivery assistants, and diet aides; helps with research projects

Alternate Title(s): Clinical Dietitian; Registered Dietitian; Executive Dietitian

Salary Range: $40,000 to $80,000

Employment Prospects: Good

Advancement Prospects: Good

Best Geographical Location(s): Anywhere in North America where there are health-care facilities, airline hubs, major high-tech production facilities, and prisons

Prerequisites:

Education or Training—Bachelor's degree in nutrition and dietetics, a completed internship, and American Dietetic Association registration as a registered dietitian

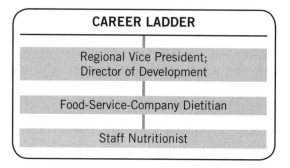

CAREER LADDER

Regional Vice President; Director of Development

Food-Service-Company Dietitian

Staff Nutritionist

Experience—Food-preparation experience, food-service experience, and experience as a clinical dietitian

Special Skills and Personality Traits—Good communication skills, including listening and writing; computer skills; ability to be a good team motivator and player; understanding of business and financial management; love of food and health and an ability to impart those to help people understand what they need to eat and that your company can provide what they need

Position Description

Many hospitals, prisons, retirement residences, airlines and corporations hire commercial food service companies to prepare and deliver packaged meals or run their kitchens, cook, make up patient or client trays, supply cafeterias, and basically manage the human resources segment of hiring, training, and firing food-service employees. Other hospitals and institutions actually run their own food service and have in-house dietitians and chefs who oversee kitchen staff that cook from scratch and deliver trays to patients and clients.

An executive dietitian or Food-Service-Company Dietitian helps create a desirable and healthy food plan for an institution and then actually goes out and sells the plan to the institution as part of a marketing team. The program they try to sell includes management, research to improve dietary programs, oversight and

guidance interns, help to hire and fire other dietitians, and oversight of support staff.

Sometimes the Food-Service-Company Dietitian approaches an institution when he or she knows that company wants to improve its dietary program or change from in-house cooking to outside food-service sources, or simply cold-calls on the chance of getting a foot in the door to replace the current food service company. Such a decision on the part of the institution is often dictated by finances, so in that case the dietitian helps to convince the relevant administrators that his or her food-service company can deliver better and more nutritious food at lower cost than another company can or than the institution spends to cook in-house.

In order to develop an appropriate plan proposal, the Food Service Company Dietitian will often meet with nursing leaders or other executives, physicians, kitchen and dining room managers, and possibly a patient or client representative to find out the real needs of the institution, which may run from special diets to rehabilitative and ethnic foods.

Once the Food-Service-Company Dietitian develops a plan and proposal to run the institution's food-service program, he or she presents or pitches it to the institution's executives, including a bid to provide the service. The hospital, nursing care facility, retirement residence, or corporation will compare bids, services, and food plans and decide whether the program is developed economically and with sensitivity to their institution's needs.

Responding in some cases to public demand, some dietitians have motivated food-service companies to incorporate organic foods into their meals and even to plant vegetable gardens on the institution's or company's property.

After a company is selected to provide food services, the dietitian in charge helps place the best dietitian, nutritionist, manager, chef, and other kitchen help possible in the institution's kitchen, all within the budget. The executive dietitian also helps with hiring, and firing of food-service staff.

Food-Service-Company Dietitians also participate in research and keep up on discoveries of what foods are best to improve which physical or medical problem or situation by reading the latest information through a variety of print and online publications.

Executive dietitians also help their profession by supervising and mentoring dietitian interns, since all dietitians are required to complete six months to a year of approved medical internship before they can even apply to take certification tests. Interns need on-the-job experience in nutrition and dietetics and nutritional health care including working with the best foods to prevent or deal with cancer, diabetes, heart disease, stroke, and Alzheimer's disease among many other health challenges.

Many Food-Service-Company Dietitians have to travel a lot (which is a blessing to some and not to others) to sell their program wherever the clients are.

Salaries

As a professional who is also a salesperson, a Food-Service-Company Dietitian starts at around $40,000 while learning the business side, and progresses to $70,000 or more, depending upon financial arrangements with the company. One might also get health insurance and other benefits, bonuses, or commissions.

Employment Prospects

Health care and food care are two industries that continued to grow during recent recessions. As our population ages, baby boomers live longer, and many Americans shy away from caring for elders at home, demand for health-care and elder-care facilities will increase, as will demand for registered dietitians.

Advancement Prospects

One can advance within the food-service company into upper management, or increase the size of one's geographical territory to become regional manager and general manager at greater salary. One can also move to a higher-paying company.

Education and Training

Any dietitian needs a college degree in nutrition and dietetics, a completed internship, and registration with the American Dietetic Association (ADA) as a registered dietitian (RD).

Experience, Skills, and Personality Traits

A Food Service Company Dietitian should have food preparation experience, food service experience, and experience as a clinical dietitian. This person needs to love the job for all the right reasons and enjoy travel as well. He or she should have good communication skills, including listening and writing; computer skills; be a good team motivator and player; have an understanding of business and financial management; have a love of food and health and an ability to translate those to help people understand what they need to eat and that their company can best provide what is needed.

Unions and Associations

The ADA (www.eatright.org) is the nation's most prominent and productive group of dietitians and nutritionists. The ADA provides accreditation and certification, coordinates undergraduate and dietetian internship programs, provides networking, and online and face-to-face multidisciplinary continuing education, posts an online career center with job placements, publishes online and print periodicals, and holds conferences to help students and seasoned nutritionists and dietitians.

Tips for Entry

1. For some practical experience at nutritious food production, volunteer at a local meals-on-wheels or other community food program.
2. Contact a local or state ADA chapter and ask about scholarship help.
3. Enroll in dietetics or a nutrition program at a community or junior college. Advance your education by completing a degree in an accredited dietetics or nutrition curriculum at an accredited university.

4. Go to your local hospital or retirement residence and ask if they cook in-house or use a food-service company to plan and provide food. Make an appointment to meet with the dietitian and ask for career or next-step advice.

5. Ask for a job or apprenticeship in the food-service department.

6. Move on to a job with the food-service company and work your way up.

HOSPITAL CLINICAL DIETITIAN

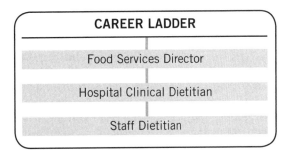
Position Description

Clinical dietitians work in many environments, especially in hospitals and residential care facilities, although they also work for clinics and health-care groups. Others work for large corporations that either manage several hospitals or provide certain services to health-care facilities on a "for hire" basis.

There are many levels of nutrition workers who support a Hospital Clinical Dietitian, such as dietary assistants, cooks, dietary clerks and managers, dietary workers who set up the food on trays in the kitchen, dietary hosts who deliver and return trays of food, and pediatric dietitians who specialize in nutrition for people 17 and younger.

In a hospital, clinical, or retirement residence setting the clinical dietitian reviews patients' records, confers with their doctors and nurses, and plans appropriate nutrition service with the food service department to serve patients' needs.

A Hospital Clinical Dietitian communicates between the doctors and food service to consider and plan what foods patients can tolerate or need to get better, whether their problems are due to chronic disease, emotional problems, accident or trauma, diabetes, hypertension, obesity, or any other condition. The dietitian researches and plans nutrition therapy according to disease and medical problems.

Working with a patient's doctors, nurses, and other medical staff, the clinical dietitian goes over a patient's medical history and immediate problems with the food service manager and nursing staff, and then follows up with nursing staff to evaluate whether the patient is eating what they should or returning it untouched and follows the patient's progress.

Constantly researching and reading both print and online publications for the latest trends and discoveries in nutrition, the clinical dietitian updates medical and other staff on the latest information and even offers seminars for hospital staff so that everyone is on the same nutritional page.

Some dietitians have motivated hospitals and retirement residences to incorporate organic foods into their meal plans and even to plant vegetable gardens on the institution's property.

A clinical dietitian in a large hospital may have other dietitians working to assist his or her goals, and may supervise an entire team from basic cooks to tray servers and cleaners. A dietitian will put on seminars for hospital staff and sometimes for patients in and out of the facilities and work with physicians, physical therapists, occupational therapists, pharmacists, speech therapists, nurses, and social workers. He or she also reports to hospital or healthcare administrators.

Many Hospital Clinical Dietitians provide nutritional consultation to individual patients, including giving them diet plans to take home, following up with phone conversations, or giving seminars for other people who may be in similar situations.

In some hospitals, the clinical dietitian is also the food-service director, in charge of food ordering, preparation, and appropriateness for standard and specialized diets.

Salaries

The head clinical dietitian in a hospital will earn from $35,000 to $60,000 depending upon advanced degrees, experience, size of the hospital, dietary budget, and whether the employer is a large corporation or a small hospital, and region of the country.

Employment Prospects

Hospitals have to feed people, and more and more hospitals try to provide the best nutrition at the lowest cost as a part of patient care. Some hospitals make the effort to provide nutritious and tasty food to encourage patients to eat properly while still under the hospital's influence.

As our population ages, clinics, medical centers, trauma centers, and hospitals, or the corporations that provide their food, need more clinical dietitians to advise them. The better your credentials, the better the opportunities and salaries.

Advancement Prospects

A hospital or care center's clinical dietitian can work up the management ladder to assistant administrator and even CEO. If working for an outside corporation that provides dietary services and food service, a dietitian can rise to overseeing several hospitals in a region, or even throughout the country and on to general management in the corporation.

If a dietitian works in a hospital setting, he or she can improve his or her salary or title sometimes by moving to a larger or better financed medical institution or research company.

Education and Training

A hospital Clinical Dietitian needs a bachelor of science degree in dietetics, nutrition, or institutional management and must have completed the required internship and obtained registered dietitian status with American Dietetic Association. One can enter the field at a lower level without these degrees.

Experience, Skills, and Personality Traits

A Hospital Clinical Dietitian will need clinical experience at various levels, and even practical food-service experience will help. A person who has worked in all parts of a facility's food-service and dietetics departments, perhaps while getting undergraduate and graduate degrees, will be even better equipped to do a good job.

A dietitian in health-care facilities should have a passion for food and nutritional science and for helping people improve their health through diet. He or she should also have great patience; good sympathetic and caring communication skills to deal with ill patients and persuade them that dietary changes might help make them better, and have great powers of persuasion to convince a patient that he or she should follow a particular regimen to improve his or her health after they leave the facility.

Unions and Associations

The American Dietetic Association (www.eatright.org) is the nation's most prominent and productive group of dietitians and nutritionists. The ADA provides accreditation and certification, coordinates undergraduate and dietetic internship programs, provides networking, features online and face-to-face multidisciplinary continuing education, posts an online career center with job placements, publishes online and print periodicals, and holds conferences to help students and seasoned nutritionists and dietitians.

The American Society of Hospital Food Service Administrators (www.ashfsa.org) has chapters throughout the United States and offers a job bank, conferences, a newsletter, scholarships, and even a cookbook.

Tips for Entry

1. Volunteer at a local meals-on-wheels or other charitable food operation to learn the basics of producing nutritious food by doing it.
2. Visit a local hospital and volunteer to work as close to the dietitian and food service as possible.

3. Enroll in the appropriate food science and nutrition courses at a local college or university.
4. Get the required B.S. degree in nutrition or dietetics and get registered with the American Dietetic Association.
5. Check relevant Web sites for job leads, such as the American Society of Hospital Food Service Administrators' site (www.ashfsa.org).

SPORTS NUTRITIONIST

Duties: Teaches athletes, groups of athletes, coaches, and teams about good nutrition in general, and specifically to fuel bodies for particular sports and expenditures of energy; teaches athletes how to use nutrition to improve their performance; translates the latest scientific nutritional information to practical advice for athletes; helps malnourished athletes (including junk food addicts) improve their diets for better health, performance, or to gain or lose weight; advises injured athletes on how to alter their diets to stay healthy and not gain weight while not training; provides nutrition education for health and wellness programs, athletic teams, and community groups; keeps up to date on skills and professional knowledge to best serve clients; develops healthy menus for "team tables"

Alternate Title(s): Sports Dietitian; Team Nutritionist or Dietitian; Trainer

Salary Range: $25,000 to $70,000

Employment Prospects: Good and improving

Advancement Prospects: Good

Best Geographical Location(s): Throughout North America where there are school sports teams or other sports competitors, serious athletics from swimming to long-distance running, or any other sports activities including race car driving

Prerequisites:

    Education and Training—Bachelor's degree in clinical nutrition, kinesiology, or food and nutrition,

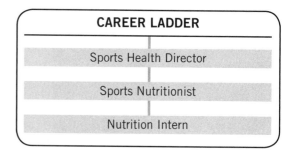

CAREER LADDER

Sports Health Director

Sports Nutritionist

Nutrition Intern

a mandatory internship, and registration with the American Dietetic Association or a master's degree in nutrition or exercise physiology from an accredited university

Experience—Two years' experience in nutrition counseling, preferably with emphasis on sports nutrition; experience working with children, teens, or any other age group to learn good communication across generations; experience with school teams as a nutritional aide, adviser, or trainer

Special Skills and Personality Traits—Great communication and counseling skills; self-motivation and the ability to work independently; good time management and organizational skills; good computer skills; knowledge and passion for food service quality and safety; ability to persuade athletes and others to change their dietary habits to improve their skills; knowledge of regional foods that athletes may have eaten all their lives that may or may not be healthy for their current purposes

Position Description

A Sports Nutritionist teaches individual athletes and groups of athletes about good nutrition in general, and specifically to condition and fuel their bodies for particular sports, and what the expenditures of energy are for recreational and professional athletes.

To do this, a Sports Nutritionist has to understand sports and the particular sport on which he or she is advising, assess body mass, fat, and muscle mass of the athlete or athletes, evaluate energy balances, and become aware of the athlete's possible eating disorders or symptoms.

In order to advise athletes on their nutritional habits, a Sports Nutritionist also has to know the rules and

regulations of each sport's league, as well as those of the National Collegiate Athletic Association, Anti-Doping Agency of the USDA, and the World Anti-Doping Agency to know which drugs and dietary supplements are banned or restricted.

Sports Nutritionists might act as consultants to individual athletes, all teams within a school, or several teams in just one sport, or to athletic programs, coaches, parents, and athletic trainers.

A Sports Nutritionist explains to athletes the reasons why proper diet and nutrition serve their interests by improving performance, speed, and endurance. With sensitivity to and knowledge of regional or ethnic dietary habits and personal allergies, a Sports Nutritionist teaches athletes how to use optimal nutrition and hydration (water) to improve their performance. Sometimes this means changing an athlete's eating habits drastically after appropriate testing, which is where tact and communication skills come in handy, perhaps creating personalized meal and snack plans to improve athletic performance and long-term health.

Some individuals and sports require intake of lots of carbohydrates to keep up energy during strenuous training or a race while others may require more protein. Some athletes have superstitious eating practices from which they won't vary no matter how it might improve their performance. One race car driver consumes nutrition-free little candies and cola before a race because that is her habit and her good-luck meal. Other athletes require wild non-farmed salmon, or pasta with a special tomato sauce.

Many athletes know how to eat at home, but have dietary problems on the road when they travel to races or games, which is exactly when they need the best foods as recommended by their nutritionist.

Some famous athletes carry their foods or chefs with them on trips, while others have been known to eat from other athletes' trays. A Sports Nutritionist could advise these athletes on proper snacks to take along for their athletic survival and, to have peak energy before their event, to avoid fatty burgers and fries, which are many Americans' security foods away from home.

Many athletes diet often to keep their weight down and their fat mass ratio under control, witch can lead to malnourishment. A Sports Nutritionist can improve athletes' diets for better health, performance, or to gain or lose weight while preserving their strength and energy.

Athletes who stop their normal training activity due to injury or retirement can gain useless weight if they continue to consume the same calories as when they were exercising, since they are not burning their normal number of calories. It is always hard to eat less if you are used to consuming lots of food. The Sports Nutritionist tries to teach the inactive athlete what foods to eat and which ones to avoid during this period, or for life if he or she retires from the sport.

Sports Nutritionists might also recommend vitamin and dietary supplements within the league rules and the law, may develop training table menus, and helps plan budgets for purchase and preparation of appropriate foods. Some Sports Nutritionists even write cookbooks aimed at all sorts of athletes, family members, sports fans, and casual sports enthusiasts.

A Sports Nutritionist translates the latest scientific nutritional information to practical use for athletes and keeps up to date on skills and professional knowledge to best serve his or her clients. He or she often provides nutrition education for health and wellness programs, athletic teams, and community groups, and even athletes' family members.

A Sports Nutritionist might even teach an athlete or a whole team how to cook at home, such as how to make pasta with sauces and prepare salads and fruits, always advising not to drink alcohol, all with varied success except with the most serious athletes.

Salaries

Sports Nutritionists' earnings vary greatly, from $25,000 to around $70,000 or more, depending upon the size of the team, the school if one is involved, and the prominence of the athletes. Some Sports Nutritionists freelance and give nutritional advice to various teams or companies and have a private consultancy or training business on the side to supplement their income.

Employment Prospects

A nutritionist might work for a group specializing in various disciplines of sports medicine, or freelance while working for a team or school. More athletes are aiming for sports careers, so nutritionists who follow news of natural foods and supplements and diet to improve performance are in high demand. One might get hired by a company that provides nutrition advice to sports teams or clubs.

Advancement Prospects

One can always move up in the management of a team, health club or chain of health clubs, or company that provides sports nutrition services, or even write one's own cookbook with nutrition advice.

Education and Training

A Sports Nutritionist needs a bachelor's degree in clinical nutrition or food and nutrition, a required internship, and registration with the American Dietetic Association or a master's degree in nutrition or exercise physiology from an accredited university.

Experience, Skills, and Personality Traits

A Sports Nutritionist should have two years' experience in nutrition counseling, preferably with an emphasis on sports nutrition; experience working with children, teens, or any other age group to learn good communication with them; and experience with school teams as a nutritional aide, adviser, or trainer.

Such a nutritionist might also have to teach teenagers and college students that they need to change their sleeping and eating habits, which takes adaptable communication and counseling skills and the ability to talk athletes into believing all of this is good for them and their athletic future.

A Sports Nutritionist also needs to be self-motivated and have the ability to work independently; possess good time management and organizational skills; have good computer skills; have knowledge and a passion for food service quality and safety; have the ability to persuade athletes and others to change their dietary habits to improve their skills; and should have knowledge of regional foods that athletes may have eaten all their lives that may or may not be healthy for their current purposes.

Unions and Associations

The National Association of Sports Nutrition (www.nasnutrition.com) issues licenses lists college and university sports nutrition degree programs, sports nutrition job openings, and seminars.

The International Society of Sports Nutrition (www.sportsnutritionsociety.org) puts on sports and performance nutrition conferences, a newsletter, and certification tests.

The American Dietetic Association (ADA; www.eatright.org) is the nation's most prominent and productive group of dietitians and nutritionists. The ADA provides accreditation and certification, coordinates undergraduate and dietetian internship programs, and provides career networking, online and face-to-face multidisciplinary continuing education, an online career center with job placements, online and print periodicals, and conferences to help students and seasoned nutritionists and dietitians.

Tips for Entry

1. If you are a school athlete or serious sports fan, get to know a local team nutritionist or team or school trainer and offer to help at games or races to learn from that person by participation.
2. Ask a local trainer or Sports Nutritionist what nearby schools offer basic courses to get you started into the nutrition field.
3. Work at a local restaurant that features locally grown or organic foods to learn the chef's outlook on nutrition.
4. Look up sports nutrition clinics online or in your local yellow pages, drop in, and ask if you could volunteer or work for them while you start necessary courses at a nearby college or university.
5. Volunteer to help coaches of local teams.

CULINARY OR BEVERAGE COMPUTER SERVICES

WEBMASTER AND SOCIAL MEDIA DIRECTOR, CULINARY BUSINESS

CAREER PROFILE

Duties: Consults with clients on what they can achieve with a Web site and blog, or through Facebook and Twitter and other social media to appeal to and communicate with a larger public and increase business; designs Web site or blog or both; teaches pertinent people at the client business how to operate and update the Web site, blog, or Facebook page; possibly sets up sales order mechanisms such as a "shopping cart" on a Web site or blog; creates electronic social network of ever-expanding "friends" who will know more and communicate with one another about the culinary or wine business

Alternate Title(s): Web Designer; Web Consultant; Social Media Consultant

Salary Range: $34,000 to $150,000 or more annually, with hourly fees from $90 to $200

Employment Prospects: Excellent

Advancement Prospects: Very good

Best Geographical Location(s): Big cities where there are sophisticated restaurants, nearby wine regions, and almost anywhere, and food and wine–related Web design opportunities around the world, which can be accomplished from one's or home

Prerequisites:

    Education or Training—Computer and social network device training from all sorts of sources, rang-

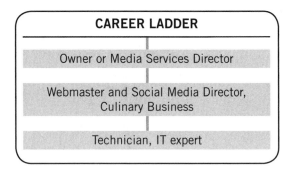

CAREER LADDER

Owner or Media Services Director

Webmaster and Social Media Director, Culinary Business

Technician, IT expert

ing from self-taught to high school, community and junior colleges, extension classes, to undergraduate to graduate degrees in communications or computer science

    Experience—Work for a busy Web designer or with friends or a marketing director of a food establishment or winery

    Special Skills and Personality Traits—Knowledge of the sophisticated computer programs and willingness to constantly check the latest developments; ability to work mostly alone but get along with others; excitement at working in the food or wine worlds; enjoyment of net spying on competing food or wine businesses; ability to keep up on latest design and marketing theories and techniques; love of graphic arts and design; patience with clients who are not net-savvy; and excellent computer skills

Position Description

All culinary businesses need some sort of Web presence these days, including farmers, restaurants, chefs, food packagers, food and wine magazines, and food distributors, to say nothing of wineries and wine brokers. Local, national, and international culinary organizations also need Web sites and blogs, and all of the above either have or are having someone develop social networking capabilities via Facebook or Twitter. Restaurants, farmers' markets, cooking schools, culinary travel consultants, and wineries all can advertise their events and schedules and can book reservations with credit cards online.

All of these methods are highly efficient ways to communicate and expand exposure of a food entity at low cost. The only real cost is the Webmaster and Social Media Director.

In-house webmasters often work in the marketing department, with more complicated parts of Web development farmed out to outside consultants. Outside freelance Web consultants can work for several clients and don't have to work in the culinary business every day. They may need good "work-from-home" skills as they may run a business from their home office or bedroom—which may be the same room.

Some webmasters will also set up blogs for the client to encourage interactive conversations among consumers, or will set up a blog instead of a Web site. To get the Web site, blog, or Facebook profile development in process, the Webmaster and Social Media Director meets extensively with the client, spends time at the culinary or winery business getting to know it and how it works, and thinks about how best to accomplish the client's goals.

Webmaster/Social Media Directors often need to educate clients about the benefits of the Web and blogs, as well as Facebook, Twitter, and other social networking sites, while explaining design needs (which may involve tactics different from those used to create a printed brochure), helping the client check out competing or exemplary Web sites, and describing the intricacies of e-tailing, or selling and maximizing sales on the Internet.

While designing someone's Web site or blog, the webmaster might create a new company logo or incorporate an existing one, or even include logos of other companies the business owns with "click-throughs" or links that go directly to each entity's Web site and, as links, increase traffic, business, and income for all of the sub-businesses.

Webmasters and blog designers need to keep up to date on the latest computer programs, shortcuts, and ways to move their clients' Web sites and blogs to high placement on search engines.

The webmaster or blog designer and client come together again to view designs the webmaster or designer has created and discuss whether they are best suited to achieve the client's goals. The final design might include a blog, ads for the company or related companies, and a "store" or "checkout" by which Web site or blog visitors can purchase the company's food or wine or make a reservation. Sites that sell alcohol directly must have means to avoid sales to underage consumers or to areas that prohibit alcohol sales by mail.

Salaries

An in-house Webmaster or Social Media Director can earn $34,000 to $150,000 or even more, depending on the person's experience, the size of the company, whether the project is starting from scratch, and whether the person works full time or part time.

Freelance webmasters and social media consultants make from $90 to $200 per hour and beyond and can have multiple clients.

Several Web design companies specialize in restaurant, food, and winery Web sites and blogs.

Employment Prospects

Everyone in every business seems to need a webmaster, and with the movement toward organic, sustainable, and biodynamically grown vegetables, more growers need Web sites to tell how they use these methods, as do restaurants that use "clean" food and wineries. A Web, blog, Facebook, and Twitter expert with extensive knowledge of food and wine will be in great demand because this kind of technology is usually not a specialty of food and wine people.

Advancement Prospects

A person with great knowledge of food or wine and the ability to build a Web site or blog and get a business onto Facebook and Twitter will find all sorts of advancement possibilities, either within the company, doing work for all of a large business's sub-labels, or as a freelancer doing work for several businesses. One can always move to a larger company with higher salaries, bigger benefits, and more perks.

Education and Training

A webmaster, blog designer, and social networking media consultant needs computer and social network device training from all sorts of sources, ranging from self-learning to high school, community and junior colleges, extension classes, degrees in communications or computer science, picking up skills on the Internet, or learning from friends and colleagues.

One also needs some graphic design training that includes some tutorials on Web design programs, university extension classes at night or on weekends, and some apprenticelike work with an experienced webmaster.

Experience, Skills, and Personality Traits

Experience working for a successful webmaster or designer, particularly one that does work for a marketing director of a food establishment or winery, would be ideal, as are a passion for detail and a willingness to be a team player.

One should know sophisticated computer programs and love to constantly check and monitor the latest developments in design and programming. One needs to like to work mostly alone but get along with others; have excitement for the worlds of food and wine; enjoy net spying on competing food or wine businesses; love to keep up on the latest design and marketing theories and techniques; have an eye for graphic arts and design; have patience with clients who are not net-savvy; have the ability to become so absorbed in a project that one can work all night; and have excellent computer skills.

Experience in the food and wine fields—from cooking to sweeping winery floors—will make a webmaster or blog designer even more successful because he or she will understand the terminology and the ambiance of any culinary or wine business.

Unions and Associations

There are several new organizations that provide resources, online programming courses, conferences, and job banks for webmasters and designers. They include the: HTML Writers Guild (www.hwg.org), Web Design and Development Association (www.wdda.org), and AIGA (formerly the American Institute of Graphic Arts) (www.aiga.org).

Tips for Entry

1. Take classes in high school, adult continuing ed programs, community or junior colleges, universities, or online to develop your webmaster and design skills, as well as the ability to communicate via Facebook and Twitter.

2. Talk to the school counselor or instructor about job possibilities.

3. Visit your favorite restaurants and wineries or local food producers and offer to work for them. If they have not been thinking of hiring a webmaster or Facebook consultant, create something to fix their needs (but not a complete project) to intrigue them, showing them how valuable you can be.

4. Monitor all pertinent Web sites to learn as much as you can about the latest Web site and social media developments.

5. Develop an attractive résumé or portfolio, both in content and design and including several other Web sites you worked on before or simply created as samples.

ONLINE CULINARY CATALOG DESIGNER

CAREER PROFILE

Duties: Designs Web sites and online catalogs of kitchenware, menus, books, and other products; works with the client to define and refine the message he or she wants to convey and what the company wants to accomplish; prepares sample layouts with graphics, colors, merchandise and a "checkout" or "buy now" feature; works with the client's merchandise, and marketing managers; chooses and installs appropriate software and hardware at the company; keeps up to date on the latest pertinent programs; trains staff on how to fulfill catalog orders, making sure the warehouse has stock of or access to the merchandise; remains available for updating, troubleshooting, and training of staff

Alternate Title(s): Web Designer; Catalog Programmer

Salary Range: $35,000 to $100,000 annually, or $20 to $200 per hour

Employment Prospects: Excellent

Advancement Prospects: Good

Best Geographical Location(s): Anywhere

Prerequisites:

  Education or Training—Constantly updated computer training; graphic design courses; work experience with online or print catalog designer

CAREER LADDER

Owner/Client of Business

Online Culinary Catalog Designer

Graphic Designer or IT technician

Experience—Any and all computer experience and graphic design, and some experience working with merchandise suppliers and their marketing teams

Special Skills and Personality Traits—Ability to work mostly alone but able to communicate with marketing departments and merchandise producers; creativity, with new ideas for online appeal; knowledge of merchandise groupings and the psychology of colors, sales, and graphic design

Position Description

Online culinary catalogs sell a variety of products and often specialize in certain fields. Some sell cooking school courses or culinary tours, while others sell organic foods, cookware, cookbooks, recipes, or all of the above combined with aprons, pans, and even kitchen garden equipment and seeds.

Some online catalogs present all of the cookware and merchandise created in the name of a television superstar chef and project a specialized image of the salesperson or chef, while others pull together cookware of a special interest, such as clay pots or antique utensils, depending upon the client's interest, store, television program, or goals.

Initially, an Online Culinary Catalog Designer meets with the clients and their marketing and merchandizing managers if they have them. Together they figure out what the clients' goals are, what kind of merchandise they want to sell and how much of it, how wide or broad an appeal they want to project, and whether the business that could be created with an online catalog can be backed up with existing or warehoused merchandise. Some online catalogs actually function to determine what quantities of an item should be manufactured according to the orders that come in.

Ultimately, the designer creates Web sites and online catalogs of kitchenware, menus, books, and other products; works with the client to define and refine the message he or she wants to convey and what the company wants to accomplish.

They also need to decide what kind of a "checkout" or "buy now" feature the client wants, and whether the client wants payment through an online service, through credit cards, or through offering to send paper bills to customers reticent to give out credit card information.

Some payment formats may require making arrangements at a local bank for that function to work.

After agreeing on a basic format, the designer prepares sample layouts with graphics, colors, merchandise, and a "checkout," "add to shopping cart," or "buy now" feature. The designer figures out where to "house" the site, what other businesses the company might want to link to and from, what related businesses' or advertisers' logos will show (if any), and where Google ads (if any) will figure into the general design.

The designer then works closely with the marketing director or copywriter to coordinate copy (the words, or text) with the graphic art. He or she also chooses and installs appropriate software and hardware at the company, keeps up to date on the latest pertinent programs, and trains staff on how to fulfill catalog orders, and works with the merchandise manager to make sure the client's warehouse has stock of or access to merchandise or with a cooking school manager to maker sure that the school's classes can handle the signups.

The designer might also set up regular e-mail blitzes to attract customers to the Web site or blog.

In some cases the Online Culinary Catalog Designer has to make sure merchandise is available, particularly if the designer works full time for the company. Freelance designers usually work with someone within the client company who has that responsibility.

The Online Culinary Catalog Designer has to make himself or herself available for updating, troubleshooting, and the training of staff, and answering what may seem like pesky or simple questions that appear complex and mysterious to those who are not computer designer professionals.

Salaries

There are many jobs in the design line, with the Online Culinary Catalog Designer at the top. Depending upon experience, the region of the country where they work, and the size of the client company, a full-time designer might make between $35,000 and $100,000 a year, or $20 to $200 per hour. Freelance designers or consultants, who can work for many clients at the same time but usually with no health or retirement benefits, work for $20 an hour to $200 an hour.

Employment Prospects

As the U.S. economy suffered in recent years, more culinary enterprises have turned to Web sites and online catalogs for communication, from cooking school class schedules and restaurant menus and reservations to giant cookware companies and cable television networks and stars. At the same time, these businesses want to pay less for the service.

Hence, a freelance Online Culinary Catalog Designer might have to work for more clients—but there are more clients who need help throughout North America.

Advancement Prospects

Full-time in-house online catalog designers have every chance to rise within the marketing and merchandising departments. They can also move to a company that will produce more catalogs for which they can do the online design work, or to a larger company with a bigger catalog of merchandise to try to sell online.

Freelance designers may earn more by going to work in-house for a company, by getting more clients, by slowly growing their business to serve better and bigger catalog merchandisers, and by hiring assistant designers to enable them to take on more work. Advancement often depends on demonstrated quality of design as well as originality.

Education and Training

A successful Online Culinary Catalog Designer will need to constantly update his or her skills with computer training, graphic design courses, and programming, and work with an experienced online or print catalog designer to learn as a sort of apprentice. Constant practice and monitoring others' work is essential.

Experience, Skills, and Personality Traits

An Online Culinary Catalog Designer needs a mastery of any and all computer and graphic design skills and some experience working with merchandise suppliers and their marketing teams. Such a designer has to enjoy working mostly alone but also communicating with marketing departments and merchandise producers, be creative with new ideas for online appeal, have knowledge of merchandise groupings and the psychology of colors, and understand the relationship between sales and graphic design.

Unions and Associations

There are several new organizations that provide resources, online programming courses, conferences, and job banks for webmasters and designers. They are the HTML Writers Guild (www.hwg.org), the Web Design and Development Association (www.wdda.org), and AIGA, a designers' organization (www.aiga.org).

Tips for Entry

1. Seek out your favorite online catalogs and notice at the bottom of the page who the designer is

and contact him or her for advice or guidance on entering the field.

2. Take high school and community or junior college courses in graphic design, catalog design, and computer skills to learn the basics.

3. Talk to teachers to ask for suggestions or references for local Web site and blog designers.

4. Approach local Web site and blog designers and ask if you might volunteer or work for them to learn what they know in the design field.

5. Approach the designers of your favorite Web sites and blogs and ask for a job, either paid or as a volunteer.

6. Approach a cooking school, bakery, cookware shop, or restaurant and offer to design a sample Web site and catalog of their courses, products, services, or merchandise.

7. Prepare an attractive résumé and portfolio with samples of your work.

CULINARY ASSOCIATION DATABASE MANAGER

Duties: Develop, expand and customize a culinary association's database and e-mail list, sometimes with subdivisions by specialized interests; gather as much information as possible on members and potential members or potential customers; enter vital communication data in the database including name, address, e-mail address, Web sites, and phone numbers; compile data for mailing labels for snail mail as well as e-mail addresses to send information and membership and renewal forms; program software to ask for renewal fees and to mine culinary blogs for participants

Alternate Title(s): Computer Manager; Membership Manager

Salary Range: $15 per hour to $100,000 per year

Employment Prospects: Limited

Advancement Prospects: Limited

Best Geographical Location(s): Many computer database or design jobs can be done from home anywhere in the world. To manage a culinary association database, it might help to be close to cooking schools, restaurants, hotels, and even sauce or cookware manufacturers, but not necessary.

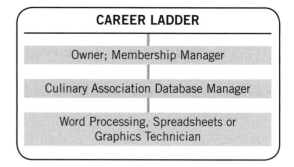

CAREER LADDER

Owner; Membership Manager

Culinary Association Database Manager

Word Processing, Spreadsheets or Graphics Technician

Prerequisites:

Education or Training—Database computer training (which can be self-taught) from community colleges or online sources and graphic design classes, along with the latest updates for avoiding spam and integrating data

Experience—Any computer database experience, either informal or professional, bringing together and merging a variety of lists

Special Skills and Personality Traits—Must love detailed work, minutiae, and working alone; have the ability to listen to culinary association leaders and discern what they want and need and translate that into a useful database

Position Description

As more and more people get involved with and interested in their food, its sources, and how to grow it, more interest groups are organizing to share information and form associations of common food interests.

At the same time, giant Web sites and blogs are communicating about food and food sources and creating enormous databases of people, e-mail addresses, and similar interest Web sites and blogs.

Cooking schools need databases of customers who like to take classes or potential learners to whom they e-mail news and bulletins to sell enrollment, as well as aprons, books, and other items. Restaurants develop databases of customers or anyone who has ever shown a hint of interest in their restaurant(s) and to whom they might sell merchandise and cookbooks.

Even local culinary societies, made up of food fans and gourmands who like to eat and cook, need help developing and updating their membership databases. Other local culinary associations may be made up of local chefs, growers and purveyors, food writers, or pastry chefs.

Some large box stores create databases of customers or members who are interested in organic foods, so there is enormous potential if one wants to help develop and manage culinary databases.

Culinary associations might use their databases to send out newsletters, cooking class schedules, culinary tasting schedules, kitchen gardening class schedules, or to announce a new book or blog, or even a text message.

The database manager might work with the newsletter or catalog editor, copywriter, and the president of the association to plan how to meet the group's needs and possibly how to set up the database so that the association members can maintain it.

Culinary associations can either use and pay a member who knows how to create a database, hire a full-time database manager, or hire someone part time to do the work, possibly continuing on contract to maintain and update the data.

The Culinary Association Database Manager will develop, expand, and customize a database and e-mail list, sometimes with subdivisions by specialized interests. He or she will gather as much information as possible on members and potential members or potential customers, include vital communication data in the database including name, address, e-mail address, Web sites, and cell phone numbers, compile data for mailing labels for snail mail as well as e-mail addresses to send information and membership and renewal forms, and will program the database to ask for renewal fees and to mine culinary blogs for participants.

Information put into the database might also include members' or customers' fax numbers, their professional affiliations, personal data if they wish, services they might like to market, and personal food profiles including preferred specialties.

Such a database should be programmed to know what month of the year members last paid their dues and trigger an automatic snail mail or e-mail asking them to renew their membership, often with not-too-subtle sales pitches for merchandise or new classes.

Many organizations are moving from print newsletters to e-mail to save money, paper, and trees, but each database should be capable of printing address labels or sending e-mails to announce meetings or personalized e-mails to individual members or customers.

As databases grow, organizations and associations may need to decide whether to keep maintenance in-house or whether to hire an outside database manager. When the organization gets truly big, members might want to divide into subgroups, with some members joining more than one. The database manager will need to integrate these interests so that members with more than one interest will receive all the information they want as efficiently as possible.

The Culinary Association Database Manager might also emerge into the role of setting up a blog for members to communicate about a wide range of food-related topics.

Salaries

As a freelancer or full-time staffer, a Culinary Association Database Manager earns from $12 an hour to $100,000 annually, if the freelancer or full-timer assembles several good clients, based partly on the size of the membership to be integrated into the database and how complicated and how many levels of data the information includes. Database managers employed full time earn annual salaries of $50,000 to $100,000.

Employment Prospects

A person with up-to-date database expertise can become known as easy to work with and efficient with time and pick up lots of freelance work in a certain geographic area. As economic times get tough, organization memberships drop out because people save their money and hold off on renewing memberships, which means the association needs all the more help in eking those necessary membership dues out of its remaining group. While associations and organizations may need more help, they tend to cut back and want more work for less. As the economy improves, directors get excited and optimistic and are more willing to hire database managers.

Advancement Prospects

As the economy improves and as associations and organizations grow, officers may be willing to pay more to freelancers for more work. If a database manager works within a culinary organization or company, he or she can think up other marketing roles to perform, possibly either saving his or her job or increasing both pay and a role in the company. This person might also work up to marketing manager and even to an executive post in a large association or company.

A freelance culinary Database Manager can approach every food-related concern in his or her immediate geographic area to expand clientele, or pitch services to individual culinary members of the association, such as a chef with a restaurant or a winemaker with a winery.

Education and Training

One should have database computer training (which can be self-taught) from community colleges or online sources and graphic design classes, along with the latest updates in avoiding spam and integrating data. Training in the latest versions of database software such as File-Maker Pro and Microsoft Access spreadsheet programs like Micrsoft Excel and Lotus 1-2-3, as well as familiarity with the newest association management software and membership software are important. Server database applications like Oracle and Microsoft SQL Server may be used. A background in data management and bookkeeping could also be helpful.

Experience, Skills, and Personality Traits

It would be ideal to have computer database experience, either informal or professional. The ability to bring together and merge a variety of lists and keep careful records of agreements and sources of lists will be handy.

Love for food and food-related organizations and associations makes this job easier. A Culinary Association Database Manager must also love detail work and working alone. He or she should also have the ability to listen to culinary association leaders and discern what they want and need and translate that into a useful database. One needs to be flexible to handle a variety of changes in goals and ideas from association officers and have a personal need to meet deadlines and be on time.

Unions and Associations

Data Management International (www.dama.org) offers conferences, courses, certification, an online diction-ary of database terms, and international conferences in some interesting places. Also check out the California Data Base Management Association (www.cdbma.org).

Tips for Entry

1. Learn everything you can either at schools or online about database management.
2. Get as familiar as possible with the latest programs mentioned above.
3. Find a database manager in your community and ask to help, either as a volunteer or as an apprentice, hopefully in the culinary or wine fields.
4. Approach culinary groups, restaurants, cooking schools, or cookware stores in your area and talk your way into creating a database for them.

WRITING AND PUBLISHING

COOKBOOK AUTHOR

CAREER PROFILE

Duties: Develops expertise on a culinary topic or the ability to research the topic thoroughly; writes a book proposal and submits it to an agent or cookbook publisher; writes the book while testing all of the recipes; submits the manuscript and then edits or adapts it according to the editor's wishes after some negotiation; coordinates photo shoots with a photographer and food stylist; reads and corrects galleys; works on index; helps coordinate publicity tours and travels

Alternate Title(s): Cookbook Writer

Salary Range: $5,000 to $15,000 for first book; up to $100,000 to $1,000,000 if a famous chef or television star chef

Employment Prospects: Limited

Advancement Prospects: Good

Best Geographical Location(s): Anywhere in the world

Prerequisites:

    Education or Training—General education, English, journalism, creative writing, and reading for style and content

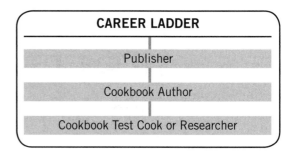

CAREER LADDER

Publisher

Cookbook Author

Cookbook Test Cook or Researcher

Experience—Restaurant chef experience, kitchen gardening experience, food writing for newspapers or magazines, teaching cooking classes, and writing original recipes or adapting recipes by other chefs or authors

Special Skills and Personality Traits—Ability to know one's market or adapt to the potential reading market; enjoyment of working alone; almost obsessive accuracy; a willingness to test and retest recipes to get them right; a love of precision; enjoyment meeting people and helping them enjoy cooking

Position Description

Cookbook publishers want to know what a potential author's "credentials" are as an expert in whatever cooking genre he or she proposes to describe in a book. It helps tremendously to teach cooking classes with a specialty, cook at a specialized restaurant, maximize one's national origin or ethnic background, or write about food in or from a distinct part of the country.

Initially a Cookbook Author develops expertise on a culinary topic or demonstrates the ability to research the topic thoroughly. You can collect recipes from a place where you cook as a volunteer, such as a local meals-on-wheels organization; collect recipes from restaurant chefs for a regional cookbook; collect recipes and adapt them for your own cooking classes; collect recipes while cooking for a teen center or Boys & Girls Club; adapt recipes to cook from your own kitchen garden; or travel and study the culture of cooking in another country, especially one not already the topic of a cookbook.

The first thing you should do is check online booksellers to find out if there are already books written and

published on the same cookbook topic as your idea, noticing the date of publication or how long ago the potentially competing cookbook was published, who wrote it, and who published it.

Your next job is to write a book proposal and submit it to an agent or cookbook publisher. These days, publishers like to use literary agents as first screeners of book proposals. Many agents have contacts with or worked for cookbook publishers, while a few agents specialize in cookbook representation.

Ask someone you know who has a cookbook published, or a cooking school director or teacher, what agent he or she uses or who his or her contact or editor is at a cookbook publishing house. Using other people's contacts and connections is usually much more successful than just sending a manuscript "blind," without any contacts or references whom the recipient knows.

If you are fortunate and get representation by a legitimate agent, first try out your ideas on that person, draft a proposal and a sample chapter, and send it to the agent for comments and suggestions, both by e-mail and with a hard copy by snail mail. Check your pride at some nearby door and follow the agent's recommendations for any changes. A good agent knows what publishers want to see and what tickles their imagination.

If you are a first-time book author, you can find books on how to write a book proposal or read good ideas online. Generally, a good book proposal should include an overall description of your concept with persuasive discussion of why it will become popular and sell well; an outline or table of contents of chapters and recipe divisions; some tasty sample recipes to make the editor drool on first reading with descriptions that show you can write; sample photographs; and a selective résumé that shows your irresistible expertise and experience in your field of choice.

Make the proposal double-spaced with numbered pages and correct grammar and spelling.

Once the agent is satisfied with your proposal, he or she will send it to the editor(s) for whom he or she thinks the book is most suitable. Do not hold your breath waiting to hear from your agent. The sale could take months or years, so go on with your life and improve your credentials. A good agent will negotiate the best deal for you, but be sure to ask all the questions you have.

Once you have a contract, you now have to actually write the book while testing all of the recipes, thinking of potentially beautiful photo shots along the way. An author's recipe testing can be expensive because the ingredients may have to be specially ordered and because if a recipe doesn't work you might have to purchase the ingredients more than once and adapt the recipe to one that does work for home use. Some Cookbook Authors invite friends whose palates they respect to sample the food and comment, then adapt the recipe using their critiques. Others just share the food with neighbors or with a local food pantry.

Some already successful Cookbook Authors hire assistants to do prep and cleanup work, and even shopping, but this assistant really needs to know food to get the right ingredients the first time. When writing cookbooks about cuisines of other countries, a cookbook author might need to hire a translator to interpret a recipe or list of ingredients from another language.

After completing the cookbook, the author submits the manuscript and then edits or adapts it according to editor's wishes after some negotiation. The publisher's art director will help coordinate photo shoots with the photographer and a food stylist, if the latter is needed. Occasionally the photography expense comes out of the author's advance against eventual royalties.

If the photo shoots are done in the author's home, he or she might either prepare the food or watch while a food stylist arranges the food and lighting. If the photos are taken in the publisher's test kitchen, the author may not choose to be there.

After the book is set in type, which is now done by computer, the publisher sends the galleys (page printouts) to the author, who then reads and corrects galleys and sends the whole bundle back to the publisher, all of which is done according to a publishing schedule. There probably is no time to add recipes or new ideas to the book at this stage.

The author works on the index, which is much easier than it used to be due to the "sort" features in most publishing applications. If the author doesn't want to work on the index, the publisher might hire an indexer at the author's expense.

Before the book is published and distributed to bookstores, the publisher helps coordinate publicity tour plans, if the company can afford to send the author on tour. If not, the author should contact bookstores, starting with his or her home area, and set up his or her own book signings and cooking demonstrations if possible. If you set up this tour yourself, be sure to arrange interviews with local food editors and radio and television news stations. You can also announce your book or your appearances via social media sites such as Facebook and Twitter, as well as by e-mail to personal and professional lists of contacts.

Salaries

Authors receive an "advance on royalties," meaning a figure that calculates to the agreed-upon percentage of what the total book sales the publisher expects, according to the contract. Print runs (numbers of copies printed) usually are around 3,000 for a first-time author, and increase with second printings if initial sales are brisk or as an author becomes better known and more popular. Advances for first books range from $5,000 to $15,000, and up to $100,000 to $1,000,000 and more if the author is a famous chef or television star chef, with an agent keeping about 15 percent of everything.

Employment Prospects

Independent cookbook writing is almost always freelance, except if one writes for a series, which may be for a set fee and may exclude royalty payments. During tough economic times especially, a freelancer needs to be an expert in a culinary field or be a prominent food writer to get a book deal.

Advancement Prospects

Success breeds success in the cookbook world. One book that does well leads to opportunities to write more cookbooks and magazine articles. Such success may also lead to teaching in cooking classes or receiving higher pay, appearing on television shows, and garnering larger book advances.

Education and Training

As a Cookbook Author one needs a good general education, including English, journalism, or creative writing. The best writers have lived a bit and read a lot. Cookbook Authors should study successful cookbook writers' work and learn from it, including the recipes and cultural information.

Experience, Skills, and Personality Traits

To be a successful Cookbook Author, or even get a cookbook published, one should have restaurant chef experience, kitchen gardening experience, food writing experience for newspapers or magazines, or be a veteran teacher of cooking classes, writer of original recipes, or expert in adapting recipes by other chefs or authors.

One should have the ability to know one's market or adapt to the potential reading market; enjoy working alone; be almost obsessively accurate; be willing to test and retest recipes to get them right; love precision; and enjoy meeting people and helping them enjoy cooking.

Unions and Associations

The International Association of Culinary Professionals (www.iacp.com) is the best organization of its kind, with the most services and a terrific annual conference where one can make loads of contacts and learn from others.

Tips for Entry

1. Become an expert in a culinary specialty, or begin to research a field about which little, if anything, has been written.
2. Find local chefs and food editors in your area who have written a cookbook and contact those persons, perhaps asking if you can interview them and even assist them in preparation or cleanup for their next book to learn as you help.
3. Find out the names of these writers' agents and editors for future contact.
4. Ask someone you meet or know to suggest names of agents or editors you should contact for help.
5. Find literary agents who specialize in cookbooks or in reference books at your local public library and contact them.
6. Check out agents on the IACP Web site as well and contact them, enticing them to look at and represent your book to publishers.
7. Look online for writing coaches who specialize in cookbook development.

COOKBOOK EDITOR

CAREER PROFILE

Duties: Reads book proposals and selects those he or she thinks have potential; presents favorites as well as new book ideas to the publisher's acquisitions committee, including the marketing department; contacts successful cookbook authors and proposes new book ideas; helps negotiate book contracts; works with authors and advises them on how to make their books better, including rewrites; reviews manuscripts and sends them out to copy editors; works with marketing, graphics, and photography professionals and sometimes plans tour schedules with the marketing department

Alternate Title(s): Senior Editor; Assistant Editor; Editor-in-Chief

Salary Range: $28,000 to $100,000 or more

Employment Prospects: Limited

Advancement Prospects: Limited

Best Geographical Location(s): New York City and San Francisco Bay area

Prerequisites:

    Education or Training—College major in English, creative writing, journalism, or communications;

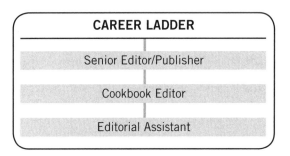

CAREER LADDER

Senior Editor/Publisher

Cookbook Editor

Editorial Assistant

passion for good food; basic cooking knowledge; passion for learning more about food; knowledge of food chemistry; familiarity with good literature; knowledge of editing, grammar, and copyediting

Experience—Any publishing experience; recipe writing; cooking experience

Special Skills and Personality Traits—Passion for detail; the sensitivity to know what the public is looking for in advance of them looking for it; an ability to deal with writers without hurting their feelings but getting constructive revisions out of them; a passion for seeing a project to completion

Position Description

Within the realm of cookbook and other book editors there are several positions under the title "editor," including editor in chief, senior editor, editor, acquisitions editor, assistant editor, and copy editor.

Some editors perform many or all of these functions, while others have more specific responsibilities. Being an editor does not necessarily mean one actually edits books.

Generally, a Cookbook Editor reads book proposals and selects those he or she thinks have potential, often being the first screener of an incoming book. The editor receives proposals and manuscripts from literary agents and cookbook authors, and may even advise the author how to revise a proposal before the editor takes it to the acquisitions committee.

An editor may present a proposal and new book ideas he or she finds worthy of publication to a senior editor and to marketing department specialists before actually showing it to the publisher's acquisitions com-

mittee in order to make it as salable as possible to the committee and then as a published book to the cookbook market in the real world. Editors should check as well as possible to make sure the work is original and not plagiarized.

A Cookbook Editor might initiate a book by contacting successful cookbook authors and proposing new book ideas that the editor thinks the writer may be the best person to write, either because of the author's expertise, the region of country where the author lives, his or her ability to research new topics, or his or her past success at writing other cookbooks.

Once a proposal or cookbook is approved by higher-ups, the editor relays a financial offer and deadlines to the author's agent or directly to the author for the start of negotiations. The editor may ask the author for more work samples or a complete chapter with recipes to make sure the writer is capable of bringing in original recipes. (Julia Child once said, however, "There is no such thing as a new recipe.")

When the parties agree to terms, the contract is finalized, with deadlines, and sent to the author for him or her to sign first. A contract can still be withdrawn up until the moment the publisher's representative or editor signs it after the author sends his or her signed copy back to the publisher.

As the writer faces the reality of actually having to write and pull the book together, the editor usually is available for advice and consultation and may request the book in chapters or batches to look it over as the writer goes along. This way the editor can advise the author early on of any possible adjustments in writing style, voice, and attitude and whether they are appropriate for the market.

The editor works with authors and advises them on how to make their books better, including rewrites, and an author should always try to accept editors' suggestions whether he or she likes them or not. One has to trust one's editor, and editors should earn authors' trust, which requires gentle handling. After all, the editor liked the work well enough to gamble his or her reputation on the book's success.

When the Cookbook Editor receives the full manuscript, he or she reads all of it slowly, making suggestions for consistency of style, explanations of culinary terms, recipe directions, and literary abilities.

An editor might work with marketing, graphics, and photography department to create the appropriate layout and image for the cookbook. The editor marshals the book through the design and production process and sometimes even helps plans a tour schedule with the marketing department and author. Regardless of how long it takes the author to write the cookbook, the gestation period of the book after it is submitted to the publisher is usually nine to 18 months before it comes out.

Salaries

Editors' salaries range from as low as $25,000 to as high as $200,000 depending on length of experience, success of previous books, contacts with existing successful authors, ability to spot and bring in hot new authors, and the editor's newness or status on the publishing house ladder.

Employment Prospects

As more people get recipes off the Internet and fewer cookbooks are published, the prospects for finding work as a Cookbook Editor narrow. While there is a plethora of English graduates from excellent universities, some of them have to start their publishing climb at the front reception desk.

Some Cookbook Editors work for the few publishers that produce only cookbooks, while others work for large publishers that do everything from fiction and nonfiction to how-to books in the cookbook department or publisher's imprint. Even specialized cookbook publishers are getting gobbled up by large houses.

Advancement Prospects

Much like the old stories of movie stars being discovered at soda fountains, Cookbook Editors can start at the reception desk and become an editor. It is, indeed, possible to start as a receptionist and rise to editor if one has the right university credentials and keen interest and abilities.

As a Cookbook Editor develops a list of reliably successful authors who repeatedly write popular books or have or develop television shows, that editor may be promoted within the publishing house. More and more agents will bring new authors to this sort of editor, and with good judgment and hard work the editor can move up the publishing ladder. A good editor might also advance by moving to a better, bigger, or smaller specialized publisher.

Education and Training

A college major in English, creative writing, journalism, or communications and a good general education will be necessary, because so many editorial applicants have those qualities.

Experience, Skills, and Personality Traits

Any publishing, recipe writing, and cooking experience will be helpful, along with editing experience, no matter how informal or formal and including your high school or college newspaper or yearbook, a local newspaper, magazines, and even as a food or wine editor for a local publication.

One needs a passion for good food, basic cooking knowledge, a desire to learn more about food, knowledge of food chemistry, familiarity with good literature, knowledge of editing, grammar, and copyediting, a passion for detail, sensitivity to know what public is looking for in advance of them looking for it, the ability to deal with writers without hurting their feelings but getting constructive revisions out of them, and a passion for seeing a project to completion.

An editor needs an extra sensor to know what authors and which books will be popular and lasting, meaning the editor needs to know the potential market extremely well.

Unions and Associations

Without a real union for cookbook authors and editors, many may meet lots of people and keep up on the latest trends by joining the International Association of Culinary Professionals (www.iacp.com) among other culinary organizations. You might also find other Cookbook Editors on Facebook or Twitter.

Tips for Entry

1. Take any job at all in a publishing house, whether it is at a food or wine magazine company, a small local publisher, or a large corporate publisher of cookbooks and other books. Receptionist jobs are great positions in which to learn how the business works and maybe get a little editing or reading thrown your way.
2. Work your way up to editorial assistant, to assistant editor, and then to editor.
3. Attend book fairs wherever they are, especially those that feature food and wine books and cookbooks, such as the Book Exposition of America. Learn from publisher exhibitors and ask lots of questions, perhaps making valuable contacts.
4. Take a look at your favorite cookbooks; look inside and find the publishing company, check its Web site, learn as much as you can about it, and approach the company for a job, any job.
5. Ask your local librarians and bookstore owners what cookbooks and cookbook authors sell well and approach their publishers. You might consider checking online bookstores that rank overall sales of all books and then apply for a job.
6. Ask local chefs what cookbooks inspire them and if they know cookbook authors or editors whom you can contact to learn from.

FOOD EDITOR

CAREER PROFILE

Duties: Coordinates style and balance of subject matter within the food section of a newspaper, magazine, cable television and radio programs, phone apps, and Web sites; brings in freelance writers occasionally; writes stories on food; edits other people's work in the field within the publication or show; works with graphic artists to select or set up photography to go with stories; represents the publication or station before the public; occasionally hires, supervises, or coordinates staff and freelance writers

Alternate Title(s): Food and Wine Editor

Salary Range: $100 to $100,000, depending on size of institution

Employment Prospects: Limited

Advancement Prospects: Limited

Best Geographical Location(s): Throughout the country

Prerequisites:

Education or Training—Study of language, grammar, and style; expertise in communications and various computer publishing programs, food chemistry, wine, and nutrition

Experience—Writing and editing; culinary experience, ranging from home cooking to catering, restaurant work, teaching, and writing cookbooks

Special Skills and Personality Traits—Passion for food and possibly wine; knowledge of food ingredients and recipes and how they work; familiarity with various cuisines; interest in sustainably grown and organic ingredients; relationships with local chefs and food sources; interest in food trends, both local and international; ability to get along with and motivate freelance writers

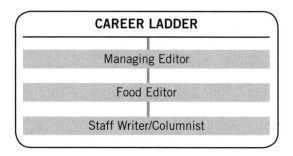

CAREER LADDER

Managing Editor

Food Editor

Staff Writer/Columnist

Position Description

Working with the managing editor, editor in chief, and possibly publisher, the Food Editor coordinates the style and balance of subject matter within the food section of a newspaper, magazine, cable television or radio programs, phone app, or Web sites, and usually writes stories as well. Such subject matter or balance might include restaurant and chef gossip, restaurant reviews, recipes, kitchen gardening, and possibly wine and cocktails.

Food Editors need to know their publication's or station's audience or market, the vernacular of the community, the financial income of the audience, and the audience's level of education, food awareness, and taste. Some food editors set out to raise a community's food awareness.

Some readers and listeners prefer *Saveur, Food & Wine* or *Cooks Illustrated*, some Facebook and the Food Network, while others prefer Fox or auto racing television and publications. Each of these outlets will have different audiences with different tastes, as will small community newspapers compared to *New York Times* readers.

Food Editors consider the season, and even the weeks, as they plan and write stories they hope will be of greatest interest to their readers, listeners, and viewers. They also have to think about the kinds of foods their community prefers, whether it is pork and corn, lobster and clams, or vegetables and artisan breads.

The Food Editor sets the theme or focus of each edition, with many newspapers traditionally publishing their food sections on Wednesdays. Some newspapers have several staff writers in the food section, while others have one person who either does it all or develops a network of freelance writers, often with distinct interests or specialties.

A Food Editor will edit all of the stories submitted to him or her by freelancers and staff writers, consult on other stories in the publication or program that deal with food or wine, select outside material from wire services or press releases, and locate other "filler" material as needed. Few Food Editors accept blind submissions, that is, unsolicited articles from writers with no connection to the editor.

Food Editors also write stories, personalized columns, and occasionally save the best subjects or events to cover for themselves. Some Food Editors have a particular interest in the food field and may write a regular or even weekly story or report electronically on that subject.

Food Editors also may alter content for the publication or network's Web site to make material more relevant to audiences outside their locale and of more general interest to those people.

Food Editors also work with staff and freelance photographers to capture the best of food and food events for publication, Web viewing, and television. They also decide which photos or drawings should be used, and may even work with a food stylist and photographer to set up the photos and page designers to lay out print or Web site pages.

When copy and photos are done, the Food Editor makes sure they go together and sends them on to composing and layout, which is nearly all done by computer and people who specialize in these crafts.

Food Editors need to dine at various restaurants, spreading the business within the food community. A few Food Editors still get expense accounts or company credit cards to do this, but many do not. If the Food Editor doubles as wine editor, he or she may also get lots of tasting opportunities and complimentary bottles of wine that come with the winery's expectation that the editor will write about them favorably.

A wide range of magazines may have Food Editors, from food magazines to those focusing on gardening, cars, wine, fashion, lifestyle, and even entertainment.

Food Editors also represent the publication or station before the public at events, which helps develop a reputation for the editors and the company they represent. Such activities include food festivals, radio and television food show appearances, phone apps and Facebook-like entities, as well as judging at cook-offs and wine tastings. Some Food Editors sit on panels, both local and national, on farming and food supply, and work to influence local, state, and federal elected officials on decisions about food policy.

In the few remaining real food section departments, the Food Editor sets work schedules, reviews writers' performances, recommends promotions and salaries, sets freelancer fees, and nurtures various writers to make their work better.

Salaries

For some small-town community newspapers and radio and television stations, the Food Editor actually performs editing functions for free, aside from whatever he or she is paid as a writer, because the local entity cannot afford to pay for a Food Editor.

In the last few years, some Food Editors' and staff writers' salaries have been cut or eliminated, and some magazines have even shut down entirely.

Typical salaries might range from zero up to $100,000 or more for top magazines and electronic media, depending on the size of the town or city, circulation numbers, viewers, and location or region of the country.

Employment Prospects

Food Editor jobs in print publications are decreasing as newspapers and magazines disappear, while Food Editor jobs on the Internet proliferate. You can even start your own blog or Web site and name yourself Food Editor.

Advancement Prospects

You can always approach your local newspaper if it doesn't have a food section or Food Editor and propose that you start one, telling company officers that it will draw advertisers.

If you talk them into starting a food section, or already work at one, you can work your way up to Food Editor or from Food Editor to lifestyle editor, managing editor, and maybe even editor in chief. Or you can simply move to a larger publication or network with better pay and circulation, more listeners or viewers, and specialized departments.

Starting a blog or Web site with connections to Facebook and links to other food sites can propel you into prominence in the food world.

Education and Training

To be a successful Food Editor, one should be well-informed on language, grammar, and style; study communications and various computer publishing programs and be familiar with graphic design; know food chemistry; have wine expertise; and be familiar with basic nutrition.

Experience, Skills, and Personality Traits

Writing, editing, and culinary experience, ranging from home cooking to catering, restaurant work, teaching, and writing cookbooks or other books will all be helpful.

A good Food Editor should have a passion for food and possibly wine; knowledge of food ingredients and recipes and how they work; familiarity with various cuisines; interest in sustainably grown, organic, and locally grown ingredients and sustainable and organic growing practices; have good relationships with local chefs and food sources; an interest in food trends, both local and international; and the ability to get along with, motivate, and nurture freelance writers.

Unions and Associations

The Association of Food Journalists (www.afjonline.com) brings together full-time, part-time, and freelance food journalists who spend most of their time writing about food.

Tips for Entry

1. Take writing and editing courses either through an adult school or community colleges if you have not graduated with a bachelor's degree in English, journalism, creative writing, or communications.

2. Contact the Food Editor, if there is one, at your local newspaper and see if she or he could use some volunteer or slightly paid help as a great way for you to learn.

3. If your local paper doesn't have a food writer, section, column, or blog, talk them into letting you start one, partly on the basis that it will attract advertisers from the restaurant and wine industries.

4. Establish your own food blog, Web site, Facebook page, or Twitter or other social media presence.

FOOD WRITER

CAREER PROFILE

Duties: Develops expertise on local foods or specialty foods, restaurants, recipes, and food festivals to write stories and articles for newspapers, magazines, and Web sites and occasionally for radio, television, and cable TV food shows

Alternate Title(s): Food Journalist; Food Editor; Food and Wine Writer; Food and Wine Editor

Salary Range: $10,000 to $80,000

Employment Prospects: Fair

Advancement Prospects: Good

Best Geographical Location(s): Almost anywhere in North America, with major cities most likely to host newspapers with food sections and magazines

Prerequisites:

Education and Training—General education with creative writing, English, journalism, or communications major; kitchen experience; kitchen garden experience; familiarity with local restaurants and chefs

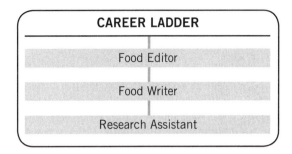

CAREER LADDER

Food Editor

Food Writer

Research Assistant

Experience—Any writing and editing experience; experience writing recipes; word processing experience; home cooking, restaurant, or food gardening experience all will be helpful

Special Skills and Personality Traits—Passion for food and telling people about food discoveries; knowledge of the food industry, both organic and conventional; enthusiasm for food activities in the region or nationally; deep curiosity about what's going on in the local food and wine community and all of its gossip; an ability to cook is handy but not required

Position Description

Food writing is a specialization within journalism and communications that requires a passion for food and how it works.

Food Writers write for daily, weekly, and biweekly newspapers, magazines, Web sites, and even for broadcast stations including radio and television.

For a local or regional newspaper, a successful Food Writer needs to either live in the area or be a very quick study from a distance of the food scene. Every region has food styles, some of which derive from the countries of origin from which residents or their ancestors came. Also, every region can grow crops defined by soil, weather, and tradition. Often local or regional specialties develop according to what is grown in the area and what people have to cook and eat at the least expense.

Food Writers need to know the details of what is grown, cooked, and sought after in their area, as well as food trends in the area and elsewhere that their audience might learn from or appreciate.

Food Writers need to keep track of all chefs in their geographic area and have an ear for gossip about the musical-chairs movement of kitchen chefs from job to

job, about prominent leaders in the community, and about winery owners and winemakers, and be open to community members' dining experience reports.

Food sections traditionally have employed food writing staff, although as newspapers struggle with a downturn in advertising, they turn to freelance Food Writers more and more often since freelancers do not receive any benefits such as health insurance and therefore cost less than staff Food Writers.

Food Writers develop expertise on local foods or specialty foods. They also need to know how to write recipes or occasionally translate a chef's recipe from large quantities to amounts usable in a home kitchen. Food Writers should be able to tell readers where ingredients are available locally or online. The also need to be up on any food festivals to write stories and articles (sometimes called "pieces") for newspapers, magazines, and Web sites and occasionally for radio, television, and cable TV food shows.

Food editors in every medium figure out what stories they need and assign them to staff Food Writers or freelancers, sometimes with plenty of advance notice and sometimes with very little. A large city newspaper might reach out to a Food Writer across the country to write about local foods in his or her home state to juice up the food section's content and make it more interesting to readers.

Writers also get their assignments based on the food editors' familiarity with the writers' specialties and food knowledge. Editors also work with writers to perfect stories after submission.

The Food Writer writes the story, checks facts, and hopefully tests all recipes before submitting it to the editor. Occasionally the editor will return the story to the writer with suggestions or orders for changes, which can frustrate the writer. Occasionally such changes can either make the story better or inaccurate.

Salaries

Freelance Food Writers' income varies widely from around $10,000 to $100,000, depending upon how long they have been writing, their reputation, and the size of the publication or program for which they write. A small-town Food Writer usually gets paid per story in the $25 to $200 range, while a well-known freelancer who sells stories to big glossy magazines can make much more. If a Food Writer has a contract for regular periodic writing, he or she can count on a certain income, unless of course the magazine folds.

Employment Prospects

Most newspapers have once-a-week food sections, often on Wednesdays, that they need to fill, since many restaurants and grocery stores advertise their specials in coordination with the food section. While some newspapers get their food stories from wire services or online "feeds," they often also want a local angle, which gives local food writers a chance to fill in the gaps.

Food magazines and magazines focused on travel, cars, home décor, fashion, and all sorts of other interests accept stories on food. Food networks, PBS, and local television programs need someone to write the scripts for food-oriented shows. Even radio stations sometimes allow food shows. Unfortunately, during recent economic problems, all media have cut back on all writers.

Advancement Prospects

If you start a food section and write for it in a local newspaper, you may advance to food editor. Otherwise, food editor positions only open when a person working in that job retires or leaves for whatever other reason. Once established as a food editor, one could move into other editing positions at the media outlet, or create one's own food blog.

Education and Training

To be a successful Food Writer, one needs a general college education with a creative writing, English or other language, journalism, or communications major. One should have kitchen experience, kitchen garden experience, and familiarity with local restaurants and chefs. Working under editors, both helpful and annoying, will teach a Food Writer how to do and not to do things.

Experience, Skills, and Personality Traits

Any and all writing and editing experience, experience writing recipes, word processing experience, home cooking, restaurant, or food gardening experience will be helpful. To be able to demonstrate your experience, keep all of your published articles (several copies) and any online links to blogs and Web sites for which you have written.

A good Food Writer needs a passion for food and for telling people about food discoveries; knowledge of the food industry, both organic and conventional; enthusiasm for food activities in the region or nationally; and a deep curiosity about what's going on in the local food and wine community and all of its gossip. An ability to cook and test recipes is important but not required. Some famous food and restaurant critics rarely cook and dine at home on ice cream and chocolate chip cookies.

Unions and Associations

The Association of Food Journalists (www.afjonline. com) brings together full-time, part-time, and freelance food journalists who spend most of their time writing about food. The American Institute of Wine and Food (www.aiwf.org), the International Association of Culinary Professionals (www.iacp.com) are two other organizations that Food Writers may join.

Tips for Entry

1. Write on a blog or start a food blog to try out your skills and warm up.
2. If you have greater aspirations, talk your way into writing a monthly or weekly column for your local newspaper, accept all advice the editors give you, and gradually move your way up.
3. Be willing to write for free in your local newspaper to get started.
4. Join local food groups, dining groups, or food or cuisine societies to get to know people and offer to write for their newsletters.
5. Join the Association of Food Journalists, the American Institute of Wine and Food, and the International Association of Food Journalists.

LITERARY AGENT

CAREER PROFILE

Duties: Guides authors and writers to perfect their book proposals, advising on proposal design and content; usually has a representation contract with writer; tries to connect the food writer with best food editor for him or her at the publishing house most likely to take the book; presents the proposal and sells it to one or more editors; compares offers if there is more than one and discusses pluses and minuses with the writer; negotiates for better money and conditions of contract than those initially offered; encourages and nudges writer through the book writing process

Alternate Title(s): Agent; Book Agent; Representative

Salary Range: $10,000 to $100,000+; 15 percent of all earnings (including advance and royalties) of each book, sometimes including foreign and electronic rights

Employment Prospects: Limited

Advancement Prospects: Fair

Best Geographical Location(s): Agents work from anywhere in the world, but New York, Boston, and the San Francisco Bay area are publishing centers

Prerequisites:

  Education or Training—Bachelor's degree in liberal arts, English, creative writing, journalism, or other

CAREER LADDER

Agency Owner

Literary Agent

Agent Assistant/Editorial Assistant

languages and literature; internship in publishing houses to understand how the business works and to make contacts that carry through to wherever in publishing the contact moves

Experience—Work with publishers and editors or have fabulous contacts with them

Special Skills and Personality Traits—Skills at mentoring writers; picking winners among manuscripts and authors; love of gossip and the musical chairs qualities of publishing houses; appreciation for language; love of food and appreciation for different approaches to food, recipes, and food culture

Position Description

Literary Agents are the supermarketers or marketeers of book proposals and books to publishers on behalf of writers, including food writers. Agents nurture and coach writers to improve their proposals, often tailored to a particular specialized editor in the food-book publishing world.

In the process of coaching a writer, Literary Agents may seem harsh in their "constructive criticism," which may be hard for a new writer to take. The agent has the writer's and his or her own best interest at heart, for the better the proposal, the better the publisher's offer, and the more money the writer and agent make.

A writer must trust his or her literary agent and take his or her advice, or move on to another agent. If the agent cannot mold a writer to suit his or her ideas of what needs to be done to a proposal to make it salable, the agent might drop the client. Agents and writers must share trust and respect for a good working relationship.

Agents may make suggestions about style, grammar, and the order of chapters, as well as whether a book is truly a new or good idea—and sometimes they are not, much to the shock of the author.

Literary Agents serve as cheerleader, moral supporter, mother and father, sister and brother, nurse and super salesperson, making the writer and his or her proposal irresistible.

Literary Agents often circulate at literary events, book conventions, and even cooking conferences and food writing workshops to meet new authors and keep up connections with food-related publishing editors. Food writers often talk to other food writers and friends for recommendations of their agents, especially if these acquaintances are successful.

Many agents require a contractual relationship with their writers, which usually stipulate that the agent gets 15 percent of all revenue from the book, including the advance on royalties, royalties themselves, foreign rights, electronic rights, and maybe even any television or film rights.

Once a proposal is complete, the Literary Agent tries to connect the food writer with the best food editor for the project at the publishing house most likely to take the book. The agent presents the proposal and tries to sell it to one or more editors. If there are multiple offers, the agent discusses them with the client and negotiates for better money and conditions of contract than those offered initially. If there is only one offer, the agent and writer talk about whether to accept it and how to improve it, after which the agent goes back to the editor to negotiate for better terms and eventually signs the contract. The writer and agent may also turn down the offer.

It is also important that Literary Agents encourage and nudge writers through the book writing process, from bringing writers out of depression and writer's block to cheering them on when they are doing great and gently motivating them to work harder and faster when behind on deadlines. Good Literary Agents will see the writers through the entire process, including demanding payment from publishers when necessary and making sure sales and royalties are reported properly.

Salaries

Agents usually collect 15 percent of all income from a book, so their payment can range from a few hundred dollars for a first cookbook to $15,000 for a well-known cookbook author, or even $150,000 for a top television network star's book—that being 15 percent of $1,000,000, which is rare.

Advances are paid in increments, generally one-third upon signing, one-third when the manuscript is submitted, and the final third when the book is complete. Alternatively, an advance may come in two parts, one upon signing and the other upon completion and submission of the manuscript. Usually the publisher's check goes directly to the agent, who takes his or her cut and then writes a check to the writer for his or her 85 percent.

Employment Prospects

Independent agents often are people who worked for large publishers or literary agencies and struck out on their own for one reason or another. They have to be patient as they build up clientele and sell their first few books.

If a Literary Agent works for a large agency, he or she usually starts with a base salary and may get commission on top of that.

As the economy suffers and book sales decrease, publishing houses get smaller as do literary agencies.

Advancement Prospects

Once a Literary Agent gets a reputation for finding successful authors and selling great books, he or she is in great demand, both among writers and by publishers who count on agents for the first level in the screening process.

If a Literary Agent represents consistent winners, meaning cookbook or food authors who win James Beard House, International Association of Culinary Professional, or other awards for their books, authors will clamor to get into their stable of writers. Both of these groups and the Culinary Institute of America publish member and participant directories that list agents and their contact information.

Education and Training

A great Literary Agent for food writers should have a bachelor's degree in liberal arts, English, creative writing, journalism, or other languages and literature; have worked in publishing houses to understand how the business works and to make contacts that carry through to wherever the contact moves; or have worked with magazines and newspapers or in public relations and advertising firms.

Experience, Skills, and Personality Traits

An ideal Literary Agent should have worked with publishers and editors or have fabulous contacts with them; love to work with food writers and nurture them into being excellent writers; have a knack for picking winners among manuscripts and authors; have a love of gossip and understanding of the musical-chairs qualities of publishing houses; have an appreciation for language; and love food and different approaches to food, recipes, and food culture.

A great agent will also be a great marketer and understand legal and marketing language and terms.

Unions and Associations

The Association of Authors' Representatives (www.aaronline.org) is the largest literary and dramatic agents' organization in the country. Food writer agents often belong to the International Association of Culinary Professionals (www.iacp.com) and the Women Chefs and Restaurateurs (www.womenchefs.org) and attend the Fancy Food Shows in New York and San Francisco, sponsored by the National Association for the Specialty Food Trade (www.specialtyfood.com).

Tips for Entry

1. Get low-level jobs in or around writing or editing, even at a local newspaper, to build experience and a résumé.

2. Find a literary agency in your area (see www.aaronline.org) who works with chefs and culinary authors and approach the agency for any volunteer or entry level work so you can learn the agency business and possibly work your way into a job.

3. Once you are into the agency, ask to work with food or cookbook agents and gradually work your way up the cookbook ladder.

FOOD HISTORIAN

Duties: Researches and chronicles history of food, locally or around the world; conducts oral history interviews of folk cooks and cultural chefs; collects old photos, recipes, stories about food and cooking, and other documentation; collects old cookbooks and studies social aspects of food; collects old recipes, cooking utensils, and pamphlets; consults with museums, television shows, movie scriptwriters, and directors; writes books and magazine articles about food history

Alternate Title(s): None

Salary Range: Freelancers earn from $200 an hour to $3,000 a day as consultants, while the few college or university level posts pay from $30,000 to $60,000 annually, with book advances and royalties separate

Employment Prospects: Limited

Advancement Prospects: Limited

Best Geographical Location(s): Anywhere for writing food historians, but freelance lecturers and consultants should be able to travel to where services are needed

Prerequisites:

Education and Training—Either a degree in history or an advanced degree in another subject will

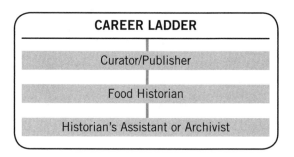

CAREER LADDER

Curator/Publisher

Food Historian

Historian's Assistant or Archivist

be required to teach at the college or university level or to get substantial research grants, with a master's degree or Ph.D. in progress

Experience—Working on a research project for an historian, food historian, or academic or media project; work as an assistant to a researcher in almost any subject to get research process experience

Special Skills and Personality Traits—Passion for detailed research and organization; computer skills such as word processing and spreadsheet creation; a good memory; skills in asking questions that draw out historical experiences; energy to dig deep into old files and go anywhere to interview subjects; ability to write clearly and grammatically

Position Description

Food Historians thrive on discovering new old facts about foods, their origins, and how they have been grown, harvested, and cooked through history.

Food is part of culture, whether it is a regional or national culture. We think categorically of French and Italian food in general. But each little region and even town in France and Italy has its specialties, often based upon what grows best in the area.

As nations primarily of immigrants, the United States and Canada have food specialties and traditions that stem from where our ancestors came from, where the residents of a community came from, what is grown where we live, and whether we live on the coasts or near lakes and rivers with access to fish and seafood.

All of these factors can be bases for research by Food Historians, on a local, regional, or national basis. Using computer research one can even investigate the food history of a place far away, although one needs to be in

the geographic locale to do on-site interviews and truly absorb the "flavor" of a region's cuisine and culinary history. A Food Historian holds oral history interviews of folk cooks and cultural chefs, which means traveling to where those sources live.

It is also important for a Food Historian to try to recreate recipes as closely as possible using the same level of ingredients and kitchen implements as in the period about which he or she is researching and writing.

Food Historians collect old photos, recipes, stories about food, old lifestyle books and cooking, and other documentation. If they do not have all of this kind of documentation they need, local libraries and museums are good sources, and more and more small museums include a small kitchen set up to look like a historic kitchen in the area. Collecting old recipes, cooking utensils, and pamphlets has become increasingly popular and will be handy to do good research. Local historic societies also gather culinary history and can be excellent sources of information. Some local, regional, and state museums include old mills that have historic milling and bread making information, for example.

Occasionally Food Historians get hired to write brochures and pamphlets for museums, state parks, and landmarks or as consultants to museums to assure the accuracy of their food history section.

The best Food Historians work with "original" sources, meaning doing personal interviews, reading firsthand diaries, locating cookbooks or finding old recipes, or digging up personal accounts of the food culture of a period.

Some Food Historians research and write or consult about the entire food history of a geographic area, while others select a time period, and research and write about the history of a region's food during that period, or look into one food item's use throughout history.

While many historians learned their research skills in college, research techniques have changed substantially. Few libraries have well-fingered card files and most everything one needs is somehow available on the Internet, except for most of those rare old dusty cultural out-of-print books that food researchers need.

If a Food Historian writes a book about food history that includes old recipes with ingredients now hard to find, it is important to update those ingredients to the closest things available and adapt the recipe, perhaps printing it next to the original recipe to show the difference.

Occasionally Food Historians consult with museums and curate kitchen exhibits, or hire a designer or model maker to help carry out their plans. Food Historians even get hired to consult on animated films and other movies and television shows to authenticate terms, utensils, recipes, and general kitchen design.

Well-known Food Historians often have the chance to lead travel groups to interesting culinary destinations around the world.

Salaries

Most Food Historians work as freelancers, meaning per job, whether it is writing an article or a book; advising television or movie writers, producers, and directors; putting together a show or display for a museum; or leading travel groups to specific regions around the world. Freelancers earn from $200 an hour to $3,000 a day as consultants. The few college or university level posts pay from $30,000 to $60,000 per year, with book advances and royalty income separate.

Employment Prospects

There are few jobs for Food Historians, although one can create a personal or regional specialty, especially where nothing has been researched or written before. One can develop a good reputation for accurate research and good speaking skills, build a following, and improve one's employment prospects. One can also start one's own historic food blog or Web site.

Advancement Prospects

As one builds a reputation and following, one can become in greater demand both for university and casual lectures to historical societies, as a consultant to museums or more than one museum, or actually get a teaching job at a culinary school or university.

Education and Training

To be successful, Food Historians need either a degree in history or an advanced degree in another subject to teach at the college or university level or to get substantial research grants, with a master's degree or Ph.D. in progress. Experience cooking and culinary research will be most helpful to give practical working advice as a consultant.

Experience, Skills, and Personality Traits

Any experience working on a research project for a historian, Food Historian, or academic or media project, whether paid or not, will help. One can work as an assistant to a researcher in almost any subject to get research process experience and learn how to catalog records and photos, both in files and on a computer.

A good Food Historian needs a passion for detailed research and organization; computer skills such as word processing and spreadsheets programs; a good memory; skills in asking questions that draw out historical experiences; energy to dig deep into old files and go anywhere to interview subjects; and true love of old food ways and cultural culinary history.

Unions and Associations

There are no real unions or associations for Food Historians, but the American Folklore Society (www.afsnet.org) has a "Foodways" section that offers publications, while Oldways (www.oldwayspt.org) connects old basic food and culinary practices and principles to modern day needs. The International Association of Culinary Professionals (www.iacp.com) has a food history committee, and Food History News (www.foodhistorynews.com) is essentially a one-woman food history event source.

Tips for Entry

1. Read everything you can in old cookbooks and at the library on the history of food culture or culinary history.
2. Get to know any local food history buff or professional and offer to volunteer or assist this person.
3. Visit any local museums you can get to and learn all you can, offering to put together a local food or kitchen section if they don't have one.
4. Read food histories and contact the authors to ask all the questions you can, even offering to help with their next project.
5. Attend any events where you might learn more about food history and research, or where publishers' representatives will speak or appear.

FOOD PHOTOGRAPHER

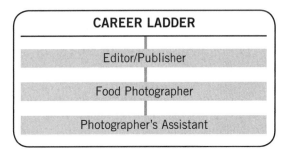
Position Description

Food Photographers are professional or commercial photographers who focus on photographing food for magazines, newspapers, cookbooks, blogs, Web sites, advertisements for foods or kitchen gadgets, and even for television food shows and movie scenes.

Food Photographers generally work on a freelance basis and are hired by art directors, marketing directors, layout specialists, and even get recommended by cookbook authors who know their work or who know another author whose publisher used their work.

The photographer often selects a food stylist to set up the food if the cookbook author or chef whose work is being photographed does not want to set up his or her creation for the photograph. Photographers may have and use their own specialized studio equipped with the best appliances and countertops, or they may have a favorite commercial or restaurant kitchen they like to use. Another alternative is to photograph in the cookbook author's or chef's home or restaurant kitchen.

It is rarely required for a Food Photographer to have a darkroom these days, but a fine digital camera is essential, as is lighting equipment. One also needs a setup with culturally-appropriate pans and utensils, dishes, glassware, and linens, although a food stylist may well provide these props. Some good friends to pose enjoying the repast will also come in handy for some situations; sometimes models or actors are used.

One thing that separates Food Photographers from others is a specialized knowledge of lighting and how various elements of food, from texture to colors and reflections, influence the photo and how they can be manipulated to enhance the outcome.

Once all the arrangements have been made, including an advance trip to the site of the photo shoot, getting to know the cookbook author or chef, and planning alterations in angles and lighting depending on the setting, Food Photographers have to work long days to get just a few good photos. With digital cameras, Food Photographers often take hundreds or thousands of images to get the best usable photos. And if they want to use only natural lighting, they work from sunrise from sunset.

If working with an art director and food stylist, the Food Photographer participates in planning the shots, possibly with a photographic assistant to move lights, clean and deliver the appropriate lenses, and assemble the pans, utensils, table linens, and glassware, and even move things around or out of the way on a cookbook author's kitchen counter.

The food stylist or the cookbook author might cook the food to be photographed, and the photographer and assistant set up a pretend scene to measure lighting and other needs. Some Food Photographers, especially those who have been to culinary school, serve as the food stylist on shoots as well.

When Polaroid film was still available, Food Photographers used to take preliminary shots to test the scene setup. With digital cameras, that step is no longer necessary and they can just click, click, click and see an instant view of what they will get in the photo and determine what lighting and other adjustments need to be made.

After the shoot, Food Photographers work at their computers, tweaking the shots with photo enhancement programs, and then e-mail their best efforts to the cookbook author, marketing director, art director, or other client for selection or approval.

Since the first senses that can be triggered in food appeals are sight and smell, Food Photographers need to be up-to-date and even ahead of popular food trends to attract the public's eye. Stacked foods, recycled paper packaging, and heart-healthy trends can influence purchases through photography. Photographers have to seduce consumers into wanting to look deep into a cookbook, read information on a cereal package, or even visit a restaurant's Web site.

As newspapers' budgets tighten, there are more opportunities for freelance writers to also take their own photos and get them published with their stories.

Salaries

Most Food Photographers are freelancers, meaning they work for themselves, work sporadically, and sometimes are in great demand. Food photography is a true specialty, so if one is good, one can do very well.

A well-established Food Photographer may have assistants and charge for their time while collecting a percentage of those charges. He or she has to invest in equipment, and works intensely for a few days at a time. Most earn between $15,000 to $80,000 or more annually.

Employment Prospects

Lots of food photography is done for Web sites, blogs, magazines, newspapers, cookbooks, video, television, and even movies, although some of it is done by "unofficial" or "technically unqualified" photographers who do it for free just to get their work on the Web.

Many photographers who focused on other subjects and topics have turned to food photography because of opportunity—there is always someone trying to sell food-related products. Food writers can occasionally double as photographers with some newspapers as editors have less money to spend on staff or freelance photographers. Writers taking their own photos may receive a small fee for their photos.

Anyone who gets photography published should ask for credits, whether he or she gets paid or not.

Advancement Prospects

As a Food Photographer's skill and reputation get to be better known, his or her work comes into greater demand, and he or she can charge more under the old supply-and-demand economic system. As one's skills increase, so do the calls and e-mails for more work.

Education and Training

An ambitious Food Photographer should study at an art school and emphasize photography; go to a specialized photography school, either as an undergraduate or graduate; work at apprenticeships or as an assistant with a major professional photographer; and have familiarity and comfort with Adobe Photoshop or other photo-perfecting computer programs.

Experience, Skills, and Personality Traits

Any photographic experience that contributes to a portfolio is valuable, either digital or in print. Work as an apprentice or volunteer with professional photographers, preferably Food Photographers, learning different styles and values from different experts, always helps.

One needs artistic talents to see light, angles, color relationships, shadows, and highlights, and know how to manipulate them. One should have a love for food and photography; have a passion for chefs and what they do; have the ability to develop great contacts and working relationships with food stylists, art directors, editors, and producers; have the ability to coax clients into helping and making the most of what is to be photographed; and have good communication skills to understand what the client wants, what the medium's goals are, who the audience is, and be able to explain to the client how to get to those goals; and be able to work as part of an artistic and marketing team, with the ability to take criticism and deal with artistic personalities.

Unions and Associations

The Advertising Photographers of America (www.apanational.com) offers professional forums, competitions, health insurance access, a credit union, and financial advice. The American Society of Magazine Photographers (www.asmp.org) is a trade organization that offers information on rights protection, ethics, and promotion standards as well as camaraderie. The International Association of Culinary Professionals (www.iacp.com) has a photography section. Local chapters of some groups offer more localized information and forms.

Tips for Entry

1. Approach any local publication, whether it is a newspaper, cooking school with a catalog, or periodic color magazine and offer to take photos, even for free.
2. Find a photographer of any kind in your area and ask to apprentice or assist them to learn, possibly for free, occasionally for pay.
3. Take any and all photography classes you can find, especially those that focus on food or other "still" photography.
4. Watch Web sites and food blogs for trends in photography.
5. Watch forward-looking chefs in local restaurants and observe what direction their creativity takes them.
6. Study the work of successful food photographers and contact them.
7. Study food photographs published in magazines and on food packages, including in advertisements.

FOOD STYLIST

Duties: Works with photographer, author, art director, editors, and directors to plan food to be photographed; shops for the food; cooks or arranges food for the shoot; provides props for the shoot along with any extra equipment from tables to umbrellas to the guests for television, movies, blogs, Web sites, slick magazines, and newspapers

Alternate Title(s): Photographer

Salary Range: $25,000 to $150,000 annually or $450 to $1,000 per day; possibly more

Employment Prospects: Limited

Advancement Prospects: Limited

Best Geographical Location(s): Anywhere or in urban or wine areas where major food and wine publications are located or where television programs and movies are produced

Prerequisites:

Education or Training—Culinary training; study at a culinary school; photographic training in

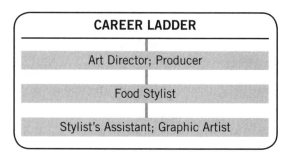

still, print, television, or movie photography or filming

Experience—Work as a chef for restaurants, caterers, or cooking schools

Special Skills and Personality Traits—Artistic flair; knowledge of colors and tricks for how to fake them; patience and precision; physical stamina to stand for long hours; knowledge of other tricks of the trade; constant alertness and focus on the job

Position Description

Food Stylists combine visual art and design with culinary art and science to cook, arrange, and display food for photos, video, movies, brochures, blogs, and Web sites. This may involve television commercials, stars' guest appearances on news or reality shows, photo shoots for cereal boxes, kitchen or buffet scenes for movies, cookbook illustrations, dramatic dining scenes, display art for magazines and newspapers or blogs and Web sites, print catalogs for cookware stores, and even for stand-up cardboard display racks.

Sometimes the Food Stylist, and even some cookbook authors, shop for the food to be used in a photographic shoot and prepare it only as well-cooked as absolutely necessary, color ingredients to enhance their appearance, and arrange the food in the most advantageous way possible to maximize or minimize light and color to make the product even more appealing than it may be in real life.

Food Stylists work with photographers and therefore need to keep up good relations with them, as well as with art directors and layout and set designers. Some photographers hire Food Stylists directly, so the two

might work consistently with each other if they work well together and are successful. Alternatively, the photographer might be full-time staff on a publication or with a television show production company and hire the Food Stylist as a freelancer.

When a job is contracted, the Food Stylist confers with the photographer and designer and then purchases the food, cooks it, arranges it, and sees through the whole session until the entire shoot is complete. Food Stylists do not just simply cook what is in a recipe. They often have to find unusual ingredients that might not even be in the recipe but will enhance the appearance of the food.

In styling food for photography, the look of the food is much more important than its true taste, and a Food Stylist needs to know tricks to highlight the food as subject matter. Some of these tricks include using heavy cream instead of milk on cereal, adding powdered aspirin to make champagne fizz more, and putting red lipstick on less-than-perfect strawberries.

Food Stylists work long, rigorous days (10 to 12 hours) when they work, often creating the same dish over and over to get just the right light, color, and texture relationships that the photographer or director have in mind. As hours progress, the food may need to be prepared again and again if it flops, dents, cracks, collapses, or changes color. Altering design placement of pomegranate or sesame seeds with tweezers is a common use of tools of the trade.

In the world of cookbooks, Food Stylists may get to work with art directors and designers to plan out the shape of the text to feature the dish photographed.

Occasionally a Food Stylist may suggest another ingredient that will make the dish look better in a photograph, and the cookbook author may or may not want to incorporate that addition into his or her recipe.

Food Stylists should have agreement ahead of time with others involved in a photo shoot and know exactly what will be prepared and photographed in order to shop for and perhaps practice cooking the dish, and have all props organized to take to the photo session. They should also have a vast stored collection of china, bowls, glasses, place mats, tablecloths, picnic supplies, silverware, and even appropriate looking "guests." Sometimes a stylist will rent appropriate props from a local rental center. Other handy tools might include tweezers, knives, cotton swabs, bamboo skewers, pins, dental floss, scissors, paintbrushes, needles and thread, a blowtorch, toothpicks, and eyedroppers. Don't forget the first aid kit.

The photo shoot might be in the photographer's studio, the author's kitchen, in a publication's test kitchen, or even in a restaurant kitchen, which the photographer should scope out ahead of time. Some Food Stylists employ architects and craftspeople to help design food sets.

Salaries

Food Stylists can earn $25,000 to $150,000 or more per year working full time, or $450 to $1,000 per day as a freelancer. Full-time Food Stylists often get benefits and have to work on other food testing and arranging projects in a company's kitchen.

Employment Prospects

One can do fairly well as a freelance Food Stylist in some areas, especially if one knows successful photographers and is willing to work for blogs and Web sites in addition to magazines, restaurants, newspapers, ad agencies and television and movie directors and pursue work through other avenues.

Advancement Prospects

Food Stylists may do so well and become so popular and in such high demand that they can either work for an agency or company full time or raise their freelance fees.

Education and Training

A successful Food Stylist needs professional culinary training including study at a culinary school; photographic training in still, print, television or movie photography, or filming, and even classes specifically in food styling or nutrition.

Experience, Skills, and Personality Traits

To be a great Food Stylist one needs to have worked as a chef for restaurants, caterers, and cooking schools, have trained as a photographer, and maybe even worked with or for successful photographers, directors, and film camera people. Some hotel banquet staffers get special training in how to improve a buffet or food display.

One needs to have an artistic flair and think of food as fashion; know colors and the tricks of how to fake reality; have patience and precision; know other tricks of the trade; and have great stamina to stand for long hours and be constantly alert and focused on the job. One also needs to be constantly curious about food trends and ingredients, fads in table accessories, and know what ingredients and other appearance enhancers are available at what stores.

Unions and Associations

The International Association of Culinary Professionals (www.iacp.com) is the best place to find other Food Stylists, as well as networking, conferences, general information, and camaraderie.

Tips for Entry

1. Go to cooking school and/or work for a good chef.
2. Find a Food Stylist, especially a successful one, and offer to work as an assistant, apprentice, or intern for free or for pay.
3. If that Food Stylist has too many clients, happily accept any he or she wants to toss your way and make the most of the opportunity.
4. Enjoy combining your artistic and culinary skills into a single career.
5. Watch food magazine trends for food (fashion) styling and technique changes.
6. Ask your local chamber of commerce or advertising club if any photographers specialize in food, and ask them if they would like to take a budding Food Stylist under their wing.

RECIPE DEVELOPER

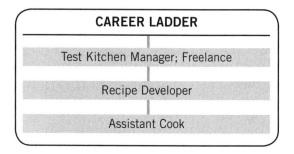

Position Description

Food producing and packaging companies all have Recipe Developers who work in test kitchens to create recipes using the company's products. In fact, some hire Recipe Developers and food chemists to create the recipes that sometimes become the food products themselves.

Food, gardening, and other lifestyle magazines hire Recipe Developers to come up with new recipes and perfect them in the company's test kitchen. In these cases, the Recipe Developer will either have to write the recipes or work with a recipe writer to present a recipe the public can actually understand.

Some public relations firms that specialize in marketing foods, food products, and the packaging of food-related merchandise have Recipe Developers to create food images in the firm's test kitchen.

Smaller food producers might retain a Recipe Developer who has his or her own locally certified test

kitchen when the food company can't afford to have a full-time person or its own kitchen. Hence, a well-equipped freelance recipe consultant can do well.

Recipe Developers create the best looking foods possible that include a company's products so that a food stylist or photographer can reproduce the dish or food and use the image to sell the product. They also develop recipes for cereal boxes, frozen food packages, blender manufacturers, flour and sugar bags and boxes, or even to sell artichokes and olive oil.

Recipe Developers need to be able to look ahead and project themselves into their audience's or the consumer's life to imagine what that person is looking for, what will attract consumer's eye in a marketplace, and what will seduce the consumer into buying one particular product over another. Thus, a Recipe Developer has to be up to date on food trends and in some cases set food trends by making recipes and foods irresistible. At the same time, the Recipe Developer has to consider cost, flavors, colors, availability of ingredients, preference for organic or conventional ingredients, food chemistry, and how ingredients work together, and how all of this blends with the company's product, if there is one.

Recipe Developers also have to consider their target audience and make sure whoever that is can obtain ingredients easily, prepare them easily, and recreate the recipe photo in a nutritious way.

Recipe Developers also work for supermarket chains that offer hot or cold prepared foods, baked goods, "grab 'n' go" foods, and even frozen burritos and toaster pastries. With the help of a food chemist, some try to find ways to make foods last without using preservatives and chemicals that may be harmful to one's health.

Some Recipe Developers and companies focus on special-diet foods and ingredients, using organic foods, natural spices and nothing with a name that consists of more than two syllables, while others specialize in recipes for weight-watching consumers and figure out how to load the food with flavorful ingredients to replace the fat people may like or expect.

Recipe Developers may experiment with sauces, spices, meats, vegetables, milk products and substitutes, and baking ingredients to come up with the latest product that can be sold to the public as "the greatest thing since sliced bread." One may take many attempts at creating something new before achieving one's goal. Other developers specialize in regional or ethnic cuisines for national or special markets.

Occasionally, Recipe Developers are employed to adapt a name chef's restaurant recipe to work in mass-market packaging and sales.

As Julia Child said, "There is no such thing as a new recipe." However, one can amplify and adapt recipes that exist and change them to meet new needs and goals and to use and create new products.

Tasters at the publishing company, food producer, kitchen equipment manufacturer, marketing and packaging company, or public relations firm all will taste each version of a new recipe until it is perfected by the Recipe Developer and his or her assistants to set the taste trend or fad of the near future.

Recipe Developers must take meticulous notes of what they put into each attempt, documenting heat, times, and altitude of cooking in order to develop a formula for larger scale production. One also has to include comments made by other testers and tasters to get the best result.

A developer or food chemist may actually write the recipe for a brochure, ads, boxes, labels, and wrappers, as well as for magazines, newspapers, blogs, and Web sites. Then recipe testers will follow the recipe and find out if they or home cooks can recreate the dish the way it is supposed to be. If not, the Recipe Developer and editors have to go back and retest and rewrite the recipe so that it can be accomplished in a home kitchen.

While some cookbook authors, chefs, and Recipe Developers use the latest high-tech equipment, many use appliances and equipment similar to what most consumers have at home to replicate real-life cooking.

Toward the end of the process, a Recipe Developer may work with a marketing department, an art director or designer, a photographer, a food stylist, and even a Web site or blog designers to help convey the new recipe to the public in the most attractive manner possible.

Recipe Developers might also write their own cookbooks—cookbook authors often develop their own recipes. They might also create special recipes for a television show or movie, as well as for posting on their own blog.

Salaries

Full-time Recipe Developers in a test kitchen might make between $25,000 to $70,000 or more, while freelancers and part-time consultants can make less or more if they can amass several clients. Test kitchen staff or assistants to Recipe Developers make less, usually in the range of $10 to $25 an hour. "Name" chefs with television shows can practically demand their price as Recipe Developers, especially if they lend their name to the product or if it is developed specifically to be marketed under their names.

Employment Prospects

Big food companies also need Recipe Developers and their assistants to create new products to sell to the public to keep up with food trends and increase or maintain the company's share of the market. Over decades we have seen the fruits of their labors from development of canned and frozen foods to microwavable diet meals and dinner kits.

On the other hand, food producers, like many other companies, try to cut jobs and pare down staff during economic hard times.

Advancement Prospects

Once one is a Recipe Developer, it is fairly easy to move up the test kitchen ladder. It's possible to become manager of the kitchen, a cookbook author, director or publications or marketing, or even achieve a higher management spot within the company.

Sometimes such promotions take a chef out of the kitchen, much as a teacher often leaves the classroom when becoming an administrator.

One can also move to another company that pays more or start one's own independent test kitchen where there is a possibility of working for many clients.

Education and Training

Most sophisticated test kitchens expect prospective Recipe Developers to have a degree from a culinary school or accredited cooking program, or a college degree in nutrition, home economics, food science, or chemistry, and have knowledge of varied ingredients from many countries, both organic and conventional. Professional restaurant chefs, especially big names, can develop recipes but will need test kitchen developers to translate the restaurant recipe to quantities suitable either for home cooking or massive commercial production.

Experience, Skills, and Personality Traits

Recipe Developers should have the experience of cooking in a restaurant or for a caterer and have an excellent palate to which they apply imagination and creativity, which can only be done with familiarity with potential ingredients.

One has to be patient and able to deal with many other people's suggestions and brilliant ideas and employ a great deal of tact. It's also handy to be able to come up with recipes that look so good when cooked that the company doesn't need to hire a food stylist before photographing.

It helps if a person has worked for food publications as a writer, taster, or tester. Working for a freelance food consultant, food stylist, or chef is also great experience.

One needs great writing and communication skills, the ability to juggle writing and cooking under pressure and assume the "voice" (attitude, language, and style) of the particular publication or company for which one works. It helps for you to be good self-starter and enjoy experimentation, be able to keep good records, be flexible and able to get along with people in other departments, and make good relationships with chefs, publishers, editors and producers so that they ask you back to do more work if you are a freelancer.

Unions and Associations

Food scientists, food chemists, home economists, and chefs are organized through the International Association of Culinary Professionals (www.iacp.com). Home economists belong to the American Association of Family and Consumer Sciences (www.aafcs.org), which has credentialing and educational programs as well as conferences where loads of networking goes on.

Tips for Entry

1. Try working with sauces, spices, and baking materials at home and amplifying other people's recipes to find out if you really like the work.

2. Plan to achieve an associate's degree or higher in culinary arts, nutrition, or home economics, study food history and ingredients, and go to a school with a good job placement reputation.

3. Write any food stories or articles you can for publications and include your original and well-tested recipes. Some editors will test the recipes themselves, but testing is your responsibility at the entry level.

4. Enter recipe and cooking contests and learn from other entrants, using your success to get you a first Recipe Developer job. Ingredient manufacturers often sponsor cook-offs or other cooking contests.

5. Offer to work as an intern or apprentice at a culinary school, for a food producing company, or even an organic grower to learn all you can.

6. Look for your perfect Recipe Developer job, get an entry-level position at the company as an assistant no matter how far down the kitchen ladder, and work your way up.

7. Start your own food blog and post your recipes on it.

RECIPE TESTER

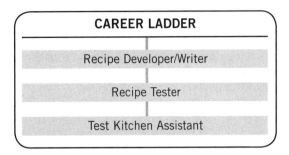
Position Description

After a recipe developer delivers what he or she thinks is the perfect recipe or formula, Recipe Testers try out the recipe to find out if and how it works, with the ultimate goal of making sure the recipe developer's instructors produce what he or she thinks it does or if it matches photos someone wants to use on food packages, in magazines, in newspapers, or on blogs and Web sites.

Whether working in a fully equipped professional test kitchen or at home, a Recipe Tester tries the recipe, sometimes several times, to make it work for the home cook, who is usually the target market.

Sometimes recipes don't work due to altitude of cooking, ingredient conflicts or quantities, ingredient omissions, overcooking or undercooking, or simply errors in the direction.

Cookbook authors sometimes look to friends they know can cook to test recipes, or to an online chat room with which they are familiar to find Recipe Testers. In many such cases, volunteers are all too happy to somehow contribute to an author's efforts, and may receive no payment besides fun, or they may get a copy of the cookbook once the book is published.

Many food magazines use their own test kitchens, although with expenses rising and profits dropping, several are soliciting volunteer Recipe Testers on their Web sites and via e-mail.

When a recipe is designed to use a particular product, say for a food manufacturer, the recipe might call by name for other ingredients produced by the same company. Recipe Testers have to make sure all of those ingredients are available to home cooks in the regional market where the product will be distributed, or nationwide if that is pertinent.

If one writes about food for a newspaper or magazine, or even about wine where recipes are included, one will either test recipes or the publication will test them in their test kitchen. Travel guide authors who include recipes also need to either test recipes submitted, adjust the formulas, make many calls to straighten out confusion on quantities, or hire someone else to test recipes.

Recipe Testers need to be honest and brave enough to subtly tell chefs, authors, and recipe developers that their work might be imperfect by asking picky little questions. Testers must point out when something is left out of the ingredient list but shows up in the recipe directions, or where directions are unclear, as a recipe that calls for chopped scallions (green onions) without specifying whether the recipe developer or chef means the white bottoms, green tops, or entire plant.

Home Recipe Testers have to face being asked to test a baked goods recipe with a hot oven in the middle of summer, a summer zucchini squash or outdoor barbecue recipe in the snows of winter, or use fruits or vegetables when they are just plain out of season.

In some cases, Recipe Testers will see if packaged processed foods work in home cooking, or how organic grains bake into breads and into gluten-free pizza. A freelance Recipe Tester may specialize in gluten-free, sugar-free, wheat-free, or organically grown foods.

Most home Recipe Testers have to shop for ingredients, keep careful track of quantities purchased and their cost, test each recipe two or three times or until it works perfectly more than once as written or rewritten, and make recommendations to the client.

Salaries

Full-time Recipe Testers work for food product companies, big magazines and newspapers, and for food stylists for television and movies where those jobs still exist, with salaries up to around $30,000.

Freelancers work for around $10 to $15 an hour, or may be offered a flat fee that includes food, time, transportation, and communications costs.

Volunteer Recipe Testers, of which there are many, work for the fun of participating in the process with fine cookbook authors, magazine editors, and even food stylists, and may or may not receive the author's new cookbook as compensation.

Employment Prospects

Where magazines and food corporations, fast-food corporations, chain grocery stores, and equipment manufacturers develop recipes, they probably have a test kitchen and need Recipe Testers, for which there are often ads online.

Freelance opportunities abound but pay less on a part-time basis.

Advancement Prospects

Once a Recipe Tester is employed, he or she can climb the test kitchen ladder possibly to recipe developer, kitchen manager, marketing director, designer, or into other management positions.

Freelancers can gain a reputation for excellence and accuracy and come into greater demand, allowing them to work more often and charge more, or even get full-time jobs. Cookbook recipe testing should be done in a home environment, since book purchasers will mostly be using home kitchens.

Education and Training

While degrees are rarely required for Recipe Testers, one should have extensive food and cooking knowledge; a high school diploma, with special interest in the high school's culinary program if possible; and basic reading, writing, and comprehension skills in English.

Experience, Skills, and Personality Traits

Extensive home cooking or experience as an intern or volunteer at a cooking school or meals-on-wheels program would be helpful, as would any restaurant experience.

Basic cooking skills such as sautéing, roasting, baking, braising, and frying. The ability to write clearly, trustworthiness to fulfill commitments on time, ability to use language that is suitable for the project, familiarity with ingredients and any new products available and where to find them, and curiosity about how food works and how recipes work are all crucial. One should also never be afraid to ask the cookbook author or recipe developer questions that might improve the recipe or its presentation.

Unions and Associations

There are no specific unions for Recipe Testers, but large corporations where test kitchens exist may have unions that cover various departments. Local and regional culinary associations may offer networking and seminars, as does the International Association of Culinary Professionals (www.iacp.com).

Tips for Entry

1. Offer to test recipes for your local newspaper if they print them, either for pay or as a volunteer to build your experience and résumé.
2. Attend local culinary or chef society meetings to meet people who might need recipes tested or who might know suppliers or authors who do.
3. Look online for several recipe-testing opportunities, some paid and some volunteer.
4. Ask local growers and food manufacturers or specialized local canners if they could use a Recipe Tester.
5. Contact publishing houses that produce cookbooks and ask if they need Recipe Testers or if any of their cookbook authors do.

6. Contact large corporate food companies, canners, and even coffee chains to find out if they need Recipe Testers.
7. Try local television stations to find out if they can use Recipe Testers for any food shows or to work with their chef guests.
8. Anyone with a food blog or Web site may need a Recipe Tester.
9. Start your own food blog or Web site and be your own recipe developer and tester.

APPENDIXES

APPENDIX I
CULINARY SCHOOLS AND ACADEMIES

ALABAMA

Bishop State Community College
414 Stanton Street
Mobile, AL 36617
Phone: (251) 405-7000
E-mail: mlombard@bishop.edu
http://www.bscc.cc.al.us

Culinard—The Culinary Institute of Virginia College
436 Palisades Boulevard
Birmingham, AL 35209
Phone: (205) 943-2136
http://www.culinard.com

Faulkner State Community College
1900 Highway 31 South Bay
Minette, AL 36507
Phone: (800) 231-3752
E-mail: rkoetter@faulknerstate.edu
http://www.faulkner.cc.al.us

Jefferson State Community College
The Culinary Arts and Hospitality Institute
2601 Carson Road
Birmingham, AL 35221
Phone: (205) 853-1200
E-mail: jmitchell@jeffstateonline.com
http://www.jscc.cc.al.us

Lawson State Community College
3060 Wilson Road SW
Birmingham, AL 35221
Phone: (205) 925-2515
http://www.ls.cc.al.us

Trenholm State Technical College
1225 Air Base Boulevard
Montgomery, AL 36108-3105
Phone: (866) 753-4544
http://www.trenholmtech.cc.al.us

Wallace State Community College
P.O. Box 2000
Hanceville, AL 35077-2000
Phone: (866) 350-WSCC
http://www2.wallacestate.edu

ALASKA

Alaska Vocational Technical Center (AVTEC)
P.O. Box 889
Seward, AK 99664-0889
Phone: (800) 478-5389
E-mail: robert.wilson@avtec.edu
http://www.avtec.alaska.edu

Chez Alaska Cooking School
2092 Jordan Avenue
Suite 585
Juneau, AK 99801
Phone: (907) 790-2439
E-mail: laraine@chezalaska.com
http://www.chezalaska.com

University of Alaska —Tanana Valley Campus
3750 Geist Road
Fairbanks, AK, 99701
Phone: (907) 455-2800
E-mail: fffud@uaf.edu
http://www.tvc.uaf.edu

ARIZONA

Arizona Culinary Institute
10585 North 114th Street
Suite 401
Scottsdale, AZ 85259
Phone: (866) 294-2433
http://www.azculinary.com

Arizona Western College
Box 929
Yuma, AZ 85364
Phone: (888) 293-0392
http://www.azwestern.edu

Central Arizona College
8470 North Overfield Road
Coolidge, AZ 85228
Phone: (800) 237-9814
E-mail: carol.bennett1@centralaz.edu
http://www.centralaz.edu

International Culinary School at The Art Institute of Phoenix
2233 West Dunlap Avenue
Phoenix, AZ 85021-2859
Phone: (602) 331-7500
E-mail: jlavilla@aii.edu
http://www.aipx.aii.edu

International Culinary School at The Art Institute of Tucson
5099 East Grant Road
Suite 100
Tucson, AZ 85712
Phone: (866) 690-8850
http://www.artinstitutes.edu

Phoenix College
1202 West Thomas Road
Phoenix, AZ 85013
Phone: (602) 285-7800
E-mail: scott.robinson@pcmail.maricopa.edu
http://www.pc.maricopa.edu

Pima Community College— Desert Vista Campus
5901 South Calle Santa Cruz
Tucson, AZ 85709
Phone: (520) 206-4500

E-mail: barry.infuso@pima.edu
http://www.pima.edu

Scottsdale Community College
9000 East Chaparral Road
Scottsdale, AZ 85256-2626
Phone: (480) 423-6241
E-mail: karen.chalmers@sccmail.
    maricopa.edu
http://www.scottsdalecc.edu

Scottsdale Culinary Institute— Le Cordon Bleu program
8100 East Camelback Road
Suite 1001
Scottsdale, AZ 85251
Phone: (480) 990-3773
E-mail: mary.mules@scichefs.com
http://www.chefs.edu

ARKANSAS

Ozarka College
218 College Drive
P.O. Box 10
Melbourne, AR 72556
Phone: (870) 368-7371
http://www.ozarka.edu

Pulaski Technical College Arkansas Culinary School
13000 Interstate 30
Little Rock, AR 72210
Phone: (501) 812-2860
E-mail: todd@arkansaschef.com
http://www.pulaskitech.edu

CALIFORNIA

American River College
4700 College Oak Drive
Sacramento, CA 95841
Phone: (916) 484-8011
E-mail: info@arc.losrios.edu
http://www.arc.losrios.edu

Art Institute of California– San Francisco
1170 Market Street
San Francisco, CA 94102
Phone: (415) 865-0198
http://www.artinstitutes.edu/
    sanfrancisco

Bakersfield College
1801 Panorama Drive
Bakersfield, CA 93305-1299
Phone: (661) 395-4011
http://www.bakersfieldcollege.edu

Bauman College Holistic Nutrition and Culinary Arts Natural Chef Training Program–Berkeley
901 Grayson St.
Berkeley, CA 94710
Phone: (800) 987-7530
E-mail: inquiry@baumancollege.org
http://www.baumancollege.org

Bauman College Holistic Nutrition and Culinary Arts Natural Chef Training Program–Penngrove
P.O. Box 940
Penngrove, CA 94951
Phone: (800) 987-7530
E-mail: inquiry@baumancollege.org
http://www.baumancollege.org

Bauman College Holistic Nutrition and Culinary Arts Natural Chef Training Program–Santa Cruz
3912 Portola Drive
Suite 10
Santa Cruz, CA 95062
Phone: (800) 987-7530
E-mail: inquiry@baumancollege.org
http://www.baumancollege.org

Cabrillo College
6500 Soquel Drive
Aptos, CA 95003
Phone: (831) 479-6100
http://www.cabrillo.edu

California Capitol Chefs Association
P.O. Box 214171
Sacramento, CA 95821
Phone: (916) 326-5020
E-mail: chefdoncec@cs.com
http://www.capitolchefs.org

California Culinary Academy
350 Rhode Island Street
San Francisco, CA 94103

Phone: (415) 216-4376
E-mail: admissions@baychef.com
http://www.baychef.com

California School of Culinary Arts–Hollywood
6370 West Sunset Boulevard
Hollywood, CA 90028-7323
Phone: (866) 230-9450
http://www.csca.edu

California School of Culinary Arts–Pasadena
521 East Green Street
Pasadena, CA 91101
Phone: (626) 229-1300
E-mail: bmomary@csca.edu
http://www.csca.edu

Chaffey College
5897 College Park Avenue
Chino, CA 91710
Phone: (909) 652-8000
E-mail: daniel.swift@chaffey.edu
http://www.chaffey.edu

Charles A. Jones Skills and Business Education Center
5451 Lemon Hill Avenue
Sacramento, CA 95824
Phone: (916) 433-2600, ext. 1000
http://www.scusd.edu/adult_
    education

Chef Eric's Culinary Classroom
2366 Pelham Avenue
Los Angeles, CA 90064
Phone: (310) 470-2640
E-mail: cheferic@culinaryclassroom.
    com
http://www.culinaryclassroom.com

Chef Is Chef Culinary School
4100 Cahuenga Boulevard
North Hollywood, CA 91602
Phone: (800) 708-9512
E-mail: info@chefischef.com
http://www.chefischef.com

City College of San Francisco
50 Phelan Avenue
San Francisco, CA 94112
Phone: (415) 239-3154

E-mail: ehamilto@ccsf.edu
http://www.ccsf.edu

College of the Desert
43-500 Monterey Avenue
Palm Desert, CA 92260
Phone: (760) 773-2571
http://www.collegeofthedesert.edu

Columbia College
11600 Columbia College Drive
Sonora, CA 95370
Phone: (209) 588-5135
E-mail: wombleg@yosemite.cc.ca.us
http://www.columbia.yosemite.cc.
ca.us

Contra Costa College
2600 Mission Bell Drive
San Pablo, CA 94806
Phone: (510) 235-7800, ext. 4408
E-mail: NSharkes@contracosta.edu
http://www.contracosta.cc.ca.us

Culinary Institute of America–Greystone
2555 Main Street
Saint Helena, CA 94574
Phone: (800) 333-9242
http://www.ciachef.edu

Cypress College–Anaheim Campus
1830 West Romneya Drive
First Floor
Anaheim, CA 92801
Phone: (714) 808-4640
E-mail: hrcdept@nocccd.edu
http://www.cypresscollege.edu

Diablo Valley College
321 Golf Club Road
Pleasant Hill, CA 94523
Phone: (925) 685-1230, ext. 252
E-mail: beustes@dvc.edu
http://www.dvc.edu

Epicurean School of Culinary Arts–Anaheim
270 South Clementine Street
Anaheim, CA 92805
Phone: (310) 659-5990
E-mail: info@epicureanschool.com

Epicurean School of Culinary Arts—West Hollywood
8500 Melrose Avenue
Los Angeles, CA 90069
Phone: (310) 659-5990
E-mail: info@epicureanschool.com
http://www.epicureanschool.com

Glendale Community College
1500 North Verdugo Road
Glendale, CA 91208
Phone: (818) 240-1000
E-mail: afeldman@glendale.edu
http://www.glendale.edu

Grossmont College
8800 Grossmont College Drive
El Cajon, CA 92020
Phone: (619) 644-7550
E-mail: michele.martens@gcccd.edu
http://www.grossmont.edu

Institute of Technology–Clovis
564 West Herndon Avenue
Clovis, CA 93612-0105
Phone: (559) 323-4216
E-mail: dcwaddell@it-email.com
http://www.it-colleges.edu/clovis.php

Institute of Technology–Modesto
5737 Stoddard Road
Modesto, CA 95356-9000
Phone: (209) 545-3100
E-mail: ptopping@it-email.com
http://www.it-colleges.edu/modesto.
php

Institute of Technology–Roseville
333 Sunrise Avenue
Suite 400
Roseville, CA 95661-3482
Phone: (916) 797-6337
E-mail: ddickinson@it-email.com
http://www.it-colleges.edu/roseville.
php

International Culinary School at The Art Institute of California–Los Angeles
2900 31st Street
Santa Monica, CA 90405

Phone: (310) 752-4700
E-mail: ailaadmin@aii.edu
http://www.artinstitutes.edu/
losangeles

International Culinary School at The Art Institute of California–Orange County
3601 West Sunflower Avenue
Santa Ana, CA 92704-7931
Phone: (714) 830-0200
http://www.artinstitutes.edu/
orangecounty

International Culinary School at The Art Institute of California–Sacramento
2850 Gateway Oaks Drive
Suite 100
Sacramento, CA 95833
Phone: (916) 830-6320
http://www.artinstitutes.edu/
sacramento

International Culinary School at The Art Institute of California–San Diego
7650 Mission Valley Road
San Diego, CA 92108
Phone: (858) 598-1200
http://www.artinstitutes.edu/sandiego

International Culinary School at The Art Institute of California–Sunnyvale
1120 Kifer Road
Sunnyvale, CA 94086
Phone: (408) 962-6400
http://www.artinstitutes.edu/
sunnyvale

International Culinary School at The Art Institute of California–Inland Empire–San Bernardino
630 East Brier Drive
San Bernardino, CA 92408
Phone: (909) 915-2100
http://www.artinstitutes.edu/
inlandempire

Kitchen Academy–Hollywood
6370 West Sunset Boulevard

Los Angeles, CA 90028
Phone: (323) 460-4022, (866) 548-2223
http://www.kitchenacademy.com

Kitchen Academy–Sacramento
2450 Del Paso Road
Sacramento, CA 95834
Phone: (888) 807-7222
http://www.kitchenacademyca.com

Laguna Culinary Arts
845 Laguna Canyon Road
Laguna Beach, CA 92651
Phone: (949) 494-4006
E-mail: admission@lagunaculinary
arts.com
http://www.lagunaculinaryarts.com

Lake Tahoe Community College
1 College Drive
South Lake Tahoe, CA 96150
Phone: (530) 541-4660 ext. 334
E-mail: fernald@ltcc.edu
http://www.ltcc.edu

Laney College
900 Fallon Street
Oakland, CA 94607
Phone: (510) 834-5740
http://www.laney.peralta.edu

Long Beach City College
4901 East Carson Street
Mailstop R15
Long Beach, CA 90808
Phone: (562) 938-4111
http://www.lbcc.edu

Los Angeles Mission College
13356 Eldridge Avenue
Sylmar, CA 91342
Phone: (818) 354-7665
http://www.lamission.edu

Los Angeles Trade-Tech College
400 West Washington Boulevard
Los Angeles, CA 90015
Phone: (213) 763-7331
E-mail: kasmarsl@lattc.edu
http://www.lattc.edu

Modesto Junior College
435 College Avenue
Modesto, CA 95350
Phone: (209) 575-6789
http://www.mjc.edu

Napa Valley Cooking School at Napa Valley College
2277 Napa-Vallejo Highway
Napa, CA 94558
Phone: (207) 253-3000, (800) 826-1077
Upper Valley Campus
1088 College Ave
Saint Helena, CA 94574-1366
Phone: (707) 967-2900
E-mail: acounihan@napavalley.edu
http://www.napavalley.edu

National Culinary and Bakery School
8400 Center Drive
La Mesa, CA 91942
Phone: (619) 461-2800
E-mail: natlschools@national
schools.com
http://www.nationalschools.com

The New School of Cooking
8690 Washington Boulevard
Culver City, CA 90232
Phone: (310) 842-9702
E-mail: annesmith@newschoolof
cooking.com
http://www.newschoolofcooking.com

Orange Coast College
2701 Fairview Road
Costa Mesa, CA 92626
Phone: (714) 432-0202
E-mail: kballinger@occ.cccd.edu
http://www.orangecoastcollege.edu

Oxnard College
4000 South Rose Avenue
Oxnard, CA 93033
Phone: (805) 986-5800
E-mail: fhaywood@vcccd.edu
http://www.oxnardcollege.edu

Professional Culinary Institute
700 West Hamilton Avenue
Suite 300

Campbell, CA 95008
Phone: (866) 318-CHEF
E-mail: admissions@pcichef.com
http://www.pcichef.com/3.html

San Diego Culinary Institute
8024 La Mesa Boulevard
La Mesa, CA 91941
Phone: (619) 644-2100
E-mail: info@sdci-inc.com
http://www.sdci-inc.com

San Francisco Baking Institute
480 Grandview Drive
South San Francisco, CA 94080
Phone: (650) 589-5729
E-mail: contact@sfbi.com
http://www.sfbi.com

San Francisco Culinary/Pastry Program
California Apprenticeship
Coordinators Association
760 Market Street
Suite 1066
San Francisco, CA 94102
Phone: (415) 989-8726
http://www.calapprenticeship.org

San Francisco State University (Hospitality & Tourism Management)
1600 Holloway Avenue
San Francisco, CA 94132
Phone: (415) 405-7700 (press 5)
E-mail: sfsuce@sfsu.edu

San Joaquin Delta College
5151 Pacific Avenue
Stockton, CA 95207
Phone: (209) 954-5516
E-mail: rhalabicky@sjdccd.cc.ca.us
http://www.deltacollege.org

Santa Barbara City College
721 Cliff Drive
Santa Barbara, CA 93109-2394
Phone: (805) 965-0581
E-mail: bublitz@sbcc.net
http://www.sbcc.net

Santa Rosa Junior College
1501 Mendocino Avenue
Santa Rosa, CA 95401

Phone: (707) 527-4685
http://www.santarosa.edu
E-mail: msalinger@santarosa.edu

Shasta College
11555 Old Oregon Trail
P.O. Box 496006
Redding, CA 96049-6006
Phone: (530) 242-7500
http://www.shastacollege.edu

Tante Marie's Cooking School
271 Francisco Street
San Francisco, CA 94133
Phone: (415) 788-6699
E-mail: peggy@tantemarie.com
http://www.tantemarie.com

University of San Francisco
McLaren School of Business
2130 Fulton Street
Malloy Hall
San Francisco, CA 94117-1045
Phone: (415) 422-6236
E-mail: costellot@usfca.edu
http://www.usfca.edu

Westlake Culinary Institute
4643 Lakeview Canyon Road
Westlake Village, CA 91361
Phone: (818) 991-3940
E-mail: lgcookin@aol.com
http://www.letsgetcookin.com

COLORADO

Colorado Mountain Culinary Institute
831 Grand Avenue
Glenwood Springs, CO 81601
Phone: (800) 621-8559
http://www.coloradomtn.edu

Cook Street School of Fine Cooking
1937 Market Street
Denver, CO 80202
Phone: (303) 308-9300
http://www.cookstreet.com

Culinary Institute of Colorado Springs
5675 South Academy Boulevard
CC17

Colorado Springs, CO 80906
Phone: (719) 502-3300
E-mail: rob.hudson@ppcc.edu
http://www.ppcc.edu

Culinary School of the Rockies
Table Mesa Shopping Center
637 South Broadway
Suite H
Boulder, CO 80305
Phone: (303) 494-7988
http://www.culinaryschoolrockies.
com

The International Culinary School at The Art Institute–Colorado
1200 Lincoln Street
Denver, CO 80203
Phone: (800) 557-7216
E-mail: mjbennett@aii.edu
http://ai.cookingschools.com/
artinstitutes/colorado.php

Johnson and Wales University at Denver
7150 Montview Boulevard
Denver, CO 80220
Phone: (303) 256-9300
http://www.jwu.edu/denver

Pueblo Community College
900 West Orman Avenue
Pueblo, CO 81004
Phone: (719) 549-3071
E-mail: Carol.Himes@pueblocc.edu
http://www.pueblocc.edu

School of Natural Cookery
P.O. Box 19466
Boulder, CO 80308-2466
Phone: (303) 444-8068
E-mail: info@naturalcookery.com
http://www.naturalcookery.com

University of Denver
Daniels College of Business
2101 South University Boulevard
Denver CO 80208
Phone: (303) 871-3416
E-mail: bpemble@du.edu
http://www.daniels.du.edu

Warren Occupational Technical Center
13300 West 2nd Place
Lakewood, CO 80228
Phone: (303) 982-8600
E-mail: dbochman@jeffco.k12.co.us
http://sc.jeffco.k12.co.us

CONNECTICUT

Gateway Community College
60 Sargent Drive
New Haven, CT 06511
Phone: (203) 285-2154
E-mail: arandi@gwcc.commnet.edu
http://www.gwcc.commnet.edu

Institute of Gastronomy and Culinary Arts
University of New Haven
300 Orange Avenue
West Haven, CT 06516
Phone: (203) 932-7362
http://www.newhaven.edu

Lincoln Culinary Institute–Branch Campus
1760 Mapleton Avenue
Suffield, CT 06078
Phone: (866) 672-4337
E-mail: suffieldinfo@ctculinary.com
http://www.ctculinary.com

Lincoln Culinary Institute—Main Campus
85 Sigourney Street
Hartford, CT 06105
Phone: (800) 762-4337
E-mail: admissions@ctculinary.com
http://www.ctculinary.com

Lincoln Technical Institute Center for Culinary Arts–Cromwell
106 Sebethe Drive
Cromwell, CT 06416
Phone: (860) 613-3350
http://www.lincolnedu.com

Lincoln Technical Institute Center for Culinary Arts–Shelton
8 Progress Drive

Shelton, CT 06484
Phone: (203) 929-0592
http://www.lincolnedu.com

Manchester Community College
Great Path
Manchester, CT 06045
Phone: (860) 512-3000
E-mail: jpearson@mcc.commnet.edu
http://www.mcc.commnet.edu

Naugatuck Valley Community College
750 Chase Parkway
Waterbury, CT 06708
Phone: (203) 575-8040
http://www.nvcc.commnet.edu

Norwalk Community College
188 Richards Avenue
Norwalk, CT 06854
Phone: (203) 857-7000
E-mail: tconnolly@ncc.commnet.edu
http://www.ncc.commnet.edu

DELAWARE

Delaware Technical and Community College
400 Stanton-Christiana Road
Newark, DE 19713
Phone: (302) 453-3757
E-mail: dnolker@dtcc.edu
http://www.dtcc.edu/stanton-wilmington

University of Delaware
Hotel, Restaurant, and Institutional Management
Raub Hall
14 West Main Street
Newark, DE 19716
Phone: (302) 831-6077
E-mail: hrim-dept@udel.edu
http://www.hrim.udel.edu

FLORIDA

The Art Institute of Tampa
Parkside at Tampa Bay Park
4401 North Himes Avenue
Suite 150
Tampa, FL 33614

Phone: (813) 873-2112
http://www.artinstitutes.edu/tampa

Atlantic Technical Center
4700 Coconut Creek Parkway
Coconut Creek, FL 33063
Phone: (754) 321-5100
E-mail: martin.wilcox@browardschools.com
http://www.atlantictechcenter.com

Charlotte Technical Center
18150 Murdock Circle
Port Charlotte, FL 33948
Phone: (941) 255-7500
http://charlottetechcenter.ccps.k12.fl.us/index.cfm

Daytona State College
1200 West International Speedway Boulevard
Daytona Beach, FL 32114
Phone: (386) 506-3000
E-mail: conklij@daytonastate.edu
http://www.daytonastate.edu

First Coast Technical College–A Division of St. Augustine Technical Center
2980 Collins Avenue
St. Augustine, FL 32095
Phone: (866) 462-3284
E-mail: dbearl@fcti.edu
http://www.fcti.org

F. K. Marchman Technical Education Center
7825 Campus Drive
New Port Richey, FL 34653-1211
Phone: (727) 774-1700
http://mtec.pasco.k12.fl.us

Florida Community College at Jacksonville
4501 Capper Road
Jacksonville, FL 32218
Phone: (904) 766-6703
E-mail: wmark@fccj.edu
http://www.fccj.edu

The Florida Culinary Institute–A Division of Lincoln College
2410 Metrocentre Boulevard
West Palm Beach, FL 33407-3155

Phone: (561) 842-8324
E-mail: dpantone@floridaculinary.com

Gulf Coast Community College
5230 West Highway 98
Panama City, FL 32401
Phone: (850) 769-1551
http://www.gc.cc.fl.us

Hillsborough Community College
Dale Mabry Campus
P.O. Box 30030
Tampa, FL 33630-3030
Phone: (813) 253-7202
E-mail: fjaeger@hccfl.edu
http://www.hccfl.edu

The International Culinary School at The Art Institute of Fort Lauderdale
1799 Southeast 17th Street
Fort Lauderdale, FL 33316
Phone: (954) 463-3000
http://www.aifl.artinstitutes.edu

Johnson and Wales University at North Miami
1701 Northeast 127th Street
North Miami, FL 33181
Phone: (305) 892-5310
E-mail: admissions.mia@jwu.edu
http://www.jwu.edu

Keiser University Center for Culinary Arts–Melbourne Campus
900 South Babcock Street
Melbourne, FL 32901
Phone: (321) 255-2255
http://www.keiseruniversity.edu/culinary

Keiser University Center for Culinary Arts–Sarasota Campus
6151 Lake Osprey Drive
Sarasota, FL 34240
Phone: (866) 534-7372
http://www.keiseruniversity.edu/culinary

Keiser University Center for Culinary Arts–Tallahassee Campus
1700 Halstead Boulevard
Tallahassee, FL 32309
Phone: (850) 906-9494
E-mail: kevink@keiseruniversity.edu
http://www.keiseruniversity.edu/culinary

Lake Technical Center–Eustis
2001 Kurt Street
Eustis, FL 32726
Phone: (352) 589-2250
E-mail: koenigk@lake.k12.fl.us
http://www.laketech.org

Lincoln College of Technology–West Palm Beach Campus
2410 Metrocentre Boulevard
West Palm Beach, FL 33407-3155
Phone: (561) 842-8324
http://www.lincolnedu.com

Manatee Technical Institute
5603 34th Street West
Bradenton, FL 34210-3509
Phone: (941) 751-7900, ext.2018
E-mail: parrisht@fc.manatee schools.net
http://www.manateetechnical institute.org/CulinaryArts

Mid Florida Technical Institute
2900 West Oak Ridge Road
Orlando, FL 32809
Phone: (407) 251-6000
http://www.mft.ocps.net

Notter School of Pastry Arts
8204 Crystal Clear Lane
Suite 1600
Orlando, FL 32809
Phone: (407) 240-9057
E-mail: info@notterschool.com
http://www.notterschool.com

Orlando Culinary Academy
8511 Commodity Circle
Suite 100
Orlando, FL 32819
Phone: (407) 888-4000
http://www.orlandoculinary.com

Pensacola Junior College
1000 College Boulevard
Suite 12
Pensacola, FL 32504
Phone: (850) 484-1641
E-mail: therr@pjc.edu
http://www.pjc.edu

Pinellas Technical Education Center–Clearwater
6100 154th Avenue
North Clearwater, FL 33760
Phone: (727) 538-7167
E-mail: guldenschuhc@pcsb.org
http://www.myptec.org

Pinellas Technical Education Center–Saint Petersburg
901 34th Street South
Saint Petersburg, FL 33711-2298
Phone: (727) 893-2500
http://www.myptec.org

Robert Morgan Vocational Technical Institute
18180 Southwest 122nd Avenue
Miami, FL 33177
Phone: (305) 253-9920
E-mail: rarmand@dadeschools.net
http://rmec.dadeschools.net

Sarasota County Technical Institute
4748 Beneva Road
Sarasota, FL 34233
Phone: (941) 924-1365
E-mail: scti_answers@srqit.sarasota.k12.fl.us
http://www.sarasotatech.org

Sheridan Technical Center
5400 Sheridan Street
Hollywood, FL 33201
Phone: (754) 321-5400
E-mail: kim.curry@broward schools.com
http://www.sheridantechnical.com

South Florida Community College
600 West College Drive
Avon Park, FL 33825

Phone: (863) 453-6661
http://www.southflorida.edu

Southeastern Academy
233 Academy Drive
Kissimmee, FL 34742-1768
Phone: (407) 847-4444

Valencia Community College
P.O. Box 3028
Orlando, FL 32802
Phone: (407) 299-5000
http://www.valenciacc.edu

William T. McFatter School of Culinary Arts
6500 Nova Drive
Davie, FL 33317
Phone: (754) 321-5700
E-mail: marsha.williams@ browardschools.com
http://www.mcfattertech.com

GEORGIA

Atlanta Area Technical School
1560 Metropolitan Parkway Southwest
Atlanta, GA 29866
Phone: (404) 225-4575
E-mail: jperrymo@atlantatech.edu
http://www.atlantatech.org

Augusta Technical College
3200 Augusta Tech Drive
Augusta, GA 30906
Phone: (706) 771-4000
E-mail: kfervan@augustatech.edu
http://www.augustatech.edu

Chattahoochee Technical College–Mountain View Campus
2680 Gordy Parkway
Marietta, GA 30066
Phone: (770) 509-6349
E-mail: gslivenik@chattcollege.com
http://www.chattcollege.com

College of Coastal Georgia
3700 Altama Avenue
Brunswick, GA 31520

Phone: (912) 279-5700
http://www.cgcc.edu

The International Culinary School at the Art Institute of Atlanta
6600 Peachtree Dunwoody Road NE
Atlanta, GA 30328
Phone: (770) 394-8300
http://www.artinstitutes.edu

Le Cordon Bleu–Atlanta
College of Culinary Arts
1927 Lakeside Parkway
Tucker, GA 30084
Phone: (888) 549-8222
E-mail: tkazenske@atlantaculinary.
com
http://www.atlantaculinary.com

North Georgia Technical College–Blairsville Campus
121 Meeks Avenue
Blairsville, GA 30512
Phone: (706) 439-6300
http://www.northgatech.edu

North Georgia Technical College–Currahee Campus
8989 Highway 17 South
Toccoa, GA 30577
Phone: (706) 779-8100
E-mail: info@northgatech.edu
http://www.northgatech.edu

Savannah Technical Institute
5717 White Bluff Road
Savannah, GA 31405
Phone: (912) 443-5700
http://www.savannahtech.edu

Ursula's Cooking School, Inc.
1764 Cheshire Bridge Road
Atlanta, GA 30324
Phone: (404) 876-7463
E-mail: Ursula@UrsulaCooks.com
http://www.ursulacooks.com

HAWAII

Hawaii Community College–Hilo Campus
200 West Kawili Street

Hilo, HI 96720
Phone: (808) 974-7611
E-mail: hawccinf@hawaii.edu
http://www.hawaii.hawaii.edu

Kapiolani Community College
4303 Diamond Head Road
Honolulu, HI 96816
Phone: (808) 734-9466
E-mail: culinary@hawaii.edu
http://www.kcc.hawaii.edu

Kauai Community College
3-1901 Kaumualii Highway
Lihue, HI 96766-9591
Phone: (808) 245-8311
http://www.kauai.hawaii.edu

Leeward Community College
96-045 Ala Ike
Pearl City, HI 96782
Phone: (808) 455-0011
E-mail: tlbenave@hawaii.edu
http://www.lcc.hawaii.edu

Maui Culinary Academy at Maui Community College
310 West Kaahumanu Avenue
Kahului, HI 96732
Phone: (808) 984-3225
E-mail: santosro@hawaii.edu
http://www.mauiculinary.com

IDAHO

College of Southern Idaho
315 Falls Avenue
P.O. Box 1238
Twin Falls, ID 83303-1238
Phone: (208) 733-9554
E-mail: info@csi.edu
http://www.csi.edu

Idaho State University
921 South 8th Avenue
Pocatello, ID 83209
Phone: (208) 282-3327
E-mail: milldav1@isu.edu
http://www.isu.edu/ctech

North Idaho College
1000 West Garden Avenue
Coeur d'Alene, ID 83814

Phone: (208) 769-3300
E-mail: Rick_Schultz@nic.edu
http://www.nic.edu

Selland College at Boise State University
MS 2005
1910 University Drive
Boise, ID 83725
Phone: (208) 426-1431
E-mail: sellandemss@boisestate.edu
http://www.selland.boisestate.edu

ILLINOIS

College of Dupage
425 Fawell Boulevard
Glen Ellyn, IL 60137
Phone: (630) 942-2592
E-mail: thielman@cod.edu
http://www.cod.edu

College of Lake County–Grayslake, Vernon Hills, Waukegan
19351 West Washington Street
Grayslake, IL 60030
Phone: (847) 543-2823
E-mail: mdowling@clcillinois.edu
http://www.clcillinois.edu

Cooking and Hospitality Institute of Chicago, Inc.
361 West Chestnut
Chicago, IL 60610
Phone: (312) 944-0882
http://www.chicnet.org

Elgin Community College
1700 Spartan Drive
Elgin, IL 60123
Phone: (847) 697-1000
E-mail: mzema@elgin.edu
http://www.elgin.edu

French Pastry School
226 West Jackson Boulevard
Suite 106
Chicago, IL 60603
Phone: (312) 726-2419
E-mail: info@frenchpastryschool.
com
http://www.frenchpastryschool.com

The International Culinary
School at the Illinois
Institute of Art Chicago
350 North Orleans Street
Chicago, IL 60654-1593
Phone: (312) 280-3500
http://www.ilic.artinstitutes.edu

Joliet Junior College
1215 Houbolt Road
Joliet, IL 60431-8938
Phone: (815) 280-2542
E-mail: kvonhoff@jjc.edu
http://www.jjc.edu

Kendall College
900 N. North Branch Street
Chicago, IL 60642
Phone: (866) 667-3344
E-mail: ckoetke@kendall.edu
http://www.kendall.edu

Lexington College
310 South Peoria Street
Chicago, IL 60607
Phone: (312) 226-6294
http://www.lexingtoncollege.edu

Lincoln Land Community
College
5250 Shepherd Road
Springfield, IL 62794-9256
Phone: (217) 786-2200
http://www.llcc.edu

Moraine Valley Community
College
9000 West College Parkway
Palos Hills, IL 60465-0937
Phone: (708) 974-4300
http://www.morainevalley.edu

Robert Morris College–Insitute
of Culinary Arts
401 South State Street
Chicago, IL 60605
Phone: (312) 935-6800
E-mail: enroll@robertmorris.edu
http://www.robertmorris.edu

Southwestern Illinois College
2500 Carlyle Avenue
Belleville, IL 62221

Phone: (618) 235-2700
E-mail: leisa.brockman@swic.edu
http://www.southwestern.cc.il.us

Triton College
2000 Fifth Avenue
River Grove, IL 60171
Phone: (708) 456-0300, ext. 3624
E-mail: jdrosos@triton.edu
http://www.triton.edu

William Rainey Harper
College
1200 West Algonquin Road
Palatine, IL 60067
Phone: (847) 925-6707
http://www.harpercollege.edu

INDIANA

Ivy Tech Community College of
Indiana–East Central
Campuses in Anderson, Marion,
Muncie (main campus)
4301 South Cowan Road
Muncie, IN 47307-9448
Phone: (765) 289-2291
http://www.ivytech.edu/eastcentral

Ivy Tech Community College of
Indiana–Indianapolis
50 West Fall Creek Parkway North
Drive
Indianapolis, IN 46208-5752
Phone: (317) 921-4516
E-mail: jbricker@ivytech.edu
http://www.ivytech.edu/
indianapolis

Ivy Tech Community College–
Northeast
3800 North Anthony Boulevard
Fort Wayne, IN 46805
Phone: (888) 489-5463
http://www.ivytech.edu/fortwayne

Ivy Tech Community College of
Indiana–Northwest
Campuses in East Chicago, Gary
(main campus), Michigan City,
Valparaiso
1440 East 35th Avenue
Gary, IN 46409

Phone: (219) 981-1111
http://www.ivytech.edu/northwest

Ivy Tech State College–
North Central
220 Dean Johnson Boulevard
South Bend, IN 46601
Phone: (574) 289-7001, ext. 5325
E-mail: tcarriga@ivytech.edu
http://www.ivytech.edu/
southbend

Vincennes University
1002 North First Street
Vincennes, IN 47591
Phone: (800) 742-9198
E-mail: prichardson@vinu.edu
http://www.vinu.edu

IOWA

Des Moines Area Community
College–Ankeny Campus
2006 South Ankeny Boulevard
Ankeny, IA 50023
Phone: (515) 964-6200
http://www.dmacc.edu

Indian Hills Community
College
525 Grandview
Building #7
Ottumwa, IA 52501
Phone: (800) 726-2585
E-mail: mkivlaha@indianhills.edu
http://www.ihcc.cc.ia.us

Iowa Lakes Community
College–Emmetsburg
Campus
3200 College Drive
Emmetsburg, IA 50536
Phone: (712) 852-3554
E-mail: rhalverson@iowalakes.edu
http://www.iowalakes.edu

Iowa Western Community
College
2700 College Road
Council Bluffs, IA 51503
Phone: (712) 325-3200
E-mail: admissions@iwcc.edu
http://iwcc.cc.ia.us

Kirkwood Community College
6301 Kirkwood Boulevard
  Southwest
Cedar Rapids, IA 52404
Phone: (319) 398-5517
E-mail: mgerman@kirkwood.edu
http://www.kirkwood.cc.ia.us

Scott Community College
500 Belmont Road
Bettendorf, IA 52722
Phone: (563) 441-4001
E-mail: bscott@eicc.edu
http://www.eicc.edu

KANSAS

American Institute of Baking
1213 Bakers Way
P.O. Box 3999
Manhattan, KS 66505-3999
Phone: (785) 537-4750
E-mail: info@aibonline.org
http://www.aibonline.org

Johnson County Community
  College
12345 College Boulevard
Overland Park, KS 66210-1299
Phone: (913) 469-8500
E-mail: lrobinson@jccc.edu
http://www.jccc.edu

Kansas City Kansas Community
  College Technical Education
  Center
2220 North 59th Street
Kansas City, KS 66104
Phone: (913) 627-4100
http://www.kckats.com

KENTUCKY

Bowling Green Technical College
1845 Loop Street
Bowling Green, KY 42101
Phone: (270) 901-1000
E-mail: mike.riggs@kctcs.edu
http://www.bowlinggreen.kctcs.edu

Elizabethtown Community and
  Technical College
610 College Street Road

Elizabethtown, KY 42701
Phone: (270) 706-8702
http://www.elizabethtown.kctcs.edu

Jefferson Community and
  Technical College
109 East Broadway
Louisville, KY 40202
Phone: (502) 213-5333
E-mail: ryan.tomes@kctcs.edu
http://www.jefferson.kctcs.edu

Owensboro Community and
  Technical College
4800 New Hartford Road
Owensboro, KY 42303
Phone: (270) 686-4400
http://www.octc.kctcs.edu

Sullivan University–Lexington
  Campus
2355 Harrodsburg Road
Lexington, KY 40504
Phone: (859) 276-4357
http://www.sullivan.edu/lexington

Sullivan University–Louisville
  Campus
(includes: National Center for
  Hospitality Studies)
3101 Bardstown Road
Louisville, KY 40205
Phone: (502) 456-6505
E-mail: thickey@sullivan.edu
http://www.sullivan.edu/louisville

West Kentucky Community
  and Technical College
4810 Alben Barkley Drive
P.O. Box 7380
Paducah, KY 42002-7380
Phone: (270) 554-9200
E-mail: CulCoord@ti.westkentucky.
  kctcs.edu
http://www.westkentucky.kctcs.edu

LOUISIANA

Bossier Parish Community
  College
6220 East Texas Street
Bossier City, LA 71111
Phone: (318) 678-6000

E-mail: edickson@bpcc.edu
http://www.bpcc.edu

Chef John Folse Culinary
  Institute at Nicholls State
  University
107 Gouaux Hall
P.O. Box 2099
Thibodaux, LA 70310
Phone: (985) 449-7091
E-mail: veronica.veillion@nicholls.
  edu
http://www.nicholls.edu/jfolse

Delgado Community College
615 City Park Avenue
New Orleans, LA 70119-4399
Phone: (504) 671-5012
E-mail: mbart@dcc.edu
http://www.dcc.edu

Louisiana Culinary Institute
5837 Essen Lane
Baton Rouge, LA 70810
Phone: (225) 769-8820
http://www.louisianaculinary.com

Louisiana Technical College–
  Baton Rouge Campus
3250 North Acadian Thruway
East Baton Rouge, LA 70805
Phone: (225) 359-9204
E-mail: mtravasos@ltc.edu
http://www.ltc.edu

Louisiana Technical College–
  Lafayette Campus
1101 Bertrand Drive
Lafayette, LA 70506
Phone: (337) 262-5962
http://www.ltc.edu

Louisiana Technical College–
  Shreveport/Bossier Campus
2010 North Market Street
Shreveport, LA 71107
Phone: (318) 676-7811
E-mail: dbeavers@ltc.edu
http://www.ltc.edu

Nunez Community College
3700 La Fontaine Street
Chalmette, LA 70043

Phone: (504) 278-7467
http://www.nunez.edu

MAINE

Eastern Maine Community College

354 Hogan Road
Bangor, ME 04401
Phone: (800) 286-9357
E-mail: demers@emcc.edu
http://www.emcc.edu

Southern Maine Community College

2 Fort Road
South Portland, ME 04106
Phone: (207) 741-5500
E-mail: wberiau@smccME.edu
http://www.smccme.edu

York Community College

112 College Drive
Wells, ME 04090
Phone: (207) 646-9282
E-mail: contact@yccc.edu
http://www.yccc.edu

MARYLAND

Allegany College of Maryland

12401 Willowbrook Road
Southeast Cumberland, MD 21502-2596
Phone: (301) 784-5005
E-mail: dsanford@allegany.edu
http://www.allegany.edu

Anne Arundel Community College

101 College Parkway
Arnold, MD 21012-1895
Phone: (410) 777-1999
E-mail: askaacc@aacc.edu
http://www.aacc.edu

Baltimore International College

17 Commerce Street
Baltimore, MD 21202
Phone: (410) 752-4710, ext. 120
http://www.bic.edu

L'Academie de Cuisine

16006 Industrial Drive
Gaithersburg, MD 20877
Phone: (301) 670-8670
E-mail: info@lacademie.com
http://www.lacademie.com

Lincoln College of Technology–Columbia Campus

9325 Snowden River Parkway
Columbia, MD 21046
Phone: (410) 290-7100
http://www.lincolnedu.com

MASSACHUSETTS

Berkshire Community College

1350 West Street
Pittsfield, MA 01201
Phone: (413) 499-4660
http://www.berkshirecc.edu

Boston University

808 Commonwealth Avenue
Boston, MA 02215
Phone: (617) 353-9852
E-mail: cularts@bu.edu
http://www.bu.edu

Bristol Community College–Fall River Campus

777 Elsbree Street
Fall River, MA 02720
Phone: (508) 678-2811
E-mail: jcaressi@bristol.mass.edu
http://www.bristol.mass.edu

Bunker Hill Community College

250 New Rutherford Avenue
Boston, MA 02129-2925
Phone: (617) 228-2000
http://www.bhcc.mass.edu

The Cambridge School of Culinary Arts

2020 Massachusetts Avenue
Cambridge, MA 02140
Phone: (617) 354-2020
http://www.cambridgeculinary.com

Holyoke Community College

303 Homestead Avenue

Holyoke, MA 01040
Phone: (413) 538-7000
E-mail: admissions@hcc.mass.edu
http://www.hcc.mass.edu

International Institute of Culinary Arts

215 Bank Street
Fall River, MA 02720
Phone: (508) 675-9305
E-mail: info@iicaculinary.com
http://www.iicaculinary.com

Massasoit Community College

One Massasoit Boulevard
Brockton, MA 02302
Phone: (508) 588-9100
E-mail: admoffice@massasoit.mass.edu
http://www.massasoit.mass.edu

Newbury College

129 Fisher Avenue
Brookline, MA 02445
Phone: (617) 730-7076
E-mail: brookline@newbury.edu
http://www.newbury.edu

North Shore Community College

562 Maple Street
Hathorne, MA 01937
Phone: (978) 774-0050
E-mail: ltirrell@northshore.edu
http://www.northshore.edu

MICHIGAN

Baker College of Muskegon

1903 Marquette Avenue
Muskegon, MI 49442-3404
Phone: (231) 777-5200
http://www.baker.edu

Grand Rapids Community College–Secchia Institute for Culinary Education

151 Fountain Street Northeast
Grand Rapids, MI 49503
Phone: (616) 234-3690
E-mail: rsahajda@grcc.edu
http://www.grcc.edu

Henry Ford Community College
5101 Evergreen Road
Dearborn, MI 48128
Phone: (313) 845-6390
E-mail: dennis@hfcc.edu
http://www.henryford.cc.mi.us

The Macomb Culinary Institute at Macomb Community College
44575 Garfield Road
Clinton Township, MI 48038-1139
Phone: (586) 445-7999
E-mail: answer@macomb.edu
http://www.macomb.edu

Monroe County Community College
1555 South Raisinville Road
Monroe, MI 48161
Phone: (734) 384-4150
E-mail: kthomas@monroeccc.edu
http://www.monroeccc.edu

Mott Community College
1401 East Court Street
Flint, MI 48503
Phone: (810) 762-0200
E-mail: grace.alexander@mcc.edu
http://www.mcc.edu

Northern Michigan University
1401 Presque Isle Avenue
Marquette, MI 49855
Phone: (906) 227-1000
http://www.nmu.edu

Northwestern Michigan College
Great Lakes Culinary Institute
1701 East Front Street
Traverse City, MI 49686
Phone: (231) 995-1197
E-mail: flaughlin@nmc.edu
http://www.nmc.edu

Oakland Community College
The Culinary Studies Institute
27055 Orchard Lake Road
Farmington Hills, MI 48334-4579
Phone: (248) 522-3700
E-mail: kmenrigh@oaklandcc.edu
http://www.oaklandcc.edu/culinary

Schoolcraft College
18600 Haggerty Road
Livonia, MI 48152
Phone: (734) 462-4400
E-mail: sloving@schoolcraft.edu
http://www.schoolcraft.edu

Washtenaw Community College
4800 East Huron River Drive
Ann Arbor, MI 48106-0978
Phone: (734) 973-3300
E-mail: therrera@wccnet.edu
http://www.wccnet.edu

MINNESOTA

The Art Institutes International Minnesota
15 South 9th Street
Minneapolis, MN 55402-3105
Phone: (612) 332-3361
http://www.aim.artinstitutes.edu

Hennepin Technical College–Brooklyn Park Campus
9000 Brooklyn Boulevard
Brooklyn Park, MN 55445
Phone: (952) 995-1300
E-mail: deisenreich@hennepintech.edu
http://www.hennepintech.edu

Hennepin Technical College–Eden Prairie Campus
13100 College View Drive
Eden Prairie, MN 55347
Phone: (952) 995-1300
E-mail: rick.forpahl@hennepintech.edu
http://www.hennepintech.edu

Hibbing Community College
1515 East 25th Street
Hibbing, MN 55746
Phone: (218) 262-7200
E-mail: danlidholm@hibbing.edu
http://www.hcc.mnscu.edu

Le Cordon Bleu College of Culinary Arts Minneapolis/ St. Paul
1315 Mendota Heights Road
Mendota Heights, MN 55120

Phone: (888) 348-5222
http://www.twincitiesculinary.com

Minnesota State Community and Technical College–Moorhead
1900 28th Avenue South
Moorhead, MN 56560
Phone: (218) 299-6500
E-mail: kim.brewster@minnesota.edu
http://www.minnesota.edu

Saint Cloud Technical College
1540 Northway Drive
Saint Cloud, MN 56303
Phone: (320) 308-5000
E-mail: jthomas@sctc.edu
http://www.sctc.edu

Saint Paul College
235 Marshall Avenue
Saint Paul, MN 55102
Phone: (651) 846-1600
http://www.saintpaul.edu

South Central Technical College–North Mankato Campus
1920 Lee Boulevard
North Mankato, MN 56003
Phone: (507) 389-7200
E-mail: jim.hanson@southcentral.edu
http://www.southcentral.edu

MISSISSIPPI

Hinds Community College
3925 Sunset Drive
Jackson, MS 39213-5899
Phone: (601) 366-1405
E-mail: smporter@hindscc.edu
http://www.hindscc.edu

Mississippi University for Women Culinary Arts Institute
W-Box 1639
Columbus, MS 39701
Phone: (662) 241-7472
E-mail: cularts@muw.edu
http://www.muw.edu/culinary

MISSOURI

East Central College
1964 Prairie Dell Road
Union, MO 63084
Phone: (636) 583-5193
http://www.eastcentral.edu

Ozark Technical College
1001 East Chestnut Expressway
Springfield, MO 65802
Phone: (417) 447-7500
http://www.otc.edu

St. Louis Community College–Forest Park
5600 Oakland Avenue
St. Louis, MO 63110
Phone: (314) 644-9100
E-mail: rhertel@stlcc.edu
http://www.stlcc.edu

MONTANA

University of Montana–College of Technology in Missoula
909 South Avenue West
Missoula, MT 59801
Phone: (406) 243-7882
E-mail: thomas.campbell@umontana.edu
http://www.cte.umt.edu

NEBRASKA

Central Community College–Hastings Campus
550 South Technical Boulevard
P.O. Box 1024
Hastings, NE 68902-1024
Phone: (402) 463-9811
http://www.cccneb.edu

Metropolitan Community College–The Institute for the Culinary Arts
P.O. Box 3777
Omaha, NE 68103-0777
Phone: (402) 457-2400
E-mail: jtrebbien@mccneb.edu
http://www.mccneb.edu

Southeast Community College
8800 O Street
Lincoln, NE 68520-1299
Phone: (402) 471-3333
E-mail: jtaylor@southeast.edu

NEVADA

Community College of Southern Nevada
3200 East Cheyenne Avenue
North Las Vegas, NV 89030-4428
Phone: (702) 651-4060
E-mail: john.metcalfe@ccsn.edu
http://www.csn.edu

Creative Cooking School of Las Vegas
7259 West Sahara Ave
Suite 2
Las Vegas, NV 89117
Phone: (702) 294-0600
http://www.creativecookingschool.com

The International Culinary School at The Art Institute of Las Vegas
2350 Corporate Circle
Henderson, NV 89074-7737
Phone: (702) 369-9944
http://www.artinstitutes.edu/lasvegas/culinary

Le Cordon Bleu College of Culinary Arts–Las Vegas
1451 Center Crossing Road
Las Vegas, NV 89144
Phone: (888) 551-8222
http://www.vegasculinary.com

Truckee Meadows Community College
7000 Dandini Boulevard
Reno, NV 89512-3999
Phone: (775) 673-7000
E-mail: KCannan@tmcc.edu
http://www.tmcc.edu

University of Nevada–Las Vegas
William F. Harrah College of Hotel Administration
Box 456013
4505 Maryland Parkway
Las Vegas, NV 89154-6013
Phone: (702) 895-1052
E-mail: pat.moreo@unlv.edu
http://www.unlv.edu

NEW HAMPSHIRE

Atlantic Culinary Academy–McIntosh College
23 Cataract Avenue
Dover, NH 03820
Phone: (800) 624-6867
http://www.mcintoshcollege.edu

The Balsams Culinary Apprenticeship Program
Balsams Resort Hotel
1000 Cold Spring Road
Dixville Notch, NH 03576
Phone: (877) 225-7267
E-mail: jlmorris@dncinc.com
http://www.thebalsams.com

Southern New Hampshire University
2500 North River Road
Manchester, NH, 03106
Phone: (800) 668-1249
E-mail: s.owens@snhu.edu
http://www.snhu.edu

White Mountains Community College
2020 Riverside Drive
Berlin, NH 03570
Phone: (603) 752-1113 or
(800) 445-4525
http://www.wmcc.edu

NEW JERSEY

Atlantic Cape Community College
5100 Black Horse Pike
Mays Landing, NJ 08330-2699
Phone: (609) 343-5000
E-mail: mcleod@atlantic.edu
http://www.atlantic.edu

Bergen Community College
400 Paramus Road
Paramus, NJ 07652
Phone: (201) 447-7195
E-mail: admsoffice@bergen.edu
http://www.bergen.cc.nj.us

Brookdale Community College–Culinary Education Center
101 Drury Lane
Asbury Park, NJ 07712
Phone: (732) 988-3299
http://www.brookdale.cc.nj.us

Hudson County Community College
161 Newkirk Street
Room E222
Jersey City, NJ 07306
Phone: (201) 360-4640
E-mail: cai@hccc.edu
http://www.hccc.edu

Middlesex County College
2600 Woodbridge Avenue
Edison, NJ 08818-3050
Phone: (732) 548-6000
E-mail: MMaciolek@middlesexcc. edu
http://www.middlesexcc.edu

Morris County School of Technology
400 East Main Street
Denville, NJ 07834
Phone: (973) 627-4600
http://www.mcvts.org

Passaic County Technical Institute
45 Reinhardt Road
Wayne, NJ 07470
Phone: (973) 790-6000
http://www.pcti.tec.nj.us

Salem County Vocational Technical Schools
880 Route 45
P.O. Box 350
Woodstown, NJ 08098
Phone: (856) 769-0101
http://www.scvts.org

NEW MEXICO

Central New Mexico Community College
525 Buena Vista Drive Southeast
Albuquerque, NM 87106

Phone: (505) 224-3000
http://www.cnm.edu

Santa Fe Community College
6401 Richards Avenue
Santa Fe, NM 87508-4887
Phone: (505) 428-1435
E-mail: info@sfccnm.edu
http://www.sfccnm.edu

NEW YORK

Adirondack Community College
640 Bay Road
Queensbury, NY 12804
Phone: (518) 743-2200
E-mail: info@sunyacc.edu
http://www.sunyacc.edu

Alfred State College
10 Upper College Drive
Alfred, NY 14802
Phone: (607) 587-4215
E-mail: SantorJM@alfredstate.edu
http://www.alfredstate.edu

The Culinary Institute of America at Hyde Park
1946 Campus Drive
Hyde Park, NY 12538-1499
Phone: (845) 452-9430
E-mail: admissions@culinary.edu
http://www.ciachef.edu

Erie Community College– City Campus
121 Ellicott Street
Buffalo, NY 14203
Phone: (716) 842-2770
http://www.ecc.edu

Erie Community College– North Campus
6205 Main Street
Williamsville, NY 14221
Phone: (716) 634-0800
http://www.ecc.edu

The French Culinary Institute
462 Broadway
New York, NY 10013-2618
Phone: (212) 219-8890 or
(888) FCI-CHEF

E-mail: admission@ frenchculinary. com
http://www.frenchculinary.com

The Institute of Culinary Education
50 West 23rd Street
New York, NY 10010
Phone: (212) 847-0701
http://www.iceculinary.com

The International Culinary School at The Art Institute of New York City
75 Varick Street
16th Floor
New York, NY 10013-1917
Phone: (212) 226-5500
E-mail: ainycadm@aii.edu
http://ainyc.artinstitutes.edu

Jefferson Community College
1220 Coffeen Street
Watertown, NY 13601
Phone: (315) 786-2277
E-mail: avickers@sunyjefferson. edu
http://www.sunyjefferson.edu

Mohawk Valley Community College
1101 Floyd Avenue
Rome, NY 13440
Phone: (315) 339-3470
http://www.mvcc.edu

Monroe College
434 Main Street
New Rochelle, NY 10801
Phone: (914) 632-5400
http://www.monroecollege.edu

Monroe Community College
1000 East Henrietta Road
Rochester, NY 14623
Phone: (585) 292-2000
http://www.monroecc.edu

The Natural Gourmet Cooking School
48 West 21st Street
New York, NY 10010
Phone: (212) 645-5170

E-mail: info@naturalgourmet
school.com
http://www.naturalgourmetschool.
com

New School Culinary Arts
131 West 23rd Street
New York, NY 10079
Phone: (212) 255-4141
http://www.newschool.edu

New York City College of Technology
300 Jay Street
Brooklyn, NY 11201
Phone: (718) 260-5500
E-mail: hospitalitymgmt@citytech.
cuny.edu
http://www.citytech.cuny.edu

New York Food and Hotel Management School
154 West 14th Street
New York, NY 10011
Phone: (212) 675-6655
http://www.nyfoodandhotelschool.
com

New York Institute of Technology
300 Carleton Avenue
Central Islip, NY 11722-9029
Phone: (631) 348-3000
E-mail: ggrossma@nyit.edu
http://www.nyit.edu

Niagara County Community College
3111 Saunders Settlement Road
Sanborn, NY 14132
Phone: (716) 614-6222
E-mail: mistrine@niagaracc.suny.edu
http://www.niagaracc.suny.edu

Onondaga Community College
4585 West Seneca Turnpike
Syracuse, NY 13215-4585
Phone: (315) 498-2622
E-mail: occinfo@sunyocc.edu
http://www.sunyocc.edu

Paul Smith's College
P.O. Box 265

Routes 30 and 86
Paul Smiths, NY 12970-0265
Phone: (518) 327-6227
E-mail: admiss@paulsmiths.edu
http://www.paulsmiths.edu

Schenectady County Community College
78 Washington Avenue
Schenectady, NY 12305
Phone: (518) 381-1200
E-mail: strianaj@sunysccc.edu
http://www.sunysccc.edu

State University of New York Cobleskill Agriculture and Technical College
State Route 7
Cobleskill, NY 12043
Phone: (518) 255-5700
E-mail: CAHT@cobleskill.edu
http://www.cobleskill.edu

State University of New York Delhi College of Technology
2 Main Street
Delhi, NY 13753-9978
Phone: (607) 746-4400
E-mail: busnhosp@delhi.edu
http://www.delhi.edu

Sullivan County Community College
112 College Road
Loch Sheldrake, NY 12759
Phone: (845) 434-5750
E-mail: mbel@sullivan.suny.edu
http://www.sullivan.suny.edu

Westchester Community College
75 Grasslands Road
Valhalla, NY 10595
Phone: (914) 606-6600
E-mail: admissions@sunywcc.edu
http://www.sunywcc.edu

NORTH CAROLINA

Alamance Community College
P.O. Box 8000
Graham, NC 27253

Phone: (336) 578-2002
http://www.alamancecc.edu

The Art Institute of Charlotte
Three Lake Pointe Plaza
2110 Water Ridge Parkway
Charlotte, NC 28217-4536
Phone: (704) 357-8020
http://www.artinstitutes.edu/charlotte

Asheville Buncombe Technical College
340 Victoria Road
Asheville, NC 28801
Phone: (828) 254-1921
E-mail: stillman@abtech.edu
http://www.abtech.edu

Cape Fear Community College
411 North Front Street
Wilmington, NC 28401
Phone: (910) 362-7000
http://www.cfcc.edu

Central Piedmont Community College
P.O. Box 35009
Charlotte, NC 28235
Phone: (704) 330-2722
http://www1.cpcc.edu

Durham Community College– Chez Bay Cooking School
1921 North Pointe Drive
Durham, NC 27705-2672
Phone: (919) 477-7878
http://chezbaygourmet.com

Guilford Technical Community College
P.O. Box 309
Jamestown, NC 27282
Phone: (336) 334-4822
http://www.gtcc.edu

Johnson and Wales University
801 West Trade Street
Charlotte, NC 28202
Phone: (980) 598-1000
http://www.jwu.edu

Lenoir Community College
P.O. Box 188

231 Highway 58
South Kinston, NC 28502-0188
Phone: (252) 527-6223
E-mail: jyourdon@lenoircc.edu
http://www.lenoircc.edu

Sandhills Community College

3395 Airport Road
Pinehurst, NC 28374
Phone: (910) 692-6185
E-mail: oelfket@sandhills.edu
http://www.sandhills.edu

Southwestern Community College

447 College Drive
Sylva, NC 28779
Phone: (828) 586-4091
E-mail: ceretta@southwesterncc.edu
http://www.southwesterncc.edu

Wake Technical College

9101 Fayetteville Road
Raleigh, NC 27603
Phone: (919) 866-5990
E-mail: jjhadley@waketech.edu
http://www.waketech.edu

Wilkes Community College

P.O. Box 120
1328 South Collegiate Drive
Wilkesboro, NC 28697
Phone: (336) 838-6100
E-mail: kimrey.jordan@wilkescc.
edu
http://www.wilkescc.edu

NORTH DAKOTA

North Dakota State College of Science

800 Sixth Street North
Wahpeton, ND 58076-0002
Phone: (800) 342-4325
http://www.ndscs.nodak.edu

OHIO

Cincinnati State–Midwest Culinary Institute

3520 Central Parkway
Cincinnati, OH 45223
Phone: (513) 569-1621

E-mail: Jeffrey.Sheldon@cincinnati
state.edu
http://culinary.cincinnatistate.edu

Columbus State Community College

550 East Spring Street
Columbus, OH 43215
Phone: (614) 287-5353
E-mail: msteiska@cscc.edu
http://www.cscc.edu

Cuyahoga Community College

2900 Community College Avenue
Cleveland, OH 44115
Phone: (216) 987-4000
E-mail: Thomas.Capretta@tri-c.edu
http://www.tri-c.edu

Hocking College

3301 Hocking Parkway
Nelsonville, OH 45764
Phone: (740) 753-3591
E-mail: admissions@hocking.edu
http://www.hocking.edu

The Loretta Paganini School of Cooking

8613 Mayfield Road
Chesterland, OH 44026
Phone: (440) 729-1110
E-mail: lpscinc@msn.com
http://www.lpscinc.com

Owens Community College

P.O. Box 10,000
Toledo, OH 43699-1947
Phone: (567) 661-7000, ext. 7000
http://www.owens.edu

Sinclair Community College

444 West Third Street
Dayton, OH 45402-1460
Phone: (937) 512-3000
E-mail: steve.cornelius@sinclair.edu
http://www.sinclair.edu

University of Akron

302 Buchtel Common
Akron, OH 44325
Phone: (330) 972-7111
E-mail: admission@uakron.edu
http://www.uakron.edu

Zane State College

1555 Newark Road
Zanesville, OH 43701
Phone: (740) 454-2501
E-mail: madornetto@zanestate.
edu
http://www.zanestate.edu

OKLAHOMA

Culinary Institute of Platt College

2727 West Memorial Road
Oklahoma City, OK 73134-8034
Phone: (405) 749-2433
http://www.plattcollege.org

Meridian Technology Center

1312 South Sangre Road
Stillwater, OK 74074-1899
Phone: (405) 377-3333
E-mail: careers@meridian-
technology.com
http://www.meridian-technology.
com

Metro Tech, South Bryant Campus

4901 South Bryant Avenue
Oklahoma City, OK 73129
Phone: (405) 424-8324
http://www.metrotech.org

Oklahoma State University– School of Technology

1801 East 4th Street
Okmulgee, OK 74447
Phone: (918) 293-4678
E-mail: rene.jungo@okstate.edu
http://www.osuit.edu

Pioneer Technology Center

2101 North Ash
Ponca City, OK 74601
Phone: (580) 762-8336
http://www.pioneertech.org

Tri-County Technical School

6101 South East Nowata Road
Bartlesville, OK 74006
Phone: (918) 331-3333
http://www.tctc.org

OREGON

Cascade Culinary Institute–Central Oregon Community College
2600 Northwest College Way
Bend, OR 97701
Phone: (541) 383-7700
E-mail: jkress@cocc.edu
http://www.culinary.cocc.edu

International School of Baking
1971 Northwest Juniper Avenue
Bend, OR 97701
Phone: (541) 389-8553
E-mail: marda@schoolofbaking.com
http://www.schoolofbaking.com

Lane Community College
4000 East 30th Avenue
Eugene, OR 97405-0640
Phone: (541) 463-3503
E-mail: kellyb@lanecc.edu
http://www.lanecc.edu

Linn-Benton Community College
6500 Pacific Boulevard Southwest
Albany, OR 97321
Phone: (541) 917-4811
E-mail: anselms@linnbenton.edu
http://www.linnbenton.edu

Oregon Coast Culinary Institute–Southwestern Oregon Community College
1988 Newmark Avenue
Coos Bay, OR 97420
Phone: (541) 888-7195
E-mail: shanlin@socc.edu
http://www.occi.net

Oregon Culinary Institute–Pioneer Pacific College
1717 Southwest Madison Street
Portland, OR 97205
Phone: (503) 961-6200
E-mail: oci-info@pioneerpacific.edu
http://www.oregonculinaryinstitute.com

Western Culinary Institute
600 Southwest 10th Avenue
Suite 400
Portland, OR 97205
Phone: (503) 223-2245
http://www.westernculinary.com

PENNSYLVANIA

Bucks County Community College
275 Swamp Road
Newtown, PA 18940
Phone: (215) 968-8000
http://www.bucks.edu

Commonwealth Technical Institute
Hiram G. Andrews Center
727 Goucher Street
Johnstown, PA 15905-3092
Phone: (814) 255-8200
http://www.dli.state.pa.us/landi/cwp/view.asp?a-128&Q-188338

Community College of Allegheny County–Allegheny Campus
808 Ridge Avenue
Pittsburgh, PA 15212-6097
Phone: (412) 237-2511
http://www.ccac.edu

Community College of Allegheny County–Boyce Campus
595 Beatty Road
Monroeville, PA 15146-1396
Phone: (724) 325-6614
http://www.ccac.edu

Community College of Beaver County
1 Campus Drive
Monaca, PA 15061
Phone: (724) 775-8561, ext. 261
http://www.ccbc.edu

Community College of Philadelphia
1700 Spring Garden Street
Philadelphia, PA 19130
Phone: (215) 751-8010
http://www.ccp.edu

Drexel University–Goodwin College of Professional Studies
One Drexel Plaza
3001 Market Street
Suite 100
Philadelphia, PA 19104
Phone: (215) 895-2159
E-mail: goodwin@drexel.edu
http://www.drexel.edu/goodwin

Harrisburg Area Community College
One HACC Drive
Harrisburg, PA 17110-2999
Phone: (717) 780-2300
E-mail: gwkassah@hacc.edu
http://www.hacc.edu

Indiana University of Pennsylvania–Academy of Culinary Arts
1012 Winslow Street
Punxsutawney, PA 15767
Phone: (800) 438-6424
E-mail: culinary-arts@iup.edu
http://www.iup.edu

The International Culinary School at The Art Institute of Philadelphia
1622 Chestnut Street
Philadelphia, PA 19103-5119
Phone: (215) 567-7080 or (800) 275-2474
http://www.artinstitutes.edu/philadelphia

The International Culinary School at The Art Institute of Pittsburgh
420 Boulevard of the Allies
Pittsburgh, PA 15219-1301
Phone: (412) 263-6600
http://www.artinstitutes.edu/pittsburgh

JNA Institute of Culinary Arts
1212 South Broad Street
Philadelphia, PA 19146
Phone: (215) 468-8800
http://culinaryarts.com

Keystone College
One College Green
La Plume, PA 18440
Phone: (570) 945-8000
http://www.keystone.edu

Lehigh County Vocational-Technical School
4500 Education Park Drive
Schnecksville, PA 18078
Phone: (610) 799-2300
E-mail: hoffmant@lcti.org
http://www.lcti.org

Mercyhurst North East–The Culinary and Wine Institute
16 West Division Street
North East, PA 16428
Phone: (814) 725-6100
http://www.northeast.mercyhurst.edu

Northampton Community College
3835 Green Pond Rd
Bethlehem, PA 18020
Phone: (610) 861-5300
E-mail: dhowden@northampton.edu
http://www.northampton.edu

Orleans Technical Institute–Northeast Campus
1330 Rhawn Street
Philadelphia, PA 19111-2899
Phone: (215) 728-4700
E-mail: culinary@jevs.org
http://www.orleanstech.edu

Pennsylvania College of Technology
1 College Avenue
Williamsport, PA 17701
Phone: (570) 326-3761
E-mail: fbecker@pct.edu
http://www.pct.edu

Pennsylvania Culinary Institute
717 Liberty Avenue
Pittsburgh, PA 15222
Phone: (412) 566-2433
http://www.chefs.edu/pittsburgh

Reading Area Community College
10 South Second Street
P.O. Box 1706
Reading, PA 19603-1706
Phone: (610) 372-4721
http://www.racc.edu

The Restaurant School at Walnut Hill College
4207 Walnut Street
Philadelphia, PA 19104
Phone: (215) 222-4200
E-mail: info@walnuthillcollege.edu
http://www.therestaurantschool.com

Westmoreland County Community College
145 Pavilion Lane
Youngwood, PA 15697
Phone: (724) 925-4000
http://www.wccc.edu

Winner Institute of Arts and Sciences
One Winner Place
Transfer, PA 16154
Phone: (724) 646-2433
http://www.winner-institute.edu

York Technical Institute–Lancaster Campus
3050 Hempland Road
Lancaster, PA 17601
Phone: (717) 295-1100
http://www.yti.edu

Yorktowne Business Institute and School of Culinary Arts
West 7th Avenue
York, PA 17404
Phone: (717) 846-5000
E-mail: chef@ybi.edu
http://www.yorkchef.com

RHODE ISLAND

Johnson and Wales University
8 Abbott Park Place
Providence, RI 02903
Phone: (800) 342-5598
http://www.jwu.edu

SOUTH CAROLINA

The Art Institute of Charleston
24 North Market Street
Charleston, SC 29401-2623
Phone: (843) 727-3500
http://www.artinstitutes.edu/charleston

Culinary Institute at the University of South Carolina
USC–McCutchen House
902 Sumter Street
Building 10
Columbia, SC 29208
Phone: (803) 777-8225
http://www.hrsm.sc.edu/McCutchen-house

Culinary Institute of Charleston at Trident Technical College
P.O. Box 118067 (mailing address)
Charleston, SC 29423-8067
7000 Rivers Avenue (main campus)
North Charleston, SC 29406
Phone: (843) 574-6111
http://www.tridenttech.edu

Culinary Institute of the Carolinas at Greenville Technical College
506 South Pleasantburg Drive
Greenville, SC 29607
Phone: (864) 250-8111
E-mail: alan.scheidhauer@gvltec.edu
http://www.gvltec.edu

Horry-Georgetown Technical College
2050 Highway 501 East
Conway, SC 29526
Phone: (843) 347-3186
http://www.hgtc.edu

Spartanburg Community College
P.O. Box 4386
Spartanburg, SC 29305
Phone: (864) 592-4800
http://www.sccsc.edu

SOUTH DAKOTA

Mitchell Technical Institute
821 North Capital Street
Mitchell, SD 57301
Phone: (800) MTI-1969
E-mail: randy.doescher@
mitchelltech.edu
http://www.mitchelltech.edu

TENNESSEE

Gaylord Opryland Culinary Institute
2800 Opryland Drive
Nashville, TN 37214
Phone: (615) 458-2776
http://www.gaylordhotels.com

International Culinary School at The Art Institute of Tennessee–Nashville
100 Centerview Drive
Suite 250
Nashville, TN 37214-3439
Phone: (615) 874-1067
http://www.artinstitutes.edu/
nashville

Memphis Culinary Academy
1252 Peabody Avenue
Memphis, TN 38104
Phone: (901) 722-8892
http://www.memphis.com
(also program at Shelby County
Correction Center)

Nashville State Community College
120 White Bridge Road
Nashville, TN 37209
Phone: (615) 353-3783
E-mail: culinary.arts@nscc.edu
http://www.nscc.edu

Walters State Community College–Rel Maples Institute For Culinary Arts
1720 Old Newport Highway
Sevierville, TN 37876
Phone: (865) 774-5826
E-mail: catherine.hallman@ws.edu
http://www.ws.edu

TEXAS

Austin Community College– Eastview Campus
3401 Webberville Road
Austin, TX 78702
Phone: (512) 223-5173
E-mail: bhay@austin.cc.tx.us
http://www.austin.cc.tx.us

Culinary Academy of Austin
6020-B Dillard Circle
Austin, TX 78752
Phone: (512) 451-5743
E-mail: info@culinaryacademyof
austin.com
http://www.culinaryacademyof
austin.com

Culinary Institute LeNôtre
7070 Allensby Street
Houston, TX 77022
Phone: (713) 692-0077
E-mail: lenotre@culinaryinstitute.
edu
http://www.culinaryinstitute.edu

Del Mar College
101 Baldwin Boulevard
Corpus Christi, TX 78404
Phone: (361) 698-2809
E-mail: mcarpen@delmar.edu
http://www.delmar.edu

El Centro College
801 Main Street
Dallas, TX 75202
Phone: (214) 860-2000
http://www.ecc.dcccd.edu

El Paso Community College
9050 Viscount Boulevard
El Paso, TX 79928
Phone: (915) 831-3722
E-mail: eWebb1@epcc.edu
http://www.epcc.edu

Galveston College–Culinary Arts Academy
4015 Avenue Q
Galveston, TX 77550
Phone: (409) 944-4242
E-mail: pmitchell@gc.edu
http://www.gc.edu

Houston Community College
3100 Main Street
Houston, TX 77002
Phone: (713) 718-6045
E-mail: nicholas.boland@hccs.edu
http://www.hccs.edu

The International Culinary School at The Art Institute of Dallas
8080 Park Lane
Suite 100
Dallas, TX 75231-5993
Phone: (214) 692-8080
http://www.aid.aii.edu

The International Culinary School at The Art Institute of Houston
1900 Yorktown Street
Houston, TX 77056-4197
Phone: (713) 623-2040
http://www.aih.aii.edu

Lamar University
P.O. Box 10035
Beaumont, TX 77710
Phone: (409) 880-8663
E-mail: dahmmj@hal.lamar.edu
http://www.lamar.edu

The Natural Epicurean Academy of Culinary Arts
1701 Toomey Road
Austin, TX 78705
Phone: (512) 476-2276
E-mail: culinary@naturalepicurean.
com
http://www.naturalepicurean.com

Odessa College
201 West University
Odessa, TX 79764
Phone: (432) 335-6400
E-mail: plewis@odessa.edu
http://www.odessa.edu

Remington College–Dallas
1800 Eastgate Drive
Garland, TX 75041
Phone: (800) 560-6192
http://www.remingtoncollege.edu

Saint Philip's College
1801 Martin Luther King Drive
San Antonio, TX 78203
Phone: (210) 531-3315
E-mail: mkunz@mail.accd.edu
http://www.accd.edu/spc

San Jacinto College Central
8060 Spencer Highway
Pasadena, TX 77505
Phone: (281) 476-1501
http://www.sjcd.edu

San Jacinto College North
5800 Uvalde
Houston, TX 77049
Phone: (281) 458-4050
http://www.sjcd.edu

Texas Culinary Academy
11400 Burnet Road
Suite 2100
Austin, TX 78758
Phone: (512) 837-2665
http://www.tca.edu

Texas State Technical College Harlingen
1902 North Loop 499
Harlingen, TX 78550
Phone: (956) 364-4755
http://www.harlingen.tstc.edu

Texas State Technical College Waco
3801 Campus Drive
Waco, TX 76705
Phone: (800) 792-8784
E-mail: debby.defee@tstc.edu
http://www.waco.tstc.edu

Texas State Technical College West Texas
300 Homer K. Taylor Drive
Sweetwater, TX 79556
Phone: (325) 235-7300
http://www.westtexas.tstc.edu

UTAH

Bridgerland Applied Technology Center
1301 North 600 West

Logan, UT 84321
Phone: (435) 753-6780
http://www.batc.edu

Salt Lake Community College
4600 South Redwood Road
Salt Lake City, UT 84123
Phone: (801) 957-4550
E-mail: ricco.renzetti@slcc.edu
http://www.slcc.edu

Utah State University
1400 Old Main Hill
Logan, UT 84322-1400
Phone: (435) 797-1000
http://www.usu.edu

Utah Valley State University
800 West University Parkway
Orem, UT 84058
Phone: (801) 863-7054
E-mail: thatchco@uvsc.edu
http://www.uvsc.edu

VERMONT

New England Culinary Institute
56 College Street
Montpelier, VT 05602
Phone: (877) 223-6324,
   (877) 223-6324 (toll free)
E-mail: info@neci.edu
http://www.neci.edu

VIRGINIA

The International Culinary School at The Art Institute–Washington
1820 North Fort Myer Drive
Arlington, VA 22209-1802
Phone: (703) 358-9550
http://www.artinstitutes.edu/arlington

J. Sargeant Reynolds Community College
Center for Culinary Arts, Tourism, and Hospitality
700 East Jackson Street
Richmond, VA 23219

Phone: (804) 371-3000
E-mail: hospitality@reynolds.edu
http://www.jsr.vccs.edu

Northern Virginia Community College
8333 Little River Turnpike
Annandale, VA 22003-3796
Phone: (703) 323-3457
E-mail: bwong@nvcc.edu
http://www.nvcc.edu

Stratford University
7777 Leesburg Pike
Falls Church, VA 22043
Phone: (703) 821-8570,
   (888) 444-0804 (toll free)
E-mail: gwalden@stratford.edu
http://www.stratford.edu

Tidewater Community College–Norfolk Campus
300 Granby Street
Norfolk, VA 23510
Phone: (757) 822-1110
http://www.tcc.edu

Virginia Intermont College
1013 Moore Street
Bristol, VA 24201
Phone: (800) 451-1VIC
http://www.vic.edu

WASHINGTON

Bates Technical College
1101 South Yakima Avenue
Tacoma, WA 98405
Phone: (253) 680-7000
http://www.bates.ctc.edu

Bellingham Technical College
3028 Lindbergh Avenue
Bellingham, WA 98225
Phone: (360) 752-8345
E-mail: admissions@btc.ctc.edu
http://www.btc.ctc.edu

Clark College
1933 Fort Vancouver Way
Vancouver, WA 98663
Phone: (360) 699-6398
http://www.clark.edu

Edmonds Community College
20000 68th Avenue West
Lynnwood, WA 98036
Phone: (425) 640-1459
E-mail: sloreen@edcc.edu
http://www.edcc.edu

**The International Culinary
School at The Art Institute
of Seattle**
2323 Elliott Avenue
Seattle, WA 98121-1642
Phone: (206) 448-6600
http://www.artinstitutes.edu/seattle

**Lake Washington Technical
College**
11605 132nd Avenue Northeast
Kirkland, WA 98034
Phone: (425) 739-8300
E-mail: Paul.Pavsidis@lwtc.edu
http://www.lwtc.ctc.edu

**North Seattle Community
College**
9600 College Way North
Seattle, WA 98103
Phone: (206) 527-3663
E-mail: ARRC@sccd.ctc.edu
http://www.northseattle.edu

Olympic College
1600 Chester Avenue
Bremerton, WA 98337-1699
Phone: (360) 792-6050
E-mail: ngiovanni@olympic.edu
http://www.oc.ctc.edu

Renton Technical College
3000 Northeast 4th Street
Renton, WA 98056
Phone: (425) 235-2352
E-mail: jfisher@rtc.edu
http://www.renton-tc.ctc.edu

**Seattle Central Community
College–Seattle Culinary
Academy**
1701 Broadway
Room BE2120
Seattle, WA 98122
Phone: (206) 587-5424
E-mail: LChauncey@sccd.ctc.edu
http://www.seattleculinary.com

Skagit Valley College
2405 East College Way
Mount Vernon, WA 98273
Phone: (360) 416-7600 or
  (877) 385-5360
E-mail: dani.cox@skagit.edu
http://www.skagit.edu

**South Puget Sound
Community College**
2011 Mottman Road Southwest
Olympia, WA 98512
Phone: (360) 596-5347
http://www.spscc.ctc.edu

**South Seattle Community
College**
6000 16th Avenue Southwest
Seattle, WA 98106
Phone: (206) 764-5344
E-mail: awitt@sccd.ctc.edu
http://www.southseattle.edu

**Spokane Community College–
Inland Northwest Culinary
Academy**
1810 North Greene Street
Spokane, WA 99217-5399
Phone: (509) 533-7000 or
  (800) 248-5644
E-mail: DFisher@scc.spokane.edu
http://www.scc.spokane.edu

Walla Walla Community College
500 Tausick Way
Walla Walla, WA 99362
Phone: (509) 527-4227
E-mail: steven.walk@wwcc.edu
http://www.wwcc.edu

WEST VIRGINIA

Mountain State University
609 South Kanawha Street
Beckley, WV 25801
Phone: (866) 367-6781
E-mail: hgilbert@mountainstate.edu
http://www.mountainstate.edu

**Pierpont Community and
Technical College**
1201 Locust Avenue
Fairmont, WV 26554

Phone: (304) 367-4892
E-mail: bfloyd@fairmontstate.edu
http://www.pierpont.edu

**West Virginia Northern
Community College**
1704 Market Street
Wheeling, WV 26003
Phone: (304) 233-5900
E-mail: mgrubor@wvncc.edu
http://www.wvncc.edu

WISCONSIN

Blackhawk Technical College
6004 South County Road G
Janesville, WI 53546-9458
Phone: (608) 758-6900
E-mail: counseling@blackhawk.edu
http://www.blackhawk.edu

Fox Valley Technical College
1825 N. Bluemound Drive
P.O. Box 2277
Appleton, WI 54912-2277
Phone: (920) 735-5600
E-mail: igel@fvtc.edu
http://www.fvtc.edu

**Gateway Technical College–
Elkhorn Campus**
400 County Road H
Elkhorn, WI 53121
Phone: (262) 741-8200
http://www.gtc.edu

**Gateway Technical College–
Kenosha Campus**
3520 30th Avenue
Kenosha, WI 53144
Phone: (262) 564-2200
http://www.gtc.edu

**Gateway Technical College–
Racine Campus**
1001 South Main Street
Racine, WI 53403
Phone: (262) 619-6200
http://www.gtc.edu

Madison Area Technical College
3550 Anderson Street
Madison, WI 53704

Phone: (608) 246-6100
http://www.matcmadison.edu

Milwaukee Area Technical College
700 West State Street
Milwaukee, WI 53233
Phone: (414) 297-6000
E-mail: info@matc.edu
http://www.matc.edu

Moraine Park Technical College
235 North National Avenue
Fond du Lac, WI 54935

Phone: (920) 922-8611
http://www.morainepark.edu

Nicolet Area Technical College
5364 College Drive
Rhinelander, WI 54501
Phone: (715) 365-4410
http://www.nicoletcollege.edu

Southwest Wisconsin Technical College
1800 Bronson Boulevard
Fennimore, WI 53809
Phone: (800) 362-3322

E-mail: jdombeck@swtc.edu
http://www.swtc.edu

Waukesha County Technical College
800 Main Street
Pewaukee, WI 53072
Phone: (262) 691-5566
E-mail: tgraham@wctc.edu
http://wctc.edu

APPENDIX II
WINE AND BEER CLASSES AND SCHOOLS

Affairs of the Vine
696 Elliot Lane
Sebastopol, CA 95472
Phone: (707) 874-1975
E-mail: info@affairsofthevine.com
http://www.affairsofthevine.com

American Brewer's Guild
1001 Maple Street
Salisbury, VT 05769
Phone: (800) 636-1331
E-mail: abg@abgbrew.com
http://www.abgbrew.com

**American Institute of
 Wine and Food**
26364 Carmel Rancho Lane
Suite 201
Carmel, CA 93923
Phone: (831) 250-7739
Fax: (831) 622-7783
E-mail: info@aiwf.org
http://www.aiwf.org

**American Sommelier
 Association**
580 Broadway
Suite 716
New York, NY 10012
Phone: (212) 226-6805
Fax: (212) 226-6407
E-mail: office@americansommelier.
 org
http://www.americansommelier.
 org

The Art Institute of Atlanta
6600 Peachtree Dunwoody Road
 Northeast
Atlanta, GA 30328
Phone: (770) 394-8300
www.artinstitutes.edu/atlanta

**The Art Institute of California–
 San Francisco**
1170 Market Street
San Francisco, CA 94102
Phone: (415) 865-0198
http://www.artinstitutes.edu/
 SanFrancisco

The Art Institute of Charleston
24 North Market Street
Charleston, SC 29401-2623
Phone: (843) 727-3500
http://www.artinstitutes.edu/
 charleston

The Art Institute of Tampa
Parkside at Tampa Bay Park
4401 North Himes Avenue
Suite 150
Tampa, FL 33614
Phone: (813) 873-2112
http://www.artinstitutes.edu/tampa

The Art Institute of Washington
1820 Fort Myer Drive
Suite 1
Arlington, VA 22209
Phone: (703) 358-9550
http://www.artinstitutes.edu/
 arlington

**Boston Center for Adult
 Education**
122 Arlington Street
Boston, MA 02116
Phone: (617) 267-4430
E-mail: info@bcae.org
http://www.bcae.org

**Boston University/Elizabeth
 Bishop Wine Resource
 Center**
Special Programs
808 Commonwealth Avenue

Boston, MA 02215
Phone: (617) 353-9852
E-mail: wineeduc@bu.edu
http://www.bu.edu/foodandwine/
 wine_programs

Bruce Cass Wine Lab
804 Avalon Avenue
San Francisco, CA 94112
Phone: (415) 839-5313
E-mail: classes@brucecasswinelab.
 com
http://brucecasswinelab.com

**California Polytechnic State
 University**
College of Agriculture–Wine and
 Viticulture Program
1 Grand Avenue
San Luis Obispo, CA 93407
Phone: (805) 756-2161
E-mail: wvit@calpoly.edu
http://www.cafes.calpoly.edu

**California State University,
 Chico**
College of Agriculture
400 West First Street
Chico, CA 95929-0310
Phone: (530) 898-5844
E-mail: AgOutreach@csuchico.edu
http://www.csuchico.edu/ag

**California State University–
 Fresno**
Viticulture and Enology
 Department
2360 East Barstow
Fresno, CA 93740
Phone: (559) 278-2089
Fax: (559) 278-4795
http://www.cast.csufresno.edu/ve/
 index.htm

Chicago Wine School
1942 South Halsted Street
Chicago, IL 60608
Phone: (312) 491-0284
E-mail: PWFegan@aol.com
http://www.wineschool.com

City College of San Francisco
50 Phelan Avenue
San Francisco, CA 94112
Phone: (415) 239-3000
http://www.ccsf.edu

Cornell University–Enology and Viticulture
College of Agriculture and Life Sciences
177 Roberts Hall
Ithaca, NY 14853
Phone: (607) 255-2036
http://www.grapesandwine.cals. cornell.edu

The Court of Master Sommeliers, American Chapter
Kathleen Lewis, Executive Director
P.O. Box 6170
Napa, CA 94581
Phone: (707) 255-5056
E-mail: klewis@mastersommeliers. org
http://www.mastersommeliers.org

The Culinary Institute of America at Greystone, California
2555 Main Street
Saint Helena, CA 94574
Phone: (800) 333-9242
http://www.ciachef.edu

The Culinary Institute of America at Hyde Park, New York
1946 Campus Drive
Hyde Park, NY 12538
Phone: (845) 452-9600
http://www.ciachef.edu

Discover Wine and Spirits, LCC
Fort Mason Center

Landmark Building A
San Francisco, CA 94123
Phone: (415) 879-2787
E-mail: info@discoverwineand spirits.com
http://www.discoverwineandspirits. com

French Culinary Institute
462 Broadway
New York, NY 10013
Phone: (212) 219-8890
http://www.frenchculinary.com

Institute of Masters of Wine
2/3 Philpot Lane
London, United Kingdom
EC3M 8AN
Phone: +44 (0) 20 7621 2830
Fax: +44 (0) 20 7929 2302
E-mail: clive@mastersofwine.org
http://www.mastersofwine.org

International Sommelier Guild
4109 Northwest 88th Avenue
Suite 101
Coral Springs, FL 33065
Phone: (866) 412-0464
Fax: (954) 272-7377
E-mail: info@international sommelier.com

The International Wine Center
350 7th Avenue
Suite 1201
New York, NY 10001
Phone: (212) 239-3055
Fax: (212) 239-3051
E-mail: info@internationalwine center.com
http://www.internationalwinecenter. com

International Wine Guild
Metropolitan State College of Denver Campus
P.O. Box 173362
Denver, CO 80217-3362
Phone: (303) 296-3966
Fax: (303) 904-3245
http://www.internationalwineguild. com

Harriet Lembeck's Wine and Spirits Programs
203 East 29th Street
New York, NY 10016
Phone: (212) 252-8989
Fax: (718) 263-3750
E-mail: h.lembeck@wineandspirits program.com
http://www.wineandspiritsprogram. com

James Beard Foundation–Food and Wine Program
167 West 12th Street
New York, NY 10011
Phone: (212) 675-4984
Fax: (212) 645-1438
E-mail: programs@jamesbeard.org
http://www.jamesbeard.org

Kevin Zraly's Windows on the World Wine School
83 South Chestnut Street
New Paltz, NY 12561
Phone: (845) 255-1456
Fax: (845) 255-2041
http://www.kevinzraly.com

Leiths School of Food and Wine Limited
16-20 Wendell Road
London W12 9RT
United Kingdom
Phone: +44 (0)20 8749 6400
E-mail: info@leiths.com
http://www.leiths.com

McCutchen House at University of South Carolina
902 Sumter Street
Building 10
Columbia, SC 29208
Phone: (803) 777-8225
http://www.hrsm.sc.edu/culinary

Mendocino College Community Extension
1000 Hensley Creek Road
Ukiah, CA 95482
Phone: (707) 468-3063
Fax: (707) 468-3008
E-mail: mcComEx@mendocino.edu
http://www.mendocino.edu

Mission College in Santa Clara
3000 Mission College Blvd
Santa Clara, CA 95054
Phone: (408) 988-2200
http://www.missioncollege.org

New England Wine School
P.O. Box 1157
Bristol, RI 02809
Phone: (401) 487-9678
E-mail: info@newenglandwine
school.com
http://www.newenglandwineschool.
com

**Professional Culinary Institute–
Certified Sommelier
Program**
700 West Hamilton Avenue
Suite 300
Campbell, CA 95008
Phone: (866) 318-CHEF
Fax: (408) 370-9186
E-mail: admissions@pcichef.com
http://www.pcichef.com/3.html

San Francisco State University
1600 Holloway Avenue
San Francisco, CA 94132
Phone: (415) 338-1111
http://www.sfsu.edu

Society of Wine Educators
1212 New York Avenue Northwest
Suite 425
Washington, DC 20005
Phone: (202) 408-8777
Fax: (202) 408-8677
http://www.societyofwineeducators.
org

Sommelier Society of America
P.O. Box 20080
West Village Station
New York, NY 10014
Phone: (212) 679-4190
Fax: (212) 255-8959
E-mail: info@sommeliersocietyof
america.org or info@winestudy.
org
http://www.sommeliersocietyof
america.org or www.winestudy.
org

Sonoma State University
The Wine Business Program of
the School of Business and
Economics
1801 East Cotati Avenue
Rohnert Park, CA 94928
Phone: (707) 664-2260
E-mail: winebiz@sonoma.edu
http://www.sonoma.edu/winebiz

**South Seattle Community
College Northwest Wine
Academy**
6000 16th Avenue Southwest
Seattle, WA 98106
Phone: (206) 764-5300
http://nwwineacademy.com

**United States Sommelier
Association**
Executive Offices
6039 Collins Avenue
Suite 504
Miami Beach, FL 33140
Phone: (305) 867-3226
E-mail: info@ussommelier.com
http://www.ussommelier.com

**University of California–
Berkeley, Extension**
1995 University Avenue
Suite 110
Berkeley, CA 94704-7000
Phone: (510) 642-4111
E-mail: info@unex.berkeley.edu
http://www.unex.berkeley.edu

**University of California–Davis,
Department of Viticulture &
Enology**
One Shields Avenue
Davis, CA 95616-5270
Phone: (530) 752-0380
Fax: (530) 752-0382
http://wineserver.ucdavis.edu

**University of California–Davis,
Extension**
1333 Research Park Drive
Davis, CA 95618
Phone: (800) 752-0881 or
(916) 757-8777
Fax: (916) 757-8558

E-mail: aginfo@unexmail.ucdavis.
edu
http://extension.ucdavis.edu

**University of Utah, Department
of Continuing Education,
Lifelong Learning**
Main Office–Annex Building
1901 East South Campus Drive
Salt Lake City, UT 84112-9359
Phone: (801) 581-6461
Fax: (801) 585-5414
http://continue.utah.edu/lifelong

**Walla Walla Community
College**
500 Tausick Way
Walla Walla, WA 99362
Phone: (509) 522-2500
http://www.wwcc.edu/CMS

Washington State University
Viticulture/Enology Program
Department of Horticulture and
Landscape Architecture
College of Agricultural, Human,
and Natural Resource Sciences
149 Johnson Hall
P.O. Box 646414
Pullman, WA 99164-6414
Phone: (509) 335-9502
E-mail: hobart@wsu.edu
http://www.wsu.edu

**The Wine School of
Philadelphia**
2008 Fairmount Avenue
Philadelphia, PA 19144
Phone: (800) 817-7351, ext. 11
E-mail: info@vinology.com
http://www.vinology.com

Wine Spectator School
387 Park Avenue South
New York, NY 10016
Phone: (212) 481-8610, ext.1-302
Fax: (212) 684-5424
E-mail: winespectatorschool@
mshanken.com
http://www.winespectatorschool.
com

APPENDIX III
CULINARY ORGANIZATIONS, PROFESSIONAL SOCIETIES, AND TRADE ASSOCIATIONS

Advertising Photographers of America (APA)
APA Membership Office
560 4th Street
San Francisco, CA 94107
Phone: (800) 272-6264
Fax: (415) 882-9781
http://www.apanational.com

American Association of Family and Consumer Sciences (AAFCS)
400 North Columbus Street
Suite 202
Alexandria, VA 22314
Phone: (703) 706-4600
Fax: (703) 706-4663
http://www.aafcs.org

American Association of Nutritional Consultants
401 Kings Highway
Winona Lake, IN 46590
Phone: (888) 828-2262
Fax: (574) 268-2120
http://www.aanc.net
E-mail: registrar@aanc.net

American Bakers Association (ABA)
1300 I Street Northwest
Suite 700 West
Washington, DC 20005
Phone: (202) 789-0300
Fax: (202) 898-1164
E-mail: info@americanbakers.org
http://www.americanbakers.org

American Cheese Society (ACS)
455 South 4th Street

Suite 650
Louisville, KY 40202
Phone: (502) 583-3783
Fax: (502) 589-3602
E-mail: acs@hqtrs.com
http://www.cheesesociety.org

American Culinary Federation (ACF)
180 Center Place Way
Saint Augustine, FL 32095
Phone: (904) 824-4468
Fax: (904) 825-4758
http://www.acfchefs.org

American Dairy Association and Dairy Council, Inc.
219 South West Street
Suite 100
Syracuse, NY 13202
Phone: (315) 472-9143
Fax: (315) 472-0506
http://www.adadc.com

American Dietetic Association (ADA)
120 South Riverside Plaza
Suite 2000
Chicago, IL 60606-6995
Phone: (800) 877-1600
http://www.eatright.org

American Farm Bureau Federation (AFBF)
600 Maryland Avenue SW
Suite 1000W
Washington, DC 20024
Phone: (202) 406-3600
Fax: (202) 406-3602
http://www.fb.org

American Folkloric Society, Foodways Sections (AFS)
1501 Neil Avenue
Columbus, OH 43201-2602
Phone: (614) 292-3375
E-mail: lloyd.100@osu.edu
http://www.afsnet.org/sections/foodways

American Herb Association
P.O. Box 1673
Nevada City, CA 95959
Phone: (530) 265-9552
http://www.ahaherb.com

American Homebrewers Association
736 Pearl Street
Boulder, CO 80302
Phone: (303) 447-0816
Fax: (303) 447-2825
info@brewersassociation.org
http://www.beertown.org

American Hospital Association (AHA)
Chicago Headquarters
1 North Franklin
Chicago, IL 60606-3421
Phone: (312) 422-3000
http://www.aha.org

American Hospital Association (AHA)
Washington Headquarters
325 7th Street, NW
Washington, DC 20004
Phone: (202) 638-1100
http://www.aha.org

American Hotel and Lodging
 Association (AH&LA)
1201 New York Avenue NW
Suite 600
Washington, DC 20005-3931
Phone: (202) 289-3100
Fax: (202) 289-3199
E-mail: informationcenter@ahla.com
http://www.ahla.com

American Institute of Baking
 (AIB)
1213 Bakers Way
P.O. Box 3999
Manhattan, KS 66505-3999
Phone: (785) 537-4750
Fax: (785) 537-1493
E-mail: membership@aibonline.org
http://www.aibonline.org

American Institute of Wine and
 Food (AIWF)
26364 Carmel Rancho Lane
Suite 201
Carmel, CA 93923
Phone: (800) 274-AIWF (2493)
Fax: (831) 622-7783
E-mail: info@aiwf.org
http://www.aiwf.org

American Personal and Private
 Chef Association (APPCA)
4572 Delaware Street
San Diego, CA 92116
Phone: (619) 294-2436
E-mail: info@personalchef.com
http://www.personalchef.com

American Society of Brewing
 Chemists (ASBC)
3340 Pilot Knob Road
Saint Paul, MN 55121
Phone: (651) 454-7250
Fax: (651) 454-0766
http://www.asbcnet.org

American Society for Enology
 and Viticulture (ASEV)
P.O. Box 1855
Davis, CA 95617
Phone: (530) 753-3142
Fax: (530) 753-3318
http://www.asev.org

American Society for
 Healthcare Food Service
 Administration (ASHFSA)
455 South 4th Street
Suite 650
Louisville, KY 40202
Phone: (502) 583-3783
Fax: (502) 589-3602
E-mail: swingfield@hqtrs.com
http://www.ashfsa.org

American Society of Interior
 Designers (ASID)
608 Massachusetts Avenue NE
Washington, DC 20002-6006
Phone: (202) 546-3480
Fax: (202) 546-3240
E-mail: asid@asid.org
http://www.asid.org

American Society of Media
 Photographers (ASMP)
150 North 2nd Street
Philadelphia, PA 19106
Phone: (215) 451-2767
Fax: (215) 451-0880
E-mail: info@asmp.org
http://www.asmp.org

American Society of Travel
 Agents (ASTA)
1101 King Street
Alexandria, VA 22314
E-mail: askasta@asta.org
http://www.asta.org

American Sommelier
 Association
580 Broadway
Suite 716
New York, NY 10012
Phone: (212) 226-6805
Fax: (212) 226-6407
E-mail: office@americansommelier.
 org
http://www.americansommelier.org

American Vegan Society
P.O. Box 369
Malaga, NJ 08328
Phone: (856) 694-2887
Fax: (856) 694-2288
http://www.americanvegan.org

Association for Dressings and
 Sauces (ADS)
1100 Johnson Ferry Road
Suite 300
Atlanta, GA 30342
Phone: (404) 252-3663
Fax: (404) 252-0774
E-mail: ads@kellencompany.com
http://www.dressings-sauces.org

Association of Food Industries
 (AFI)
3301 Route 66
Suite 205
Building C
Neptune, NJ 07753
Phone: (732) 922-3008
Fax: (732) 922-3590
E-mail: info@afius.org
http://afi.mytradeassociation.org

Association of Food Journalists
 (AFJ)
7 Avenida Vista Grande
Suite B7 #467
Santa Fe, NM 87508
Phone: (505) 466-4742
E-mail: caroldemasters@yahoo.com
http://www.afjonline.com

Association of Fundraising
 Professionals (AFP)
4300 Wilson Boulevard
Suite 300
Arlington, VA 22203
Phone: (703) 684-0410
Fax: (703) 684-0540
http://www.afpnet.org

The Authors Guild
31 East 32nd Street
7th Floor
New York, NY 10016
Phone: (212) 563-5904
Fax: (212) 564-5363
E-mail: staff@authorsguild.org
http://www.authorsguild.org

The Bakery, Confectionery,
 Tobacco Workers and Grain
 Millers Union
10401 Connecticut Avenue
Kensington, MD 20895

Phone: (301) 933-8600
http://www.bctgm.org

The Beer Institute
122 C Street NW
Suite 350
Washington, DC 20001
Phone: (202) 737-2337
Fax: (202) 737-7004
E-mail: info@beerinstitute.org
http://www.beerinstitute.org

The Biodynamic Farming and Gardening Association
25844 Butler Road
Junction City, OR 97448
Phone: (888) 516-7797
Fax: (541) 998-0106
E-mail: info@biodynamics.com
http://www.biodynamics.com

Black Culinarians Alliance (BCA)
P.O. Box 2044
North Babylon, NY 11703
Phone: (212) 714-3132
http://www.bcaglobal.org

Bread Bakers Guild of America (BBGA)
670 West Napa Street
Suite B
Sonoma, CA 95476
Phone: (707) 935-1468
Fax: (707) 935-1672
E-mail: info@bbga.org
http://www.bbga.org

Chaîne des Rotisseurs USA (CHAINE)
National Office
Confrérie de la Chaîne des Rôtisseurs
Chaîne House at Fairleigh
   Dickinson University
285 Madison Avenue
Madison, NJ 07940-1099
Phone: (973) 360-9200
Fax: (973) 360-9330
E-mail: chaine@chaineus.org
http://www.chaineus.org

Chefs Collaborative
89 South Street

Lower Level
Boston, MA 02111
Phone: (617) 236-5200
Fax: (617) 236-5272
E-mail: ChefsCollaborative@chefs
   collaborative.org
http://www.chefscollaborative.org

Chez Panisse Foundation
1517 Shattuck Avenue
Berkeley, CA 94709
Phone: (510) 843-3811
Fax: (510) 843-3880
E-mail: info@chezpanissefoundation.
   org
http://www.chezpanissefoundation.
   org

Commercial Food Equipment Service Association
2216 West Meadowview Road
Suite100
Greensboro, NC 27407
Phone: (336) 346-4700
Fax: (336) 346-4745
E-mail: cstrickland@cfesa.com
http://www.cfesa.com

Data Management International
19239 North Dale Mabry Highway
Suite 132
Lutz, FL 33548
http://www.dama.org
E-mail: info@dama.org

Direct Marketing Association (DMA)
1120 Avenue of the Americas
New York, NY 10036-6700
Phone: (212) 768-7277
Fax: (212) 302-6714
http://www.the-dma.org

Farmers Market Coalition (FMA)
P.O. Box 4089
Martinsburg, WV 25402
Phone: (877) 362-0553
http://www.farmersmarketcoalition.
   org

Food Marketing Institute (FMI)
2345 Crystal Drive
Suite 800
Arlington, VA 22202
Phone: (202) 452-8444
Fax: (202) 429-4519
http://www.fmi.org

Food Processing Suppliers Association
1451 Dolley Madison Boulevard
Suite 200
McLean, VA 22101
Phone: (703) 761-2600
http://www.iafis.org
E-mail: info@fpsa.org

Foodservice Consultants Society International
144 Parkedge Street
Rockwood, ON N0B 2K0
Canada
Phone: (519) 856-0783
Fax: (519) 856-0648
http://www.fcsi.org

The Gluten Intolerance Group of North America (GIG)
31214 124th Ave Southeast
Auburn, WA 98092-3667
Phone: (253) 833-6655
Fax: (253) 833-6675
E-mail: info@gluten.net
http://www.gluten.net

Green Restaurant Association
89 South Street
Suite LL02
Boston, MA 02111
Phone: (858) 452-7378
E-mail: gra@dinegreen.com
http://www.dinegreen.com

The Grocery Manufacturers Association (GMA)
1350 I Street, NW
Suite 300
Washington, DC 20005
Phone: (202) 639-5900
Fax: (202) 639-5932
E-mail: info@gmaonline.org
http://www.gmaonline.org

**Hospitality Sales and
Marketing Association
International (HSMAI)**
1760 Old Meadow Road
Suite 500
McLean, VA 22102
Phone: (703) 506-3280
Fax: (703) 506-3266
E-mail: info@hsmai.org
http://www.hsmai.org

HTML Writers Guild
119 East Union Street
Suite F
Pasadena, CA 91103
Phone: (626) 449-3709
Fax: (626) 449-8308
http://www.hwg.org

Institute of Culinary Education
50 West 23rd Street
New York, NY 10010
Phone: (888) 354-CHEF
http://www.iceculinary.com

**Institute of Food Technologists
(IFT)**
525 West Van Buren
Suite 1000
Chicago, IL 60607
Phone: (312) 782-8424
Fax: (312) 782-8348
E-mail: info@ift.org
http://www.ift.org

Institute of Masters of Wine
2/3 Philpot Lane
London United Kingdom
EC3M 8AN
Phone: +44 (0) 20 7621 2830
Fax: +44 (0) 20 7929 2302
E-mail: clive@mastersofwine.org
http://www.mastersofwine.org

**International Association of
Culinary Professionals (IACP)**
1100 Johnson Ferry Road
Suite 300
Atlanta, GA 30342
Phone: (404) 252-3663
Fax: (404) 252-0774
E-mail: info@iacp.com
http://www.iacp.com

**International Brotherhood of
Teamsters**
25 Louisiana Avenue NW
Washington, DC 20001
Phone: (202) 624-6800
http://www.teamster.org

**International Cake Exploration
Société (ICES)**
http://www.ices.org

International Chili Society (ICS)
P.O. Box 1027
San Juan Capistrano, CA 92693
Phone: (949) 496-2651
Fax: (949) 496-7091
E-mail: ics@chilicookoff.com
http://www.chilicookoff.com

**International Council on Hotel,
Restaurant & Institutional
Education (CHRIE)**
2810 North Parham Road
Suite 230
Richmond, VA 23294
Phone: (804) 346-4800
Fax: (804) 346-5009
http://www.chrie.org

**International Culinary Tourism
Association (ICTA)**
4110 Southeast Hawthorne
Boulevard
Suite 440
Portland, OR 97214
Phone: (503) 750-7200
http://www.culinarytourism.org

**International Dairy Foods
Association (IDFA)**
1250 H Street NW
Suite 900
Washington, DC 20005
Phone: (202) 737-4332
Fax: (202) 331-7820
http://www.idfa.org

**International Foodservice
Editorial Council (IFEC)**
P.O. Box 491
Hyde Park, NY 12538
Phone: (845) 229-6973
Fax: (845) 229-6993

E-mail: ifec@ifeconline.com
http://ifeconline.com

**International Foodservice
Executives Association
(IFSEA)**
500 Ryland Street
Suite 200
Reno, NV 89502
Phone: (775) 825-2665
Fax: (775) 825-6411
http://www.ifsea.com

**International Food, Wine and
Travel Writers Association
(IFWTWA)**
1142 South Diamond Bar Boulevard
Suite 177
Diamond Bar, CA 91765-2203
Phone: (877) 439-8929
Fax: (909) 396-0014
E-mail: admin@ifwtwa.org
http://www.ifwtwa.org

**International Interior Design
Association (IIDA)**
Headquarters
222 Merchandise Mart Plaza
Suite 567
Chicago, IL 60654-1103
Phone: (312) 467-1950
Fax: (312) 467-0779
E-mail: iidahq@iida.org
http://www.iida.org

**International Society of Sports
Nutrition**
c/o Maelu Fleck
600 Pembrook Drive
Woodland Park, CA 80863
Phone: (866) 740-4776
Fax: (719) 687-5184
E-mail: issn@sportsnutrition
society.org
http://www.sportsnutritionsociety.
org

International Wine Guild
Metropolitan State College of
Denver Campus
P.O. Box 173362
Denver, CO 80217
Phone: (303) 296-3966

Fax: (303) 904-3245
http://www.internationalwineguild.
com

James Beard Foundation
167 West 12th Street
New York, NY 10011
Phone: (212) 675-4984
Fax: (212) 645-1438
E-mail: info@jamesbeard.org
http://www.jamesbeard.org

Jewish Vegetarians of North America
49 Patton Drive
Newport News, VA 23606
Phone: (718) 761-5876
http://www.jewishveg.com

Les Dames d'Escoffier International (LDEI)
P.O. Box 4961
Louisville, KY 40204
Phone: (502) 456-1851
Fax: (502) 456-1821
E-mail: ldei@aecmanagement.com
http://www.ldei.org

Manufacturers' Agents for the Food Service Industry
1199 Euclid Avenue
Atlanta, GA 30307
Phone: (404) 214-9474
Fax: (404) 522-0132
E-mail: info@mafsi.org
http://www.mafsi.org

Master Brewers Association of the Americas
3340 Pilot Knob Road
Saint Paul, MN 55121-2097
Phone: (651) 454-7250
Fax: (651) 454-0766
E-mail: mbaa@mbaa.com
http://www.mbaa.com

Meals on Wheels Association of America (MOWAA)
203 South Union Street
Alexandria, VA 22314
Phone: (703) 548-5558
Fax: (703) 548-8024
http://www.mowaa.org

Meeting Professionals International (MPI)
3030 Lyndon B. Johnson Freeway
Suite 1700
Dallas, TX 75234-2759
Phone: (972) 702-3000
Fax: (972) 702-3070
E-mail: feedback@mpiWeb.org
http://www.mpiWeb.org

National Association for the Specialty Food Trade, Inc. (NASFT)
120 Wall Street
27th Floor
New York, NY 10005
Phone: (212) 482-6440
Fax: (212) 482-6459
http://www.specialtyfood.com

National Association of Career Travel Agents
1101 King Street
Suite 200
Alexandria, VA 22314
Phone: (703) 739-6826
Fax: (703) 739-6861
E-mail: nacta@nacta.com
http://www.nacta.com

National Association of Catering Executives (NACE)
9881 Broken Land Parkway
Suite 101
Columbia, MD 21046
Phone: (410) 290-5410
Fax: (410) 290-5460
http://www.nace.net

National Association of College and University Food (NACUFS)
2525 Jolly Road
Suite 280
Okemos, MI 48864-3680
Phone: (517) 332-2494
Fax: (517) 332-8144
http://www.nacufs.org

National Association of Sports Nutrition
7710 Balboa Avenue
Suite 227 B

San Diego, CA 92111
Phone: (858) 694-0317
E-mail: nasn@nasnutrition.com
http://www.nasnutrition.com

National Association of Wholesaler-Distributors (NAW)
325 G Street NW
Suite 1000
Washington, DC 20005-3100
Phone: (202) 872-0885
Fax: (202) 785-0586
E-mail: naw@naw.org
http://www.naw.org

National Farmers Union (NFU)
400 North Capitol Street NW
Suite 790
Washington, DC 20001
Phone: (202) 554-1600
Fax: (202) 554-1654
http://nfu.org

National Kitchen and Bath Association (NKBA)
687 Willow Grove Street
Hackettstown, NJ 07840
Phone: (800) THE-NKBA
Fax: (908) 852-1695
E-mail: feedback@nkba.org
http://www.nkba.org

National Restaurant Association (NRA)
1200 17th Street NW
Washington, DC 20036
Phone: (202) 331-5900
Fax: (202) 331-2429
www.nationalrestaurantassociation.
org

National Writer's Union (NWU)
NWU National Office
113 University Place
6th Floor
New York, NY 10003
Phone: (212) 254-0279
Fax: (212) 254-0673
E-mail: nwu@nwu.org
http://www.nwu.org

North American Brewers Association
http://www.northamericanbrewers.org
info@northamericanbrewers.org

North American Farmers' Direct Marketing Association (NAFDMA)
62 White Loaf Road
Southampton, MA 01073
Phone: (413) 529-0386
Fax: (413) 529-9101
http://www.nafdma.com

North American Food Equipment Manufacturers
161 North Clark Street
Suite 2020
Chicago, IL 60601
Phone: (312) 821-0201
Fax: (312) 821-0202
E-mail: info@nafem.org
http://www.nafem.org

Oldways Preservation and Exchange Trust
266 Beacon Street
Boston, MA 02116
Phone: (617) 421-5500
Fax: (617) 421-5511
E-mail: oldways@oldwayspt.org
http://www.oldwayspt.org

Prepared Foods Network
1050 IL. Route 83
Suite 200
Bensenville, IL 60106
Phone: (630) 694-4353
http://www.preparedfoods.com

Professional Convention Management Association (PCMA)
2301 South Lake Shore Drive
Suite 1001
Chicago, IL 60616-1419
Phone: (312) 423.7262
Fax: (312) 423-7222
http://www.pcma.org

Professional Photographers of America (PPA)
229 Peachtree Street Northeast
Suite 2200
Atlanta, GA 30303
Phone: (404) 522-8600
Fax: (404) 614-6400
E-mail: csc@ppa.com
http://www.ppa.com

Retail Bakers of America
8400 Westpark Drive
2nd Floor
McLean, VA 22102
Phone: (703) 610-9035
Fax: (703) 610-0239
E-mail: Info@RBAnet.com
http://www.rbanet.com

Share Our Strength (SOS)
1730 M Street NW
Suite 700
Washington, DC 20036
Phone: (202) 393-2925
Fax: (202) 347-5868
E-mail: info@strength.org
http://www.strength.org

Slow Food USA
Slow Food USA National Office
20 Jay Street
Suite M04
Brooklyn, NY 11201
Phone: (718) 260-8000
Fax: (718) 260-8068
E-mail: info@slowfoodusa.org
http://www.slowfoodusa.org

Snack Food Association
1600 Wilson Boulevard
Suite 650
Arlington VA 22209
Phone: (703) 836-4500
Fax: (703) 836-8262
E-mail: sfa@sfa.org
http://www.sfa.org

Society of Flavor Chemists
3301 Route 66
Suite 205
Building C
Neptune, NJ 07753
Phone: (732) 922-3393
Fax: (732) 922-3590
E-mail: administrator@flavor chemist.org
http://www.flavorchemist.org

Society of Wine Educators (SWE)
1212 New York Avenue NW
Suite 425
Washington, DC 20005
Phone: (202) 408-8777
Fax: (202) 408-8677
http://www.societyofwineeducators.org

Specialty Travel Agents Association (STAA)
12381 Fenton Road
Fenton, MI 48430
Phone: (810) 629-2386
http://www.specialtytravelagents.com

Southern Foodways Alliance (SFA)
Center for the Study of Southern Culture
P.O. Box 1848
Barnard Observatory
University, MS 38677
Phone: (662) 915-5993
Fax: (662) 915-5814
E-mail: sfamail@olemiss.edu
http://www.southernfoodways.com

United Farm Workers of America (UFW)
National Headquarters
P.O. Box 62
29700 Woodford-Tehachapi Road
Keene, CA 93531
Phone: (661) 823-6250
E-mail: execoffice@ufw.org
http://www.ufw.org

United Food and Commercial Workers (UFCW)
International Office
1775 K Street NW
Washington, DC 20006-1598
Phone: (202) 223-3111
http://www.ufcw.org

United States Personal Chef Association (USPCA)
610 Quantum
Rio Rancho, NM 87124
Phone: (505) 994-6372
http://www.uspca.com

United States Sommelier Association
8362 Pines Boulevard
Suite 247
Pembroke Pines, FL 33024
Phone: (305) 867-3226
E-mail: info@USsommelier.com
http://www.ussommelier.com

Unite Here
Headquarters
275 7th Avenue
New York, NY 10001-6708
Phone: (212) 265-7000
http://www.unitehere.org

Vegetarian Nutrition Dietetic Practice Group (VN DPG)
American Dietetic Association
120 South Riverside Plaza
Suite 2000
Chicago, IL 60606-6995
Phone: (800) 877-1600, x4816
E-mail: practice@eatright.org
http://www.vegetariannutrition.net

The Vegetarian Resource Group
P.O. Box 1463
Baltimore, MD 21203
Phone: (410) 366-8343
E-mail: vrg@vrg.org
http://www.vrg.org

Web Design and Developers Association
8515 Brower

Houston, TX 77017
Phone: (435) 518-9784
Fax: (734) 448-5384
E-mail: wdda@wdda.org
http://www.wdda.org

Wine Institute
San Francisco Office
425 Market Street
Suite 1000
San Francisco, CA 94105
Phone: (415) 512-0151
Fax: (415) 442-0742
http://wineinstitute.org

Women Chefs and Restaurateurs (WCR)
P.O. Box 1875
Madison, AL 35758
Phone: (256) 975-1346
E-mail: admin@womenchefs.org
http://www.womenchefs.org

Women for WineSense
P.O. Box 10549
Napa, CA 94581
Phone: (800) 204-1616
http://www.womenforwinesense.org

Women's Foodservice Forum (WFF)
1650 West 82nd Street
Suite 650
Bloomington, MN 55431
Phone: (952) 358-2100 or (866) 368-8008

Fax: (952) 358-2119
E-mail: lpharr@womensfoodserviceforum.com
http://www.womensfoodserviceforum.com

Women's National Book Association (WNBA)
Susannah Greenberg Public Relations
c/o Women's National Book Association–New York City Chapter
P.O. Box 237
FDR Station
New York, NY 10150-0231
Phone: (212) 208-4629
Fax: (212) 208-4629
http://www.wnba-books.org

The World Association of Chefs Societies (WACS)
Vice President Hilmar Jonnson
Corporate Chef, Key Impact Sales
6244 Sommerset Lane
Williamsburg, VA 23188
Phone: (757) 303-2493
E-mail: hjonsson@kisales.com
http://www.wacs2000.org

APPENDIX IV
MAGAZINES AND PERIODICALS

AIB Research Technical Bulletin
AIB International, Inc.
1213 Bakers Way
P.O. Box 3999
Manhattan, KS 66505-3999
Phone: (785) 537-4750
Fax: (785) 537-1493
E-mail: techbulletins@aibonline.org
http://www.aibonline.org
Bimonthly bulletin. Subscriptions:
$20 to $220, may order print
subscriptions, individual
bulletins or a complete online
archive. Published by AIB's
research department staff and
guest contributors. Topics
range from bakery ingredients,
products, and operations to pest
control and other operation and
food safety issues.

All About Beer Magazine
501 Washington Street
Suite H
Durham, NC 27701
Phone: (919) 530-8150 or customer
service: (800) 999-9718
Fax: (919) 530-8160
E-mail: editor@allaboutbeer.com
http://allaboutbeer.com
Bimonthly magazine. Subscriptions:
$19.99/year. American beer
magazine featuring articles
about beer, brewing beer, and
beer news. Some articles also
available online.

American Cake Decorating
2594 Rice Street
Saint Paul, MN 55113
Phone: (651) 293-1544
http://www.
americancakedecorating.com
Bimonthly magazine. Subscriptions:
$28.00/year. Provides detailed

pictures and instructions,
information about tools and
materials, and reviews of new
products.

American Herb Association
Quarterly Newsletter
P.O. Box 1673
Nevada City, CA 95959
Phone: (530) 265-9552
http://www.ahaherb.com
Quarterly newsletter. Included
in AHA membership at $20/
year. Also online. Reports on
scientific studies, new books,
international herb news, legal
and environmental issues, and
national and international herb-
related events.

***American Vegan* magazine**
P.O. Box 369
Malaga, NJ 08328
Phone: (856) 694-2887
Fax: (856) 694-2288
http://www.americanvegan.org
Quarterly magazine published by
the American Vegan Society.
Subscription included in the
$20/year membership fee ($10
for students/low income).
Includes information about
living a vegan lifestyle.

Art Culinaire
40 Mills Street
Morristown, NJ 07960
Phone: (973) 993-5500 or (800) SO-
TASTY
Fax: (973) 993-8779
E-mail: info@
ArtCulinaireMagazine.com
http://www.getartc.com
Quarterly hardcover magazine.
Subscriptions: $59.00/year.

Provides techniques and
contemporary topics for
professionals, students, and
consumers.

Art of Eating
P.O. Box 242
Peacham, VT 05862
Phone: (800) 495-3944
E-mail: mail@artofeating.com
http://www.artofeating.com
Quarterly newsletter. Subscriptions:
$48/year. There is no advertising.
Along with in-depth articles,
there are recipes, letters, a wine
review, restaurant reviews, book
reviews, and more.

Baking Innovations Newsletter
Lallemand Inc.
1620 Préfontaine
Montreal, QC H1W 2N8
Canada
Phone: (514) 522-2133
Fax: (514) 522-2884
E-mail: info@lallemand.com
http://www.lallemand.com
Available online at no charge. A
new series of publications about
innovations in the baker's yeast
market. Available in French.

The Baking Sheet Newsletter
King Arthur Flour
58 Billings Farm Road
White River Junction, VT 05001
Phone: (800) 827-6836
Fax: (800) 343-3002
http://www.kingarthurflour.com
Bimonthly publication.
Subscriptions: $21.95/year.
Includes baking with kids of
all ages, recipe makeovers, and
baking ideas. Online newsletter
also available.

Baking Update Newsletter
Lallemand Inc.
1620 Préfontaine
Montreal, QC H1W 2N8
Canada
Phone: (514) 522-2133
Fax: (514) 522-2884
E-mail: info@lallemand.com
http://www.lallemand.com
Available online at no charge.
Read about various baking
applications and techniques.

Beard Bites
James Beard Foundation
167 West 12th Street
New York, NY 10011
Phone: (212) 675-4984
Fax: (212) 645-1438
http://www.jamesbeard.org
Biweekly e-newsletter. No charge.
Features information about
upcoming events, recipes and
photos from the Beard House,
scholarship news, restaurant
news from around the country,
and the latest on other
foundation goings-on.

Beer Magazine
P.O. Box 15896
North Hollywood, CA 91616
Phone: (866) 456-0410
Fax: (818) 487-4550
E-mail: beer@pubservice.com
http://www.thebeermag.com
Bimonthly magazine. Subscriptions:
$19.99/year. Includes beer taste
tests, recipes, and event coverage.
Digital subscriptions for the
same price are also available.

Bon Appétit
Condé Nast Publications
4 Times Square
New York, NY 10036
Phone: (212) 286-2860
http://www.bonappetit.com
Monthly magazine. Subscriptions:
$12 to $15/year. Includes recipes,
cooking tips, tools, ingredients,
restaurant reviews, and regional
cuisine.

Brew Your Own
5515 Main Street
Manchester Center, VT 05255
Phone: (802) 362-3981
Fax: (802) 362-2377
http://www.byo.com
Eight issues/year. Subscriptions:
$28/year. A how-to homebrew
beer magazine for all levels of
brewers.

Catering Magazine
GP Publishing
609 East Oregon Avenue
Phoenix, AZ 85012
Phone: (602) 265-7778
Fax: (602) 265-7771
http://www.cateringmagazine.com
Bimonthly. Subscriptions: $35/
year. Provides ideas and
information on all the business
aspects pertaining to off-
premise catering in the United
States.

Catersource magazine
250 Marquette Avenue
Suite 550
Minneapolis, MN 55401
Phone: (612) 870-7727
Fax: (612) 870-7106
E-mail: info@catersource.com
http://www.catersource.com
Bimonthly magazine. No charge
for qualified catering, event,
foodservice, and hospitality
professionals. A trade
publication focusing on
education, products, and news
for professional caterers.

Chef magazine
20 West Kinzie Street
Suite 1200
Chicago, IL 60654
Phone: (312) 849-2220
Fax: (312) 849-2174
http://www.chefmagazine.com
Eleven issues per year.
Subscriptions: $32/year print,
online free. Trade publication for
food service professionals.

Chile Pepper magazine
Goodman Media Group
250 West 57th Street
Suite 710
New York, NY 10107
Phone: (212) 262-2247
Fax: (212) 400-8620
http://www.chilepepper.com
Bimonthly magazine. Subscriptions:
$26.99/year. For spicy food
lovers. Includes recipes, new
cooking gadgets, planning
vacations, and learning how to
grow chiles in the garden.

Cook and Tell
298 Hendricks Hill Road
Southport, MN 04576
http://www.cookandtell.com
Online newsletter. Ten issues per
year. Subscriptions: $20.00/year.
Folksy newsletter with recipes,
kitchen trivia, readers' feedback,
and art.

Cooking for Profit magazine
CP Publishing, Inc.
P.O. Box 267
Fond du Lac, WI 54936-0267
Phone: (920) 923-3700
http://www.cookingforprofit.com
comments@cookingforprofit.com
Monthly magazine. Subscriptions:
$30/year. A trade magazine
directed to owners, managers,
and chefs of foodservice facilities.
Published by Gas Foodservice
Equipment Network.

Cooking Light magazine
P.O. Box 1748
Birmingham, AL 35201
Phone: (205) 445-6000
Fax: (205) 445-6600
http://www.cookinglight.com
Monthly magazine. Subscriptions:
$15/year. A food and fitness
magazine. Includes recipes,
nutrition advice, and food and
fitness tips.

Cooking with Paula Deen
Hoffman Media, LLC

1900 International Park Drive
Suite 50
Birmingham, AL 35243
Phone: (205) 995-8860
Fax: (205) 991-0071
http://www.pauladeenmagazine.com
Six issues per year. Subscriptions:
$19.98/year. Includes recipes,
shopping tips, kitchen design
and gardening news.

Cook's Country magazine

17 Station Street
Brookline, MA 02445
Phone: (800) 526-8442
http://www.cookscountry.com
Bimonthly magazine. Subscriptions:
$19.95/year. American home
cooking, including recipes,
recommended kitchen tools,
cookware, and supermarket
ingredients.

Cook's Illustrated

17 Station Street
Brookline, MA 02445
Phone: (800) 526-8442
http://www.cooksillustrated.com
Bimonthly magazine. Subscriptions:
$24.95/year. Online edition also
available. Professional how-tos,
recipes, taste tests, and reviews
of cookware and food products.

Cuisine at Home

P.O. Box 842
Des Moines, IA 50304-9961
Phone: (800) 311-3995
Fax: (515) 283-0447
E-mail: cuisineathome@cuisineat
home.com
http://www.cuisineathome.com
Bimonthly magazine. Subscriptions:
$28/ two years to start. A
"cooking class" magazine with
step-by-step recipe photos,
cooking tips and techniques,
kitchenware reviews, Q&A from
readers, and no advertising.

Culinary online

1900 Folsom Street
Suite 210

Boulder, CO 80302 USA
Phone: (303) 447-3334
http://www.culinary-online.com
Ten online issues per year.
Subscriptions: $29/year.
Dedicated to culinary
professionals and food lovers.
Includes recipes, reviews of
culinary Web sites, opinions and
ideas from professionals, and
tips to promote your Web site or
business online.

Culinary Trends

503 Vista Bella
Suite 12
Oceanside, CA 92057
Phone: (760) 721-2500
Fax: (760) 721-0294
E-mail: subscriptions@
culinarytrends.net
http://www.culinarytrends.net
Bimonthly magazine. Subscriptions:
$35.00/year. Also available
online. Includes recipes from
executive chefs, sources for
high-quality or hard to find
ingredients, book reviews, and
news about new trends.

Diabetic Cooking

Publications International, Ltd.
7373 North Cicero Avenue
Lincolnwood, IL 60712
Phone: (800) 777-5582
http://www.diabeticcooking.com
Bimonthly magazine. Subscriptions:
$14.95/year, $24.95/two years.
Features recipes that meet the
needs of a diabetic diet along
with cooking tips.

Digest: An Interdisciplinary Study of Food and Foodways

c/o Lucy Long
Department of Popular Culture/
American Folklore Society
Bowling Green State University
Bowling Green, OH 43403
Phone: (419) 372-7862
E-mail: lucyl@bgnet.bgsu.edu
http://www.afsnet.org/sections/
foodways/digest.htm

One volume per year, $15.00 per
volume. Presents scholarship
from a variety of disciplines:
culinary history, nutritional
sciences, cultural and nutritional
anthropology, sociology, and
folklore. Also may include
information about books,
conferences, exhibits, festivals,
museums, and films.

Eating Well magazine

823A Ferry Road
P.O. Box 1010
Charlotte, VT 05445
Phone: (802) 425-5700
Fax: (802) 425-3700
E-mail: editor@eatingwell.com
http://eatingwell.com
Bimonthly magazine. Subscriptions:
$14.97/year. Includes recipes,
nutritional and health
information, and kitchen tips
and techniques. E-newsletters
also available.

Epicurious

Condé Nast Publications
4 Times Square
New York, NY 10036
Phone: (212) 286-2860
http://www.epicurious.com
Online Web site offering recipes,
cooking features, video
demonstrations, plus links to
Bon Appétit magazine. No
charge to access information on
Web site.

Fine Cooking

The Taunton Press, Inc.
63 South Main Street
P.O. Box 5506
Newtown, CT 06470-5506
Phone: (203) 426-8171
Fax: (203) 426-3434
http://www.finecooking.com
Bimonthly magazine. Subscriptions:
$29.95/year. Also available
online. Step-by-step recipes
with photos, Q&A column, and
reviews.

Flavor and Fortune

P.O. Box 91
Kings Park, NY 11754
E-mail: flavorandfortune@hotmail.com
http://www.flavorandfortune.com
Quarterly magazine. Subscriptions: $21.50/year. Information about Chinese cuisine with articles and book, food, and restaurant reviews.

Food & Wine magazine

P.O. Box 62665
Tampa, FL 33662
Phone: (800) 333-6569
http://www.foodandwine.com
Monthly magazine. Subscriptions: $19.99/year. Also available online. Includes recipes, menus, wine reviews, and articles about innovations in the food world. Features chats with food experts.

Food Arts

M. Shanken Communications, Inc.
387 Park Avenue South
New York, NY 10016
Phone: (212) 684-4224
http://www.foodarts.com
Ten issues per year. No charge; subscriptions subject to publisher's acceptance. For food and beverage industry professionals. Coverage of trends and industry news that includes restaurant openings, business-building tips from colleagues, menu and food trends, how-to culinary demos, tabletop and equipment innovations, marketing ideas, and recipes.

Food Reflections

c/o Alice Henneman, Extension Educator
University of Nebraska–Lincoln in Lancaster County
444 Cherrycreek Road
Suite A
Lincoln, NE 68528
Phone: (402) 441-7180

http://lancaster.unl.edu/FOOD/food-reflections.shtml
Free monthly e-mail newsletter. Provides information on food, nutrition, and food safety for health professionals, educators, and consumers. Past newsletters are archived on the Internet.

Foodservice and Hospitality magazine

Toronto Office
Kostuch Publications Limited
01-23 Lesmill Road
Toronto, ON M3B 3P6
Canada
Phone: (416) 447-0888
Fax: (416) 447-5333
http://www.foodserviceworld.com
Monthly publication. Published in Canada for the foodservice and hospitality markets. Subscriptions: Complimentary for Canada residents; $60 (CDN) for U.S. residents.

Food Technology

525 West Van Buren
Suite 1000
Chicago, IL 60607
Phone: (312) 782-8424
Fax: (312) 782-8348
E-mail: info@ift.org
http://www.ift.org
Monthly publication. Included in membership in the Institute of Food Technologists (membership rates vary) or $190 for one year for nonmembers. Covers food science and technology including research developments, industry news, consumer product innovations, and professional opportunities.

Foodwatch Newsletter

6800 Galway Drive
Edina, MN 55439
Phone: (612) 819-1052
E-mail: info@foodwatchtrends.com
http://www.foodwatchtrends.com

Bimonthly e-newsletter. One-time $60 registration fee. Tracks contents of 21 consumer magazines and 12 major metropolitan newspapers and item information from more than 450 chain and independent restaurant menus. Analyzes data on current and future food trends.

Fresh Cup Magazine

P.O. Box 14827
Portland, OR 97293-0827
Phone: (503) 236-2587
Fax: (503) 236-3165
E-mail: subscriptions@freshcup.com
http://www.freshcup.com
Monthly magazine. Subscriptions: $48/year for U.S. residents. Print magazine for specialty coffee and tea professionals. Includes the latest coffee and tea news, business and marketing tips, profiles of industry veterans, firsthand views of coffee- and tea-growing regions, and more.

Gastronomica: The Journal of Food and Culture

Darra Goldstein, Editor in Chief
Williams College
North Academic Building
85 Mission Park Drive
Williamstown, MA 01267
E-mail: gastronomica@williams.edu
http://www.gastronomica.org
Published four times per year. Individual subscriptions: $48/year. Available both in print and online, but online subscriptions are only available for institutions, not individuals. Includes studies, humor, fiction, poetry, and visual imagery, using food as an important source of knowledge about different cultures and societies.

Gig Newsletter

The Gluten Intolerance Group of North America (GIG)
31214 124th Avenue Southeast
Auburn, WA 98092-3667

Phone: (253) 833-6655
Fax: (253) 833-6675
E-mail: info@gluten.net
http://www.gluten.net
Quarterly newsmagazine. Included in membership to GIG at $35/year. Detailed information about celiac disease and gluten intolerance.

Gorgeless Gourmet
Ferris Robinson, Editor
208 Oberon Trail
Lookout Mountain, GA 30750
http://dinnercoop.cs.cmu.edu/
     dinnercoop/special/FatFree.html
Monthly online newsletter. $12/year. Features fat-free or nearly fat-free recipes.

Gourmet News
65 West Commercial Street
Suite 207
Portland, ME 04101
Phone: (207) 775-2372
http://www.gourmetnews.com
Monthly publication. Subscriptions: $65 /year. A business newspaper for the gourmet industry.

Gourmet Retailer
770 Broadway
New York, NY 10003-9595
Phone: (847) 763-9050
Fax: (847) 763-9037
http://www.gourmetretailer.com
Monthly print magazine. Subscriptions: $83/year for U.S. residents. Online newsletter also available. For owners, operators, executives, and managers of gourmet, specialty food, and kitchenware stores, as well as coffee stores, department stores, and upscale supermarkets. Includes news, national and international sources of specialty foods and innovative housewares, consumer trends, new product ideas, creative merchandising, and education of store personnel for specialty retailing.

Gravy
Southern Foodways Alliance (SFA)
Center for the Study of Southern
     Culture
P.O. Box 1848
Barnard Observatory
University, MS 38677
Phone: (662) 915-5993
Fax: (662) 915-5814
E-mail: sfamail@olemiss.edu
http://www.southernfoodways.com
Online quarterly newsletter. No charge for subscriptions. Covers the South's newest books, eateries, raconteurs, and more.

Healthy Cooking magazine
Reiman Publications
5400 South 60th Street
Greendale, WI 53129
Phone: (800) 344-6913
http://www.tasteofhome.com/
     Healthy-Cooking-Magazine
Bimonthly magazine. Subscriptions: $14.98/year. Recipes and lifestyle tips for healthy and special diets.

Healthy Exchanges
P.O. Box 80
DeWitt, IA 52742-0080
Phone: (563) 659-8234
Fax: (563) 659-2126
E-mail: customer_service@
     healthyexchanges.com
http://www.healthyexchanges.com
Monthly newsletter. Subscriptions: $25/year. Features low-fat, low sugar, low sodium recipes, tips on healthy living, and advice on healthy lifestyles.

The Herb Companion
Ogden Publications, Inc.
1503 Southwest 42nd Street
Topeka, KS 66609-1265
Phone: (785) 274-4357
http://www.herbcompanion.com
Bimonthly magazine. Subscriptions: $19.95/year. A guide to the uses and pleasures of herbs.

The Herb Quarterly
4075 Papazian Way

Suite 208
Fremont, CA 94538
Phone: (510) 668-0268
http://www.herbquarterly.com
Quarterly magazine. Subscriptions: $19.97/year. Provides tips on hard to grow herbs, new herbs, recipes built around herbs, herbal lore, and more.

Jewish Vegetarians of North America Newsletter
49 Patton Drive
Newport News, VA 23606-1744
Phone: (718) 761-5876
http://www.jewishveg.com
Weekly e-mail newsletter. No charge for subscriptions. Articles related to Jewish vegetarianism.

Journal of the American Dietetic Association
Elsevier, Inc.
1600 John F. Kennedy Boulevard
Suite 1800
Philadelphia, PA 19103-2899
Phone: (215) 239-3733
Fax: (215) 239-3734
http://www.adajournal.org
Monthly publication. Subscriptions: $268/year. Also available online. Peer-reviewed journal presenting articles about nutritional science, medical nutrition therapy, public health nutrition, food science and biotechnology, foodservice systems, leadership and management, and dietetics education.

Kitchenware News
65 West Commercial Street
Portland, ME 04101
Phone: (207) 775-2372
Fax: (207) 775-2375
http://www.kitchenwarenews.com
Monthly magazine. No charge for qualified subscribers. A business-to-business publication covering the specialty foods and kitchenwares market. Also available online.

La Cucina Italiana magazine
Quadratum Publishing
512 Seventh Avenue
41st floor
New York, NY 10018
Phone: (800) 584-2043
E-mail: info@quadratumusa.com
http://www.lacucinaitaliana
    magazine.com
Eight issues yearly. Subscriptions:
    $24.00/year. Italian food and
    cooking, including recipes,
    guides to ingredients and
    sources, reviews of restaurants,
    and travel tips.

Living Without
800 Connecticut Avenue
Norwalk, CT 06854
Phone: (800) 474-8614
http://www.livingwithout.com
Bimonthly magazine. Subscriptions:
    $23/year. Recipes and
    information for people with
    food allergies and sensitivities.

The Monthly Slice
2594 Rice Street
St. Paul, MN 55113
Phone: (651) 293-1544
http://www.americancake
    decorating.com
Free monthly e-newsletter from
    American Cake Decorating.
    Includes ideas, projects,
    discounts, tips, and tricks for
    cake decorators.

National Barbecue News
P.O. Box 981
Douglas, GA 31534-0981
Phone: (800) 385-0002
http://www.barbecuenews.com
info@barbecuenews.com
Monthly magazine. Subscriptions:
    $20/year. Includes barbecue
    recipes and news.

The National Culinary Review
American Culinary Federation
180 Center Place Way
Saint Augustine, FL 32095
Phone: (800) 624-9458

Fax: (904) 825-4758
E-mail: acf@acfchefs.net
http://www.acfchefs.org
Monthly magazine. Subscrip-
    tions: $19.99 to $50/year.
    Magazine of the American
    Culinary Federation (ACF).
    Contains chef-tested recipes,
    industry news, and culinary
    techniques.

Nation's Restaurant News
425 Park Avenue
6th Floor
New York, NY 10022
Phone: (800) 453-2427
http://www.nrn.com
Print magazine; 48 issues per year.
    Subscriptions: $49.95/year.
    Online newsletter also available.
    For foodservice professionals.
    Offers menu ideas, creative
    marketing promotions, and
    news about food trends, food
    safety, and more.

New England Cheesemaking Supply Company Newsletter
P.O. Box 85
Ashfield, MA 01330
Phone: (413) 628-3808
Fax: (413) 628-4061
E-mail: info@cheesemaking.com
http://www.cheesemaking.com
Online newsletter. No charge.
    News and information on
    cheese making and related
    recipes, reviews, conferences,
    and workshops, along with a
    classified ads section.

Nutrition Action Healthletter
1875 Connecticut Avenue NW
Suite 300
Washington, DC 20009-5728
Phone: (202) 332-9110, ext. 393
E-mail: circ@cspinet.org
http://www.cspinet.org/nah
Ten issues per year. Subscriptions:
    $24/year. Presents research and
    practical advice on nutrition,
    diet, and related health issues.

Prepared Foods
P.O. Box 2147
Skokie, IL 60076-9785
Phone: (847) 763-9534
Fax: (947) 763-9538
E-mail: PF@halldata.com
http://www.preparedfoods.com
Monthly magazine. Both print
    and online versions are
    available. Print subscriptions
    to Prepared Foods are free to
    persons residing in the United
    States and Canada. Non-U.S.
    and Canadian residents may
    subscribe at no charge to the
    digital edition or purchase a
    paid subscription to the printed
    magazine. Includes information
    on new product introductions,
    culinary trends, ingredient
    technology, and practical
    applications for product
    developers.

One+
3030 Lyndon B. Johnson Freeway
Suite 1700
Dallas, TX 75234-2759
Phone: (972) 702-3000
Fax: (972) 702-3096
E-mail: publications@mpiWeb.org.
http://www.mpiWeb.org
Monthly magazine. Included
    in membership to Meeting
    Professionals International
    (MPI). Nonmembers may
    subscribe for $99/year.
    Publication for meeting and
    event professionals. Online
    edition and news also available.

Quarterly Review of Wines
24 Garfield Avenue
Winchester, MA 01890
Phone: (781) 729-7132
Fax: (781) 721-0572
http://www.qrw.com
Four issues per year. Subscriptions:
    $17.95/year. The nation's oldest
    wine quarterly covering wines,
    some selected spirits and beers,
    gourmet foods, and other wine-
    related topics.

Restaurants and Institutions magazine

Reed Business Information
8878 Barrons Boulevard
Highlands Ranch, CO 80129-2345
Phone: (800) 446-6551
http://www.rimag.com
Monthly magazine. Available online at no charge; free subscription to print version at no charge subject to publisher's approval. Paid subscriptions are available by contacting customer service. A source for food industry professionals for food and business trend information and research.

Santé magazine

On-Premise Communications, Inc.
100 South Street
Bennington, VT 05201
Phone: (802) 442-6771
Fax: (802) 442-6859
http://www.santemagazine.com
Santé magazine is currently published eight times a year, with double issues in January/February, March/April, July/August and October/November. The magazine is free to those in the restaurant and hospitality industry. An online edition is also available.

Saveur magazine

15 East 32nd Street
8th Floor
New York, NY 10016
Phone: (212) 219-7400
http://www.saveur.com
Nine issues per year. Subscriptions: $19.95/year. Digital version and online newsletter also available. Includes food and drink recipes, essays, reviews, cooking techniques, and information about culinary travel.

Simple Cooking

Editor: John Thorne
P.O. Box 778
Northampton, MA 01061-0778
Phone: (413) 586-6594
E-mail: johnandmatt@outlawcook.com
http://www.outlawcook.com
Newsletter. Published irregulary; issues are sent out when finished. Subscriptions: $25 for five issues; $45 for ten issues. Includes essays on food and cooking with illustrative recipes and food, book, and product reviews.

Specialty Food Magazine

120 Wall Street
27th Floor
New York, NY 10005
Phone: (212) 482-6440
Fax: (212) 482-6459
http://www.specialtyfood.com
Nine issues per year. Free to qualified specialty food businesses in the United States or Canada. Subscriptions: $50/year (more for international subscribers). Online newsletter also available. Covers products and trends in the specialty food business.

Tea, A Magazine

3 Devotion Road
P.O. Box 348
Scotland, CT 06264
Phone: (860) 456-1145
Fax: (860) 456.1023
E-mail: teamag@teamag.com
http://www.teamag.com
Quarterly magazine. Subscriptions: $17/year. All about tea, both as a beverage and for its cultural significance in art, music, literature, history, and society.

Today's Diet and Nutrition magazine

Great Valley Publishing
3801 Schuylkill Road
Spring City, PA 19475
Phone: (610) 948-9500
Fax: (610) 948-4202
http://www.todaysdietandnutrition.com
Bimonthly magazine. Subscriptions: $9.99/year. A resource for guidance on healthy food and fitness.

Urban Agricultural Notes

City Farmer–Canada's Office of Urban Agriculture
Box 74567, Kitsilano RPO
Vancouver, BC V6K 4P4
Canada
Phone: (604) 685-5832
http://www.cityfarmer.org
cityfarm@interchange.ubc.ca
Online newsletter. No charge. E-mail updates available. Articles on how to grow food in the city, compost waste, and take care of a home landscape in an environmentally responsible way.

Vegetarian Journal

The Vegetarian Resource Group
P.O. Box 1463
Baltimore, MD 21203
Phone: (410) 366-8343
E-mail: vrg@vrg.org
http://www.vrg.org
Quarterly magazine. Included with $25 membership fee to join the Vegetarian Resource Group, a nonprofit educational organization. Contains articles, recipes, book reviews, notices about vegetarian events, product evaluations, hints on where to find vegetarian products and services, and travel tips. Does not accept paid advertising.

Vegetarian Newsletter

University of Florida
Horticultural Sciences Department
1117 Fifield Hall
P.O. Box 110690
Gainesville, FL 32611-0690
Phone: (352) 392-1928
Fax: (352) 392-5653
http://www.hos.ufl.edu/vegetarian
Monthly online newsletter. No charge for subscriptions. Produced as a service to

extension agents, farmers, growers, gardeners and the general public.

Vegetarian Nutrition Update

American Dietetic Association (ADA)
120 South Riverside Plaza
Suite 2000
Chicago, IL 60606-6995
Phone: (800) 877-1600, ext. 4816
E-mail: practice@eatright.org
http://www.vegetariannutrition.net
Quarterly newsletter. Published by the Vegetarian Nutrition (VN) Dietetic Practice Group and distributed free of charge to all VN members. If not eligible for membership in the American Dietetic Association may subscribe for $30/year. Includes articles, reviews of scientific literature, book reviews, spotlights on members, and other news and events related to vegetarian topics.

Vegetarian Times

Active Interest Media
300 North Continental Boulevard
Suite 650
El Segundo, CA 90245
Phone: (310) 356-4100
Fax: (310) 356-4110
http://www.vegetariantimes.com
Nine issues per year.
  Subscriptions: $14.95/year.
  Online edition also available.
  Includes recipes and resources for vegetarian, vegan, low-fat, wheat-free, dairy-free, and other specialized cooking.

Wine Advocate

P.O. Box 311
Monkton, MD 21111
Phone: (410) 329-6477
E-mail: wineadvocate@erobert parker.com.
http://www.erobertparker.com
Bimonthly magazine.
  Subscriptions: $99/year.
  Detailed information about all aspects of wine purchasing and consumption.

Wine and Spirits Magazine

2 West 32nd Street
Suite 601
New York, NY 10001
Phone: (212) 695-4660
E-mail: info@wineandspirits magazine.com
http://www.wineandspirits magazine.com
Seven issues per year. Subscriptions: $29.95/year. Includes wine tasting results, restaurant polls, and news and tips about what's new in the field of food, wine, and spirits.

Wine Enthusiast Magazine

333 North Bedford Road
Mt. Kisco, NY 10549
Phone: (914) 345-8463
Fax: (914) 218-9186
http://www.winemag.com
Fourteen issues per year.
  Subscriptions: $29.95/year. A source for ratings and reviews of wine and spirits currently available in the marketplace, as well as wine accessories news, food pairings, and commentary on wine trends, vintages, and wine regions.

Wine Spectator

M. Shanken Communications
387 Park Avenue South
New York, NY 10016
Phone: (212) 684-4224
http://www.winespectator.com
Fifteen issues per year.
  Subscriptions: $49.95/year.
  Online version also available.
  Features stories fine wine and dining, cooking, entertaining, travel, and the arts.

Wines & Vines magazine

1800 Lincoln Avenue
San Rafael, CA 94901
Phone: (415) 453-9700
Fax: (415) 453-2517
E-mail: info@winesandvines.com
http://www.winesandvines.com
Monthly magazine. Subscriptions: $38.00/year. Includes wine industry news, feature articles, editorial opinion, and buyer's guide.

Zymurgy Magazine

736 Pearl Street
Boulder, CO 80302
Phone: (303) 447-0816
Fax: (303) 447-2825
http://www.shop.beertown.org
Bimonthly magazine. $38/year.
  Published by the American Homebrewers Association. Includes do-it-yourself equipment building, explanations of brewing science, and presentations of brewing techniques.

BIBLIOGRAPHY

BOOKS AND ARTICLES

Brennan, Georgeanne. "Singing Salumi's Praises." *San Francisco Chronicle*, 3 December 2008.

Chalmers, Irena. *Food Jobs.* New York: Beaufort Books, 2008.

Chmelynski, Carol Caprione. *Opportunities in Restaurant Careers.* New York: McGraw-Hill, 2004.

Donovan, Mary. *Opportunities in Culinary Careers.* New York: McGraw-Hill, 2004.

Elias, Peter. "Better Wine through Chemistry, Though Some Complain about Taste." *USA Today*, 11 September 2006.

Gibson, Richard. "Sizing Up Salaries Inside Franchisers," *Wall Street Journal*, 30 December 2008.

The Guide to Cooking Schools 2005. 17th ed. New York: Shaw Guides, 2004.

"Healthier Pizza." *Science Daily*, 1 July 2007. Available online. URL: www.sciencedaily.com/videos/2007/0802-healthier_pizza.htm.

Hill, Kathleen. "Saucier than Thou." *Sonoma Valley Sun: Fine Life*, 15 September 2007.

Hunter, Marnie. "A Growing Taste for Culinary Travel." CNN, 1 September 2006. Available online at http://cnn.travel.

Manuel, Dennis. "Boutique Wines." Supermarket Guru. Available online. URL: www.supermarketguru.com/page.cfm/199.

Marcello, Martin, and Julie Garden-Robinson. "The Art and Practice of Sausage Making." North Dakota State University Agriculture and University Extension, 2004. Available online. URL: www.ag.ndsu.edu/pubs/yf/foods/he176w.htm.

Meneou, Candace. "Cook's 2009 Buyers Guide and Restaurant Supply Catalog Focus on New Products." Articlesbase, 6 February 2009. www.articlesbase.com/print/760016.

Parsons, Russ. "The ABCs of Salumi." *Los Angeles Times*, 30 August 2006. Available online. URL: http://articles.latimes.com/2006/aug/30/food/fo-charcuterie30.

Reilly, Richard Byrne. "Butchers' Union Beef." *New York Post*, 19 May 2008.

Rozhon, Tracie. "Upstairs, Downstairs and Above the Garage." *New York Times*, 18 March 2008.

Smith, Andrew F., ed. *The Oxford Companion to American Food and Drink.* New York: Oxford University Press, 2007.

U.S. Travel Association. "Comprehensive Culinary Travel Survey Provides Insights on Food and Wine Travelers," Travel Industry Association, 14 February 2007. Available online. URL: www.tia.org/pressmedia/pressrec.asp?Item=750 or www.usdm.net.

WEB SITES

Agricultural Career Guide
http://www.khake.com/page39.html

Agritourism World
http://www.agritourismworld.com

American Chemical Society
http://portal.acs.org

American Institute of Baking International
http://www.aibonline.org

American Society for Enology and Viticulture
http://www.asev.org

Apprentice Chef Information: Chef Mario's Inc.
http://www.chefmario.com

Apprentice Chef Information from Columbus State Community College (Ohio)
http://www.cscc.edu/Hospitality?chefapprenticeshipmajor.html

Apprentice Chef Information from Johnson County Community College (Kansas)
http://www.jccc.edu

Apprentice Chef Information from Red Rocks Community College (Colorado)
http://www.rrcc.edu/culinary/index.html

Bakery, Confectionary, Tobacco Workers & Grain Millers (AFL-CIO)
http://www.bctgm.org

Baking and Pastry Arts Instructor Information
http://www.winecountryjobs.com

Baking Job Descriptions
http://careers.stateuniversity.com

Beer-Related Web Site Lists
http://www.beerstuff.com

Biodynamic Farming and Gardening Association
http://www.biodynamics.com

Brigade de Cuisine Descriptions
http://www.acfchefs.org/Content/
Education/Certification/Levels/
default.htm

California Wine Institute
http://www.wineinstitute.org

CareerPlanner.com
http://Careerplanner.com

Catering Job Descriptions
http://www.caterer.com/
SearchBySpecialism.aspx

Club Managers Association of America (Restaurant Equipment)
http://http://cmaa.
officialbuyersguide.net

Commis Chef Information
http://www.geebo.com

Court of Master Sommeliers of the United Kingdom
http://www.mastersommeliers.org

Culinary Institute of America
http://www.prochef.com

Culinary Instructor Information
http://www.ihirechefs.com

Culinary School Information
http://www.acfchefs.org
http://www.allculinaryschools.com
http://www.cookingschool.com
http://www.artinstitutes.edu
http://www.iacp.com

Eco Destination Management Services (International Culinary Destination Management Information)
http://www.edodms.com

Farmers Market Coalition for (State Farmers' Markets)
http://www.farmersmarketcoalition.
org

Farmers' Market Federation of New York
http://www.nyfarmersmarket.com

Feeding America (Formerly America's Second Harvest)
http://www.feedingamerica.org

Food Historian Information
http://foodhistorynews.com

Food Photographer Information
http://www.foodphotography.com

Food Service Equipment Distributors Association
http://www.feda.com/resources

Food Service Manager and Food Service Management Teacher Information
http://www.braintrack.com/
colleges-by-career/food-service-
managers

Food Stylist Information
http://www.culinaryschools.com/
being-a-food-stylist

French Culinary Institute at the International Culinary Center (for Pastry Jobs)
http://www.frenchculinary.com/
pastry_chef_jobs.html

Gallo Winery Jobs
http://gallo.com

Garde-Manger Information
http://www.gardemanger.com

Hospitality and Restaurant Jobs Information
http://www.allculinaryschools.com

Hospitality Pro Search
http://www.hcareers.com

International Association of Culinary Professionals
http://www.iacp.com

International Culinary Tourism Association
http://www.culinarytourism.org

Local Harvest
http://www.localharvest.org

Magazine and Periodical Information
http://www.globalgourmet.com

Master Brewers Association of the Americas
http://www.mbaa.com

Master of Wine Certification
http://www.tasting-wine.com/
articles/print/sommelier-
definition/wine-master.htm

Meals on Wheels Association of America
http://www.mowaa.org

Monster.com
http://www.monster.com

National Agricultural Library of the United States Department of Agriculture: Community Supported Agriculture
http://www.nal.usda.gov/afsic/pubs/
csa/printPHP2.php

National Sustainable Agriculture Information Service: How to Organize a New Farm or Market
http://www.attra.ncat.org

North American Farmers' Direct Marketing Association
http://www.familyfarms.com

North Carolina Cooperative Extension Chatham County Center: Community Supported Agriculture (CSA) Resource Guide for Farmers
http://www.ces.ncsu.edu/chatham/ag/SustAg/csaguide.html

Nutrition Counseling (University Level) Information from NorthShore University HealthSystem (Illinois)
http://www.northshore.org

Ontario Culinary Tourism Alliance
http://www.ontarioculinarytourism.com

Pacific Coast Farmers' Market Association
http://www.pcfma.com

Professional Organizations
http://www.iceculinary.com
http://www.victoriapacking.com/culinaryorginfo.html

Recipe Developer Information
http://www.ehow.com

Recipe Tester Information
http://americastestkitchen.qualtrics.com

Restaurant Equipment Supply Information
http://www.applerestaurantsupply.com/buying-guide-pages/resource.html
http://www.jeansrestaurantsupply.com/Cooking-Equipment-C2.aspx
http://www.restaurantequipment.net

Retail Food Job Descriptions
http://http://jobs5-wholefoods.icims.com/jobs/36022/job?sn=simplyhired.com
http://newyork.craigslist.org/mnh/fbh/1095248217.html

San Diego Culinary Institute: Commis Programs
http://sdco-inc.com/commis_programs.html

Snack Food Association
http://www.sfa.org

Society of Flavor Chemists
http://www.flavorchemist.org/about

Society of Wine Educators
http://www.societyofwineeducators.org/public/education_and_certification/index.aqspx

Sommelier Information
http://www.chiff.com/wine/sommelier.htm

Sonoma Gourmet
http://www.sonomagourmet.com

Sports, Cardiovascular, and Wellness Nutritionists
http://www.scandpg.org/sporsdietitianjobdescription.php

United Food and Commercial Workers International Union
http://www.fucw.org

United States Department of Agriculture–Agricultural Marketing Service
http://www.ams.usda.gov/farmersmarket

United States Sommelier Association
http://www.ussommelier.com

Vocational Schools Database
http://www.rwm.org

Wine Jobs
http://www.thejobnetwork.com
http://www.vinoenology.com

Wine Schools Information
http://www.internationalsommelier.com
http://www.wineinstitute.org

Winemaker, Viticulturalist, Vintner, and Oenologist Information: Australian Government
http://www.myfuture.edu.au

Wine Marketing and Sales Jobs
http://www.jobmonkey.com/winejobs/marketing-jobs.html

Winery Job Descriptions for Advertising, Marketing Sales Manager at Various Wineries
http://www.winebusiness.com

Wine Spectator Magazine and Professional Courses
http://www.winespectatorschool.com

INDEX

Page numbers in **boldface** indicate main articles.

$ 49.50

CONNETQUOT PUBLIC LIBRARY
760 Ocean Avenue
Bohemia, NY   11716
631-567-5079

Library Hours:

Monday - Friday	9:00 - 9:00
Saturday	9:00 - 5:00
Sunday (Oct. - May)	1:00 - 5:00

GAYLORD M